OXFORD MONOGRAPHS IN INTERNATIONAL LAW

The Identity of Governments in International Law

OXFORD MONOGRAPHS IN INTERNATIONAL LAW

The aim of this series is to publish important and original pieces of research on all aspects of international law. Topics that are given particular prominence are those which, while of interest to the academic lawyer, also have important bearing on issues which touch the actual conduct of international relations. Nonetheless the series is wide in scope and includes monographs on the history and philosophical foundations of international law.

RECENT TITLES IN THE SERIES

Access to Courts for Asylum Seekers and Refugees
State Obligations under the 1951 Refugee Convention
Emma Dunlop

International Law Obligations on Climate Change Mitigation
Benoit Mayer

Coastal State Jurisdiction over Living Resources in the Exclusive Economic Zone
Camille Goodman

International Law and Corporate Actors in Deep Seabed Mining
Joanna Dingwall

The Concept of an International Organization in International Law
Lorenzo Gasbarri

Necessity and Proportionality and the Right of Self-Defence in International Law
Chris O'Meara

Neutrality in Contemporary International Law
James Upcher

Geographical Change and the Law of the Sea
Kate Purcell

Statehood and the State-Like in International Law
Rowan Nicholson

Confronting the Shadow State
Henri Decoeur

Irresolvable Norm Conflicts in International Law
The Concept of a Legal Dilemma
Valentin Jeutner

The Identity of Governments in International Law

NIKO PAVLOPOULOS
Associate Legal Officer, International Court of Justice, Netherlands (the)

OXFORD
UNIVERSITY PRESS

OXFORD
UNIVERSITY PRESS

Great Clarendon Street, Oxford, OX2 6DP,
United Kingdom

Oxford University Press is a department of the University of Oxford.
It furthers the University's objective of excellence in research, scholarship,
and education by publishing worldwide. Oxford is a registered trade mark of
Oxford University Press in the UK and in certain other countries

Published in the United States of America by Oxford University Press
198 Madison Avenue, New York, NY 10016, United States of America

British Library Cataloguing in Publication Data
Data available

Library of Congress Control Number: 2023948492

ISBN 978–0–19–888292–3

DOI: 10.1093/9780191991509.001.0001

Pod

General Editors' Preface

It was long said that a political entity claiming to be the government of a state was to be considered that state's government for the purposes of international law if it exercised effective control over the territory and population of the state. This putative statement of the law, however, never explained the recognition by other states of 'governments in exile'. Moreover, the received wisdom came under challenge in the 1990s from the claim that 'democratic legitimacy' was instead becoming the international legal touchstone of governmental status. When both effective control and democratic legitimacy appeared to take a beating from state and international organizational practice over the following decades, the exasperated cry went up that no rules as to the identity of a state's government existed any longer under customary international law. On this view, whether a political entity was the government of a state for the purposes of international law was in the eye of the beholder, with other states free to treat as that government whichever competing entity they pleased, absent specific prohibition to the contrary. Unruly practice had supposedly trampled principle underfoot.

In *The Identity of Governments in International Law*, Niko Pavlopoulos begs to differ. He argues that practice in the recognition of governments, while messy, nonetheless continues to reflect principle. Such principle, however, is now subtly but significantly different from the effectivity thesis, while not supporting the democratic thesis either. Proceeding from the presumptive sovereign freedom of each state—as a juridical construct distinct from its people—to choose its own government, Dr Pavlopoulos scrutinizes a wealth of historic and contemporary practice to conclude that the identity of the government of a state remains an objective international legal question and that, in determining this identity, customary international law today privileges constitutionality, as distinct from democratic representativity, over effective control. As long as it asserts and maintains a claim to being the government and is autonomous of foreign states, a 'constitutional' claimant can today become and remain the government of a state under international law even where a rival, 'unconstitutional' claimant enjoys effective control over the territory and population. Only where no 'constitutional' claimant maintains a claim can an 'unconstitutional' claimant in effective control become the government of the state as a matter of international law. Notwithstanding this, Dr Pavlopoulos cautions, it may be that the rules, which include the established practice, of an international organization permit the organization to accept for certain purposes the representation of a member state by an entity other than the entity that qualifies as the state's government under international law.

The Identity of Governments in International Law is a work of modern international legal positivism of the very highest quality. It combines a painstaking, discerning analysis of the practice of states and international organizations with an insightful, original account of underlying principle. Its framing of the formal end of the criteria of government under international law as the ascertainment in unstraightforward cases of the state's own choice is inspired. The book makes a magisterial contribution to the international legal literature on government and its relation to statehood, on the representation of states, on recognition, and on the practice and powers of international organizations *vis-à-vis* their member states. It deserves to become a classic.

RO'K, CR
Milan and Oxford
October 2023

Preface

The author is an Associate Legal Officer at the International Court of Justice. The views expressed in this book are personal and do not necessarily reflect those of the International Court of Justice.

The book is up to date as at 31 August 2023. All websites were last accessed on this date. All translations are the author's own unless otherwise indicated.

Niko Pavlopoulos
The Hague
January 2024

Acknowledgements

A number of persons and institutions made possible and pleasant the completion of this work. I am very grateful to them all.

During my doctoral studies at University College London (UCL), in which this book has its origins, Roger O'Keefe was an inspirational and formative principal supervisor. My thesis and I benefited enormously from his meticulous and candid engagement with my work. It was a pleasure and privilege to be his supervisee. Much the same goes for Alex Mills, my secondary supervisor, whose steadfast support and critical consideration of my work throughout the doctoral process contributed in many significant ways to my thesis. Further, both he and Kimberley Trapp made the 'upgrade viva' a constructive and encouraging experience. Marko Milanovic and Martins Paparinskis held a rigorous and incisive viva, which enabled me to further refine the work. Other academics at UCL engaged meaningfully with aspects of my work, including Drs Danae Azaria and Ralph Wilde.

The Economic and Social Research Council and the UCL Faculty of Laws provided the necessary financial support that allowed me to undertake my doctoral studies. Cambridge University and the Lauterpacht Centre for International Law welcomed me during an academic stay which was of substantial benefit to my research.

Beyond the PhD, Brad Roth, Jure Vidmar, and Luca Ferro kindly provided incisive feedback on a draft of the manuscript. Several exchanges with Federica Paddeu on the topic were also fruitful. Cyril Emery's impressive document-finding abilities allowed me to locate certain underexamined materials. At Oxford University Press, Merel Alstein, Robert Cavooris, Louise Karam, and Kim Vollrodt supported the project and guided me through the publication process. Two reviewers furnished valuable and detailed comments. The team at Newgen KnowledgeWorks facilitated the copy-editing process.

More generally, friends and colleagues contributed to a warm and stimulating academic environment at UCL and beyond. I am fortunate enough to have met more kind persons than can be mentioned here by name, but the convivial and supportive PhD community at UCL Laws merits special mention. This includes Chiara Armeni, Joe Atkinson, Joseph Crampin, Conor Crummey, Allie Hearne, Andrew McLean, Gaiane Nuridzhanian, Lea Raible, Sara Razai, Ed Robinson, Priya Urs, and Eugenio Velasco Ibarra. I would be remiss not to mention also the cherished love and support of other friends during the preparation of the book, in particular that of Madeleine Barrow, Maria De la Cruz, Emilie Fitzsimons, James Lincoln, Michael Murphy, Lucy Page, and Camilla Pickles. The same is true for my parents, Fani and Alekos, and my sister, Maria.

Contents

Table of Cases

Table of Instruments

1. INTERNATIONAL AGREEMENTS

2. OSTENSIBLE CONSTITUTIONAL DOCUMENTS, LEGISLATIVE INSTRUMENTS, AND DECLARATIONS BY CLAIMANT GOVERNMENTS

3. DOCUMENTS OF INTERNATIONAL ORGANIZATIONS

3.1 African Union and the Organization of African Unity

3.1.1 AU ASSEMBLY

3.1.2 AUPSC

3.1.3 OAU ASSEMBLY

3.1.4 OTHER

3.2 Council of Europe

3.3 European Union and European Community

3.4 International Criminal Court

3.5 Organization of American States

3.5.1 OASGA

3.5.1.1 Documents

3.5.1.2 MEETING RECORDS

3.5.2 OASPC

3.5.2.1 Documents

3.5.2.2 Meeting records

3.5.3 SECRETARIAT

3.5.4 OTHER

3.6 United Nations

3.6.1 ECONOMIC AND SOCIAL COUNCIL

3.6.2 General Assembly

3.6.2.1 DOCUMENTS

3.6.2.2 Meeting records

3.6.3 INTERNATIONAL COURT OF JUSTICE

3.6.4 INTERNATIONAL LAW COMMISSION

3.6.4.1 *Draft articles and draft conclusions*

3.6.6 SECURITY COUNCIL

3.6.6.1 *Documents*

3.6.6.2 *Meeting records*

3.6.7 CONFERENCE DOCUMENTS

3.7 Miscellaneous

4. OTHER

List of Abbreviations

AC	Appeal Cases, Law Reports, England and Wales
AFDI	*Annuaire française de droit international*
AfJIL	African Journal of International Law
AJIL	American Journal of International Law
All ER	All England Law Reports
Annuaire IDI	*Annuaire de l'Institut de Droit International*
ARSIWA	Articles on the Responsibility of States for Internationally Wrongful Acts
art	Article
AU	African Union
AU Assembly	Assembly of the African Union
AUILR	American University International Law Review
AUPSC	Peace and Security Council of the African Union
AYIL	Australian Yearbook of International Law
BFSP	British and Foreign State Papers
BYIL	British Yearbook of International Law
CA	Court of Appeals (England and Wales)
CERD	Committee on the Elimination of Racial Discrimination
CFLN	*Comité français de liberation nationale*
CGDK	Coalition Government of Democratic Kampuchea
Ch	Chancery Division of the High Court of Justice, Law Reports (England and Wales)
CILSA	Comparative and International Law Journal of Southern Africa
CJIL	Chinese Journal of International Law
CJTL	Columbia Journal of Transnational Law
CLC	Commercial Law Cases (England and Wales)
col	Column
Comm	Commercial Court
CRPH	Committee Representing Pyidaungsu Hluttaw
CSM	Convention on Special Missions
CUP	Cambridge University Press
CYIL	Canadian Yearbook of International Law
CYILA	Chinese (Taiwan) Yearbook of International Law and Affairs
DCER	Documents on Canadian External Relations
Doc	Document
DSB	Department of State Bulletin
ECommHR	European Commission of Human Rights
ECOSOC	United Nations Economic and Social Council

ECOWAS	Economic Community of West African States
EHRR	European Human Rights Reports
EJIL	European Journal of International Law
EU	European Union
EWCA Civ	England and Wales Court of Appeal, Civil Division
EWHC	England and Wales High Court
F Supp	Federal Supplement
F.2d	Federal Reporter, 2nd series
FAO	Food and Agriculture Organization of the United Nations
FPGK	Free Provisional Government of Kuwait
FRUS	Foreign Relations of the United States
FRY	Federal Republic of Yugoslavia (Serbia and Montenegro)
Gaceta Legislativa	*Gaceta Legislativa de la Asamblea Nacional* (Venezuela)
GCI	Governing Council of Iraq
GNA	Government of National Accord
GRUNK	Royal Government of the National Union of Kampuchea (*Gouvernement royal d'union nationale du Kampuchéa*)
Hague *Recueil*	*Recueil des cours de l'Académie de Droit International de la Haye*
HC Debs	UK Parliamentary Debates, House of Commons
HL Debs	UK Parliamentary Debates, House of Lords
HR Debs	Australia Parliamentary Debates, House of Representatives
IADC	Inter-American Democratic Charter
ICC	International Criminal Court
ICJ	International Court of Justice
ICJ Rep	ICJ Reports
ICLQ	International and Comparative Law Quarterly
ICSID	International Centre for Settlement of Investment Disputes
IJCL	International Journal of Constitutional Law
ILC	International Law Commission
ILC Report	*Report of the International Law Commission*
ILM	International Legal Materials
ILO	International Labour Organization
ILR	International Law Reports
IYIL	Italian Yearbook of International Law
JAIL	The Japanese Annual of International Law
JUFIL	Journal on the Use of Force and International Law
KB	King's Bench Reports (England and Wales)
Keesing's	*Keesing's Contemporary Archives: Record of National and International Current Affairs with Continually Updated Indexes*
LJIL	Leiden Journal of International Law
LLR	Liverpool Law Review
LNOJ	League of Nations Official Journal
LNTS	League of Nations Treaty Series
MJIL	Melbourne Journal of International Law

MPEPIL	Max Planck Encyclopedia of Public International Law
MPUNYB	Max Planck United Nations Yearbook
NILR	Netherlands International Law Review
NLD	National League for Democracy
No	number
NTC	National Transitional Council
NUCC	National Unity Consultative Council
NUG	National Unity Government
NYIL	Netherlands Yearbook of International Law
NYUJILP	New York University Journal of International Law and Politics
NZLR	New Zealand Law Review
OAS	Organization of American States
OASGA	Organization of American States General Assembly
OASPC	Permanent Council of the Organization of American States
OAU	Organization of African Unity
OUP	Oxford University Press
PSC Protocol	Protocol Relating to the Establishment of the Peace and Security Council
QB	Queen's Bench Reports (England and Wales)
RBDI	*Revue Belge de Droit International*
res	resolution
RMPA	*Revista Mexicana de Política Exterior*
SAC	State Administration Council
SADR	Saharan Arab Democratic Republic
SLORC	State Law and Order Restoration Council
SNC	Supreme National Council
Supp	Supplement
SYIL	Spanish Yearbook of International Law
UAE	United Arab Emirates
UK	United Kingdom of Great Britain and Northern Ireland
UKMIL	United Kingdom Materials on International Law
UKSC	Supreme Court of the United Kingdom
UN	United Nations
UN Charter	Charter of the United Nations
UNGA	United Nations General Assembly
UNHRC	United Nations Human Rights Council
UNJYB	United Nations Juridical Yearbook
UNRIAA	United Nations Reports of International Arbitral Awards
UNSC	United Nations Security Council
UNTS	United Nations Treaty Series
USA	United States of America
USSR	Union of Soviet Socialist Republics
VCCR	Vienna Convention on Consular Relations
VCDR	Vienna Convention on Diplomatic Relations

VCLT	Vienna Convention on the Law of Treaties
VCRSIO	Vienna Convention on the Representation of States in their Relations with International Organizations of a Universal Character
vol	volume
WA	Written Answers
WLR	Weekly Law Reports (England and Wales)
WTO	World Trade Organization
Ybk ILC	Yearbook of the International Law Commission
Ybk World Aff	Year Book of World Affairs

1
Introduction

1.1 Setting the Scene

As a matter of international law, a state is an abstract juridical construct which can act only through the instrumentality of human beings.[1] This raises the question who qualifies as a state representative or, in other words, who has the capacity[2] to represent that state for one or more purposes of international law. In general, it appears that whether or not international law accepts as effective for its purposes the ostensible representation of a state depends principally, although perhaps not exclusively, on whether a particular person or collectivity of persons comprises at least part of or acts under the authority of the government of that state.[3] Indeed, uncertainty over the identity of a state's government appears capable of rendering problematic the assessment of virtually every matter to which the will or view of that state is relevant.

One such matter is whether a state is party to a treaty, a question which might arise where a state's ostensible government purports to express either that state's consent to be bound by a treaty or that state's intention to denounce or withdraw from a treaty. An example of disagreement as regards the effectiveness of the ostensible consent of a state to be bound by a treaty relates to the ostensible consent of China in 1961 to be bound by the Vienna Convention on Diplomatic Relations (VCDR) as expressed through the nationalist ostensible government of China at a time when the communist ostensible government of China exercised control over most of China's territory and population.[4] When the treaty in respect of which a state has ostensibly become or ceased to be a party is the constituent instrument of an international organization, the state's status as a party to that treaty may also affect that state's membership of the organization. Illustrative in this regard is the question of Poland's membership of the International Civil Aviation Organization

[1] See eg *German Settlers in Poland, Advisory Opinion* (1923) PCIJ, Series B, No 6, 5, 22; Kelsen, *Pure Theory of Law* (Knight tr, 2nd edn, University of California Press 1967) 290–312.

[2] It is worth clarifying that international law grants capacities to states, not their governments. The present work uses the term 'capacity' in this context merely as shorthand to refer to the possession by a person or collectivity of persons of the ability to represent a state for one or more purposes of international law. On the distinction between a state and its government, see eg Crawford, *The Creation of States in International Law* (2nd edn, CUP 2006) 33–5, 678–80, including n 46; Moore, *Digest of International Law*, vol 1 (US Government Printing Office 1906) 249; Marek, *Identity and Continuity of States in Public International Law* (Librairie Droz 1954) 24–5, 30–45.

[3] See further sections 2.3.1 and 5.3.2.

[4] See chapter 2, n 75 and accompanying text.

The Identity of Governments in International Law. Niko Pavlopoulos, Oxford University Press. © Niko Pavlopoulos 2024.
DOI: 10.1093/9780191991509.003.0001

in 1945[5] and the disagreement as to Venezuela's continued membership in the Organization of American States (OAS) since 2019, when Juan Guaidó purported to annul Venezuela's denunciation of the Charter of the Organization of American States (OAS Charter).[6] Other questions involving the ostensible representation of a state to which the identity of a state's government appears to be relevant include, for example, whether a state has consented to the use of force on its territory by another state[7] and whether a state has waived its entitlement to see itself or one or more of its officials benefit from immunity from proceedings before a foreign municipal court.[8] Further recent incidents that demonstrate the significance of the identity of the government of a state to the representation of the state include the uncertainty as regards the effectiveness of Egypt's ostensible consent in 2013 to the exercise of jurisdiction by the International Criminal Court over crimes allegedly committed on the territory of Egypt[9] and of the ostensible initiation of proceedings by Honduras against Brazil at the International Court of Justice (ICJ) in 2009,[10] as well as the disagreement as to the identity of Venezuela's representatives in the context of arbitral proceedings since 2019.[11]

As the range of matters of state representation to which the identity of a state's government might be relevant indicates, disagreement or uncertainty as to the identity of the government of a state can give rise to numerous situations conducive to neither the smooth functioning of international organizations nor the development or maintenance of friendly interstate relations. Such situations do not arise only in relation to matters concerning the ostensible representation of a state but also from the fact that certain individuals comprising part of the state's government, as well as certain persons appointed by or otherwise acting under the authority of the state's government, are the beneficiaries of certain immunities and

[5] See Talmon, *Recognition of Governments in International Law with Particular Reference to Governments in Exile* (OUP 1998) 133–4.

[6] See further section 5.5.

[7] See also Brownlie, *International Law and the Use of Force by States* (OUP 1963) 317; *Military and Paramilitary Activities in and against Nicaragua (Nicaragua v USA), Merits, Judgment* [1986] ICJ Rep 14, 126, §246; Gray, *International Law and the Use of Force* (4th edn, CUP 2018) 101; Corten, *The Law against War* (2nd edn, Hart 2021) 256–63.

[8] See 'Seventh Report on Immunity of State Officials from Foreign Criminal Jurisdiction, by Concepción Escobar Hernández, Special Rapporteur' (18 April 2019) UN Doc A/CN.4/729, 23, §58. On the position of the office-holders mentioned therein as members of a state's government, see section 2.2.1.

[9] International Criminal Court (ICC), 'The Determination of the Office of the Prosecutor on the Communication Received in Relation to Egypt' (Press release, 8 May 2014) ICC-OTP-20130508-PR1003, available at <http://icc-cpi.int/Pages/item.aspx?name=pr1003>.

[10] *Certain Questions concerning Diplomatic Relations (Honduras v Brazil), Order of 12 May 2010* [2010] ICJ Rep 303 ('*Honduras v Brazil*') 303–4.

[11] See eg *ConocoPhillips Petrozuata BV, ConocoPhillips Hamaca BV and ConocoPhillips Gulf of Paria BV v Venezuela* (ICSID Case No ARB/07/30), *Decision on Rectification* (29 August 2019); *Valores Mundiales, SL and Consorcio Andino SL v Bolivarian Republic of Venezuela* (ICSID Case No ARB/13/11), *Annulment Proceeding, Procedural Resolution No 2* (29 August 2019); *Mobil Cerro Negro Holding, Ltd and others v Venezuela* (ICSID Case No ARB/07/27), *Resubmission Proceeding, Decision on the Respondent's Representation in this Proceeding* (1 March 2021).

privileges under international law. Indeed, given the far-reaching significance of the identity of a state's government, the importance for the effective functioning of international law of the international legal framework on the identity of the governments of states is difficult to overstate.

Recent examples of situations unconducive to the development or maintenance of amicable interstate relations as a result of the contested identity of a state's government include one consequence of the difference of views in 2020 between Turkey and Egypt over the identity of Libya's government. The two states provided or considered providing military support to rival political authorities in Libya in reliance on the ostensible consent of Libya as expressed by the political authority that each considers to comprise Libya's government.[12] As another recent example, in May 2020, Venezuela's Permanent Representative to the United Nations (UN) referred to the Bank of England's decision not to follow instructions by Nicolás Maduro's government as 'the greatest robbery in the modern history of the Bolivarian Republic of Venezuela'.[13] Nicolás Maduro's ostensible government had instructed the Bank to liquidate assets held with it in an account belonging to the Central Bank of Venezuela, instructions which the Bank of England did not follow on the ground that the United Kingdom of Great Britain and Northern Ireland (UK) did not recognize as the government of Venezuela the political authority operating under Nicolás Maduro's leadership. A further example relates to Iran's decision, following its acceptance of the Houthi-led claimant[14] as the government of Yemen, to accept as Yemen's diplomatic agent in Iran a person acting under the authority of that movement. The decision resulted in Yemen's Permanent Representative to the UN, acting under the rival authority of Abdrabbuh Mansur Hadi, calling on the United Nations Security Council (UNSC) in November 2019 to condemn Iran's action for what he considered to be a violation of, among other things, the VCDR.[15]

[12] See eg Ferro, 'A Libyan Playground for Foreign Powers: Presenting the Case for "Negative Equality"' (*Opinio Juris*, 26 June 2020), available at <http://opiniojuris.org/2020/06/26/a-libyan-playground-for-foreign-powers-presenting-the-case-for-negative-equality>.

[13] 'Letter Dated 26 May 2020 from the Permanent Representative of the Bolivarian Republic of Venezuela to the United Nations Addressed to the President of the Security Council' (27 May 2020) UN Doc S/2020/444, 1. See further Waseem, 'Introductory Note to *"Maduro Board" of the Central Bank of Venez v "Guaidó Board" of the Central Bank of Venez* (UKSC)' (2022) 62 ILM 120 for subsequent developments that work in favour of the rival claimant government of Juan Guaidó being given control over the assets in question. Cf the position taken recently by a municipal court in Portugal, eg as reported in 'Venezuela Says Wins Ruling to Recoup $1.5 bln in Portugal Funds' (*Reuters*, 9 August 2023), available at <http://reuters.com/world/americas/venezuela-says-wins-ruling-recoup-15-bln-portugal-funds-2023-08-09>.

[14] On 6 February 2015, the Houthi movement, through its Revolutionary Committee, issued a 'constitutional declaration' that gave rise to a claim to governmental status. In July 2016, power was transferred by the Committee to the Supreme Political Council.

[15] 'Letter Dated 21 November 2019 from the Permanent Representative of Yemen to the United Nations Addressed to the President of the Security Council' (25 November 2019) UN Doc S/2019/904, 1–2.

In the context of international organizations, disagreement over the identity of the government of a state and the representative of that state in an international organization has, for example, led other states to disengage with certain aspects of the work of an organization. Illustrative in this regard is the decision of the Union of Soviet Socialist Republics (USSR), in January 1950, to abstain from participating in the work of the UNSC in response to the continued occupation of China's seat on the Council by persons acting under the authority of the Taiwan-based ostensible government of China.[16] More recently, in June 2019, Uruguay's representative walked out of a meeting of the General Assembly of the Organization of American States (OASGA) owing to the latter's acceptance of a person acting under the authority of Juan Guaidó as the representative of Venezuela, subsequent to the ostensible annulment by Juan Guaidó of Venezuela's intention to withdraw from the OAS.[17] It is not only disagreement among states as to the identity of a state's government that has hindered the work of international organizations. In 2010, for example, in the light of apparent uncertainty as to the identity of Honduras's government, the ICJ decided not to take action on the ostensible initiation of proceedings by Honduras, through one of Honduras's claimants to governmental status, against Brazil.[18] As another example, disagreement over the identity of Venezuela's government reportedly resulted in the International Monetary Fund finding itself unable to consider Nicolás Maduro's request for funds, ostensibly in Venezuela's name, in order to deal with the coronavirus pandemic.[19]

As the above suggests, and although identifying the government of a state is ordinarily unproblematic, the qualification by a person or group of persons as the government of a state is not-infrequently contested or otherwise in doubt. Recent examples in this regard concern the identity of the respective governments of Afghanistan (2021–), Myanmar (2021–), and Venezuela (2019–). Some further examples of controversies concerning the identity of a state's government relate to the respective governments of the following states: Spain in the context of the Spanish Civil War (1936–9), Cambodia (1970–5; 1979–89, 1997–8), and Somalia (1991–2012). There exist also situations in which the identity of a state's government is generally accepted by the vast majority of, if not all, states, while the reason for such acceptance is unclear, including but not exclusively where there is more than one ostensible government of that state. Examples in this regard include the identity of

[16] UNSC, 'Official Records, 459th Meeting' (10 January 1950) UN Doc S/PV.459, 3–7.

[17] OASGA, 'Cuadragésimo Noveno Período Ordinario de Sesiones' (26–28 June 2019) Actas y Documentos, vol II, OEA/Ser.P/XLIX-O.2, 39–40; Baddour, 'Uruguay Walks Out of OAS Assembly over Guaido Envoy Inclusion' (*Al Jazeera*, 27 June 2019), available at <http://aljazeera.com/news/2019/06/uruguay-walks-oas-assembly-inclusion-guaido-envoy-190627191520096.html>. Further on this, see section 5.5.

[18] See *Honduras v Brazil* (n 10).

[19] Laya and Vazquez, 'IMF Won't Lend to Venezuela Because Maduro Lacks Recognition' (*Bloomberg*, 17 March 2020), available at <http://bloomberg.com/news/articles/2020-03-17/venezuela-requests-5-billion-from-imf-to-fight-coronavirus>.

the respective governments of Haiti (1991–4), Sierra Leone (1997), Côte d'Ivoire (2010–11), Libya (2011; 2014–), and Ukraine (2014). The existence in such situations of more than one ostensible government renders these cases examples also of the absence of an immediately-apparent reason behind the rejection of a specific claimant's governmental status, as was the case also with Afghanistan (1996–2001). The lack of clarity as to the reason for a specific claimant's enjoyment or non-enjoyment of governmental status does not facilitate the ascertainment of any framework against which the identity of a state's government may be ascertained in other cases.

In short, there is a range of state and organizational practice that demonstrates the importance of the identity of a state's government to a number of international legal matters. At the same time, substantial practice indicates that the identity of each state's government and the international legal explanation behind such identity is not always clear. This gives rise to questions concerning the identity of governments in international law, for example in relation to the recognition of governments and the extent to which states may be represented only by their governments in the context of international organizations.

Over the years, there have been attempts to ascertain aspects of the international legal regulation of governmental status. The accuracy and comprehensiveness today of some earlier works[20] and judicial decisions[21] can be questioned, not least because of practice over the past thirty or so years that appears not to accord with what is generally considered to have comprised the traditional international legal framework on the identity of the governments of states. Indeed, the 1990s saw a pursuit or perception, at least in some quarters, of a broader shift in the foundation and content of the international legal order towards greater regard for human rights and democracy.[22] This extended into matters concerning governments, including the customary international legal criteria for governmental status[23] and matters of state representation in international organizations.[24]

That said, practice in the twenty-first century has not consistently supported the ideals propounded by some at the end of the preceding century. This has contributed to confusion as regards the state of law, given the principal focus in the literature on whether the protection and promotion of democracy and human rights has supplanted what was perceived to be the traditional framework, without regard

[20] See eg Chen, *The International Law of Recognition with Special Reference to Practice in Great Britain and the United States* (Praeger 1951); Lauterpacht, *Recognition in International Law* (CUP 1947, repr 2013) Part II; Blix, 'Contemporary Aspects of Recognition' (1970) 130 Hague *Recueil* 587.

[21] See eg *Aguilar-Amory and Royal Bank of Canada Claims (Great Britain v Costa Rica)* (1923) I UNRIAA 375.

[22] See eg Reisman, 'International Law after the Cold War' (1990) 84 AJIL 859, 861; Franck, 'The Emerging Rights to Democratic Governance' (1992) 86 AJIL 46, 60.

[23] See further chapter 4, especially section 4.2.2.5.1.2.

[24] See eg chapter 5, n 298 and the accompanying text.

for other possible changes in this regard.[25] This is reflected, for example, even in the work of authors who have considered democratic representativity to be relevant to the enjoyment of governmental status as they seem unable to agree on precisely what changes have taken place. In any event, they accept the existence of practice that undermines or limits the significance of democratic representativity to the enjoyment of governmental status. Indeed, some such authors have revised their positions, accepting further limitations as to the relevance of democratic representativity, with the benefit of only a few years of additional state practice.[26] All of this apparently-discordant practice and the resultant perception of legal uncertainty has even led to the suggestion that there is no general objective customary international legal framework for the assessment of governmental status.[27] The extent to which this convincingly addresses the question how to identify the government of a state for the purposes of international law is an open question. In any event, it leaves unaddressed several other international legal issues related to governments.

Indeed, the international legal regulation of the identity of the governments of states has not received much attention beyond the criteria for governmental status. For example, little consideration has been given to questions concerning the representation of states in international organizations. When this matter has been examined, the focus has tended to be on a specific contentious incident or on one particular international organization.[28] Even the works that do engage more comprehensively with one or more legal questions concerning the identity of the governments of states do so in isolation from other aspects of the international legal framework regulating the identity of the governments of states. In this way, only a partial analysis of the relevant rules of international law are provided. For example, as valuable as it may be, a review of the meanings of recognition in the context

[25] See eg Roth, *Governmental Illegitimacy in International Law* (OUP 2000) 1 for an assessment of the customary international legal framework for the identification of a state's government with a view to determining 'the extent to which a norm of popular sovereignty has displaced the protections that international law has traditionally accorded *de facto* authorities'. Indeed, most of the recent literature on the criteria for governmental status has focused on assessing whether international law has shift towards further protection and promotion of democracy, often at the expense of other possible considerations. See, generally, section 4.2.2.5.1.2. See also section 4.2.2.5.2.

[26] See further section 4.2.2.5.1.2.

[27] See eg Redaelli, *Intervention in Civil Wars: Effectiveness, Legitimacy, and Human Rights* (Hart 2021) 119; International Law Association, 'Resolution 3/2018', available at <http://ila-hq.org/en_GB/documents/conference-resolution-sydney-2018-english>, §6. This view might be seen to be implicit also in Ruys and Ferro, 'Weathering the Storm: Legality and Legal Implications of the Saudi-Led Military Intervention in Yemen' (2016) 65 ICLQ 61, 81, who claim that 'international recognition' is one of the requirements for the enjoyment of governmental status, and in Roth, 'Secessions, Coups and the International Rule of Law: Assessing the Decline of the Effective Control Doctrine' (2010) 11 MJIL 393, 396, who suggests that 'democratic legitimacy' has 'an ad hoc quality' as regards the enjoyment of governmental status.

[28] See eg Akehurst, 'Enforcement Action by Regional Agencies, with Special Reference to the Organization of American States' (1967) 42 BYIL 175; Ciobanu, 'Credentials of Delegations and Representation of Member States at the United Nations' (1976) 25 ICLQ 351; Suttner, 'Has South Africa Been Illegally Excluded from the United Nations General Assembly?' (1984) 17 CILSA 279.

of recognition of governmental status and of the perceived significance of such recognition for the recognizing state in relation to the legal status of an ostensible 'government-in-exile' does not answer 'whether or not a recognized government in exile, in fact, qualified as a government under international law, and whether the recognizing State thus acted lawfully when recognizing it'.[29]

1.2 Scope of the Book

The overarching aim of this book is to ascertain how, if at all, international law regulates the identity of the governments of states. Put differently, its principal aim is to attempt to discern such legal principles as may underpin international practice in relation to the identity of the governments of states. In this regard, the present work examines whether and, if so, how international law provides a basis for ascertaining the identity of a state's government. It assesses also what, if any, rules of international law regulate the conduct of other states and international organizations in relation to an ostensible government of a state. To this end, the book engages considerably with state and organizational practice, which it assesses in the light of conceptual considerations concerning the identity of the governments of states as a matter of international law. In this way, the book offers an extensive analysis of the international legal rules concerning the identity of the governments of states and insights into the concept of the government of a state as a matter of international law. The focus is largely on customary international law, although certain treaties are relevant to aspects of the work.

The book does not concern itself with political, philosophical, or moral aspects of the identity of a state's government, nor does it suggest what legal principles ought to underpin international practice in relation to the governments of states. Moreover, it considers the regulation of the identity of a state's government by the municipal legal system of that state only insofar as this is relevant to the content or application of a rule of international law on the identity of the government of that state. Additionally, it excludes from its consideration the international legal regulation of the identity and capacities[30] of a person or group of persons directing the exercise of authority on behalf of a territorial-political entity other than a state, whether that be a Non-Self-Governing Territory or other colonial country,[31] a component unit of a federal state, an autonomous region within a state, or an entity enjoying some other status, including one 'legally proximate to' statehood.[32] So, for

[29] Talmon (n 5) ix.
[30] On the use of the term 'capacity' in the present context, see n 2.
[31] On the categories of 'colonial countries', see United Nations General Assembly (UNGA) res 1514 (XV) (14 December 1960) UN Doc A/RES/1514(XV).
[32] Crawford (n 2) 107.

example, the law of occupation,[33] aspects of the right to self-determination,[34] the law on international territorial administration,[35] and recognition of belligerency[36] are not addressed. Nor does the present work consider in any detail the law of statehood or the law of title to territory. It nevertheless notes the instances in which these areas of law are liable to affect the content or application of the international legal framework on the identity of the governments of states.

Even as regards the identity of the governments of states as a matter of international law, the present work does not attempt to catalogue, let alone analyse, every situation in which the identity of a state's government has been controversial or unclear. Without prejudice to the general applicability of the international legal rules discussed, situations concerning the identity of a state's government that demonstrate nothing special about the content or application of the rules on the identity of the governments of states do not feature prominently. Conversely, the book highlights certain situations where the identity of a state's government is contested or otherwise uncertain or where the reason for which an ostensible government does or does not qualify as the government of a state is not apparent. It focuses in particular on situations which contribute meaningfully to illuminating the content or application of the international legal regulation of the identity of governments of states. Moreover, the book does not address all questions on the identity of the governments of states in international law. For example, it does not fully explore the extent to which the government of a state may qualify as the representative of the people of that state. That said, the book provides a basis for further research into such matters.

1.3 Terminological Clarifications

Broadly conceived, 'the government' of a state, within the meaning of international law, refers to the individual and collective organs exercising public authority on behalf of a state. Narrowly conceived, 'the government' of a state, within the meaning of international law, refers to the person who or group of persons that directs the exercise of public authority on behalf of a state.[37] The book focuses on

33 See, generally, Dinstein, *The International Law of Belligerent Occupation* (CUP 2009); Benvenisti, *The International Law of Occupation* (2nd edn, OUP 2012).

34 See, generally, Crawford (n 2) 107–48, 565–647.

35 See, generally, Wilde, *International Territorial Administration: How Trusteeship and the Civilizing Mission Never Went Away* (OUP 2008); Stahn, *The Law and Practice of International Territorial Administration: Versailles to Iraq and Beyond* (CUP 2008).

36 See, generally, Lauterpacht (n 20) 239–55; Chen (n 20) 303–98; Sivakumaran, *The Law of Non-International Armed Conflict* (OUP 2012) 10–20; Crawford (n 2) 380–2.

37 See also Magiera, 'Governments' (2007) MPEPIL, available at <http://opil.ouplaw.com/home/mpil>, §§2–4.

'the governments' of states in the second, more specific sense.[38] Accordingly, it uses the term 'the government' of a state to refer only to the person who or collectivity of persons that directs the exercise of public authority on behalf of that state.

The characterization of a government as the 'right' or 'wrong' government refers to the qualification or non-qualification, respectively, by the ostensible government in question as the government of a state under customary international law. The terms 'claimant to governmental status' and 'ostensible government' are used interchangeably to refer to any person who or collectivity of persons that expressly claims or otherwise purports to be the government of a state.

The 'constitution' of a state, within the meaning of international law, refers broadly to the internal disposal of public power within a state.[39] The present work uses the word 'constitution', without inverted commas around the term, to refer generically to whatever internal disposal of public power exists within a state. The term 'constitutional', without inverted commas, is used in a similar way.

A '"constitutional"' government, with inverted commas, refers within the present work to an ostensible government which qualifies for governmental status under customary international law and which has a valid basis for its claim to power under the constitutional arrangement of the state that already existed before the success of its claim to governmental status. Conversely, the present work uses the term '"unconstitutional"' government to refer to a government which qualifies for governmental status under customary international law and which at the time its claim became successful had no valid claim to power in the existing constitutional arrangement of the state.[40] More broadly, a '"constitutional"' claim or claimant to governmental status refers to a claim that or claimant to governmental status whose claim to power has a valid basis in the constitutional arrangement of that state which exists at the time of that claim. An '"unconstitutional"' claim or claimant to governmental status refers to a claim that or claimant to governmental status whose claim has no valid basis in the constitutional arrangement of the state at the time of the claim. Given their use also in other senses,[41] the present work avoids the terms 'de facto government' and 'de jure government' as ways of referring to an 'unconstitutional' government and a 'constitutional' government,

[38] On the relationship between the government and the organs of a state, see section 2.2.1.

[39] See also International Law Commission (ILC), 'Draft Articles on the Law of Treaties with Commentaries' in Ybk ILC [1966] vol II, 187, 190 (art 2, comment 15); Magiera (n 37) §15. Further on the forms that a state's constitution may take, see section 4.2.2.3.

[40] In turn, the use of such punctuation in referring to an 'unconstitutional' government of a state ensures accuracy since, at the time of the success of the claim of that government, the state is taken fundamentally to have changed its constitution. Accordingly, the claim to power of that government will, upon its success, indeed have a valid claim to power in the internal disposal of public power within that state. In this regard, see further chapter 2, n 8 and accompanying text. Put differently, if the term 'unconstitutional' did not refer to the existing constitution of a state, there could never be, strictly speaking, an unconstitutional government.

[41] On the different senses in which these terms are used, see chapter 2, nn 96 and 99, including accompanying text.

respectively. For the same reason, the present work does not use the term 'legitimacy' to refer to '"constitutionality"'.[42]

A 'government-in-exile' of a state refers, within the present work, to a government of a state which is comprised of one or more persons based outside the territory of that state.

In the light of the abstract juridical character of a state, international law requires rules on the representation of a state and the attribution of conduct to that state. As used in the present book, the 'representation' of a state refers, unless otherwise specified, to the authoritative expression of the will or view of that state for one or more purposes of international law. Whether the ostensible representation of a state is effective for the purposes of international law is a question distinct from whether conduct is attributable to that state for the purposes of international law. This distinction is uncontroversial, even if the terminology does not consistently reflect it[43] and even though the content and application of the rules concerning the representation or attribution of a state may not be identical in all contexts.[44] Only the representation of a state is premised on the anthropomorphic conception of the state in its quality as an international legal person. The attribution of conduct to a state neither amounts to nor is generally dependent on the authoritative expression of the will or view of that state.[45]

The term 'effectiveness', when used in the present work to characterize the ostensible representation of a state, indicates that such ostensible representation does indeed reflect the will or view of the state. Similarly, the characterization of the acceptance of a state's ostensible representation as effective refers to the acceptance that the ostensible representation reflects the will or view of the state. The term 'effectiveness' is preferred over alternatives, such as 'validity', in order to avoid the conflation of the logically-prior question whether the ostensible representation emanates from the state with other possible questions concerning whether international law ultimately treats such representation as having legal force. In

[42] On the different senses in which the term 'legitimate' is used in relation to an ostensible government of a state, see section 4.2.2.5.1.

[43] See eg ILC, 'Articles on the Responsibility of States for Internationally Wrongful Acts' in Ybk ILC [2001] vol II(2) 31 ('ARSIWA') 73 (art 20, comment 5); *Duke Energy International Peru Investments No 1, Ltd v Republic of Peru, Award* (ICSID Case No ARB/03/28) (18 August 2008) §§247–8, 250. See also 'First Report on State Responsibility by Mr. James Crawford, Special Rapporteur' (22 July 1998) UN Doc A/CN.4/490/Add.5, §151. For the use of the term 'represent', 'representative', etc as employed in the present work, see eg Vienna Convention on the Law of Treaties (adopted 23 May 1969, entered into force 27 January 1980) 1155 UNTS 331, arts 7(1)–7(2), 51; *Armed Activities on the Territory of the Congo (New Application: 2002) (Democratic Republic of the Congo v Rwanda), Jurisdiction and Admissibility* [2006] ICJ Rep 6, 27, §46; *Arrest Warrant of 11 April 2000 (Democratic Republic of Congo v Belgium), Judgment* [2002] ICJ Rep 3, 22, §53. See also Sereni, 'La représentation en droit international' (1948) 73 Hague *Recueil* 69, 73–4.

[44] On possible variations to the rules concerning the representation of states, see sections 2.3 and 5.3.2.

[45] There may exist specific, narrow exceptions. See eg ARSIWA (n 43) 52 (art 11) (both acknowledgement and adoption appear to depend on the representation of that state).

accordance with its focus,[46] the present work uses the term 'state' to refer, unless otherwise specified, to an existing state, not a state *in statu nascendi*.

Further, more specific clarifications appear throughout the book as and when necessary.

1.4 Overview of the Book

Each of the four substantive chapters of the book focuses on particular aspects of the international legal regulation of the identity of governments of states.

Chapter 2 considers the foundational international legal characteristics and features of 'the government' of a state that enable the ascertainment and explanation of much of the rest of the international legal framework on the identity of the governments of states. It first notes the existence of certain specific organ-statuses which are occupied only by persons who belong to the government of a state before demonstrating that the government of a state is in a distinctive position to represent that state. It enjoys plenary or near-plenary capacity to represent the state. The chapter then identifies certain presumptive sovereign freedoms of a state which relate to the identity of a state's government. Most notable in this regard is the freedom of each state to choose its government. Finally, the chapter highlights a range of indications that to be the government of a state is to enjoy an objective international legal status.

Chapter 3 focuses on the recognition by states of foreign governments. After certain terminological and other clarifications, it surveys the modes of recognition of governments, providing insights into the ways in which states may recognize the governmental status of an ostensible government. Next, the chapter ascertains the rules regulating the practice concerning the recognition by states of foreign governments and the value of such practice in ascertaining the identity of a state's government as a matter of customary international law. The chapter posits that the recognition by states of foreign governments, which in certain forms is common, provides valuable evidence as to the objective basis on which the identity of a state's government is to be ascertained for the purposes of customary international law. It indicates, moreover, that, while not being under a general obligation to accord express recognition to the government of another state, a state does not enjoy unfettered discretion under international law as to whom it accepts or rejects as the government of another state.

Chapter 4 seeks to ascertain the customary international legal framework for identifying the government of a state. It does so by analysing state practice on the recognition of governments and by having regard to the analytical value of

[46] Recall section 1.2 above.

the presumptive sovereign freedoms of each state identified earlier in this work. Additionally, the chapter examines whether the criteria for governmental status under customary international law are indeed a means for ascertaining the state's choice of government. It argues that there exists a customary international legal framework for identifying the government of a state, which in general gives effect to the exercise of the presumptive sovereign freedom of each state to choose its government. According to this framework, an autonomous 'constitutional' claimant to governmental status will generally qualify as the government of a state. An autonomous 'unconstitutional' claimant can enjoy governmental status only in the absence of an autonomous 'constitutional' claim. To attain but not to retain governmental status, an autonomous 'unconstitutional' claimant must also exercise effective control over the state's territory and population.

Chapter 5 discusses legal questions concerning the identity of the governments of states in the context of international organizations. It suggests that, in general, international organizations may and do accept as effective the ostensible representation of a state by the 'right' government. At the same time, in certain circumstances, an international organization may accept as effective the ostensible representation of a state through the 'wrong' government. Additionally, international organizations are sometimes empowered to limit the participation of a state in their work on account of the latter's possession of a specific ostensible government, including when that is the 'right' government. None of this is unambivalently understood to violate any rights of the affected state. Nor is there anything in this clearly to undermine the freedom of each state to choose its government or the objective international legal existence of a state's government. At the same time, the possibility of effective representation by the 'wrong' government nuances the distinctive capacity of a state's 'right' government to represent that state. This, as well as possible limitations on state participation in the work of an international organization, indicate that the plenary or near-plenary capacity of the government of a state to represent that state may in effect be limited for at least certain purposes of international law on grounds which relate to the identity or basis of the claim to power of a state's government but which are nevertheless extraneous to the customary international legal framework for the assessment of governmental status.

Chapter 6 offers concluding remarks. It distils the main points on the significance of certain conceptual legal aspects of the identity of the governments of states to the ascertainment and understanding of the international legal rules on the identity of such governments; on the objective existence and distinctive representative function of the government of a state; on the relevance of an ostensible government's democratic representativity and its willingness to ensure compliance with international law to the identity and representation of the state by that ostensible government; and on the international legal framework for identifying the government of a state, including a conceptual justification for the particular significance that customary international law accords to the 'constitutionality' of a claim.

The central thesis of this work is that, as a means of giving effect to the choice of that state, customary international law provides an objective framework for ascertaining the identity of the government of a state. The government of a state, which performs a distinctive function in the representation of that state for the purposes of international law, appears to have an objective existence for all purposes of international law. Each other state does not enjoy unfettered discretion under international law to accept or reject whomever it wishes as the government of that state, even if the recognition by states of foreign governments is valuable evidence in ascertaining the international legal identity of a state's government. As a matter of customary international law, an autonomous ostensible government with a 'constitutional' claim to governmental status will invariably enjoy governmental status, while an autonomous 'unconstitutional' ostensible government will enjoy governmental status only in the absence of a rival 'constitutional' claim. Unlike a 'constitutional' claimant, moreover, an 'unconstitutional' claimant will attain governmental status only once it secures effective control over the state's territory and population. At the same time, while the government of a state need be neither democratically representative nor willing to ensure the state's compliance with the state's international legal obligations in order to qualify for governmental status as a matter of customary international law, such matters may result in the government of a state being unable to represent the state in the context of an international organization as a result of the exercise by that organization of a power to limit the participation by one of its members in its work. At least certain international organizations appear to have the power also to accept as effective the ostensible representation of a state by an ostensible government which does not qualify for governmental status as a matter of customary international law, including to prevent the representation by a government which is unwilling to ensure the state's compliance with certain international legal obligations of the state. Such possibilities do not necessarily undermine the objective international legal existence of a state's government or the freedom of each state to choose its government.

2
The Concept of 'the Government' of a State in International Law

2.1 Introduction

This chapter explores the fundamental conceptual aspects of the government of a state in international law. More specifically, it considers certain core aspects of the government of a state as organs of that state, the general function of a state's government in representing that state for the purposes of international law, the extent to which certain presumptive sovereign freedoms of each state relate to the framework for the identification of a state's government, and the indications concerning the objective international legal existence of a state's government. An examination of these matters sheds light on other aspects of the international legal regulation of the identity of governments of states considered later in this book. Indeed, it serves to better understand when and why something involves recognition or denial of governmental status as well as contributing to an assessment of the framework for the identification and role of the government of a state for the purposes of international law.

The present chapter finds that, possible variations to the composition of the government of a state notwithstanding, there are certain offices of a state which are invariably occupied by the person or one or more of the collectivity of persons comprising the government of that state. This reflects the distinctive position of the government of a state to represent that state for the purposes of international law since it is through these office-holders that a state is ordinarily represented for the purposes of international law. In contrast to what is sometimes suggested, the capacity of a state's government to represent that state for the purposes of international law does not generally depend on the features of that government or the circumstances in which it finds itself. Further, the chapter identifies certain presumptive sovereign freedoms of a state which relate to the international legal framework on the identity of the governments of state. More concretely, certain specific presumptions that relate to the general presumption against limitations on state sovereignty may contribute to ascertaining any objective customary international legal criteria as might exist for the identification of a state's government. Additionally, the presumptive sovereign freedom of each state to choose its government might contribute to rationalizing any such framework whilst being relevant also to the ascertainment of the existence of certain international legal rules on the conduct of

The Identity of Governments in International Law. Niko Pavlopoulos, Oxford University Press. © Niko Pavlopoulos 2024.
DOI: 10.1093/9780191991509.003.0002

other states and international organizations in respect of an ostensible government of a state. Finally, the chapter posits that there exist further indicators that to be the government of a state is to qualify for an objective international legal status.

2.2 The Person or Persons Comprising the Government of a State as State Organs

2.2.1 In General

Among the organs of a state, there are certain organ-statuses for which only a person who or collectivity of persons that possesses constitutional authority to direct at least certain aspects of executive authority on the state's behalf may qualify. In this light, and since the government of a state within the meaning of international law refers to the person who or collectivity of persons that is constitutionally empowered to exercise executive authority on a state's behalf,[1] these organ-statuses may be referred to as 'governmental offices'. Indeed, only the person or one or more of the persons comprising the government of a state as a matter of international law may qualify as the occupant of a 'governmental office', whether on a 'de facto' or 'de jure' basis. The 'governmental offices' of a state include the office of head of state and the office of head of government as well as the ministerial offices of the state.[2] As regards the qualification by one or more of the persons comprising the government of a state for these organ-statuses, seven points of clarification are the following.

First, as with state organs in general, the constitution of a state reflects the basis on which a person or collectivity of persons occupies a specific governmental office of a state for the purposes of international law. This is in part because the constitution of a state provides the basis for determining what qualifies as the municipal law of that state,[3] thus comprising the ultimate basis for identifying so-called 'de jure' state organs, that is, organs which have 'that status in accordance with the internal law of the State'.[4] The constitution of a state comprises the basis for identifying also any so-called 'de facto' organs of a state (that is, state organs which qualify as such

[1] Recall section 1.3. See further n 8 below and accompanying text.

[2] See also ILC, 'Draft Articles on Jurisdictional Immunities of States and Their Property and Commentaries Thereto' in Ybk ILC [1991] vol II(2), 13, 15 (art 2, comments 8 and 10).

[3] See Kelsen, *The Pure Theory of Law* (Knight tr, 2nd edn, University of California Press 1967) 198; Hart, *The Concept of Law* (OUP 1961) 91–6; Roth, *Governmental Illegitimacy in International Law* (OUP 2000) 52.

[4] ILC, 'Articles on the Responsibility of States for Internationally Wrongful Acts' in Ybk ILC [2001] vol II(2) 31 ('ARSIWA') 40 (art 4). For the view that the rules concerning the identification of state organs for the purposes of state responsibility are similar, if not identical, to the rules in other contexts, see ibid (art 4, comment 11 n 122); ILC, 'Draft Conclusions on Identification of Customary International Law, with Commentaries' in *ILC Report* (2018) UN Doc A/73/10, 122, 132 (conclusion 5, comment 2).

on the basis of sharing a structural link with some other organ of that state[5]) since the constitution is the 'structure' by reference to which a 'de facto' state organ qualifies as such.[6] This is so even though the evidence on the basis of which a person or collectivity of persons can qualify as a de facto state organ may vary depending on the circumstances, including on the position of the putative de facto organ within the state's constitution.[7]

Secondly, and relatedly, that the person or collectivity of persons comprising the government of a state occupies certain offices under the constitution of a state does not necessarily render a state's constitution a clear or sufficient basis for identifying the government of that state. The constitution of a state might itself be in need of identification, perhaps most notably when it has purportedly undergone a fundamental change. Indeed, a fundamental change to the constitution of a state—that is, a change to the constitution which does not take place in accordance with the existing constitution of a state and thus requires an independent reason for its constitutional force—occurs as a result of a successful claim by an 'unconstitutional' ostensible government to governmental status.[8] Even if the constitution of a state is known, it does not necessarily exhaust the considerations relevant to the identification of a state's government. Regardless of whether the constitution of a state suffices to establish that a person qualifies as a state organ for the purposes of international law, additional considerations might be—indeed, as a matter of positive international law are[9]—relevant to the qualification as a matter of international law by a person or collectivity of persons as the government of a state.

[5] See 'Summary Records of the Meeting of the Fiftieth Session (1998), 2553rd Meeting' in Ybk ILC [1998] vol I, 228, 229, §3; Momtaz, 'Attribution of Conduct to the State: State Organs and Entities Empowered to Exercise Elements of Governmental Authority' in Crawford, Pellet, and Olleson (eds), *The Law of International Responsibility* (OUP 2010) 237, 241; Crawford, *State Responsibility: The General Part* (CUP 2013) 127, for a reference to the 'structural test of ARSIWA Article 4'; *Flamingo DutyFree Shop Private Limited v Republic of Poland, Award* (12 August 2016), available at <http://italaw.com/sites/default/files/case-documents/italaw7709_3.pdf>, §§434–5.

[6] See eg ARSIWA (n 4) 40 (art 4(1), which provides that an organ has some position 'in the organization of the State').

[7] For example, 'complete dependence on . . . and control [by another state organ]' is necessary and sufficient, according to the ICJ, for a person or collectivity of persons not purporting to exercise executive authority on a state's behalf to qualify as a de facto state organ for the purposes of state responsibility (see *Military and Paramilitary Activities in and against Nicaragua (Nicaragua v USA), Merits, Judgment* [1986] ICJ Rep 14 ('*Nicaragua v USA*') 62, §109. See also *Application of the Convention on the Prevention and Punishment of the Crime of Genocide (Bosnia and Herzegovina v Serbia and Montenegro), Judgment* [2007] ICJ Rep 43 ('*Bosnia v Serbia*') 205, §§392–3. At the same time, a person can be considered a de facto state organ possessing executive authority to act on the state's behalf for at least certain purposes of international law on the basis of other evidence. See further section 2.2.2 on the identification of the occupants of 'governmental offices'.

[8] On fundamental changes to the constitution of a state, see Marek, *Identity and Continuity of States in Public International Law* (Librairie Droz 1954) 25; Kelsen (n 3) 209; ARSIWA (n 4) 49 (art 9, comment (4)). See also *Aguilar-Amory and Royal Bank of Canada Claims (Great Britain v Costa Rica)* (1923) I UNRIAA 375 ('*Tinoco*') 375, 381. Further on the overlap between the criteria for governmental status and the circumstances involving a fundamental change to a state's constitution, see section 4.2.2.3.

[9] See further chapter 4.

Thirdly, the extent to and ways in which the constitution of a state permits the government of that state to direct the exercise of authority on a state's behalf varies between states. For example, the constitutional authority of the central government of a federal state may be more limited than the authority of the government of a unitary state. Such differences do not affect the qualification of the person or collectivity of persons directing the exercise of authority on a state's behalf as the government of a state.

Fourthly, the exercise of executive authority on a state's behalf refers, in the present context, to 'inherent' authority, signifying that the authority is not delegated, devolved, or otherwise exercised under the direction of another state organ. The exercise of executive authority on a state's behalf is not to be confused with the exercise of executive functions on behalf of a state. A number of persons not comprising part of the government of a state may exercise executive functions on behalf of that state,[10] such as the persons serving as police officers of a state.

Fifthly, a governmental office is to be distinguished from an office whose occupant is constitutionally-entitled to exercise executive authority only if and when certain circumstances arise that preclude the person who or group of persons that ordinarily exercises such authority,[11] at least until those circumstances arise. For example, the Heir Apparent of Liechtenstein was not to be treated as comprising part of Liechtenstein's government until 2004, when he commenced serving as active Regent.[12] This distinction notwithstanding, the same person may occupy both a governmental office and an office that would entitle him or her to exercise additional aspects of executive authority on a state's behalf in circumstances such as death or illness of another, typically more senior member of the state's government.[13] For example, since the late 1970s, the Prime Minister of the United Arab Emirates (UAE) has generally served also as Vice-President of the UAE.

Sixthly, a person who has been elected or appointed to a particular office may not immediately assume that office. The election or appointment may be due to take effect at a later date. There is little to suggest that international law treats any such person as the occupant of the office to which he or she has been elected or appointed before the election or appointment is due to take effect. The assertion to the contrary accords substantial weight to the ICJ's apparent openness in one case to take into account a statement by a person who had been elected to but who had not yet assumed a representative governmental office when determining the

[10] See also *Propend Finance Pty Limited and others v Sing and others* (UK, Court of Appeal of England and Wales, 2 May 1997) (1999) 111 ILR 611, 648–9.

[11] Common circumstances in this regard include death, illness, and resignation. Common municipal legal titles for such office-holders include 'Regent', 'Deputy-President', 'Vice-President', 'Deputy-Prime Minister', and 'Vice-Prime Minister'.

[12] For an example of the exercise of a head of state's powers by a regent, see Jennings and Watts (eds), *Oppenheim's International Law*, vol 1 (Wildy 1992) 147, §43 n 1.

[13] Common municipal legal titles for such office-holders include 'Deputy-President', 'Vice-President', 'Deputy-Prime Minister', and 'Vice-Prime Minister'.

position of a state on a specific matter.[14] This decision alone does not conclusively demonstrate that a person elected or appointed to a governmental office is to be treated as the occupant of that office before the election or appointment is due to take effect.[15] Indeed, states generally appear to be rather careful in distinguishing between before and after the time at which a person's appointment or election is due to take effect.

Seventhly, it is irrelevant to the question whether a person or collectivity of persons occupies a governmental office that that person or group of persons also exercises other aspects of public authority on the state's behalf, perhaps collectively with other individuals. It is not uncommon for one or more members of a state's government to be part of the main legislative organ of that state, as is typical in so-called 'parliamentary systems' of government, or to have the constitutional authority to issue presidential decrees or executive orders with the force of municipal law.

Beyond these points of clarification, the scope of the constitutional authority of each governmental office-holder to direct at least certain aspects of executive authority on a state's behalf may vary between states. One notable variation is that the head of state may enjoy the constitutional authority to exercise relevant functions only ceremonially, without any real power to act of his or her own accord,[16] in which case the person or persons comprising this organ may be said to comprise part of the state's government within the international legal meaning of the term only in a notional sense.[17] The situation concerning Japan, whose head of state holds no real executive power under the constitution of Japan and who, as a constitutional matter, 'shall not have powers related to government', is one of the clearest examples in this regard. Its head of state is vested under its constitution with the power to act in respect of certain 'matters of state', including matters which involve the exercise of executive authority.[18] The constitutional requirement that Japan's head of state acts 'with the advice and approval of the Cabinet' in performing his or her 'acts in matters of state' does not preclude the head of state from comprising

[14] Foakes, *The Position of Heads of State and Senior Officials in International Law* (OUP 2014) 32 n 12, in reference to *Application of the International Convention on the Elimination of All Forms of Racial Discrimination (Georgia v Russian Federation), Preliminary Objections* [2011] ICJ Rep 70 ('*Georgia v Russia*') 105, §77.

[15] Even this one decision by the ICJ in question, in recording the absence of a 'specific follow-up' on the matter in question by or under the authority of the President-elect once he had assumed office, appears to have concerned itself with the possibility of the government of a state rendering effective its initially-ineffective ostensible representation rather than with the possible effectiveness of the ostensible representation of a state by the President-elect as such. See *Georgia v Russia* (n 14). On the possibility of a state rendering effective its initially-ineffective ostensible representation, see n 80 below and accompanying text.

[16] On the constitutional variation of the powers of heads of states of different states, see also Watts, 'The Legal Position in International Law of Heads of States, Heads of Governments and Foreign Ministers' (1994) 247 Hague *Recueil* 9, 24–5. See further section 2.2.2.

[17] See also ILC (n 2) (art 2, comment 8: 'a head of State may be equated with the central Government').

[18] Constitution of Japan (1947) arts 3–4, 6–7.

part of Japan's government for the purposes of international law. Not wholly dissimilar requirements may exist under the constitution of a state in relation to a minister, who will unquestionably comprise part of its government.

2.2.2 Characteristics of Specific Governmental Office-Holders

There are two alternative ways for the constitution of a state to reflect the basis on which a person or collectivity of persons occupies a specific governmental office of a state for the purposes of international law.

The first is the 'de jure' basis, which involves the designation by a state's municipal law of that person or collectivity of persons as the occupant of a governmental office.[19] Such designation is usually indirect, for example by specifying a process for the appointment of a person to a particular office, rather than naming a particular person as the occupant of an office. In the case of such indirect designation, the municipal law of a state enables the identification of the person or collectivity of persons comprising at least part of a state's government only to the extent that the process of designation has been carried out and has resulted in the clear indication of a person as the occupant of the office. This may not always be the case, for example if a state's constitution provides that the person entitled to occupy a particular office is to be decided by an electoral process and the result of such an election is contested, as was the case with the presidential election of Côte d'Ivoire in 2010 and of The Gambia in 2016.[20] The contested validity of an election might also create difficulties in ascertaining whom the constitution of a state designates as the occupant of a specific governmental office. It was on the basis of such contestation that rival claims to governmental status arose in Venezuela in 2019.[21]

The second is the 'de facto' basis, specifically as a result of the conferral of constitutional authority, albeit without express municipal legal basis, to exercise at least some of the functions typically exercised by the occupant or occupants of each of governmental office. For example, Muammar Qadhafi is generally accepted to have been the head of state of Libya at a time during which he appears to have held only a nominal position under the municipal law of Libya as 'Brotherly Leader and Guide of the Revolution'.[22] Support for the distinction drawn by one commentator

[19] See also Jennings and Watts (n 12) 1057, §466.

[20] See further chapter 4, n 79 and accompanying text.

[21] Further on the rival claims in respect of Venezuela, see section 4.2.2.3.

[22] See eg *Gaddafi* (France, Court of Appeal of Paris, 20 October 2000) (2004) 125 ILR 490, 495 for the view that Muammar Qadhafi was 'the highest authority in the Libyan Republic', noting in this regard that, at the relevant time, 'he exercise[d] effectively and continuously the normal functions reserved for Heads of State', although the court there had regard also to 'the constitutional proclamation giving him the title of "Guide of the Grand Revolution of 1 September"'. See also *Keesing's* [1979] 29665A on the relinquishment by Mr Qadhafi of 'all administrative duties' and on the statement that 'the revolution and authority must be separate from one another', noting also that 'the leadership of the revolution shall not be involved in any post, secretariat or people's committee, but will join the forces of the revolution and

between 'a "strong man" behind a régime' and a head of state or head of government is scarce.[23] In one of the two municipal cases on which the asserted distinction is based, the court considered only the written constitution of the state—not the actual internal disposal of public power within that state[24]—in determining whether or not the 'strong man' in question comprised the head of state.[25] In the other case, the court dismissed the claim of immunity in respect of the 'strong man' at least in part on grounds other than his non-qualification as head of state or head of government of a foreign state.[26] Indeed, the court in that case accepted that the 'strong man' was 'chief executive' of Venezuela.[27] The distinction between a 'strong man' and the occupant of a governmental office may nevertheless be valid insofar as the former is understood to refer to a person with mere influence over one or more other persons in whom executive authority vests.

The municipal legal designation of a person or collectivity of persons as the holder of a governmental office is separate, moreover, from the municipal legal title of a specific organ. Although there are certain common municipal legal titles for the holder of each governmental office,[28] the municipal legal title of a state organ may not always serve accurately to identify the constitutionally-designated occupant of each governmental office. For example, although 'President' is a common municipal legal title for a head of state, the municipal legal nomenclature of 'President' does not necessarily mean that the holder of that office is designated as head of state. The Constitution of Iran, for instance, gives Iran's head of government the title of 'President',[29] while Iran's head of state is the Leader of the Leadership Council.[30] The distinction between the municipal legal designation and the municipal legal title of a state organ collapses where the municipal law of a state designates one of its organs for one of the offices by naming that organ as the occupant of one of these offices. For example, the municipal legal title of the head of government of Andorra is 'head of Government'.[31] That said, the existence of a collective organ of a state to which the municipal law of that state refers as 'the government' does not necessarily mean that only the persons comprising that organ belong to the government of that state for the purposes of international law. Indeed, it is not

work for it (Col Kadhafi, however, retained his responsibilities as Supreme Commander of the Armed Forces)'.

[23] On the distinction, see Watts (n 16) 22 n 4.
[24] Further on the forms of a state's constitution, see section 4.2.2.3.
[25] *United States v Noriega* (1990) 746 F Supp 1506, 1519.
[26] *Jimenez v Aristeguieta*, 5th Circuit (1962) 311 F.2d 547, 558.
[27] Ibid, 557.
[28] For heads of state, these include 'President' and 'King' or 'Queen', although there are others, such as 'Governor-General', 'Emir', and 'Duke'; for heads of government, they include 'Prime Minister' and 'Chancellor', although there are again others; and for a minister of a state, they include 'Minister' and 'Secretary of State'.
[29] Constitution of the Islamic Republic of Iran (1979, as amended in 1989) art 60.
[30] Ibid, chapter VIII.
[31] Constitution of the Principality of Andorra (1993) art 73.

uncommon for the municipal law of a state to refer only to its head of government and its ministers as 'the government',[32] perhaps in reflection of where real, as opposed to nominal, executive power lies.[33]

Although the functions exercised by each governmental office-holder may vary between states,[34] the functions typically exercised by the holder of each governmental office may nevertheless provide valuable evidence in ascertaining the constitutional standing of a particular person or collectivity of persons as the occupant of a specific governmental office, especially where there is no express municipal legal designation on which to rely in this regard. The functions typically exercised by the head of state, the head of government, and the ministers of a state are as follows.

The head of state is typically the titular commander-in-chief of the state's armed forces. It is also ordinarily the head of state who formally accredits persons as diplomatic representatives of that state.[35] Additionally, insofar as the head of state is not the same person or group of persons as the head of government, the former may be involved, even if only in a formal sense, in the appointment of the latter. Not least because the internal disposal of public power within one state may vary from that of another state, the functions of heads of state may vary among states.[36] Insofar as the same person or collectivity of persons does not comprise both the head of government and head of state, real executive power may vest only in the head of government, with the head of state possessing only ceremonial powers. Alternatively, executive authority may be shared, to varying degrees and in different ways, between the head of state and the head of government. Where real executive power is shared between the head of state and head of government, it is more common than not that the head of government acts under the head of state's direction, although other arrangements are possible, including one in which the occupant of each of these two offices directs the exercise of authority on a state's behalf in respect of different matters. This is the case in France during times of *cohabitation*, where the head of government and the head of state do not belong to the same political party. If the same person or collectivity of persons acts both as head of government and head of state, as is the case with many so-called 'absolute monarchies' and 'presidential systems' of government, there is no head of government who is different from the head of state and amongst whom executive authority is to be shared.[37]

[32] Other not-uncommon municipal titles for a collective organ that is charged under the constitution of a state with exercising at least certain aspects of executive authority on behalf of that state include 'Cabinet' and 'Council of Ministers'.

[33] Further on this distinction, recall n 16 above.

[34] See Watts (n 16) 25. See also ARSIWA (n 4) 39 (chapter II, comment 6).

[35] See also Watts (n 16) 26–31; *Gaddafi* (n 22).

[36] On the variation of arrangements among states as regards the constitutional powers of heads of state and heads of government, see also Watts (n 16) 24–5, 97.

[37] See eg Constitution of the United States of America (1789, as amended in 1992) ('Constitution of the USA') art II, s1(1). See also Basic Law of Governance of Saudi Arabia of 1992, arts 55–6. But see ibid, art 65 and the designation of the 'Crown Prince' as the Deputy Prime Minister of Saudi Arabia, who, in fact, qualifies as the head of government of Saudi Arabia.

The head of government is typically the state organ which at least nominally leads the affairs of the government of that state. The precise nature and scope of the constitutional powers of a head of government vary among states. The constitutions of some states permit or require heads of government to chair government meetings while requiring the collective agreement of all ministers of a state in order for a decision to be constitutionally effective, while other heads of government possess constitutional authority to make substantive decisions on their own. The head of government is, moreover, typically involved in the appointment and dismissal of the ministers of a state and in the delimitation of ministerial portfolios, although such decisions may in substance be taken or ceremonially be performed by a head of state.[38]

A minister of a state is a person who exercises executive authority on the state's behalf in respect of specific matters. While the matters in respect of which a specific minister directs the exercise of authority on the state's behalf is left to each state's discretion, there are certain common arrangements, such as having a specific person tasked with directing the state's foreign affairs, *viz* a minister for foreign affairs.[39] It is also common for a state to have a specific minister for each of internal affairs, defence, justice, and finance. Depending on the constitutional arrangements of a state, its ministers may be involved in determining policies of the government concerning matters beyond the portfolio specifically assigned to them, especially when the head of government is *primus inter pares* among the state's ministers.[40]

Given that international law defers to the internal disposal of public power within a state in order to identify the organs of that state, and since international law does not regulate '[t]he structure of the State',[41] the number and nature of the offices that the person or collectivity of persons comprising each state's government occupies under the constitution of a state may vary.[42]

One possible variation in this regard is that two or more persons may qualify as head of state of the same state. These persons may be joint occupants of a single office, as is the case with the persons comprising the Swiss Federal Council[43] and those comprising the Sovereignty Council of Sudan between 2019 and 2021;[44] they

38 Recall n 16 above and accompanying text.

39 On ministers of foreign affairs generally, see Jennings and Watts (n 12) 1045–6, §459 and sources cited therein; Watts (n 16) 98–9; *Arrest Warrant of 11 April 2000 (Democratic Republic of Congo v Belgium), Judgment* [2002] ICJ Rep 3, 21–2, §53.

40 See eg Federal Constitution of the Swiss Confederation (1999, as amended in 2018) ('Constitution of Switzerland') art 177(1).

41 ARSIWA (n 4) 39 (chapter II, comment 6).

42 See also n 37 above and accompanying text.

43 Constitution of Switzerland (n 40) arts 174, 175(1), and 177(1). As another example, see Article V of Annex 4 of the General Framework Agreement for Peace in Bosnia and Herzegovina of 14 December 1995, attached to 'Letter Dated 29 November 1995 from the Permanent Representative of the United States of America to the United Nations Addressed to the Secretary-General' (30 November 1995) UN Doc A/50/790–S/1995/999 on the Presidency of Bosnia and Herzegovina.

44 Draft Constitutional Declaration of Sudan (2019) art 11.

may occupy distinct offices but nevertheless be constitutionally required to act on a collegial basis, as is the case in San Marino;[45] or they may each separately exercise some of the functions of the head of state, as was the case in Libya between 1979 and 2011, during which time Libya had both a de jure head of state (the General Secretary of the General People's Congress) and a de facto head of state (Muammar Qadhafi), in addition to a head of government (the Secretary-General of the General People's Committee).[46] It may be, moreover, that one person is the nominal occupant of one of these offices while only some other person who occupies a distinct office is constitutionally empowered to exercise the functions of the former office. This is the case with the states which designate the head of state of the UK as their own head of state, the constitution of each of which provides that the head of state's powers are to be exercised by another person, for example a 'Governor-General'.[47] Where two or more persons are joint occupants of a single office, there may be one person designated to speak and act in the name of this collectivity of persons for certain purposes, as a result of which the identity of a state's head of state will vary depending on the purpose for which this identity is in question. This is the case in Switzerland, where the President of the Swiss Federal Council acts as Switzerland's head of state at meetings of states at the UN, while the Swiss Federal Council as a whole accredits Switzerland's diplomatic representatives.

The rules of international law are sufficiently adaptable to accommodate such differences, as reflected, for example, in the Convention on the Prevention and Punishment of Crimes against Internationally Protected Persons, including Diplomatic Agents, which provides that for its purposes a head of state includes 'any member of a collegial body performing the functions of a Head of State under the constitution of the State concerned'.[48] At the same time, whether or not a person qualifies on his or her own as the sole occupant of a governmental office may not always be clear, as was apparently the case in respect of Alija Izetbegovic's claim as head of state of Bosnia and Herzegovina, rather than as a member of the Presidency, which as a collective body comprised the head of state of Bosnia and Herzegovina.[49]

[45] See Constitution of the Republic of San Marino (1974) art 3.

[46] See also *Keesings* (n 22) 29665A.

[47] See eg Constitution of Tuvalu (1978, as amended in 1986) ss48(1) and 51(2). A similar situation exists in Antigua and Barbuda, Australia, the Bahamas, Belize, Canada, Grenada, Jamaica, New Zealand, Papua New Guinea, Saint Kitts and Nevis, Saint Lucia, Saint Vincent and the Grenadines, and the Solomon Islands. See the list of states maintained by the UN Protocol and Liaison Service, available at <http://protocol.un.org/dgacm/pls/site.nsf/HSHGNFA.xsp>, in which 'His Majesty King Charles III' is mentioned as one of the two heads of state of each of those states. See also Watts (n 16) 21.

[48] See Convention on the Prevention and Punishment of Crimes against Internationally Protected Persons, including Diplomatic Agents (adopted 14 December 1973, entered into force 20 February 1977) 1035 UNTS 167, art 1(1)(*a*). See, not dissimilarly, Vienna Convention on the Representation of States in their Relations with International Organizations of a Universal Character (adopted 14 March 1975, not in force), reproduced in (1975) 69 AJIL 730 ('VCRSIO') art 50(1).

[49] For the divergent views in this regard compare, on the one hand, 'Letter Dated 1 March 1993 from the Prime Minister of Bosnia and Herzegovina to the Secretary-General' (5 March 1993) UN Doc A/47/899–S/25360, 3 and, on the other, *Application of the Convention on the Prevention and Punishment of*

One further possible difference among states as regards the number and nature of the offices that the person or collectivity of persons comprising the government of a state may occupy under the constitution of a state is that the roles of two or more governmental office-holders may be exercised by the same person or collectivity of persons, as with the aforementioned 'absolute monarchies' and 'presidential systems' of government. In such a case, that person or collectivity of persons qualifies as the occupant of more than one governmental office within the same state for the purposes of international law, as is the case with the President of the USA.[50] As another example, the Swiss Federal Council acts collectively, at least in certain contexts, both as head of state and head of government.[51] It is not uncommon, moreover, for a head of government permanently or temporarily to occupy a particular ministerial office, especially that of foreign affairs. It may also be that a particular person or collectivity of persons occupies a governmental office in more than one state. For example, the Constitution of the Principality of Andorra designates 'the President of the French Republic' as one of the two 'Coprinces' of Andorra and provides that the 'Coprinces are, jointly and indivisibly, the Head of State' of Andorra.[52]

2.3 The Government of a State and the Representation of That State

2.3.1 The Distinctive Role of a State's Government in the Representation of That State

Although there is no specific rule or set of international legal rules on the representation of states which is uniformly applicable to the ostensible representation of a state on all matters,[53] it is generally only the person or persons comprising the government of a state and certain persons acting under the authority of the government that can effectively represent that state for the purposes of international law, except where and insofar as states opt to vary the application of these rules *inter se*.[54]

The representative function of the government of a state is apparent from, among other things, the following three points.

the Crime of Genocide (Bosnia and Herzegovina v Yugoslavia (Serbia and Montenegro)), Order of 8 April 1993 [1993] ICJ Rep 3, 14.

[50] Constitution of the USA (n 37).
[51] See Constitution of Switzerland (n 40).
[52] Constitution of the Principality of Andorra (1993) art 43(2).
[53] See eg ARSIWA (n 4) 73 (art 20, comment 6: '[w]ho has authority to consent to a departure from a particular rule may depend on the rule').
[54] See further sections 5.3.2 and 5.5.

First, the head of state, the head of government, and the minister for foreign affairs of a state—each of whom invariably comprises at least part of that state's government[55]—possess *ex officio* plenary or near-plenary capacity as a matter of international law to represent the state for the purposes of international law. This is reflected in, among other places, rules concerning the representation of a state in specific contexts.[56] There may exist certain specific and narrow exceptions to the representative capacity of one or more of these office-holders, perhaps on account of a rule that allows for the representation of a state in some specific context by only some other person. For example, a restrictive interpretation of Article 22 of the VCDR suggests that only the head of a diplomatic mission may consent to the entry by the authorities of the receiving state onto the state's diplomatic premises,[57] although a more flexible approach might better reflect the position under customary international law.[58] An exception or limitation to the representative capacity of one or more of these office-holders might instead arise from a constitutional restriction on the representative capacity of one or more of these three office-holders being relevant for one of more purposes of international law. For instance, it has been said that, '[f]or a promise to be legally binding on a State, it is necessary that the authorities from which it emanates should be competent so to bind the State (a question of internal constitutional law and international law)'.[59] A constitutional restriction on the representative capacity of any of these three office-holders may instead serve as a basis for a state to invoke the invalidity of its ostensible representation that has taken place in contravention of such a limitation.[60] This appears to be the case in respect of the ostensible expression of a state's consent to be bound by a treaty that occurs in violation of a 'properly publicized' constitutional limitation

[55] Recall section 2.2.1.

[56] See eg Vienna Convention on the Law of Treaties (adopted 23 May 1969, entered into force 27 January 1980) 1155 UNTS 331 ('VCLT') art 7(2)(*a*). See, generally, *Armed Activities on the Territory of the Congo (New Application: 2002) Democratic Republic of the Congo* v *Rwanda, Jurisdiction and Admissibility* [2006] ICJ Rep 6 ('*DRC v Rwanda*') 27, §46; ARSIWA (n 4) 39 (chapter II, comment 5). See also Watts (n 16) 31–2, 100–1; Jennings and Watts (n 12) 1034, §445 n 3, and §446; Magiera (n 37) §31; Salmon, 'Representatives of States in International Relations' (2007) MPEPIL, available at <http://opil.ouplaw.com/home/mpil>, §§12–20. See further section 5.3.2.

[57] Vienna Convention on Diplomatic Relations (adopted 18 April 1961, entered into force 24 April 1964) 500 UNTS 95 ('VCDR').

[58] See eg Denza, *Diplomatic Law: Commentary on the Vienna Convention on Diplomatic Relations* (4th edn, OUP 2016) 123.

[59] *Nuclear Tests (Australia v France), Judgment* [1974] ICJ Rep 253, 374, §3 (Dissenting Opinion of Judge de Castro). See also ILC, 'Guiding Principles Applicable to Unilateral Declarations of States Capable of Creating Legal Obligations' in *ILC Report* (2006) UN Doc A/61/10, 369, 373–4 (Principle 4, comment 2), including on the indication of the subsequent confirmation or the absence of subsequent rejection by the state of its ostensible representation. According to the Special Rapporteur on unilateral acts, the significance of the constitutional arrangements of a state to the effectiveness as a matter of international law of a unilateral declaration purporting to bind the state is one 'of the most difficult aspects' of the rules of international law concerning unilateral declarations ('Eighth Report on Unilateral Acts of States, by Mr. Víctor Rodríguez Cedeño, Special Rapporteur' (26 May 2005) UN Doc A/CN.4/557, §189).

[60] See eg VCLT (n 56) art 46.

to act in this regard.[61] Such possibilities notwithstanding, the distinctive representative capacity of each of these three office-holders remains beyond doubt.

Secondly, other ministerial office-holders, who are also invariably members of a state's government,[62] also appear to possess *ex officio* capacity as a matter of international law to represent the state for at least certain purposes of international law. For example, the Drafting Committee of the United Nations Conference on the Law of Treaties believed that

> [i]n States where a Minister was responsible for a certain sector of foreign affairs, for example the Minister for Commonwealth Relations in the United Kingdom and the Minister for International Trade in some other countries, the reference [in what became Article 7(1)(*b*) of the VCLT] to 'practice of the States concerned' might relieve the Minister of the need to produce full powers when negotiating a treaty on a matter within his competence.[63]

Moreover, it seems to be the view of the ICJ and the International Law Commission that ministers of a state have the capacity to undertake a unilateral commitment that is binding on their state 'in respect of matters falling within their purview'.[64]

Thirdly, while a state typically has persons who possess the capacity to represent it for one or more specific purposes but who do not belong to its government,[65] such persons ordinarily act under the authority of its government. For example, the head of a diplomatic mission, who is appointed by and ordinarily acts under the instructions of the government of a state,[66] possesses the capacity as a matter of international law to represent the state for at least certain purposes of international law.[67] As another example, the government of a state may authorize a specific individual not belonging to the government to represent the state for some specific purpose, such as the adoption of a treaty, through the conferral of full powers.[68]

[61] It seems to be the ICJ's position that such publicization renders the limitation 'manifest' within the meaning of Article 46 of the VCLT and, according to the ICJ, '[t]he rules concerning the authority to sign treaties for a State are constitutional rules of fundamental importance' and thus, seemingly, are 'rule[s] of... internal law of fundamental importance' within the meaning of Article 46 of the VCLT. See *Land and Maritime Boundary between Cameroon and Nigeria (Cameroon v Nigeria: Equatorial Guinea intervening), Judgment* [2002] ICJ Rep 303, 430, §265.

[62] Recall section 2.2.1.

[63] United Nations Conference on the Law of Treaties, First Session (26 March–24 May 1968), 'Official Records, Summary Records of the Plenary Meetings and of the Committee of the Whole, 34th Plenary Meeting' (23 April 1968) UN Doc A/CONF.39/11, 185, 185–6, §5. See also VCLT (n 56) art 7(1)(*b*).

[64] *DRC v Rwanda* (n 56) 27–8, §§47–8; ILC (n 59) 374 (Principle 4, including comment 3 thereof).

[65] See, generally, Salmon (n 56) §§21–9.

[66] See further section 3.3.2.2.1.2.

[67] See eg VCLT (n 56) art 7(2)(*b*); VCDR (n 57) art 22.

[68] See VCLT (n 56) art 7(1)(*a*). For an example of the conferral of full powers in practice, albeit in relation to a minister of the state, see *Maritime Delimitation in the Indian Ocean (Somalia v Kenya), Preliminary Objections* [2017] ICJ Rep 3, 22, §43.

While the identity of a 'competent authority of a State' to confer full powers may depend on the constitution of that state,[69] a 'competent authority' will invariably be only a person or collectivity of persons comprising at least part of or perhaps acting under the authority of the state's government, given that the conferral of such powers is an exercise of executive authority.[70]

In addition to the three above points, an abundance of state practice and numerous international legal instruments reflect the capacity of the government of a state to represent that state for the purposes of international law. To give just one example in this regard, the preamble of the Charter of the United Nations (UN Charter) notes that it is 'Governments [which] have agreed to the present Charter of the United Nations and do hereby establish an international organization to be known as the United Nations'.[71]

That the government of a state is in a distinctive position to represent that state for the purposes of international law[72] arises from both the representative capacity of persons belonging to or acting under the authority of the state's government and the general inability of persons neither comprising at least part of nor acting under the actual or ostensible authority of the government of a state to represent that state for the purposes of international law.

This general inability of persons who neither belong to nor act under the authority of a state's government to represent the state for the purposes of international law is reflected in the approach of states to ostensible governments whose governmental status they deny.[73] For example,[74] the states which denied the governmental status of the nationalist ostensible government of China refused to

[69] See ILC, 'Text of Draft Articles [on Law of Treaties] 1–10 and 14–17 with Commentary' in Ybk ILC [1959] vol II, 92, 106 (art 15, comment 5).

[70] The distinctive role of the government of a state in this regard remains unaffected by the possibility that the constitution of a state may also require the approval of some other person for the constitutionally-compliant conferral of full powers, even if international law defers to such a requirement.

[71] Charter of the United Nations (signed 26 June 1945, entered into force 24 October 1945), available at <http://un.org/en/about-us/un-charter/full-text>. On the interchangeable use of 'people' and state', see chapter 4, nn 236–7 and accompanying text.

[72] See also Blix, 'Contemporary Aspects of Recognition' (1970) 130 Hague *Recueil* 587, 696; Verhoeven, *La reconnaissance internationale dans la pratique contemporaine: Les relations publiques internationales* (Pedone 1975) 65; Doswald-Beck, 'The Legal Validity of Military Intervention by Invitation of the Government' (1985) 56 BYIL 189, 190; Crawford, 'The Rights of Peoples: "Peoples" or "Governments"?' in Crawford (ed), *The Rights of Peoples* (Clarendon Press 1988) 55, 55; ILC (n 2) (art 2, comment 9); Talmon, *Recognition of Governments in International Law with Particular Reference to Governments in Exile* (OUP 1998) viii, 67 (including citations therein), and 115 (including citations therein); Kelsen, 'Recognition in International Law: Theoretical Observations' (1941) 35 AJIL 605, 615; Grant, 'Current Developments: Afghanistan Recognizes Chechnya' (1999–2000) 15 AUILR 869, 874; Crawford, *The Creation of States in International Law* (2nd edn, CUP 2006) 33–4; *Georgia v Russia* (n 14) 87, §37; *Valores Mundiales, SL and Consorcio Andino SL v Bolivarian Republic of Venezuela* (ICSID Case No ARB/13/11), *Annulment Proceeding, Procedural Resolution No 2* (29 August 2019) §42.

[73] On the use within the present work of the term 'denial' and the attendant verb in relation to governmental status, see section 3.2.3.

[74] See also Talmon (n 72) 117–20, 142–4, 149–59 in respect of the difference between so-called 'governments-in-exile' and political authorities 'in exile' that do not qualify as the government of a state.

accept as effective the ostensible signature and ostensible ratification by China of the VCDR through persons acting under the authority of that ostensible government.[75] As another example, the *Comité national français*, which the Allies considered not to be the government of France, was not invited by them to sign the 'Declaration by United Nations' of 1942.[76] As one further example, the states which denied the governmental status of the Free Provisional Government of Kuwait (FPGK) referred to this denial in asserting the illegality of Iraq's military action in Kuwait,[77] an action which Iraq claimed to take pursuant to a 'request made by the Free Provisional Government of Kuwait'.[78]

While there are certain possible exceptions pursuant to which a state may be represented not through its government, the distinctive position of the government of the state remains clear. The following three points are indicative in this regard.

First, while there are apparent specific limited exceptions where states agree *inter se* in advance to the possibility of their effective representation for one or more specific purposes of international law not through its government, such prior agreement will have been expressed through the government of each state.[79]

Secondly, the possibility that a state may, through its government, render effective for at least certain purposes of international law its ostensible representation 'by a person who cannot be considered . . . as authorized to represent a State for that purpose'[80] does not undermine—indeed, it affirms—the distinctive function of each state's government in the representation of that state for the purposes of international law. Also in this case, it is because of the conduct of a person or

[75] See eg 'Multilateral Treaties Deposited with the Secretary-General, status as at 1 April 2009' (2009) vol I, UN Doc ST/LEG/SER.E/26 ('Multilateral Treaties Deposited with the Secretary-General'), 113–14 n 4. Also in relation to the ostensible representation of China in relation to multilateral treaties, see Lauterpacht, 'The Contemporary Practice of the United Kingdom in the Field of International Law—Survey and Comment, III' (1957) 6 ICLQ 301, 302–3; Lauterpacht, 'The Contemporary Practice of the United Kingdom in the Field of International Law—Survey and Comment, IV' (1957) 6 ICLQ 506, 508–9; Lauterpacht, 'The Contemporary Practice of the United Kingdom in the Field of International Law—Survey and Comment, VI' (1958) 7 ICLQ 514, 523; Lauterpacht, 'The Contemporary Practice of the United Kingdom in the Field of International Law—Survey and Comment, VII' (1959) 8 ICLQ 146, 159.

[76] On the declaration, see 'Declaration by United Nations, Washington, January 1st, 1942, with Related Documents' (1943) 204 LNTS 381. On the exclusion of the 'Free French Movement', see DCER [1943] IX, 100. See also Talmon (n 72) 120, also on the statement by the depositary of the Declaration in relation to 'statements of adherence to its principles from appropriate authorities which are not Governments'.

[77] For reliance on the denial of the governmental status of the FPGK in opposing the legality of Iraq's action, see UNSC, 'Official Records, 2932nd Meeting' (2 August 1990) UN Doc S/PV.2932, 12–13 (USA), 19 (UK). On the distinctive position of the government of a state to request military assistance, recall also chapter 1, n 7.

[78] UNSC (n 77) 11.

[79] See further sections 5.3.2 and 5.5.

[80] See VCLT (n 56) art 8. For the view that as a matter of international law 'every person regarded as a representative of the State under Article 7 [of the VCLT] is entitled to confirm the act', see Angelet and Leidgens, 'Article 8' in Corten and Klein (eds), *The Vienna Convention on the Law of Treaties: A Commentary* (OUP 2011) 155, 160, §10.

collectivity of persons comprising at least part of or acting under the authority of a state's government that the ostensible representation of a state by some other person becomes effective.

Thirdly, while international law might provide for the effective representation of a state for some purpose not through its government and without the state's prior agreement to such representation, there would appear to remain some connection between the identity of a state's government and the effectiveness of the ostensible representation of that state. An example in this regard is the putative rule according to which the ostensible representation of a state *in statu nascendi* by the political authority which eventually comprises the government of that state is treated, upon the entity's attainment of statehood, as an effective representation of that state, at least insofar as this is not subject to the possible subsequent disavowal of its ostensible representation.[81] Another example is the possible analogous rule applicable in respect of the ostensible representation of an existing state by a political authority which subsequently comprises the government of that state. Relevant to the first of these putative rules are the views of certain states that Algeria became a party to the 1949 Geneva Conventions immediately after the states in question accepted Algeria's statehood, before the six-month period that is ordinarily required for accession to any of these conventions to become effective.[82] For its part, the ICJ did not accept Croatia's argument that Article 10(2) of the Articles on the Responsibility of States for Internationally Wrongful Acts reflects a rule of customary international law that a state may be effectively represented in such a way.[83]

While the identity of a state's government must ordinarily be known in order for the will or view of the state to be determined, there are certain situations in which the will or view of a state may be ascertained without the clear determination of a state's government. While having only infrequently occurred, this is the case where each of two or more rival ostensible governments of a state express the same ostensible position of the state.[84] The will or view of a state as a matter of international

[81] If any such rule renders effective the ostensible representation of a nascent state only if the state does not subsequently disavow its ostensible representation, then there is an additional connection between the effectiveness of the ostensible representation of a state and its government. Indeed, it is then the case that the ostensible representation of a state is effective because of the conduct of the government of the state. See, generally, Crawford (n 72) 659–61, 663–4.

[82] See eg Talmon (n 72) 124–5. For further practice of possible relevance to one or more of these putative rules, see ibid, 142–3. It is noteworthy that some of these states accepted the status of Algeria as a party to these conventions only after a statement by Algeria to the effect that it considered itself bound by these conventions on the basis of the instrument of accession deposited by the 'Provisional Government of the Algerian Republic'.

[83] *Application of the Convention on the Prevention and Punishment of the Crime of Genocide (Croatia v Serbia), Judgment* [2015] ICJ Rep 3 ('*Croatia v Serbia*'), 52, §104. Recall also chapter 1, n 43 and accompanying text on the distinction between representation of a state and attribution of conduct to a state.

[84] This was apparently the case in respect of Venezuela in connection with the rectification proceedings in *ConocoPhillips Petrozuata BV, ConocoPhillips Hamaca BV and ConocoPhillips Gulf of Paria BV v Venezuela* (ICSID Case No ARB/07/30), *Decision on Rectification*, 29 August 2019, §25.

law may be unclear, moreover, even where the identity of its government is known. This is the case, for example, where the meaning of a specific statement is ambiguous[85] or where the view expressed by one member of a state's government is contradicted by the view of another member of that state's government.[86] None of this undermines the distinctive function of a state's government in representing that state for the purposes of international law.

2.3.2 Variations in the Representative Capacity of a State's Government?

The general capacity of the government of each state to represent that state for the purposes of international law notwithstanding, it has been occasionally suggested that the representative capacity for the purposes of international law of the government of a state depends on the characteristics of that government or the circumstances in which it finds itself.

One ground on which the representative capacity of the government of a state has been said to vary is its lacking a physical presence in the territory of that state. For example, eminent commentators have suggested that a so-called 'government-in-exile' of a state can represent a state for the purposes of international law only in strict accordance with limitations imposed by that state's constitution.[87] More fundamentally, it has been said that a 'government-in-exile' cannot effectively express the consent of a state to be bound by certain types of treaties[88] or even that '[t]here is a presumption . . . that a government, even if generally recognized, cannot speak for the state if it is not in firm possession of the state's territory'.[89] But as another commentator demonstrates, where a state recognizes an ostensible 'government-in-exile' as the government of another state, the former state accepts the possession by that government of equal capacity to represent the state as a government '*in situ*' would possess.[90] Contrary to what this analysis might be taken to suggest,[91]

[85] See eg *Armed Activities on the Territory of the Congo (Democratic Republic of the Congo v Uganda), Judgment* [2005] ICJ Rep 168, 198, §51.

[86] See eg *Bosnia v Serbia* (n 7) 52–4, §§18–24; ICJ, 'Document Entitled "Application for Revision of the Judgment of 26 February 2007 in the Case Concerning the *Application of the Convention on the Prevention and Punishment of the Crime of Genocide (Bosnia and Herzegovina v Serbia)*", Statement by H.E. Judge Ronny Abraham, President of the International Court of Justice' (Press release No 2017/12, 9 March 2017).

[87] See McNair and Watts, *The Legal Effects of War* (4th edn, CUP 1966) 426.

[88] See the materials cited in Talmon (n 72) 135 n 100.

[89] See Wright, 'United States Intervention in Lebanon' (1959) 53 AJIL 112, 120. See also Ruys and Ferro, 'Weathering the Storm: Legality and Legal Implications of the Saudi-Led Military Intervention in Yemen' (2016) 65 ICLQ 61, 81–4.

[90] See Talmon (n 72) Part II, especially 144, 205. See also 'Second Issues Paper by Patrícia Galvão Teles and Juan José Ruda Santolaria, Co-Chairs of the Study Group on Sea-Level Rise in relation to International Law' (19 April 2022) UN Doc A/CN.4/752, §§138–53.

[91] A close reading of the text indicates that this suggestion should not be considered as implied in Talmon's work. See Talmon (n 72), ix.

however, the recognition, non-recognition, or denial[92] by a state of governmental status in respect of an ostensible government is not determinative of the effectiveness of the ostensible representation by the claimant vis-à-vis the state that has recognized or denied governmental status or which has not recognized the ostensible government. This is true in respect of both 'governments-in-exile' and governments '*in situ*'. What is generally determinative is the enjoyment or otherwise of governmental status.[93]

Another basis on which the representative capacity of a government has been said to vary is whether a government is recognized as a 'de jure' or a 'de facto' government.[94] But since the qualification by an ostensible government for governmental status is not dependent on its recognition as such by one or more specific states,[95] so too is the characterization of the government being recognized as 'de jure' or 'de facto' irrelevant to the representative capacity of an ostensible government which does indeed comprise the government of a state. Even if there existed a distinction in international law between a 'de jure' and a 'de facto' government,[96] evidence generally does not suggest that the representative capacity of a 'de facto' government differs from the representative capacity of a 'de jure' government.[97] Any apparent difference in the representative capacity of a 'de facto' government from that of a 'de jure' government, including, for example, as regards an entitlement to control state assets,[98] results from the fact that the

[92] On these different categories of practice in relation to recognition, see section 3.2.3.

[93] See further sections 2.5 and 3.5. But see the text accompanying n 101 below.

[94] See eg Jennings and Watts (n 12) 157, §46.

[95] See further section 3.5.1.

[96] One possibility as regards an objective basis to distinguish a 'de facto government' from a 'de jure government' insofar as both relate to the government of a state concerns the 'constitutionality' of that government. But the relevant terms have not consistently been used in a way to suggest the existence of an international legal distinction between 'de facto governments' and 'de jure governments'. On the use of these terms, see eg *Georges Pinson (France) v United Mexican States* (1928) V UNRIAA 327, 422–3, §51(2)–(3); HC Debs, 21 March 1951, vol 485, cols 2410–11 (UK); Lauterpacht, *Recognition in International Law* (CUP 1947, repr 2013) 336; Chen, *The International Law of Recognition with Special Reference to Practice in Great Britain and the United States* (Praeger 1951) 271–2; Brownlie, 'Recognition in Theory and Practice' (1982) 53 BYIL 197, 207; Jennings and Watts (n 12) 155, §46, including n 2; Talmon (n 72) 60; Crawford, *Brownlie's Principles of Public International Law* (OUP 2019) 143; *Dr Ali Mahmoud Hassan Mohamed v Mr Abdulmagid Breish and others* [2020] EWCA Civ 637, §43; 'Case on Behalf of the Foreign Secretary', submitted as part of its intervention in *The "Maduro Board" of the Central Bank of Venezuela v The "Guaidó Board" of the Central Bank of Venezuela* [2021] UKSC 57, available at <https://assets.publishing.service.gov.uk/government/uploads/system/uploads/attachment_data/file/1003665/20210818_Foreign_Secretary_s_Case_18_June_2021.pdf>, §29.

[97] See also Brownlie (n 96) 207. For the treatment by the ICJ of a specific reference to 'the responsible *de jure* or *de facto* government' as the 'state', albeit not in the context of state representation, see *Reparation for Injuries Suffered in the Service of the United Nations, Advisory Opinion* [1949] ICJ Rep 174, 177.

[98] See eg FRUS [1948] vol V(2), 1051, 1052; Jennings and Watts (n 12) 157, §46. But see also eg the recent action by the USA in respect of certain assets of Afghanistan involving the treatment of specific individuals which appear not to comprise part of any claimant to governmental status as entitled to dispose of the assets in question, 'The United States and Partners Announce Establishment of Fund for the People of Afghanistan' (Media Note, 14 September 2022), available at <https://state.gov/the-united-states-and-partners-announce-establishment-of-fund-for-the-people-of-afghanistan>.

former term is sometimes used to characterize a political authority not as the government of a state but as some other authority, for example as an occupying power or an insurrectionary political authority (also known as a 'local de facto government').[99]

State practice ultimately does not support the existence in positive international law of a general difference as regards the representative capacity of different governments. It may nevertheless be that, for some specific purpose of international law, the ostensible representation of a state is ineffective on account of some characteristic of its government or the situation in which its government finds itself. For an example of what is in effect a specific limitation to the representative capacity of a state's government, an international organization may limit a state's participation in the work of that organization, including on account of some matter directly related to a specific ostensible government of that state.[100]

As a conceptually-separate matter, international law may preclude the representation of a state from having the international legal consequences it would otherwise have when the government of a state has certain characteristics or finds itself in certain circumstances. Illustrative in this regard is the effect that international la w may give to a declaration by a state that it does not consider the treaty applicable between itself and one or more states whose governments the former state does not recognize,[101] thereby precluding the treaty from having legal effect between the declarant state and the state or states to which the declaration relates. Such a declaration might be made either during the performance by the declaring state of an act involved in the conclusion of a multilateral treaty or on the later occasion of one or more other states purporting to become party to a multilateral treaty.[102] An

[99] See Jennings and Watts (n 12) 155, §46; Lauterpacht (n 96) 289–90, 338; Talmon (n 72) 60. See also eg *Banco de Bilbao v Sancha, Banco de Bilbao v Rey* [1938] CA 176, 189 on 'the de facto Government of [a] portion of [a] State'; *Bank of Ethiopia v National Bank of Egypt and Liguori* [1937] Ch 513, 522, in which Clauson J uses the term 'de facto government' to refer to the local administration established by an occupying power in part of the occupied state's territory; *Haile Selassie v Cable and Wireless Limited (No 2)* [1939] Ch 182, 195.

[100] See further section 5.6.2.

[101] This does not mean that recognition is constitutive of governmental status. See further section 3.5. On whether acts amount to recognition or denial of governmental status, see section 3.3.

[102] On the legal effect of such statements, see eg Lauterpacht (n 96) 372; 'First Report on the Law of Treaties, by Sir Humphrey Waldock, Special Rapporteur'(26 March 1962) in Ybk ILC [1962] vol II, 27, 56 (art 13, comment 8); ILC, 'Draft Articles on the Law of Treaties' in Ybk ILC [1962] vol II, 161, 168 (art 9(4)); 'Third Report on Reservations to Treaties, by Mr. Alain Pellet, Special Rapporteur' (30 April–19 July 1998) UN Doc A/CN.4/491 and Add.1-6 ('Third Report on Reservations to Treaties'), 252, §§163(*c*)–175; ILC, 'Guide to Practice on Reservations to Treaties' in *ILC Report* (2011) UN Doc A/66/10/Add.1, 32, 96 (Guideline 1.5.1, comment 5). Cf European Commission of Human Rights (ECommHR), *Cyprus v Turkey (App No 8007/77), Report of the Commission, 4 October 1983* (1993) 15 EHRR 509, 519; Committee on the Elimination of Racial Discrimination (CERD), 'Inter-State Communication Submitted by the State of Palestine against Israel' (12 December 2019) UN Doc CERD/C/100/5, §3.13.

example is the statement by the USA that its participation in the 1941 Convention for Limiting the Manufacture and Regulating the Distribution of Narcotic Drugs

> does not involve any contractual obligation on the part of the United States of America to a country represented by a régime or entity which the Government of the United States of America does not recognise as the government of that country until such country has a government recognised by the Government of the United States of America.[103]

Another example is the statement by France that, 'not recognizing the Government of the (Democratic Kampuchea), [it] consider[ed] as being without effect the acceptance by that Government of the 1976 amendments to articles 24 and 25 of the Constitution of the World Health Organization, adopted by the Twenty-ninth World Health Assembly on 17 May 1976'.[104]

The conceptual distinction between a limit to the representative capacity of a state's government and any preclusion of the ordinary international legal consequences of the representation of a state notwithstanding, it may not always be clear in practice whether a particular rule concerns the former or the latter. An example in this regard concerns the suggestion that the consent by a state's government to foreign military force in the territory of that state during a civil war cannot render such force unwrongful.[105] This is sometimes said to arise from a limitation under international law of the capacity of the state's government effectively to represent that state in those circumstances for the purposes of consenting to the foreign use of force.[106] Others appear to take the view that some other rule, such as the prohibition on intervention or the right to self-determination, precludes another state in such a situation from relying on the consent of the state on whose territory the former uses force.[107]

[103] 'Multilateral Treaties Deposited with the Secretary-General' (n 75) 529 (USA, §6). This was discussed in 'Third Report on Reservations to Treaties' (n 102) 252, §173.

[104] See the declaration of 13 October 1983, reproduced in Amendments to Articles 24 and 25 of the Constitution of the World Health Organization (adopted 17 May 1976, entered into force 20 January 1984) 1347 UNTS 289, 295.

[105] For divergent views as to the existence of any such rule as a matter of positive international law, see eg Corten, *The Law against War* (2nd edn, Hart 2021) 274–5; Ruys and Ferro (n 89) 86–96; Gray, *International Law and the Use of Force* (4th edn, CUP 2018) 85–95.

[106] See eg Fox, 'Intervention by Invitation' in Weller (ed), *The Oxford Handbook of the Use of Force in International Law* (OUP 2015) 816, 818.

[107] See eg Doswald-Beck (n 72) 251 (but see also ibid, 243, which might be taken to suggest that the rule concerns a limitation on the representative capacity of the government); Corten (n 105) 274–8. See also Brownlie, *International Law and the Use of Force by States* (OUP 1963) 327.

2.4 The Presumptive Sovereign Freedom of Each State to Choose Its Government and Certain Related Freedoms

In accordance with the general presumption under international law against limitations on state sovereignty,[108] each state is free as a matter of international law to choose its government, subject to any prohibitive rule or specific undertaking to the contrary. Putting it another way, it is presumed that the government of a state is, as a matter of international law, whichever person or collectivity of persons the state itself considers to be its government.[109]

As an international legal person, a state is nevertheless simply a juridical construct. For the purposes of international law, moreover, the will of a state is generally expressed through its government.[110] Accordingly, the presumptive sovereign freedom of each state to choose its government is no more than a formal legal notion or, putting it another way, a legal fiction.[111] A state has no direct means of expressing its choice of government for the purposes of international law. At the same time, international law itself may possess some objective means by which to ascertain whom a state is deemed to have chosen as its government. Indeed, in order for each state to retain its presumptive sovereign freedom to choose its government, there must exist some objective basis by which it can be deemed to have chosen a specific person or collectivity of persons as its government as a matter of customary international law. In the absence of such a framework, nothing would prevent the identity of a state's government from being determined by the subjective preference of every other state, in which case a limitation would be imposed in practice, if not in law, on that state's presumptive sovereign freedom to choose its government. That said, there is no necessary reason why an objective legal framework for establishing the identity of a state's government need serve to safeguard each state's freedom in this regard. It could instead limit that freedom. Whether such a framework does indeed safeguard the presumptive sovereign freedom of each state to choose its government depends on whether the various criteria comprising it can be conceptualized as means for ascertaining that choice rather than as restrictions on that choice.[112]

[108] See *The Case of the SS Lotus (France v Turkey), Judgment* (1927) PCIJ, Series A, No 10, 3, 19.

[109] See also Kelsen (n 72); Marek (n 8) 56, n 3 and accompanying text; Peterson, *Recognition of Governments: Legal Doctrine and State Practice, 1815–1995* (Macmillan 1997) 77; Crawford, 'Sovereignty as a Legal Value' in Crawford and Koskenniemi (eds), *The Cambridge Companion to International Law* (CUP 2012) 117, 129–30. See, moreover, eg 'Declaration of Señor Don Genaro Estrada, Secretary of Foreign Relations of Mexico, Published in the Press on September 27, 1930, Relating to the Express Recognition of Governments' (1931) 25 AJIL Supp 203, 203, on 'the right of foreign nations to accept, maintain or replace their governments'; UNGA, 'Official Records, 75th Session, 83rd Plenary Meeting' (18 June 2021) UN Doc A/75/PV.83, 9 (China); and the practice cited in chapter 5, nn 161–2.

[110] Recall section 2.3.1.

[111] See also 'Fourth Report on State Responsibility, by Mr. Roberto Ago, Special Rapporteur, 30 June 1972' in Ybk ILC [1972] vol II, 71, 145, §198.

[112] See further chapter 4.

In addition to the possibility of providing a rationalization for any objective international legal framework as might exist for identifying the government of a state, the presumption against limitations on state sovereignty militates against readily inferring the existence of a framework that would restrict the freedom of each state to choose its government. Since the identity and configuration of a state's government reflects at least part of the political system and constitution of that state,[113] and since each state enjoys the presumptive sovereign freedom to choose its political system[114] and its constitution,[115] the existence of a customary international legal criterion for governmental status that would limit either of these freedoms also ought not be readily inferred. In other words, a plausible view on any customary international legal criterion as might exist for governmental status that does not undermine any of these freedoms ought to be preferred over at least an equally-plausible criterion which would limit any of these freedoms. That said, the customary international legal criteria for governmental status ultimately might, in effect, limit one or more of these presumptive sovereign freedoms of a state.[116]

Additionally, the presumptive sovereign freedom of each state to choose its government may be of substantive relevance to the existence of rules on the conduct of states and international organizations in respect of an ostensible government of a state. For example, under customary international law, states are prohibited from intervening in those affairs of another state that international law leaves to the sovereign discretion of each state, while the powers of international organizations in such matters are at least sometimes limited. At least insofar as international law places no restriction on the presumptive sovereign freedom of each state to choose its government, the choice of the identity of the government of a state is a matter in which other states are prohibited as a matter of international law from intervening and in respect of which at least some international organizations enjoy no power to intervene.[117]

The traditional position is that 'a change of [states'] rulers or in their forms of government . . . are but expressions of a change of national will'.[118] In its

[113] Recall section 2.2.1.

[114] See UNGA res 2131 (XX) (21 December 1965) UN Doc A/RES/2131(XX) §5; UNGA res 2625 (XXV) (24 October 1970) UN Doc A/RES/2625(XXV) Annex, §1. See also UNGA res 36/103 (9 December 1981) UN Doc A/RES/36/103, §2(I)(b); *Western Sahara, Advisory Opinion* [1975] ICJ Rep 12, 43–4, §94; *Nicaragua v USA* (n 7) 108, §205 and 133, §263; ARSIWA (n 4) 39 (chapter II, comment 6); and eg UNGA, 'Official Records, 1st Session, 59th Plenary Meeting' (12 December 1946) UN Doc A/PV.59, 1215 (Mexico): '[w]e are not condemning [Francisco Franco] just because he is dictatorial and anti-democratic'; UNGA, '16th session, 1079th Plenary Meeting' (14 December 1961) UN Doc A/PV.1079, §10 (USA): 'we have no objection to a communist regime if that is what the people of a certain country want for themselves'. On the conflation of 'people' and 'state', see chapter 4, n 236 and accompanying text.

[115] See eg ARSIWA (n 4) 39 (chapter II, comment 6). See also *Certain German Interests in Polish Upper Silesia (Merits), Judgment* (1926) PCIJ, Series A, No 7, 3, 19.

[116] See further chapter 4.

[117] See further sections 3.4.2 and 5.5.1.

[118] *Bolívar Railway Company Case* (1903) IX UNRIAA 445, 452. See also *Croatia v Serbia* (n 83) 493, §66.1 (Separate Opinion of Judge *ad hoc* Kreca).

ascertainment of the rules concerning the identity of governments in international law, the present book considers at each appropriate stage the explanatory, analytical, and substantive value of the presumptive sovereign freedom of each state to choose its government and of certain associated freedoms as well as the possibility of restrictions on these freedoms.

2.5 The Objective Identity of a State's Government

It is generally accepted that international law has traditionally provided some objective framework for identifying the government of a state.[119] For example, the UK has stated that 'international law . . . defines the conditions under which a Government should be recognised'.[120] Barbados has posited that there exist 'basic requirements in classical international law for recognition [of governmental status]'.[121] Australia has expressed the view that a particular ostensible government 'ha[d] not [at a particular time] satisfied the internationally accepted criteria for recognition [of governmental status]'.[122] Spain maintained that recognition of governments 'should be applied in a consistent manner without making use of double standards'.[123] In the 1923 arbitral award between Great Britain and Costa Rica in the so-called '*Tinoco Case*', moreover, the sole arbitrator referred to 'the existence of a *de facto* government . . . according to the standard set by international law'.[124]

In addition to the state practice involving more-or-less clear references to the existence of an objective international legal framework for the assessment of governmental status, at least three points suggest that customary international law continues to provide such a framework, despite the occasional suggestion to the contrary.[125]

First, the identification of a state's government is at least in part determined by reference to the constitution of a state, which itself has an objective existence in international law.[126] The relevance of the constitution of a state to the identification of a state's government is reflected in the fact that the members of a state's

[119] See further section 3.5.1.

[120] See HC Debs, 21 March 1951, vol 485, cols 2410–11. The distinction drawn by the UK Secretary of State between recognition 'de jure or de facto'—a distinction which has no international legal significance insofar as each involves recognition as the government of a state—does not detract from the basic point that there exists an objective international legal framework for the identification of a state's government. Further on the use of the terms 'de jure' and 'de facto' in relation to the ostensible governments of states, see section 2.3.2.

[121] UNGA, 'Official Records, 28th Session, 2189th Plenary Meeting' (4 December 1973) UN Doc A/PV.2189, §109 (Barbados).

[122] 'Australian Practice in International Law 1978–1980' (1983) 8 AYIL 253, 274.

[123] UNGA, 'Official Records, 20th Session, 877th Meeting of the Sixth Committee' (17 November 1965) UN Doc A/C.6/SR.877, §11 (Spain).

[124] *Tinoco* (n 8) 381.

[125] For such suggestions, recall chapter 1, n 27.

[126] This must be so at least insofar as each state continues to be free as a matter of customary international law to choose its constitution. See also n 115 above and accompanying text.

government occupy the governmental offices of that state and the occupation of such an office reflects part of the constitution of that state.[127]

Secondly, the existence of an objective customary international legal framework for ascertaining the identity of a state's government is not just compatible with the presumptive sovereign freedom that each state enjoys under international law to choose its government.[128] More to the point, such a framework is necessary for the retention by each state of this and other freedoms. In the absence of such a framework, there would be no apparent limitation on each state to treat whomever it so wishes as the government of another state, which would undermine, among other things, the presumptive sovereign freedom of each state to choose its own government.[129]

Thirdly, it is generally accepted that under customary international law a state can possess no more than one government.[130] This presupposes the existence of objective means by which to determine which of two or more rival claimants qualifies as a matter of international law as the government of the state. Insofar as an objective framework exists under customary international law for determining which of two or more rival claimants to governmental status qualified for the purposes of international law as the government of the state, this framework might also provide the basis for determining whether a sole claimant to governmental status in respect of a state qualified as a matter of international law as that state's government. Indeed, state practice in general supports the position that a state may have no government, including where there exists only one ostensible government of that state. This appears to have been the position of at least certain states in respect of Somalia after the fall in 1991 of the government led by Siad Barre.[131] This is apparently also the view of the states, which—at least retrospectively—appear to have taken the position that the Baltic states retained their personality between 1940 and 1991, despite lacking governments.[132]

[127] Recall section 2.2.

[128] The objective existence of the constitution of a state is not in any serious doubt, nor could it be insofar as each state continues to be free as a matter of customary international law to choose its constitution. Recall section 2.4.

[129] Recall section 2.4. See further section 3.5.2.

[130] See eg *Gdynia Ameryka Linie Zeglugowe Spolka Akcyjna v Boguslawski and another* [1953] AC 11, 27 (Lord Porter) and 45 (Lord Reid); Talmon (n 72) 105–6, including nn 290–1 and n 294; ARSIWA (n 4) 49 (art 9, comment 4). See also section 3.2.3 on the recognition of one claim to governmental status as the derecognition of any other previously-recognized claim.

[131] See eg 'Brief for the United States as Amicus Curiae Supporting Affirmance' in *Mohamed Ali Samantar v. Bashe Abdi Yousuf et al*, available at <http://scotusblog.com/wp-content/uploads/2010/01/08-1555_us-amicus-supporting-affirmance.pdf>, 4.

[132] See eg European Community, 'Declaration at the Brussels European Community Extraordinary Ministerial Meeting', 27 August 1991, reproduced in (1991) 62 BYIL 558, in which the European Community member states 'welcome[d] the restoration of the sovereignty and independence of the Baltic States'. For the view that those states lacked governments during that time, see eg *Re an Application by Ernst Jaakson and Aarand Roos* (UK, High Court of England and Wales, 14 December 1990) (1991) 85 ILR 53, 57, 60; UKMIL (1983) 54 BYIL 361, 384.

Other similar views have been expressed in respect of other states at other times.[133]

2.6 Conclusion

The person or collectivity of persons comprising the government of a state occupies certain specific offices. In so doing, the government of a state performs a distinctive function in the representation of that state for the purposes of international law. Indeed, it is generally only the ostensible representation of a state through its government that is effective as a matter of international law. The government's representative capacity does not vary as a general matter of international law depending on its characteristic features or the circumstances in which it finds itself.

A fundamental but often-overlooked conceptual aspect of the relationship between a state and its government is that, absent any prohibitive rule or specific undertaking to the contrary, the identity of that government is a matter that the state is free to decide for itself in the exercise of its sovereignty. This and certain related presumptive sovereign freedoms of a state may be relevant to the ascertainment of any objective international legal framework as might exist for the identification of the government of a state for the purposes of customary international law. The presumptive sovereign freedom of each state to choose its government may contribute, too, to the rationalization of any such objective international legal framework as might exist. Additionally, this presumptive sovereign freedom may inform the existence of other rules of international law concerning the conduct of other states and international organizations in relation to the government of a state. There are a range of indicators, moreover, which suggest that the identity of a state's government is to be ascertained by objective reference to international law.

[133] See eg President's Statement, 'US Severs Diplomatic Contact with Noriega Regime' (1 September 1989) in DSB [1989] vol 89, No 2152, 69.

3
The Recognition of Governments

3.1 Introduction

The present chapter considers the practice concerning recognition by states[1] of the governments of other states before ascertaining the legal value of such practice to the identity of the government of a state as a matter of customary international law. This contributes to ascertaining the possible existence and content of an objective international legal framework for identifying the government of a state. The chapter examines, moreover, the rules on the lawfulness of recognition, non-recognition, and denial of governmental status under customary international law. Much of this enables the assessment as to whether or not international law restricts the presumptive sovereign freedom of each state to choose its government. Analysis of relevant practice in the light of the concept of the government of a state in international law suggests the following.

A state may recognize or deny governmental status through a range of acts. These include official statements involving the express recognition or denial of governmental status and conduct, which implies the acceptance or denial of a specific person as the occupant of a particular office or post or as possessing the capacity to perform certain acts on behalf of a state. Whether or not an act amounts to recognition or denial of governmental status may not always be clear. One reason for such uncertainty is the different senses in which the term 'recognition' may be used. Another reason for such uncertainty is the possibility of an individual being accepted as capable of acting or being treated in a manner analogous to the government of a state.

States are under no general international legal obligation to make known their view on the identity of another state's government. Nor is a state entirely free to accept and reject whomever it wishes as the government of another state. The prohibition on intervention may limit the extent to which a state can lawfully recognize or deny governmental status to a specific claimant to governmental status. In any event, other rules of customary international law limit the extent to which a state can choose which ostensible government to treat or to refuse to treat as the government of another state. These include rules concerning state representation and the treatment owed in respect of foreign governments. Whether states are prohibited

[1] On recognition by international organizations and by states in the context of international organizations, see section 5.4.

The Identity of Governments in International Law. Niko Pavlopoulos, Oxford University Press. © Niko Pavlopoulos 2024.
DOI: 10.1093/9780191991509.003.0003

from recognizing an ostensible government which arises in consequence of, or the attainment by which of governmental status would amount to, the violation of a peremptory norm of general international law is unclear.

The recognition by a state of a specific person or collectivity of persons as the government of another state does not make that person or collectivity of persons the government of the latter state for the purposes of customary international law. Put differently, recognition of governmental status is not constitutive of that status. Nor does the denial by a state of governmental status to a specific person or collectivity of persons as the government of another state preclude that person or collectivity of persons from being the government of that latter state as a matter of international law. At the same time, both the recognition and denial of governmental status by states provides valuable evidence as to the framework for the enjoyment of governmental status as a matter of customary international law and as to the identity of a specific state's government at a specific moment in time.

3.2 Prefatory Clarifications

3.2.1 The Meanings of Recognition

For the specific purposes of international law and without prejudice to how the term is understood in any body of municipal law,[2] 'recognition' by a state of a government refers in a broad sense to the expression or other manifestation of a view by a state that a specific person or collectivity of persons comprises at least part of another state's government.[3] In addition to recognition of a person or collectivity of persons as the government of a state proper, a person or group of persons may be recognized as the occupant of a governmental office, which amounts to recognition as at least part of a state's government.[4] 'Recognition of governmental

[2] For at least certain bodies of municipal law, moreover, the term 'recognition' is reserved for acts performed by the occupant or occupants of the office or offices in which the constitutional arrangement of the state vests executive authority to act on behalf of the state. See eg *Halsbury's Laws of England: International Law and Foreign Relations* (LexisNexis 2018) §48.

[3] See also Lauterpacht, *Recognition in International Law* (CUP 1947, repr 2013) 349; Peterson, *Recognition of Governments: Legal Doctrine and State Practice, 1815–1995* (Macmillan 1997) 1; Talmon, *Recognition of Governments in International Law with Particular Reference to Governments in Exile* (OUP 1998) 29–30; Wright, 'Some Thoughts about Recognition' (1950) 44 AJIL 548, 555; HC Debs, 21 March 1951, vol 485, cols 2410–11. On recognition generally, see 'Sixth Report on Unilateral Acts of States, by Mr. Victor Rodríquez Cedeño, Special Rapporteur' (30 May 2003) UN Doc A/CN.4/534 ('Sixth Report on Unilateral Acts') §49, in which 'acknowledgement of an existing situation' is noted as one of the 'constituent elements of the definition of the act [of recognition]'; Warbrick, 'The New British Policy on Recognition of Governments' (1981) 30 ICLQ 568, 568: '[i]n international law, recognition is the acknowledgement of a set of facts or a condition of things which has legal consequences'.

[4] On governmental offices, see section 2.2.1. See also Peterson (n 3) 86; Hackworth, *Digest of International Law*, vol 1 (US Government Printing Office 1940) 167–8.

status' is used interchangeably within the present chapter with 'recognition of a government' to refer, unless otherwise specified, to the recognition by a state of a person or collectivity of persons as at least part of the government of another state. Accordingly, the phrase 'recognition of governmental status' covers also the recognition of a person or collectivity of persons as the occupant of a governmental office, even if such recognition may not always make clear the recognizing state's view as to the entire composition of the other state's government.

'Recognition' of governmental status is used within the present chapter in a broad sense. Unless otherwise specified, it includes acts that are understood for the purposes of international law to amount to the representation of a state and acts that as a matter of international law are attributable to a state but which do not amount to the authoritative expression of the position of the state.[5] It is not uncommon for a state to recognize or deny governmental status through one of those organs of state that have *ex officio* plenary or near-plenary capacity to represent the state for the purposes of international law or, more accurately, through one of those organs that, as a constitutional matter, possess executive authority to represent the state in its international relations.[6] But there is no reason to exclude from the meaning of 'recognition' as a matter of international law the position by any other state organ or state agent on the identity of another state's government, even if it does not amount to an authoritative expression of the recognizing state's view as to the identity of another state's government.[7] Nor is there any reason to reserve the term 'recognition' for the purposes of international law only for acts that authoritatively express the intention of a state.[8]

[5] On the distinction between the usual broader sense of 'recognition' and the specific narrower sense of the term relating to the establishment or maintenance of diplomatic relations, see Kelsen, 'Recognition in International Law: Theoretical Observations' (1941) 35 AJIL 605, 605–7, who uses the terms 'legal' and 'political' recognition, respectively, which may be misleading because a political decision may underlie each type of recognition and since both 'political' and 'legal' recognition are legally significant. See also Brownlie, 'Recognition in Theory and Practice' (1982) 53 BYIL 197, 201; Chen, *The International Law of Recognition with Special Reference to the Practice in Great Britain and the United States* (Praeger 1951) 129; Talmon (n 3) 21–33.

[6] See eg Hackworth (n 4) 161–16. See, generally, Chen (n 5) 224.

[7] See eg *Wulfsohn v Russian Socialist Federated Soviet Republic (RSFSR)* (USA, New York Court of Appeals, 9 January 1923) (1933) 2 ILR 39, 40–1. See also *In Re: Terrorist Attacks on September 11, 2001, Case 1:03-md-01570-GBD-SN, Memorandum Decision and Order* (filed 21 February 2023) ('*In Re: Terrorist Attacks*') 28: 'accepting the Judgment Creditors' argument as to the Taliban's control over [Afghanistan's central bank] makes the implied recognition of the Taliban as Afghanistan's government inescapable'.

[8] Cf. Hackworth (n 4) 166; 'Sixth Report on Unilateral Acts' (n 3); Crawford, *Brownlie's Principles of Public International Law* (9th edn, OUP 2019) 139. See also Institut de Droit International, 'La reconnaissance des nouveaux Etats et des nouveaux gouvernements' (1936) art 12, as reproduced in (1936) 9 *Annuaire IDI* 300, 301; 'Case on Behalf of the Foreign Secretary' submitted as part of its intervention in *The "Maduro Board" of the Central Bank of Venezuela v The "Guaidó Board" of the Central Bank of Venezuela* [2021] UKSC 57 ('*Foreign Secretary's Case*'), available at <http://assets.publishing.service.gov.uk/government/uploads/system/uploads/attachment_data/file/1003665/20210818_Foreign_Secretary_s_Case_18_June_2021.pdf>, §22(1); *The 'Maduro Board' of the Central Bank of Venezuela v The 'Guaidó Board' of the Central Bank of Venezuela* [2021] UKSC 57 ('*Maduro v Guaido*') §80; Blix, 'Contemporary Aspects of Recognition' (1970) 130 Hague *Recueil* 587, 623–4, who distinguishes

That said, insofar as a state's intention refers to something which may be expressed only by one of the organs of state which can effectively represent that state for the purposes of international law, such intention may be relevant to certain narrower understandings of the term 'recognition'. For example, such intention might well be relevant to 'recognition' when understood more narrowly to refer only to acts which render opposable the recognized entity to the recognizing state,[9] or acts which express the willingness of a state to establish or maintain diplomatic relations with the state whose government is recognized through that ostensible government,[10] or perhaps to those acts that are sometimes considered to be accompanied by political support for the recognized claimant.[11]

Any such intention is unnecessary for recognition in a broader sense. Indeed, a focus on the intention of a state in determining whether or not a state has recognized a claimant's governmental status may be misleading because it may wrongly diminish the value of the practice of certain state organs and state agents. A focus on intention could be misleading also because it could be taken to suggest that a statement by a state that it does 'not recognize' a specific ostensible government is taken necessarily to imply that state's non-acceptance of the ostensible government as the government of another state, even in the presence of evidence to the contrary. For example, such a statement may signal only a state's unwillingness to accord political support to an ostensible government.[12]

Ultimately, there is no general distinction under international law between what is covered only by recognition of governmental status in the narrower sense and what additional acts are covered by the broader sense of recognition. For example, recognition in either the narrower or the broader sense may in the same circumstances both be lawful or unlawful, and both types of recognition may have probative value in relation to the international legal framework for identifying the government of a state. That said, the precise legal consequences and significance of recognition of governmental status may vary depending on the constitutional position or representative capacity as a matter of international law of the organ or agent whose conduct amounts to recognition of governmental status. For example,

between 'cognition' and 'recognition' (for the distinction between 'cognition' and 'recognition' on an alternative and less questionable basis, see Brownlie (n 5) 204).

[9] Albeit in the context of recognition of states, see Crawford, *The Creation of States in International Law* (2nd edn, OUP 2006) 27, referring to Charpentier, *La Reconnaissance Internationale et l'Évolution du Droit des Gens* (Pedone 1956) 217–25.

[10] Further on diplomatic relations and recognition of governmental status, see section 3.3.2.2.

[11] For the view that at least certain forms of recognition of governmental status may be seen as an expression of political support for the government being recognized, see eg FRUS [1948] vol V(2), 1052; 'Australian Practice in International Law 1978–1980' (1983) 8 AYIL 273; HL Debs, 28 April 1980, vol 408, col 1121–2WA; 'Letter from the Netherlands' Minister for Foreign Affairs Sent to the Parliament of the Netherlands on 4 July 1990', reproduced in Siekmann, 'Netherlands State Practice for the Parliamentary Year 1989–1990' (1991) 22 NYIL 237, 238.

[12] See eg nn 93–4 below and accompanying text.

the weight accorded to recognition for the purposes of the identification of a rule of customary international law,[13] whether recognition renders opposable the recognized government vis-à-vis the recognizing state,[14] and the lawfulness of a specific instance of recognition[15] may all vary depending on the constitutional authority or representative capacity as a matter of international law of the organ or agent through which a state has recognized an ostensible government.

3.2.2 Recognition as What?

A person or collectivity of persons, including one claiming governmental status, can be recognized in different capacities. Recognition of a person or group of persons as the government of a state is distinct from recognition of a person or group of persons as a national liberation movement or as some other *sui generis* entity.[16] Recent examples of recognition in such other capacities include the recognition in 2012 of the National Coalition for Syrian Revolutionary and Opposition Forces 'as the sole legitimate representative of the Syrian people',[17] the recognition in 2011 of the National Transitional Council (NTC) in Libya as 'the legitimate representative of the Libyan people',[18] and the recognition of the National League for Democracy (NLD) 'as the legitimate representative of the Burmese people'.[19] Earlier examples include the recognition in 1918 of the Czecho-Slovak National Council 'as the supreme organ of the Czecho-Slovak national interests, and as the present trustee of the future Czecho-Slovak Government'[20] and as 'the supreme organ of the Czecho-Slovak Movement in Entente countries';[21] recognition in 1940 of Charles de Gaulle

[13] See eg ILC, 'Draft Conclusions on Identification of Customary International Law, with Commentaries' in *ILC Report* (2018) UN Doc A/73/10, 122, 135 (conclusion 7, comment 5). On recognition of governmental status as state practice which is relevant to the ascertainment of the customary international legal framework for identifying the government of a state, see section 3.5.2.

[14] Such opposability appears to arise only when the act of recognition amounts to the international representation of a state (on the distinction between attribution and representation, recall section 1.3). See eg 'Sixth Report on Unilateral Acts' (n 3) §49.

[15] On the possibility that the lawfulness of recognition depends on the effects of such recognition, which may in turn vary, depending on the constitutional position or representative capacity of the organ from which the recognition emanates, see section 3.5.2.

[16] On the distinction between national liberation movements and governments, see eg HL Debs, 18 June 2014, vol 754, col 76WA; ILC, 'Articles on the Responsibility of States for Internationally Wrongful Acts' in Ybk ILC [2001] vol II(2) 31 ('ARSIWA') 50 (art 10); *Halsbury's Laws of England* (n 2) §47. See also 'Sixth Report on Unilateral Acts' (n 3) §§38, 76; FRUS [1943] vol II, 173.

[17] HC Debs, 20 November 2012, vol 553, col 445. See also the statements mentioned in Talmon, 'Recognition of Opposition Groups as the Legitimate Representative of a People' (2013) 12 CJIL 219, 220–32.

[18] Talmon, 'Recognition of the Libyan National Transitional Council' (*ASIL Insights*, 16 June 2011), available at <http://asil.org/insights/volume/15/issue/16/recognition-libyan-national-transitional-council>.

[19] Burmese Freedom and Democracy Act of 2003 (USA) s 2(14).

[20] FRUS [1918] Supp 1, vol I, 823.

[21] Hackworth (n 4) 203.

'as the leader of all free Frenchmen wherever they may be';[22] and the recognition in 1943 of the *Comité français de liberation nationale* (CFLN) 'as administering those French overseas territories which acknowledge its authority'.[23]

Recognition of a specific person or collectivity of persons in some capacity other than as a government of a state includes also the recognition of a person or group of persons as some state organ, insofar as that does not amount to recognition of the person or the group of persons in question as the occupant of a governmental office. Examples in this regard include the recognition by the so-called 'Lima Group' of 'the National Assembly . . . as a democratically elected constitutional institution in Venezuela'[24] and the more recent recognition by Canada of the National Assembly of Venezuela as 'the last remaining democratically elected institution in Venezuela'.[25]

The recognition of a person as the person to have been elected or appointed to, but not yet to have assumed, a governmental office, as was the case with the recognition, albeit not by states, of Adama Barrow as President-elect of The Gambia,[26] is also distinct from recognition of governmental status.[27]

The conceptual distinction between recognition as a government and recognition in some other capacity notwithstanding, the latter may serve as a precursor to the former, as has been the case with Adama Barrow, the President of the National Assembly of Venezuela, the NTC, and the successor of each of the CFLN and the Czecho-Slovak National Council. Despite this clear conceptual distinction, moreover, whether or not a particular act is one of recognition of governmental status instead of recognition in some other capacity may not be readily apparent.

In ascertaining whether a statement of recognition involves recognition of governmental or some other status, difficulty may result from the use of ambiguous terminology. For example, the term 'de facto government' has been used in statements involving recognition of governmental status and statements involving recognition in some other capacity.[28] Recent examples of ambiguous terminology include references to the Taliban administration since its establishment of control in respect of most of Afghanistan's territory and population in 2021 as 'the de facto

[22] HC Debs, 3 July 1940, vol 362, col 385.

[23] Whiteman, *Digest of International Law*, vol 2 (US Department of State 1963) 371.

[24] 'Lima Group Declaration' (4 January 2019), available at <http://international.gc.ca/world-monde/international_relations-relations_internationales/latin_america-amerique_latine/2019-01-04-lima_groupe-groupe_lima.aspx>, §2.

[25] 'Canada's Statement on the Recent Vote by the Venezuela National Assembly to Dissolve the Interim Government' (6 January 2023), available at <http://international.gc.ca/country_news-pays_nouvelles/2023-01-06-venezuela.aspx>.

[26] 'Statement by the President of the Security Council' (21 December 2016) UN Doc S/PRST/2016/19.

[27] Recall section 2.2.1 on the distinction between the occupant of a governmental office and a person whose election or appointment to a governmental office has not yet taken effect.

[28] Recall chapter 2, n 99 and accompanying text.

Government authorities' in Afghanistan,[29] as 'de facto authorities',[30] as 'de facto cabinet members',[31] as 'the de facto Administration',[32] and as 'de facto leaders'.[33]

As regards other acts of recognition, difficulty may arise in ascertaining whether or not they amount to recognition of governmental status, for instance because of the treatment of a person as the beneficiary of capacities or of privileges and immunities approximate or virtually-identical to at least some of those enjoyed by members or appointees of a state's government. This could be as a function of either the recognizing state's domestic law or policy or as a matter of international law. An example of treatment as analogous to those owed to certain appointees of a state's government[34] is the treatment by the UK of Francisco Franco's representatives in 1937 subsequent to an agreement to grant, 'upon a basis of strict reciprocity', 'freedom for the agents and sub-agents to exercise, in the same way as consular representatives, all the normal functions of Consuls in relation to matters of commerce and navigation'.[35]

3.2.3 The Range of Practice Concerning Recognition

Practice concerning the recognition of governmental status is not limited to the recognition of governmental status. A state can instead deny that an ostensible government qualifies as the government of another state, as distinct from the mere non-recognition of governmental status. The non-recognition of governmental status refers simply to the absence of a view by a state as to the qualification or otherwise of a specific claimant to governmental status as the government of another state.[36] The term 'denial' of governmental status is used within the present work to refer to the expression or other manifestation of the view that a specific person or collectivity of persons does not comprise at least part of another state's government without suggesting that that claimant is precluded from enjoying governmental status as a matter of international law.[37] As with recognition of governmental status, a state may deny governmental status through any of its organs or

[29] UNSC, 'Official Records, 9075th Meeting' (23 June 2022) UN Doc S/PV.9075 (provisional) 25 (Russia).
[30] UNSC, 'Official Records, 9137th Meeting' (27 September 2022) UN Doc S/PV.9137 (provisional) 8 (Norway), 9 (Ghana), 16 (Albania), 17 (UAE), 19 (Russia), 24 (Iran).
[31] Ibid, 15 (Gabon).
[32] Ibid, 15 (Brazil).
[33] Ibid. See also *In Re: Terrorist Attacks* (n 7) 28.
[34] On the appointment of the consular officers of a state, see section 3.3.2.2.2.2.
[35] See n 167 below and accompanying text.
[36] See also *Legal Consequences for States of the Continued Presence of South Africa in Namibia (South West Africa) notwithstanding Security Council Resolution 276 (1970), Advisory Opinion* [1971] ICJ Rep 16, 134 (Separate Opinion of Judge Petrén).
[37] Further in this regard, see section 3.5.2.

agents acting in that capacity, not just through those persons who possess the capacity to represent the state.[38]

A specific type of denial of governmental status is the 'derecognition' by a state of governmental status, which refers to the denial by a state of governmental status in respect of a claim which that state formerly accepted.[39] Examples in this regard include Canada's decision in 1942 to cease to recognize the government at Vichy as the government of France,[40] as well as the UK's decision as of 6 July 1945 to cease to recognize 'the former Polish Government having its headquarters in London as being the Government of Poland'.[41] A more recent example in this regard concerns the UK's decision in 2011 'no longer' to recognize 'diplomats from the Qadhafi regime' 'as the representatives of the Libyan Government'.[42]

As for the denial of governmental status more generally, the recognition by a state of one claim to governmental status of another state ordinarily involves the denial by the first state of any other claim to governmental status in respect of the latter state. Indeed, in the light of the general position that a state may possess no more than one government as a matter of customary international law,[43] the recognition by a state of one claimant's governmental status might even be presumed to involve the denial by that state of any rival claimant to governmental status. In any event, such an understanding might manifest clearly in the context of the act of recognition, including by express denial of governmental status. For example,[44] the UK derecognized 'the Qadhafi regime' '[i]n line with' its decision to recognize the NTC as the government of Libya.[45]

While the parallel recognition by a state of two or more rival governments is conceptually possible, there is usually an alternative and more convincing explanation for a state's practice than its recognition of two or more rival governments. For instance, the UK executive's concurrent recognition, at the beginning of 1950, of the Central People's Government as 'the de facto government of those parts of the territory of the Republic of China over which it had established control' and of the rival nationalist government 'as being de jure government of the Republic of China'[46] did not involve the acceptance of two separate entities simultaneously

[38] On the modes of recognition and denial of governmental status, see section 3.3.

[39] On withdrawal of recognition of governments generally, see Lauterpacht (n 3) 352–5; Chen (n 5) chapter 16.

[40] See DCER [1943] vol IX, 19, 21. On withdrawal of recognition of governmental status generally, see Lauterpacht (n 3) 352–5; Chen (n 5) chapter 16.

[41] See the certificate of the UK's Foreign Secretary, reproduced in *Gdynia Ameryka Linie Zeglugowe Spolka Akcyjna v Boguslawski and another* [1953] AC 11 ('*Gdynia v Boguslawski*') 17.

[42] Hartmann, Shah, and Warbrick (eds), 'UKMIL' (2012) 82 BYIL 676, 741, 742.

[43] Recall section 2.5.

[44] As another example, see the UK executive's certificate as reproduced in *Gdynia v Boguslawski* (n 41) 17.

[45] UKMIL (2012) (n 42). On the maintenance of diplomatic relations and recognition of governmental status, see section 3.3.2.2.1.

[46] *Civil Air Transport Inc v Central Air Transport Corp* [1953] AC 70, 86–8.

enjoying governmental status in respect of the same state. Rather, only the nationalist claimant was recognized by the UK at that time as the government of China, with the communist claimant recognized as a 'local de facto government'.[47] Another historical example involving recognition of one ostensible government of a state as a 'local de facto government' within that state and recognition of another ostensible government as the government of that state concerns the UK's approach in respect of rival ostensible governments of Greece in 1916.[48] More recently, a municipal court suggested that the UK executive might have concurrently recognized each of two rival claimants as the head of state of Venezuela, with the UK executive expressly recognizing Mr Guaidó as President of Venezuela and possibly concurrently 'impliedly recogni[zing] Mr Maduro as the *de facto* President of Venezuela',[49] in the light of, among other things, the UK's 'maintenance of diplomatic relations with the Maduro regime, including through an ambassador accredited to Mr Maduro as president of Venezuela'.[50] This was dismissed on appeal on grounds relating to the conclusive character, under English law, of express recognition by the UK executive.[51] As for the purposes of international law, while the express recognition by a state's executive of one claimant to governmental status does not necessarily preclude that state's concurrent recognition of a rival claimant's governmental status, in the situation in question, the UK indeed did not appear simultaneously to have recognized the governmental status of two rival claimants.[52] In this regard, it is notable that, when the UK changed the head of its diplomatic mission in Venezuela after its recognition of Mr Guaidó, it appointed a *chargée d'affaires ad interim*.[53] Moreover, while the head of Venezuela's diplomatic mission, who had been appointed by Mr Maduro and who remained in his post after the UK executive's recognition of Mr Guaidó as President of Venezuela, 'HMG engage[d] with the Venezuela Embassy in London', this was 'on necessary routine business only, and at a junior official level'.[54] It is unclear, moreover, in exactly what capacity the UK executive had 'dealings . . . with . . . Mr Maduro's foreign minister . . . and his deputy'.[55]

[47] See also *Foreign Secretary's Case* (n 8) §31 n 28.

[48] See HC Debs, 14 November 1916, vol 87, col 55. See also *Government of the Republic of Spain v SS 'Arantzazu Mendi'* [1939] AC 256, 265, in which the court interpreted the position of the UK executive as regards the situation in Spain as involving the recognition of two separate states rather than the concurrent recognition of two rival ostensible governments of the same state. For criticism of this decision, see Lauterpacht (n 3) 288–94. On the confusion between recognition as a 'local de facto government' and recognition as the government of a state, see also chapter 2, n 99 and accompanying text.

[49] *The 'Maduro Board' of the Central Bank of Venezuela v The 'Guaidó Board' of the Central Bank of Venezuela and others* [2020] EWCA Civ 1249 ('*Maduro v Guaido* (Court of Appeal)') §126.

[50] Ibid, §123(3).

[51] *Maduro v Guaido* (n 8) §§98, 110.

[52] On recognition of governmental status in the context of diplomatic relations, see section 3.3.2.2.1.

[53] See *Maduro v Guaido* (n 8) §35.

[54] *Foreign Secretary's Case* (n 8) §63(3).

[55] Ibid, §63(1).

3.3 Modes of Recognition and Denial of Governmental Status

After considering certain general points concerning the recognition and denial by states of governmental status, this section analyses some of the specific forms and contexts in which the recognition and—to a lesser extent, at least without being accompanied by recognition of a rival claimant's governmental status—denial of governmental status occurs.

3.3.1 In General

Recognition or denial of governmental status may take various forms. A distinction is sometimes drawn between express or explicit modes of recognition, on the one hand, and what have been varyingly referred to as implied, implicit, or tacit forms of recognition on the other.[56] The former appears to refer to a statement through which an organ or agent of the state acting in that capacity expresses the view that a specific person or group of persons qualifies as at least part of another state's government. The latter appears to cover any conduct of a state organ or agent acting in that capacity from which the view as to the qualification by a specific person or group of persons for governmental status can be inferred. This distinction can be made, *mutatis mutandis*, in respect of the denial of governmental status, although the non-performance or even the refusal to act in a way which would imply recognition of governmental status does not necessarily involve denial of governmental status.[57] No such distinction can be made in respect of the non-recognition of governmental status. That said, and although non-recognition of governmental status is typically characterized by abstention, a disclaimer against recognition of governmental status may amount to a mere act of non-recognition.[58]

The distinction between express recognition and denial of governmental status, on the one hand, and implied recognition and denial of governmental status, on the other hand, is of no relevance to the evidential value of the practice of recognition in relation to the international legal identity of the governments of states.[59] Nor is the distinction always clear in practice.[60] Determining whether one state has recognized or denied the governmental status of another state's ostensible government may require the statement of a state to be considered alongside some other conduct of that state. For example, in ascertaining whether the UK had recognized the Government of National Accord (GNA) as the government of Libya, a domestic court had regard to statements by the UK government and to 'other evidence', including the maintenance

[56] See eg 'Sixth Report on Unilateral Acts' (n 3) §25; Hackworth (n 4) 166; Peterson (n 3) 86–7.
[57] See eg n 74 below and the accompanying text.
[58] Recall n 12 above and accompanying text.
[59] See also Hackworth (n 4) 166, albeit in relation to a narrower understanding of 'recognition'.
[60] See also Ando, 'The Recognition of Governments Reconsidered' (1985) 28 JAIL 29, 34 n 33.

of 'full diplomatic relations with representatives of the GNA'.[61] That said, care must be taken as regards what inferences may be drawn from the conduct of a state.[62] In any event, the distinction between express and implied recognition and denial of governmental status can serve as a general means of categorizing the different acts of recognition and denial of governmental status.

With express recognition of governmental status generally taking the form of official statements, it is other conduct by a state organ or agent acting in that capacity which may amount to implied recognition of governmental status. More specifically, recognition of governmental status is implied in any other conduct of a state which manifests the view that a specific person qualifies as the occupant of an office or post of another state which can be occupied only by a person belonging to or appointed through or acting under the authority of the government of that other state. The manifestation by a state of such a view ordinarily arises from acts which indicate one of two things.

First, a state's acceptance of the effectiveness as a matter of international law of the ostensible representation of another state in a given instance by a particular person or collectivity of persons ordinarily implies its recognition of a particular claim to governmental status in respect of that other state. This includes, for example, the state's acceptance that a particular person or collectivity of persons has made a binding unilateral statement in the other state's name, the state's reliance on consent ostensibly given in the other state's name with a view to rendering its conduct lawful or otherwise unwrongful, and the state's acceptance of the effectiveness of the other state's ostensible waiver of its international legal entitlement to jurisdictional immunity. That said, given the possible variation *inter se* by states of rules so as to permit their representation in international organizations not through their respective governments,[63] the acceptance as effective of the ostensible representation of a state in the context of an international organization might not involve recognition of governmental status.[64] In circumstances that have not arisen frequently, moreover, it may be unclear who, if anyone, a state recognizes as another state's government in accepting as effective the ostensible representation of the latter state for one or more purposes of international law. The separate possibilities of the representation of a nascent state through a political entity not yet enjoying governmental status and of two rival ostensible governments expressing the same ostensible position of the state have already been discussed.[65]

[61] See *Dr Ali Mahmoud Hassan Mohamed v Mr Abdulmagid Breish and others* [2020] EWCA Civ 637 ('*Mohamed v Breish*') §§31, 35(2), 38. See also *Maduro v Guaido* (Court of Appeal) (n 49) §§121–4. Cf *Maduro v Guaido* (n 8) §§96–8 on criticism of this approach for reasons particular to English law.

[62] Recall section 3.2.3. See also nn 68, 166–8 below and accompanying text on possible similarities between conduct that amounts to recognition of governmental status and conduct which does not amount to recognition of governmental status.

[63] Recall, generally, section 2.3.1. See further sections 5.3.2 and 5.5.

[64] See further section 5.4.1.2.

[65] See section 2.3.1.

Secondly, recognition of governmental status may be implied from a view by a state as regards the treatment it is obliged to accord a particular person. A view of a state that another state is entitled as a matter of international law to see a particular person treated in a way that as a matter of international law is due only to occupants of governmental offices (for example, to benefit from head-of-government immunity) or to state representatives, such as diplomatic agents, who are appointed by, or otherwise act under, the authority of a state's government and who are entitled to diplomatic immunity would ordinarily imply recognition of governmental status.[66] Perhaps more common is the view of a state that a particular person benefits from certain privileges or immunities under its municipal law. At least insofar as that state's municipal law accords these privileges and immunities only to persons belonging to or acting under the authority of the government of another state, the state's according of any such privilege or immunity under its municipal law generally implies its recognition of governmental status.[67] Even if a state's municipal law does not accord such privileges and immunities only to persons belonging to or acting under the authority of the government of another state, its according of any such privilege or immunity implies recognition of governmental status if it is clear that the state considers the person or collectivity of persons to benefit from particular treatment because they occupy a governmental office or a post that is reserved for persons acting under the authority of the government of a state.[68]

It is perhaps worth noting that the application by a municipal court of foreign legislation, including an executive decree promulgated by or under the authority of a claimant to governmental status, does not necessarily amount to recognition of governmental status. There are a number of examples involving the application by a municipal court of foreign legislation without implying governmental status.[69] The *Fubini Case* provides an example of a distinct situation which further demonstrates that taking cognizance of municipal legislation promulgated by an ostensible government does not necessarily amount to governmental status. In this case, the Italian–United States Conciliation Commission treated the ostensible

[66] See also n 144 below and accompanying text. For a recent example of recognition of a person as head of government in expressing the view that that person qualifies for head-of-government immunity, albeit involving also express recognition of governmental status, see 'Response to Order of the Court' (filed 17 November 2022) (Exhibit A in *Cengiz v Mohammed bin Salman* (District Court, District of Columbia, Civil Action No 20-3009)).

[67] On the evidentiary value of the determination of governmental status for the purposes of the municipal law of a state in relation to the customary international legal identity of the government of a state, see section 3.5.2.

[68] See eg Diplomatic Privileges (Extension) Act 1941, s(1)(1)(a)–(b) on the treatment of members of certain 'national committee[s]' in the same way as 'member[s] of the government of [certain] foreign Power[s]', albeit on the basis of a distinct provision.

[69] See eg Talmon (n 3) 221–31 on the treatment by municipal courts of legislation promulgated by occupying powers and 'local de facto governments' as the applicable law in respect of particular disputes.

exercise of legislative authority by what it considered to be a 'local de facto government' as 'part of the legislation in force in Italy' for the purpose of a particular treaty.[70] Indeed, there may be judicial acknowledgement of another claimant as the government of the state in respect of whose territory the legislation in question ostensibly applies that exists in parallel with the judicial cognizance of legislation promulgated by another political authority.[71] Judicial cognizance of legislation will generally also not amount to recognition of governmental status even where there is no parallel judicial acknowledgement of another claimant as the government of the state in respect of whose territory the legislation in question ostensibly applies. Judicial cognizance of an executive decree promulgated by a political authority may amount to recognition of governmental status only if there is some specific indication in this regard.

As for implied denial of governmental status, its ascertainment is straightforward in fewer circumstances than is the case for the implied recognition of governmental status. The following two points demonstrate this point.

First, a state's view that the ostensible representation of another state is ineffective does not necessarily amount to a denial of governmental status. Such a view may be based on some reason other than the non-qualification for governmental status by the ostensible government through which the ostensible representation took place.[72]

Secondly, while a state's view that a specific person does not qualify as the occupant of a governmental office of another state involves the denial of governmental status, a state's view that a specific person does not qualify as the occupant of an office or post of another state which is to be occupied by a person appointed through the government of that other state does not necessarily imply the denial of governmental status. There may be other reasons for such a view, as will be the case, for example, once a 'reasonable period' has passed since it has declared a diplomatic agent as *persona non grata*.[73] Not dissimilarly, as with diplomatic agents, representatives of a state in a special mission, and consular officers,[74] the refusal of a state to treat a person as international law or its municipal law would ordinarily require in relation to the government of another state may but need not amount to denial of governmental status. There may be a reason for such refusal that is unconnected to the view that a specific ostensible government does not enjoy governmental status. For example, the state might consider that there exists an exception to the rule requiring the treatment in question to be applicable in that case.

[70] *Fubini Case* (1959) XIV UNRIAA 420, 429–30.

[71] See eg *Banco de Bilbao v Sancha, Banco de Bilbao v Rey* [1938] CA 176 ('*Banco de Bilbao*') 195–6; *Gdynia v Boguslawski* (n 41).

[72] Recall section 2.3.2.

[73] See Vienna Convention on Diplomatic Relations (adopted 18 April 1961, entered into force 24 April 1964) 500 UNTS 95 ('VCDR') art 9.

[74] On recognition by the receiving state in relation to such persons, see sections 3.3.2.2.1.2 and 3.3.2.2.2.2.

As a separate matter, the refusal of a municipal court to accept as effective—and even the positive treatment as ineffective of—legislation ostensibly promulgated by or under the authority of a claimant to governmental status does not generally amount to denial of that authority's governmental status, not least because the acceptance as effective of such legislation does not involve recognition of governmental status. Indeed, some of the cases involving judicial cognizance of legislation that is promulgated by a 'local de facto government' or an occupying power involve the denial of the effectiveness of legislation promulgated by the government of the state.[75]

3.3.2 Specific Forms and Contexts

3.3.2.1 Official Statements

A state may recognize or deny governmental status through an official statement—that is, a pronouncement by a state organ or agent acting in that capacity. Examples in this regard include a declaration by a state organ in parliament or in a press briefing,[76] a parliamentary resolution,[77] and a judicial decision.[78] A statement of recognition or denial of governmental status may instead take the form of a treaty provision or the text of some other international instrument.[79]

A statement need include neither the term 'recognition' nor the term 'government' to amount to recognition of governmental status. It is sufficient that the wording expresses the state's acceptance of an ostensible government as the government of another state.[80] For example, the acceptance of '[t]he Supreme National Council [as] the unique legitimate body and source of authority in which . . . the sovereignty, independence and unity of Cambodia are enshrined'[81] appears

[75] See eg *Banco de Bilbao* (n 71). See also Talmon (n 3) 221–31.

[76] See also Talmon, 'Recognition of Governments: An Analysis of the New British Policy and Practice' (1992) 63 BYIL 231, 243.

[77] Presumably for constitutional reasons, the limited practice of state parliaments on questions of recognition suggests that parliaments are more likely to recommend recognition to the executive rather than to accord recognition themselves. See eg the resolution adopted by the Senate of France, '*Résolution portant sur la nécessité de reconnaître le Gouvernment d'unité nationale de Birmanie*' (5 October 2021) §13.

[78] On judicial decisions as practice concerning recognition, recall n 7 above. A court may instead affirm the executive's recognition of governmental status. See eg *Lafontant v Aristide* (USA, District Court, Eastern District of New York, 27 January 1994) 844 F Supp 128, 130.

[79] See eg Agreement on a Comprehensive Political Settlement of the Cambodia Conflict, annexed to 'Letter Dated 30 October 1991 from the Permanent Representatives of France and Indonesia to the United Nations Addressed to the Secretary-General' (30 October 1991) UN Doc A/46/608–S/23177 ('Agreement Concerning Cambodia') art 3.

[80] Peterson (n 3) 86; Brownlie (n 5) 199, 208; *Mohamed v Breish* (n 61) §35. See also Woodward, *British Foreign Policy in the Second World War*, vol 2 (Her Majesty's Stationery Office 1962) 341 for the apparent view of the UK Foreign Office that the acceptance of the French National Committee as having the 'sole competence' to represent all French interests 'would be tantamount to implying [recognition of] the Committee as the Government of France.'

[81] See Agreement Concerning Cambodia (n 79).

sufficiently clear to be a statement of recognition of governmental status. The same is true, *mutatis mutandis*, as regards the denial of governmental status. Indeed, the denial by a state of governmental status in respect of a specific claimant will ordinarily be reflected in the acceptance of a rival claim to governmental status by that state.[82]

Certain statements are clear in expressing recognition of governmental status, including those in which a person or collectivity of persons is accepted 'as the government of [another state]' or as the occupant of a governmental office in another state. Other clear statements of recognition of governmental status include the recognition by the UK of the NTC as 'the sole governmental authority in Libya [with which it will deal] on the same basis as other governments around the world',[83] the recognition by France of the NTC as the 'sole repository of governmental authority, in France's relations with the Libyan State',[84] and the recognition by Italy of the NTC 'as [Libya's] only legitimate interlocutor on bilateral relations'.[85] Other statements might be similar yet different enough so as not in themselves unambiguously to amount to recognition of governmental status. An example in this regard is the recognition of the NTC 'as the legitimate governing authority in Libya' by the so-called 'Libya Contact Group'.[86]

The context in which a statement is made may be valuable in determining whether or not that statement amounts to recognition of governmental status. Indeed, a state may clarify, in its initial statement or afterwards, that its acceptance of a person or collectivity of persons in a specific capacity does not constitute recognition of governmental status. While unnecessary in terms of ensuring that its statement did not amount to recognition of governmental status, the clarification by the USA that its recognition of the CFLN 'as administering those French overseas territories which acknowledge its authority' as 'not constitut[ing] recognition of a government of France or of the French Empire' is an example in this regard.[87] Another example is the reference, subsequent to the reiteration by the UK of its recognition of Charles de Gaulle as the leader of all free Frenchmen, to the fact that the UK retained diplomatic relations with the Vichy government.[88] Other conduct of a state may also inform the assessment of whether that state has recognized a specific claimant's governmental status. An example concerns the statement and conduct of the UK in relation to the GNA.[89]

[82] Recall section 3.2.3.
[83] UKMIL (n 45) 742.
[84] 'Libya/National Transitional Council—Statement by Alain Juppé, Ministre d'Etat, Minister of Foreign and European Affairs' (7 June 2011), available at <http://in.ambafrance.org/Libya-National-Transitional>.
[85] Talmon (n 18).
[86] See UKMIL (n 45) 742.
[87] See eg Whiteman (n 23).
[88] HC Debs, 3 July 1940, vol 362, col 385.
[89] See n 61 above and accompanying text.

As regards statements in which a state purports to disclaim the recognition of a specific ostensible government or any ostensible government as the government of another state,[90] it is necessary to determine whether the term 'recognition' is used narrowly[91] in order to ascertain the import of the statement. Depending on this and on the context in which the statement is made, the disclaiming state might indeed be denying the governmental status of an ostensible government, but it might instead simply not be recognizing or even not precluding its recognition of the governmental status of that ostensible government.

Indeed, the distinctive capacity of the government of a state to represent the state weighs in favour of a narrow understanding of the term 'recognition' in the context of a disclaimer against recognition in relation to an act of a state which otherwise implies recognition of governmental status. For example, in the context of its apparent acceptance that Angola had acceded and continued to accede to certain treaties,[92] the USA's declaration that it 'will not recognize any government in Angola'[93] may be understood as expressing an unwillingness to establish diplomatic relations with any government in Angola, not a denial of every claimant's governmental status.[94] The statement may also or instead be understood as a refusal to accord political support to any government in Angola.[95] Cameroon's statement that its signing of the 1963 Treaty Banning Nuclear Weapon Tests in the Atmosphere, in Outer Space and under Water[96] could '[u]nder no circumstances . . . have the effect of entailing recognition by Cameroon of Governments or regimes which, prior to such signing, had not yet been recognized by the Federal Republic of Cameroon according to the normal traditional procedures established by international law'[97] might be understood similarly to concern only the absence of political approval. In any event, in the context of a multilateral treaty there may be no recognition to disclaim.[98]

If a disclaimer by a state against recognition of a specific ostensible government as the government of another state is accompanied, for example, by the former state's view that the non-recognized claimant cannot represent the latter state, the disclaimer would, in the absence of any indication to the contrary, reflect the denial

[90] On such statements in the context of an international organization, see section 5.4.3.
[91] Recall section 3.2.1.
[92] On recognition of governmental status through the acceptance as effective of the consent to a treaty, see section 3.3.2.3.
[93] Clark, Jr, 'Efforts toward Peace and Reconciliation in Angola' in DSB [1989] vol 89, No 2153, 31.
[94] See also Talmon (n 3) 38–9.
[95] Recall section 3.2.1.
[96] Treaty Banning Nuclear Weapon Tests in the Atmosphere, in Outer Space and under Water (adopted 5 August 1963, entered into force 10 October 1963) 480 UNTS 43.
[97] *Status of Multilateral Arms Regulation and Disarmament Agreements* (5th edn, UN 1996) 40. This statement was discussed alongside other similar statements in 'Third Report on Reservations to Treaties, by Mr. Alain Pellet, Special Rapporteur' (30 April–19 July 1998) UN Doc A/CN.4/491 and Add.1-6, 252, §173.
[98] See further section 3.3.2.3.

of governmental status. This is to be distinguished from a statement by one state which reflects the position that a multilateral treaty lacks legal effect between itself and one or more other states whose respective ostensible governments it does not recognize.[99] Since such statements are as a matter of neither logic nor law necessarily premised on the non-qualification for governmental status, they do not, in themselves, amount to denial of governmental status. Indeed, there may be no recognition to disclaim in the first place.

At the same time, a statement may amount to the denial of governmental status without expressly purporting to disclaim against 'recognition'. Examples in this regard include the views of certain states that the ratification by the Taiwan-based authorities of the 1958 Convention on the Continental Shelf ostensibly in China's name 'represented no one . . ., there being only one Chinese State in the world, the People's Republic of China, and one Government entitled to represent it, the Government of the People's Republic of China'.[100]

The different possible meanings of 'recognition' do not leave open the possibility that a declaration expressly mentioning the 'recognition' of governmental status do not involve the acceptance of governmental status. On any of the meanings of 'recognition', a decision to recognize governmental status amounts to the acceptance of governmental status.[101] There are many ways by which a state may specify the person or collectivity of persons whose governmental status it recognizes or denies. These include the reference in a statement of recognition of governmental status to one or more individuals by name;[102] to the political party, family, or faction at least some of whose members comprise an ostensible government;[103] to the location in which the person or collectivity of persons comprising an ostensible government is based;[104] to the name of a state that a specific ostensible government of a state uses in respect of that state;[105] to the name that an ostensible government

[99] See eg chapter 2, nn 103–4 and accompanying text.

[100] 'Multilateral Treaties Deposited with the Secretary-General, status as at 1 April 2009' (2009) vol III, UN Doc ST/LEG/SER.E/26, 437 n 1.

[101] Ibid.

[102] This is rare, but see eg the 'List' compiled by the UK's Principal Secretary of State for Affairs pursuant to the Diplomatic Privileges (Extension) Act 1941, reproduced in *Edinburgh Gazette* (24 July 1942) 295, 295–9 naming the 'members of the government' of various states. The list excluded heads of state, the inclusion of which was unnecessary, given the purpose of the list and the independent acceptance in English law of the immunities of such officials. See HL Debs, 19 December 1940, vol 118, cols 191–2.

[103] See eg HC Debs, 24 November 1938, vol 341, col 1970WA on the 'Nationalist Government' of Spain.

[104] See eg the statement of Canada's Secretary of State for External Affairs (26 February 1959) reproduced in Dai, 'Recognition of States and Governments under International Law with Special Reference to Canadian Postwar Practice and the Legal Status of Taiwan (Formosa)' (1965) 3 CYIL 290, 299–30, in relation to the 'Peking government'.

[105] See eg the reference to 'Democratic Kampuchea' in relation to Pol Pot's regime ('Note verbale Dated 25 November 1980 from the Permanent Mission of the Union of Soviet Socialist Republics to the United Nations Addressed to the Secretary-General', annexed to 'Letter Dated 25 November 1980 from the Permanent Representative of the Union of Soviet Socialist Republics to the United Nations Addressed to the Secretary-General' (26 November 1980) UN Doc A/35/660) and the reference to 'the

has given itself as a political entity;[106] or to the political system that an ostensible government seeks to impose or under which it purports to operate.[107] Depending on the context, it may be that only some of these descriptors can be used to specify the ostensible government whose claim to governmental status a state recognizes. For example, two ostensible governments of the same state may both refer to that state by the same name, in which case reference by another state to that name may not indicate which, if any, ostensible government the latter state recognizes as the government of the first state. Even where each of the two ostensible governments of a state refer to the state of which they purport to be the government by a different name, the use by another state of one name in some specific context might not indicate which ostensible government the latter state recognizes as the government of the first state.[108]

The addressees of statements of recognition and of denial of governmental status vary. Potential addresses include the ostensible government being recognized,[109] a state other than the one whose ostensible government is being recognized, other organs or agents of the recognizing state,[110] and the public at large.[111]

Many states have adopted a policy, often referred to as the 'Estrada doctrine',[112] of not issuing public statements of recognition in respect of foreign governments.[113]

People's Republic of China as the legitimate Government of that country' (UNGA, 'Official Records, 15th Session, 995th Plenary Meeting' (21 April 1961) UN Doc A/PV.995, §377 (Nepal)).

[106] See eg the executive recognition of 'the National Transitional Council as the Government of Libya', reproduced in *British Arab Commercial Bank PLC v The National Transitional Council of the State of Libya* [2011] EWHC 2274 (Comm) ('*British Arab Bank v NTC*') §23.

[107] See eg Canada's Secretary of State for External Affairs (n 104) 299–30 on the recognition of 'communist China'.

[108] See eg Brown (ed), 'Australian Practice in International Law 1990 and 1991' (1992) 13 AYIL 195, 233.

[109] See eg Hackworth (n 4) 297. See also Whiteman (n 23) 244.

[110] This is the case, for example, with executive certificates issued in the context of judicial proceedings, on which see eg McLachlan, *Foreign Relations Law* (CUP 2014) 240–2, §§6.60–6.87.

[111] See eg Galbraith (ed), 'Contemporary Practice of the United States Relating to International Law' (2019) 113 AJIL 600, 602 in reference to a statement by President Trump concerning the recognition of Juan Guaidó as 'Interim President of Venezuela'.

[112] The policy derives its name from the fact that a formal policy to this effect was first proclaimed by the Mexican Secretary of Foreign Affairs, Genaro Estrada. See 'Declaration of Señor Don Genaro Estrada, Secretary of Foreign Relations of Mexico, Published in the Press on September 27, 1930, Relating to the Express Recognition of Governments' (1931) 25 AJIL Supp 203 ('Estrada doctrine') 203. For an affirmation of Mexico's continued adherence to the doctrine, see eg 'México aplica la doctrina Estrada en el caso de Venezuela' (2003) 67–8 RMPA 191, 191–2.

[113] See eg Charpentier, 'Pratique française relative au droit international law' (1966) 12 AFDI 893, 918; Salmon and Smets (eds), 'Practique du pouvoir executif et le controle des Chambres Legislatives en matiere de relations internationales' (1968) 4 RBDI 520, 541–2; Caggiano (ed), 'Diplomatic and Parliamentary Practice' (1978) 4 IYIL 212, 219; HL Debs, 28 April 1980, vol 408, cols 1121–2WA; 'Memorandum of the Legal Bureau of Ministry of External Affairs of Canada' (9 November 1988) reproduced in Lee, 'Canadian Practice in International Law at the Department of External Affairs in 1988–89/ La pratique Canadienne en Matière de Droit International Public au Ministère des Affaires Extérieures en 1988–89 (1989) 27 CYIL 373, 387–8; certificate of 28 March 1988 by New Zealand's Minister of Foreign Affairs, as reported in *Attorney-General for Fiji v Robert Jones House Ltd* (New Zealand, High Court, 4 November 1988) (1989) 80 ILR 1, 5 ('certificate of 28 March 1988'); Brown (ed), 'Australian Practice in International Law 1988 and 1989' (1992) 12 AYIL 319, 357–8; 'Spanish Diplomatic and

The popularity of this approach notwithstanding, states, including those that adopt such a policy, continue, on occasion, expressly to recognize the government of another state. Examples in this regard include the recognition by Canada of Juan Guaidó as President of Venezuela in 2019 and the recognition by the UK of the NTC in 2011.[114] In any event, they do generally continue to recognize the governmental status of ostensible governments in other ways.[115]

3.3.2.2 Interstate Diplomatic and Consular Relations

The focus here is only on bilateral interstate diplomatic relations, even though 'diplomatic relations', broadly construed, might also include the interactions states have with each other in multilateral settings.[116] The reference to 'interstate' diplomatic and consular relations serves to exclude relations between a state and some entity other than a state.[117] Perhaps needless to say, acts performed in the context of diplomatic or consular relations between a state and some entity that that entity does not treat as a state cannot, in themselves, imply recognition of governmental status. References within the present section to diplomatic or consular relations concern, unless otherwise specified, interstate diplomatic or consular relations.

3.3.2.2.1 The establishment and maintenance of interstate diplomatic relations

3.3.2.2.1.1 Recognition by the sending state

The accreditation by a sending state of a person as the head of one of its diplomatic missions requires the *agrément* of the receiving state.[118] A receiving state may give its *agrément* only through its government.[119] In this light, a request by the sending state addressed to an ostensible government of the receiving state for the latter state's consent to the accreditation of a person as the head of a diplomatic mission of the former state ordinarily amounts to the sending state's recognition of the

Parliamentary Practice in Public International Law, 1992' (1992) 2 SYIL 121, 152; Siekmann (n 11) 238. See also Talmon (n 3) 3 nn 1–2; Peterson (n 3) 180; McLachlan (n 110) 382–6, §§10.10–10.20. For an example of a state that has refrained from adopting such a policy, see Nomura, 'Recognition of Foreign Governments' (1982) 25 JAIL 67, 71.

[114] See 'Lima Group Declaration' (4 February 2019), available at <http://canada.ca/en/global-affairs/news/2019/02/lima-group-declaration-february-04-2019.html>, §1 and n 45 above, respectively. See also *Kuwait Airways Corporation v Iraqi Airways Co (Nos 4 and 5)* [2001] 3 WLR 1117, 1211, §349; *Maduro v Guaido* (n 8) §43. On the adoption by Canada and the UK of the Estrada doctrine, recall n 112 above.

[115] See also eg Crawford (n 9) 152.

[116] On recognition of governmental status in the context of international organization, see section 5.4.

[117] On the international legal capacity of other entities to enter into diplomatic relations, see eg VCDR (n 73) art 16(3) on the Holy See. See also ILC, 'Draft Articles on Special Missions' in Ybk ILC [1967] vol II, 40, 40 (art 1, comment 2(*a*)). On the exercise of consular functions by entities other than states, see n 166 below and accompanying text.

[118] VCDR (n 73) art 4(1).

[119] See also Denza, *Diplomatic Law: Commentary on the Vienna Convention on Diplomatic Relations* (4th edn, OUP 2016) 40. Recall, generally, section 2.2.2.

person or collectivity of persons through which this consent was issued as at least part of the receiving state's government. The same goes for reliance by the sending state on consent ostensibly issued on the receiving state's behalf, for example by proceeding to accredit a person as the head of its diplomatic mission on the basis of that consent.

Relatedly, the sending state may expressly acknowledge in its letter of credence the person or collectivity of persons to whom it accredits the head of its diplomatic mission as the receiving state's head of state or minister for foreign affairs since all heads of diplomatic missions are accredited either to the head of state or the minister of foreign affairs of the receiving state.[120] Regardless of such express acknowledgement, the accreditation by the sending state of an individual as the head of its diplomatic mission to another state implies the sending state's recognition of the governmental status of the claimant to which the individual is accredited. For example, the UK's

> deci[sion] to accredit an Envoy Extraordinary and Minister Plenipotentiary to Dr. Beneš as President of the Czecho-Slovak Republic . . . implied that His Majesty's Government in the United Kingdom regarded the juridical position of the President and Government of the Czecho-Slovak Republic as identical with that of the other Allied heads of States and Governments established in [the UK]

—that is, as identical with certain specific other collectivities of persons each of which the UK regarded as the government of some specific state.[121]

Moreover, the treatment by the sending state of a person as the head of its diplomatic mission, for example by considering that person to possess the capacity as a matter of international law to perform functions reserved for heads of diplomatic missions, [122] generally implies its recognition of the ostensible government to which the person's credentials were presented.[123] According to Article 13(1) of the VCDR,

[120] VCDR (n 73) art 14(1)(*a*).

[121] 'Exchange of Notes between His Majesty's Government in the United Kingdom and the Government of the Czecho-Slovak Republic concerning the Policy of His Majesty's Government in the United Kingdom in regard to Czechoslovakia' (letters exchanged and agreement entered into force 5 August 1942) 204 LNTS 377, 378.

[122] See eg VCDR (n 73) art 22(1).

[123] See also Moore, A Digest of International Law, vol 1 (US Department of State 1906) 235: 'the sending of a new minister or the retention of an old one . . . does not constitute a recognition of the new government, so long as there is no formal presentation of credentials and communications bear only an unofficial character'; Hackworth (n 4) 167–8; Lauterpacht (n 3) 381; FRUS [1948] vol V(2), 1052: '[t]he establishment of legations and the exchange of accredited diplomatic representatives between Israel and the United States would constitute recognition by the United States of the "provisional government" as the government *de jure* of Israel'; Canadian Legal Bureau, 'Approaches to Recognition of States and Governments' (1988) 26 CYIL 324, 325.

> [t]he head of the mission is considered as having taken up his functions in the receiving State either when he has presented his credentials or when he has notified his arrival and a true copy of his credentials has been presented to the Ministry for Foreign Affairs of the receiving State, or such other ministry as may be agreed.

An exception to the sending state's recognition of governmental status through its appointment and treatment of a person as the head of its diplomatic mission exists in relation to a *chargé d'affaires ad interim*.[124] A state may appoint a *chargé d'affaires ad interim* without the *agrément* of the receiving state,[125] and a *chargé d'affaires ad interim* need not have credentials presented to the receiving state in order for that person to be deemed to have taken up his or her functions. Accordingly, the sending state's appointment and treatment of a person as a *chargé d'affaires ad interim* does not as such provide evidence of its recognition of an ostensible government of the receiving state. This might be one reason why the UK, which stated in 2021 that it 'will not recognise the Taliban',[126] has since appointed only *chargés d'affaires ad interim* to Afghanistan.[127] A further recent example of such an appointment includes that of Mr Vowles, whom the UK announced first as ambassador to Myanmar and then, after the UK refused to present his credentials to the State Administration Council (one of the two ostensible governments of Myanmar at the time), as *chargé d'affaires ad interim* of its diplomatic mission in Myanmar.[128] Additionally, having recognized Guan Juaidó as the President of Venezuela in 2019, the UK replaced its Ambassador in Venezuela, who was in post between 2017 and 2021, with a *chargée d'affaires ad interim*.[129]

Not dissimilar to the situation concerning the head of a diplomatic mission is the position concerning representatives of a state in a special mission. The sending state requires the consent of the receiving state in order for an individual to qualify as a representative of the sending state in a special mission.[130] The receiving state can give its consent in this regard only through its government.[131] A request by the sending state for the receiving state's consent that is addressed to a specific claimant

[124] On *chargés d'affaires ad interim*, see VCDR (n 73) art 19(1).

[125] Denza (n 119) 40. On the distinction between a *chargé d'affaires ad interim* and a regular *chargé d'affaires*, see ibid, 99; Roberts, 'Formal Aspects of Diplomatic Relations' in Roberts (ed), *Satow's Diplomatic Practice* (7th edn, OUP 2017) 110.

[126] 'Afghanistan Response: Foreign Secretary's Statement' (6 September 2021), available at <http://gov.uk/government/speeches/foreign-secretary-statement-on-afghanistan-response>.

[127] Ibid (on Mr Martin Longden); 'Appointment of Chargé d'Affaires ad interim of the UK Mission to Afghanistan: Hugo Shorter' (18 January 2022), available at <http://gov.uk/government/news/appointment-of-charge-daffaires-ad-interim-of-the-uk-mission-to-afghanistan-hugo-shorter>.

[128] See eg 'Ministry of Foreign Affairs of Myanmar Responds to the Tweet by My. Peter Vowles' (*Eleven*, 15 July 2022), available at <http://elevenmyanmar.com/news/ministry-of-foreign-affairs-of-myanmar-responds-to-the-tweet-by-mr-peter-vowles>.

[129] *Foreign Secretary's Case* (n 8) §63(4).

[130] Convention on Special Missions (adopted on 8 December 1969, entered into force 21 June 1985) 1400 UNTS 231 ('CSM') art 3.

[131] See also ILC (n 117) 41 (art 1, comment 4). Recall section 2.2.2.

thus ordinarily implies the recognition by the former state of that claimant as the latter state's government. The sending state's reliance on the receiving state's consent in treating an individual as its representative in a special mission also implies recognition of governmental status. Indeed, the sending state's view that one or more persons qualify as its representatives to the receiving state for some particular purpose implies its recognition of any person or collectivity of persons through which the receiving state's consent was ostensibly given as at least part of the receiving state's government.

More generally, a sending state's diplomatic agent[132] or representative of the state in a special mission may accept a person's capacity to represent the receiving state, for example in the context of interstate negotiations. Such acceptance amounts to the sending state's recognition of the ostensible government through which the receiving state is ostensibly represented.[133] In contrast, interaction between a diplomatic agent or representative of a state in a special mission and a person claiming to comprise at least part of or to be acting under the authority of the receiving state's government does not amount to the sending state's recognition of governmental status where the interaction does not involve the sending state's acceptance that the person with whom interaction takes place possesses the capacity to represent the receiving state.[134] At the same time, the sending state's acceptance that one of its consular officers can perform diplomatic acts on its behalf in the receiving state implies recognition of governmental status since a consular officer can perform such functions only with the consent of the receiving state,[135] which can be given only through its government.

3.3.2.2.1.2 Recognition by the receiving state

It is only through its government that a sending state may appoint its diplomatic agents and representatives of the state in a special mission.[136] The official activities of such persons are to take place, moreover, under the direction of the government of the sending state.[137] As such, the acceptance by the receiving state of a person

[132] For the definition of 'diplomatic agent', see VCDR (n 73) art 1(*e*).

[133] See eg Marston (ed), 'UKMIL' (2001) 71 BYIL 518, 584: '[t]he new Government [of Chile] was recognized by Her Majesty's Government . . . through the medium of a Diplomatic Note from the British Embassy responding to a Note from the Ministry of Foreign Affairs'). See also Denza (n 119) 20; Roberts, 'Functions of Diplomatic Missions and Consulates' in Roberts (n 125) 71, 74–5, §5.10; Hackworth (n 4) 171.

[134] See also Lauterpacht (n 3) 388–90; Chen (n 5) 216–18; Talmon (n 3) 156–8.

[135] Vienna Convention on Consular Relations (adopted 24 April 1963, entered into force 19 March 1967) 596 UNTS 261 ('VCCR') art 17(1).

[136] The VCDR contains no provision as to who possesses the capacity as a matter of international law to appoint an individual as the head of a state's diplomatic mission. But see *Re an Application by Ernst Jaakson and Aarand Roos* (UK, High Court, 14 December 1990) (1991) 85 ILR 53, 60; Marston (ed), 'UKMIL' (1983) 54 BYIL 361, 384; Foakes and Denza, 'The Diplomatic Mission, the Corps, Breach of Relations, and Protection of Interests' in Roberts (n 125) 153, 169–70.

[137] See Jennings and Watts (eds), *Oppenheim's International Law*, vol 1 (Wildy 1992) 1045, §459; *Arrest Warrant of 11 April 2000 (Democratic Republic of Congo v Belgium), Judgment* [2002] ICJ Rep 3, 21, §53.

as the sending state's diplomatic agent or representative of the state in a special mission generally implies the receiving state's recognition of governmental status. More specifically, the person by whom the diplomatic agent or representative of the state in the special mission was appointed or under whose authority the diplomatic agent or representative of the state in the special mission currently acts will, in such circumstances, be recognized by the receiving state as at least a part of the sending state's government.[138] The denial by the receiving state of a specific person as the diplomatic agent or representative of the state in a special mission may but does not necessarily amount to the denial of governmental status.[139]

Various acts demonstrate the view by the receiving state that a person qualifies as a sending state's diplomatic agent or representative of the state in a special mission.

The clearest example in this regard is the issuance of express consent to have a person act as the head of the sending state's diplomatic mission or as a representative of the state in a special mission. Another clear example is that the receiving state express 'accept[ance of] the nomination' of a specific individual as another state's *chargé d'affaires ad interim* to the receiving state.[140]

Other acts that typically demonstrate the view by the receiving state that a person qualifies as a sending state's diplomatic agent or representative of the state in a special mission or that otherwise involve recognition of governmental status include those premised on the acceptance of a person's capacity to perform functions that, leaving aside members of the sending state's government and possibly certain other persons acting under the authority of the sending state's government, may generally be effectively performed only by the sending state's diplomatic agent or representative of the state in a special mission. This includes the acceptance of the person's capacity to represent the sending state on some specific matter[141] since it is generally such persons who are tasked with '[r]epresenting the sending State in the receiving State'.[142] In relation to recognition as the head of a diplomatic mission, a classic example is the treatment as effective by the authorities of the receiving state of the grant of consent to entry onto the premises of the mission.[143]

The receiving state's view that a person qualifies as the sending state's diplomatic agent or representative of the state in a special mission is apparent also from its treatment of the sending state as entitled under international law to see that person benefit from those privileges and immunities that as a matter of international law apply only in respect of a diplomatic agent or representative of a state in a special

138 See also FRUS [1948] vol V(2), 1052; Canadian Legal Bureau (n 123).

139 Recall section 3.3.1.

140 *British Arab Bank v NTC* (n 106) §10.

141 See also the statement by Belgium's minister for foreign affairs, reproduced in Salmon and Smets (n 113) 541–2; Hackworth (n 4) 168; Foakes and Denza (n 136) 155, §10.7.

142 VCDR (n 73) art 3(1)(*a*). See also CSM (n 130) art 1(*a*).

143 See VCDR (n 73) art 22(1).

mission.[144] Often to the same effect and perhaps more common is the acceptance by the receiving state that the person benefits under its municipal law from treatment due only in respect of a sending state's diplomatic agent or representative of the state in a special mission.[145] As with the denial of the status of an individual as a diplomatic agent or a representative of the state in a special mission, the refusal by a state of treatment due only in respect of a sending state's diplomatic agent or representative of the state in a special mission may but does not necessarily amount to the denial of governmental status.[146]

The mere presence in its territory of a person who purports to be a sending state's diplomatic agent or representative of the state in a special mission does not demonstrate the receiving state's acceptance of a particular claim to governmental status in respect of the sending state.[147] Indeed, a state may have relations with a person appointed by an ostensible government of a sending state without implying its acceptance of the person's capacity to represent the sending state or otherwise acknowledging the person's status as the sending state's diplomatic agent or representative of the state in a special mission.[148] This is so even when the state, either unilaterally or in agreement with a foreign entity, agrees to grant to persons who are not diplomatic agents of another state certain privileges and immunities approximate to those enjoyed by diplomatic agents.[149] The question pertinent to establishing whether a state's acceptance of the applicability of certain privileges and immunities constitutes implicit recognition of governmental status is whether the state views this applicability as the function either of an international legal obligation owed to another state in respect of certain persons acting under the authority of the latter state's government or otherwise of the person's status as the diplomatic agent or representative of the state in a special mission of another state.

3.3.2.2.2 The establishment and maintenance of interstate consular relations

3.3.2.2.2.1 Recognition by the sending state

The transmission by the sending state of a commission or similar instrument—that is, a document in which a state certifies the appointment of a specific person as the head of its consular post[150]—may amount to recognition by the sending state of

[144] For the codified privileges and immunities of diplomatic agents, see VCDR (n 73) arts 31, 33–40. For the conventional privileges and immunities of the representatives of a sending state in a special mission, see CSM (n 130) arts 21–36.

[145] See section 3.5.2 on the international legal significance of recognition for municipal legal purposes.

[146] Recall section 3.3.1.

[147] See also Lauterpacht (n 3) 382–3.

[148] See eg Hackworth, *Digest of International Law*, vol 4 (US Government Printing Office 1942) 416–17; Chen (n 5) 216–18; Lauterpacht (n 3) 388–90; Talmon (n 3) 156–8.

[149] See eg HC Debs, 26 February 1991, vol 186, col 459WA; HC Debs, 4 April 1938, vol 334, col 4.

[150] See VCCR (n 135) art 11(1); Foakes and Denza, 'The Appointment and Functions of Consuls' in Roberts (n 125) 120, 124–5, §8.10.

the instrument's addressee or the person under whose authority the addressee acts as at least part of the receiving state's government.[151] That said, a state may instead notify a foreign authority that a person is to act as one of its consular officers in territory controlled by that foreign authority without the notifying state recognizing anyone as another state's government. The difference in this regard lies in the form and terminology of the communication.[152]

In any event, given the general requirement that the receiving state consent to the appointment of the head of a consular post through an 'authorization . . . termed an *exequatur*' before that person can be 'admitted to the exercise of his [or her] functions'[153] and since such authorization is to be given through the receiving state's government, the sending state's view that the head of its consular post has taken up his or her functions generally implies recognition of the governmental status of the ostensible government which purported to granted the *exequatur* in the receiving state's name.[154] Similarly, a sending state's request for an *exequatur* typically implies its recognition of the addressee of the request as a person comprising at least part of or acting under the authority of the receiving state's government.[155]

There may, however, be no recognition by the sending state of any ostensible government as the government of the receiving state where the former state considers the head of a consular post to have been admitted the exercise of his or her functions 'on a provisional basis'. This is because, '[p]ending delivery of the *exequatur*, the head of a consular post may be admitted on [this] basis to the exercise of his [or her] functions'.[156] On this basis, a sending state may have a person act as the head of its consular post without recognizing any person or collectivity of persons as the government of the receiving state. For example, a number of states are said to maintain consular offices in northern Cyprus on this basis.[157] The 'passive acquiescence of the authorities in the receiving State' is still necessary, however, for that person lawfully to exercise consular functions on behalf of the sending state in the territory of the receiving state.[158] Through its respect for and response to

[151] See also VCCR (n 135) art 11(2), which provides that, in respect of the head of its consular post, the sending state 'shall transmit the commission or similar instrument . . . to the Government of the State in whose territory the head of a consular post is to exercise his [or her] functions'.

[152] See eg HC Debs, 8 November 1937, vol 328, col 1386, in which a distinction is drawn between the 'exchange of agents' and 'the appointment of new Consuls with commissions'. See also Talmon (n 3) 157.

[153] See VCCR (n 135) art 12(1). See also Foakes and Denza (n 150) 123, §8.7.

[154] See also FRUS [1920] vol III, 661; HC Debs, 8 November 1937, vol 328, col 1386; Canadian Legal Bureau (n 123). See, generally, Lee and Quigley, *Consular Law and Practice* (3rd edn, OUP 2008) chapter 5.

[155] See eg Hackworth (n 148) 689. See also Peterson (n 3) 114.

[156] VCCR (n 135) art 13. See the statement by the UK's Foreign Office dated 28 July 1952, reproduced in *Civil Air Transport Inc v Central Air Transport Corp* (n 46) 88–9 for an example of apparent non-recognition of governmental status by the sending state in establishing certain relations, through its consular officers, with an ostensible government of another state.

[157] Lee and Quigley (n 154) 102.

[158] See Foakes and Denza (n 150) 123, §8.7. See also VCCR (n 135) art 12(1), according to which the receiving state's authorization to have the sending state's head of a consular post admitted to his or her functions may take any form.

the receiving state's non-acquiescence, the sending state may recognize a specific claimant as the government of the receiving state.[159]

As a separate matter, any conduct of the sending state's consular officers by which they accept the executive authority of a specific person or collectivity of persons to act in the receiving state's name indicates the sending state's view as to the identity of at least part of the receiving state's government.[160]

3.3.2.2.2.2 Recognition by the receiving state

A sending state may appoint its consular officers only through its government.[161] The receiving state's authorization to have a person admitted as the head of a sending state's consular post therefore implies the receiving state's acceptance of the person who or collectivity of persons which appoints or under whose authority the appointment is made as at least part of the sending state's government.[162] The receiving state's authorization for the appointment of other persons as consular officers of the sending state would also imply the receiving state's recognition of an ostensible government of the sending state. Such authorization is nevertheless less common,[163] not least because the receiving state is not required to provide authorization for the appointment of the sending state's consular officers other than the head of a consular post.

The receiving state's subsequent acceptance of an individual's status as a consular officer of the sending state, for example by accepting the person's capacity to perform consular functions on the sending state's behalf or by accepting that the person benefits under its municipal law from treatment due only in respect of another state's consular officer, also implies its recognition of the person or collectivity of persons under whose authority the officer operates as at least part of the sending state's government.[164] The receiving state's consent to a consular officer's performance of diplomatic acts of the sending state[165] also amounts to the former state's

[159] See further section 3.3.2.2.3.2.

[160] Recall section 3.3.2.2.1.1 on the not-dissimilar situation concerning diplomatic agents.

[161] While the VCCR leaves it to each state to determine which of its organs is competent to appoint heads of its consular posts (see VCCR (n 135) art 10(2)), the relevant provision is worded in this way to refute '[t]he mistaken opinion . . . that only heads of State are competent to appoint consuls' (ILC, 'Draft Articles on Consular Relations, and Commentaries' in Ybk ILC [1961] vol II, 92, 161–2 (art 12, comment 2)).

[162] See eg, *a contrario*, FRUS [1920] vol III, 661: '[t]his Government cannot . . . grant an exequatur to a Consul from a non-recognized Government'; HC Debs, 8 November 1937, vol 328, col 1386; Canadian Legal Bureau (n 123).

[163] See Foakes and Denza (n 150) 125, §8.11.

[164] See also *Anglo-Czechoslovak & Prague Credit Bank v Janssen* (Australia, Supreme Court of Victoria, 23 August 1943) (1951) 12 ILR 43, 46, according to which the acceptance by the receiving state of a person as the sending state's consular officer may amount to 'recognition of a *de jure* government of [that state]'.

[165] Such consent is necessary for the performance by a consular officer of diplomatic acts: VCCR (n 135) art 17(1).

recognition of governmental status since such consent amounts to the receiving state's acceptance of a specific individual as a consular officer of the sending state.

Distinct from the acceptance of a person as a consular officer of the sending state is the acceptance of a person as performing consular functions on behalf of an entity other than a state. For example, the UK accepted passports issued by the authorities operating under Charles de Gaulle's leadership at a time when the UK did not recognize Mr de Gaulle as part of the government of a state.[166] The persons performing such functions remain distinct from consular officers of a state even if they enjoy privileges and immunities approximate to those enjoyed by the consular officers of other states, as was the case in 1937 with Francisco Franco's agents in the UK[167] and as is generally the case with Hong Kong's delegations abroad.[168] It is only where the receiving state accepts that the consular functions are exercised on behalf of another state or that the person enjoys the status of (rather than merely privileges and immunities approximate to those of) a consular officer that it recognizes another state's government by accepting the person's performance of those consular functions or enjoyment of those privileges and immunities.[169]

As with diplomatic agents and representatives of a state in a special mission, the mere presence of a sending state's consular officer in the territory of the receiving state does not imply the receiving state's recognition of anyone as the government of the sending state. Indeed, a consular officer of a sending state may operate in the territory of the receiving state without the receiving state recognizing any claim to governmental status in respect of the sending state.[170] As with diplomatic agents and representatives of the state in a special mission, moreover, the denial by a state of treatment due only in respect of a sending state's consular officers may but does not necessarily amount to the denial of governmental status.[171]

3.3.2.2.3 Severance of diplomatic or consular interstate relations

The term 'severance' of diplomatic and consular relations and the attendant verb is used within the present context merely as convenient shorthand to refer to any of the following situations: the revocation by a state of its consent to maintaining diplomatic or consular relations with another state, the revocation by the receiving

[166] DCER [1941] vol VIII, 614–15. On this possibility, see also Hackworth (n 148) 693; FRUS [1918] Supp 1, vol I, 844–5. Cf *Veysi Dag v Secretary of State for the Home Department* (UK, Immigration Appeal Tribunal, 14 March 2001) (2001) 122 ILR 529 for a different possible approach by a municipal court, albeit in a situation also involving a contested claim to statehood.

[167] HC Debs, 8 November 1937, vol 328, cols 1386–7 on the exchange of agents between the UK and the regime led by Francisco Franco on 'a basis of strict reciprocity'.

[168] See Foakes and Denza (n 150) 123, §8.8.

[169] On the acceptance of the performance of consular functions without recognition of governmental status, see eg Hackworth (n 148) 692; HC Debs, 27 May 1941, vol 371, col 1713 on the permission granted by the UK to have certain French consuls continue to function in the UK but without cypher or bag facilities and in relation only to routine consular matters. See also Talmon (n 3) 156–8.

[170] See n 169 above.

[171] Recall section 3.3.1.

state of its consent to the presence of another state's diplomatic mission or consular post on its territory, and the receiving state's notification to the sending state that a specific diplomatic agent or consular officer of the latter state is *persona non grata*.

3.3.2.2.3.1 Derecognition by the severing state?

The severance by a state of its diplomatic or consular relations with another state does not necessarily imply the former state's denial of a specific claim to governmental status in respect of the latter state. A state may sever diplomatic and consular relations with another state for any number of reasons, many of which are unrelated to its view that the ostensible government of the other state under whose authority the diplomatic agents or consular officers operate no longer comprises that state's government.[172] Indeed, the notification by a receiving state that an ostensible diplomatic agent or consular officer of another state is *persona non grata* could be seen as the receiving state's acceptance of the ostensible government under whose instructions the ostensible diplomatic agent or consular officer acts as the government of that other state.[173] At the same time, the denial by one state of the governmental status of another state's ostensible government will ordinarily result in the former state not maintaining diplomatic and consular relations with the latter state through the ostensible government in question. For example, in 1942, Canada's Prime Minister explained that 'the Canadian Government has ceased to recognize the present Government at Vichy as being the *de jure* Government of France and diplomatic relations with Vichy are accordingly terminated'.[174]

3.3.2.2.3.2 Recognition by the affected state

As a matter of international law, a state may sever diplomatic or consular relations only through its government. The response of the state with which such relations are severed may, depending on the circumstances, imply recognition of governmental status. For example, the closure by a sending state of its diplomatic mission or consular post in response to the ostensible withdrawal of consent to the mission or post by the receiving state implies the sending state's recognition of the ostensible government through which consent was revoked.[175] Similarly, the recall by

[172] See also DCER (n 40) 21: '[t]he distinction between a severance of relations with the Vichy government and withdrawal of recognition of that government as the *de jure* government of France was of fundamental importance'; Lauterpacht (n 3) 354; Crawford (n 8) 382.

[173] Compare eg the reference in Hartmann, Shah, and Warbrick (n 42) 892–3 to the expulsion by the United of 'diplomats from the Qadhafi regime' subsequent to the UK's recognition of the NTC as the government of Libya; and ibid, 891 on the earlier declaration of 'the Libyan Ambassador [as] persona non grata'.

[174] DCER (n 40) 21. Also, recall sections 3.3.2.2.1–3.3.2.2.2 on the recognition of governmental status through such relations.

[175] See, *a contrario*, the UK's disregard of the suggestion made by Laurent Gbagbo that the UK's diplomatic agents in Côte d'Ivoire 'will be asked to leave', given the UK's recognition of Mr Gbagbo's rival, Alassane Ouattara, as President of Côte d'Ivoire (Hartmann, Shah, and Warbrick (n 42) 737). Similarly, see France's apparent disregard of the request, made by the authorities led by Abdourahamane Tchiani, that the head of France's diplomatic mission in Niger departs from Niger since France recognizes the

a state of one of its diplomatic agents or consular officers on the basis that they have been declared *persona non grata* implies the sending state's recognition of the person who or collectivity of persons that made the declaration as belonging to or acting under the authority of the receiving state's government.[176]

A sending state may nevertheless close a diplomatic mission or consular post for reasons other than the ostensible termination of consent to its presence, including where such consent has indeed been revoked. Not dissimilarly, a sending state may recall one of its diplomatic agents or consular officers for its own reasons, whether or not those persons have ostensibly been declared *persona non grata*. For example, in 1946, the UNGA recommended that 'all Members of the United Nations immediately recall from Madrid their Ambassadors and Ministers plenipotentiary accredited there', in the light of the UNGA's disapproval of the conduct and basis of claim to power of 'the Franco Fascist Government of Spain'.[177]

Recognition by a sending state of governmental status as a result of its closure of a diplomatic mission or post or the withdrawal of the members of its diplomatic mission or consular office is implied only if it considers itself to lack the receiving state's consent for its diplomatic or consular presence in the receiving state. While perhaps not strictly necessary, a state may make a statement to avoid implied recognition of governmental status in such circumstances.[178]

3.3.2.3 The Conclusion of and Consent to Treaties by States

As a matter of international law, a state may perform the acts that comprise the conclusion of a treaty only through its government.[179] The acceptance by a state that a specific person or collectivity of persons has the capacity to perform any of these acts in the name of another state thus typically implies the former state's recognition of the person or persons as comprising at least part of or acting under the authority of the other state's government.[180] Such acceptance can manifest itself in various ways and at different times. Whether such acceptance is in fact manifest is

rival 'legitimate elected Nigerien authorities' as the government of Niger ('France Says Niger's Junta "Has No Authority" to Ask Ambassador to Leave' (*France 24*, 25 August 2023), available at <http://france24.com/en/live-news/20230825-%F0%9F%94%B4-niger-s-military-junta-gives-french-ambassador-48-hours-to-leave-country>).

[176] See also Weller, 'The Kuwait Crisis: A Survey of Some Legal Issues' (1991) 3 AfJIL 1, 17–18.

[177] UNGA res 39 (I) (12 December 1946) UN Doc A/RES/39(I).

[178] See eg the statement of Romania subsequent to the withdrawal of the members of its diplomatic staff from Kuwait, as discussed in Talmon (n 3) 162, which concerned not only the question of the identity of the government of Kuwait but also the more fundamental question of title to territory. (This statement also referred expressly to Romania's continued recognition of the governmental status of a rival claimant.) On withdrawal of diplomatic missions, see also Foakes and Denza (n 136) 167–8, §§10.29–10.30.

[179] Recall section 2.2.2. On the acts involved in the conclusion of a treaty, see Vienna Convention on the Law of Treaties (adopted 23 May 1969, entered into force 27 January 1980) 1155 UNTS 331 ('VCLT') Part II, Section 1.

[180] See eg Hackworth (n 4) 171.

more complicated in the context of multilateral treaties than in the context of bilateral treaties. Perhaps needless to say, the conclusion of a treaty between a state and a non-state entity does not, as such, constitute recognition by the state of any specific claim to governmental status in respect of any other state.[181]

As regards the ostensible performance of an act involved in the conclusion of a bilateral treaty between states, recognition of governmental status is clearest where the acceptance as effective of the act occurs at the same or virtually the same time as when the act is performed.[182] Such acceptance by a state is manifest in its view that the act involved in the conclusion by the treaty ostensibly performed by the other state has had the effect, in conjunction with the accepting state's act, for which international law provides the successful performance by both states of the acts involved in the conclusion of the treaty will have, for example by considering that the treaty has been adopted or has entered into force.

In circumstances that do not appear to arise often, a state may accept that a bilateral treaty between it and another state has been adopted or has entered into force as a result of an act ostensibly performed by the latter state at an earlier time. In such circumstances, it cannot be excluded that the former state has not recognized as the government of the latter state the ostensible government through which the act in question was performed since the initially-ineffective ostensible performance of an act by a state involved in the conclusion of a treaty may become effective as a result of the subsequent confirmation by that state through its government.[183] The acceptance by a state that a bilateral treaty with another state has been adopted or has entered into force can nevertheless be taken to amount to the recognition by the former state of some ostensible government of the latter state between the initial ostensible performance by the latter state of the act involved in the conclusion of a treaty and the former state's acceptance that the treaty has been adopted or entered into force.[184]

The consent of a state to be bound by a multilateral treaty among states or any other act concerned with the conclusion of such a treaty does not necessarily imply the contracting state's recognition of the ostensible government of every other state which has purported to perform or later purports to perform an act involved in the conclusion of the treaty.[185]

[181] On the capacity of entities other than states to conclude international agreements, see eg Crawford (n 9) 227–9 in respect of the Holy See. On insurrectionary movements, see eg the Agreement of 3 September 1918 between the British Government and the Czecho-Slovak National Council, reproduced in FRUS [1918] Supp 1, vol I, 844 and the Modus Vivendi between the USA and the French Committee of National Liberation on Reciprocal Aid in French North and West Africa (signed 25 September 1943, entered into force on the same date) 76 UNTS 183.

[182] See eg Hackworth (n 4) 171, 347, 354.

[183] See VCLT (n 179) art 8. Recall also chapter 2, n 80 and accompanying text.

[184] Recall section 2.2.2.

[185] See also Lauterpacht (n 3) 371–4 and many of the references contained therein; CERD, 'Inter-State Communication Submitted by the State of Palestine against Israel' (12 December 2019) UN Doc CERD/C/100/5, §3.12.

In accepting that the text of a multilateral treaty has been adopted, however, a state can generally be taken to recognize the governmental status of at least some ostensible governments of the other states participating in the adoption of the text of the treaty. This is because the adoption of the text of a treaty typically requires the consent of at least some of the states participating in its drawing up. In its view that a treaty has been adopted, a state can thus be taken to accept as effective the ostensible consent to the adoption of the treaty by however many of the other states participating in its drawing up is necessary for the treaty to be adopted.[186] The governmental status of precisely which ostensible governments has been recognized may be unclear, at least insofar as the adoption of a treaty does not depend on the consent of all states participating in its drawing up.[187] As a separate matter, uncertainty as to which ostensible governments a state has recognized can arise from the possibility that the initial ostensible consent by a state to the adoption of a treaty is treated as effective on account of the subsequent confirmation by that state of its consent to adopt the treaty.[188]

Not dissimilarly, where the entry into force of a multilateral treaty is dependent upon its ratification by a certain number of states, a state's view that the treaty has entered into force (for example, in its reliance on a right arising under that treaty) can be taken to imply its recognition of however many states must have ratified the treaty for it to enter into force. The governmental status of which claimants has been recognized may not be entirely clear. There may be uncertainty both as to the states whose ostensible governments have been recognized and as to the specific ostensible government of a state that has been recognized. The number of ratifications needed for entry into force might be lower than the number of ostensible parties to the treaty, and one ostensible government of a state may subsequently confirm the state's ostensible ratification of the treaty by a different claimant to governmental status.[189] Due also to the possible subsequent affirmation of an initially-ineffective act, the acceptance by a contracting state that it is party to a multilateral treaty vis-à-vis a specific other contracting state, including one that joined the treaty at a later date, does not necessarily amount to the former state party's recognition of the ostensible government through which the latter state's consent to be bound by the treaty was expressed.

In contrast to the apparent view of the European Commission of Human Rights (ECommHR), the lack of objection by a contracting state to a multilateral treaty to another contracting state's ostensible expression of consent to be bound by the treaty does not in itself reflect the recognition of governmental status by the former state of the person or persons through which the latter ostensibly

[186] See VCLT (n 179) art 9.
[187] Ibid, art 9(2).
[188] See n 183 above and accompanying text.
[189] Ibid.

expressed its consent to be bound by the treaty.[190] It is unclear for what reason mere non-objection could be taken to amount to recognition of governmental status. Recognition of governmental status in such circumstances arises only as a consequence of a statement to that effect or by necessary implication from some other positive act, for example the assertion as to the applicability of the treaty between itself and one or more specific other states.

While possibly unnecessary as a matter of international law, to avoid any perceived inference of recognition of governmental status from its mere performance of an act involved in the conclusion of a multilateral treaty, a contracting state may expressly declare that its performance of the act in question does not involve the recognition of one or more ostensible governments. An example is the statement by the USA that its 'signing the International Sanitary Convention . . . is not to be construed to mean that [it] recognizes a régime or entity acting as Government of a signatory or adhering Power when that régime or entity is not recognized by the United States as the Government of that Power'.[191] Such a disclaimer may instead take another form, such as a treaty provision. For example, Article 9 of the Act of the International Conference on Vietnam provides, inter alia, that '[s]ignature of this Act does not constitute recognition of any Party in any case in which it has not previously been accorded'.[192]

As a separate matter, possibly but not necessarily on the basis of its non-recognition of an ostensible government of another state, a state may declare that a multilateral treaty has no legal force between itself and that other state.[193]

That said, regardless of its form, a purported disclaimer against recognition does not necessarily amount to either the denial or even the non-recognition of governmental status. Nor does a declaration by a state that a multilateral treaty is inapplicable between itself and another state necessarily involve the denial of governmental status.[194]

The subject-matter of the treaty does not affect whether there is recognition of governmental status. Suggestions to the contrary[195] might be best understood in the light of a narrower understanding of the term 'recognition'.[196] That said, multilateral treaties requiring or otherwise involving regular interactions between states

[190] See ECommHR, 'Decision of 26 May 1975 on the Admissibility of the Applications (App Nos 6780/74 and 6950/75)', Decisions and Reports, vol 2, 125, 135.

[191] Hudson, *International Legislation*, vol 3 (Carnegie Endowment for International Peace 1931) 1975. For another example, recall n 97 above.

[192] Act of the International Conference on Vietnam (2 March 1973) art 9, reproduced in DSB [1973] vol 68, No 1761, 346.

[193] For an example in this regard, recall the text accompanying chapter 2, n 104.

[194] On both such disclaimers and declarations, recall section 3.3.2.1.

[195] See Peterson (n 3) 112–14, 128–9.

[196] On the different meanings of this term, recall section 3.2.1.

might more frequently result in an act amounting to recognition of governmental status.

3.4 The Legality of Practice Concerning Recognition of Governmental Status

3.4.1 No Customary International Legal Obligation to Recognize Governmental Status

On the whole, state practice supports the position that states are under no general customary international legal obligation to recognize the government of another state.[197] For example, '[t]he Dutch view is that there is no duty to recognise a new government'[198] and New Zealand has stated that 'formal acts of recognition in respect of new Governments in other countries are unnecessary as a matter of international law'.[199] Put differently, the refusal of recognition of governmental status of the 'right' government is not per se unlawful.[200] The widespread adoption by states of the Estrada doctrine[201] might also be seen to support this position.[202]

A number of considerations might render states reluctant to recognize a government, without this involving the violation of an international legal obligation. For example, a state may refrain from recognizing the governmental status of a specific claimant because of uncertainty as to whether that claimant qualifies for governmental status.[203] Alternatively or additionally, a state may be unwilling to accord what is sometimes seen as the 'prestige' or political 'approval' that accompanies at least certain forms of recognition.[204] Relatedly, a state may refuse to recognize the government of another state as a 'symbolic gesture',[205] for example if the state disapproves of some aspect of the composition or basis of the claim to power of

[197] See also Whiteman (n 23) 5–7; Henkin, 'Restatement of the Foreign Relations Law of the United States (Revised): Tentative Draft No. 2' (1981) 75 AJIL 987, 989. See, generally, Kelsen, *Principles of International Law* (2nd edn, Rinehart & Winston 1966) 404; 'Sixth Report on Unilateral Acts' (n 3) 39–40; Brownlie (n 5) 209; Peterson (n 3) 28–35. As noted by Whiteman (n 23) 7, the position may differ as a matter of treaty law. See further section 3.4.3.

[198] Siekmann (n 11) 238.

[199] See the certificate of 28 March 1988 (n 113) .

[200] See also Jennings and Watts (n 137) 432, §129.

[201] On the adoption of a policy of non-recognition, recall n 113 above.

[202] See also Crawford (n 9) 152.

[203] See eg UNGA, 'Official Records, 66th Session, 2nd Plenary Meeting' (16 September 2011) UN Doc A/66/PV.2, 14 on the approach of St Vincent and the Grenadines in respect of the NTC.

[204] Recall n 11 above.

[205] Crawford, 'Democracy and the Body of International Law' in Fox and Roth (eds), *Democratic Governance and International Law* (CUP 2000) 91, 108, although the case Crawford mentions concerns non-recognition by the UNGA. In any event, the governmental status of the ostensible government in question was, at least during part of this 'symbolic gesture', not beyond doubt. See chapter 5, n 84 and accompanying text.

the government in question. Moreover, a possible reason for a state's reluctance to recognize a transitional government—that is, a government which claims power under a constitution that is intended to have an interim existence, pending a reorganization of the internal disposal of public power within the state—may pertain to the possible implications recognition might be seen to have on the success of the transition. Related concerns may have informed the practice concerning recognition of the ostensible government operating under Burhanuddin Rabbani's leadership as the government of Afghanistan[206] and of the various interim authorities existing in Somalia between 1991 and 2012.[207] Similar considerations were expressed in respect of the Governing Council of Iraq (GCI) in 2003.[208] At the same time, express recognition of a transitional government may be forthcoming in other cases, as was the case with the recognition by several states of the GNA.[209] This might be especially so where a state's wish to make clear its acceptance of no other political authority as the government of a state is greater than its concern that a transitional government may not proceed, especially if expressly recognized, with the expected political transition.

Although this is less clear,[210] the denial of governmental status to the 'right' government may also be lawful in at least certain circumstances.[211] This is so especially where the denial does not amount to or result in a rejection by the denying state of the effectiveness of the representation of the other state by the 'right' government, a refusal to accord to the 'right' government the privileges and immunities owed under international law by the denying state in respect of foreign governments, or a coercive act in respect of some matter that international law leaves to the sovereign discretion of each state. Denial of governmental status to the 'right' government which amounts to or results in any of these situations will generally comprise or contribute to a violation of international law. Not entirely dissimilarly, non-recognition of the 'right' government which results in any of these situations will, in effect, contribute to a violation of international law.[212]

[206] See chapter 4, nn 247–8 and accompanying text.

[207] There may have been uncertainty as to the satisfaction of the requirement of effective control in respect of these claims. For relevant practice, see eg 'Brief for the United States as Amicus Curiae Supporting Affirmance' in *Mohamed Ali Samantar v. Bashe Abdi Yousuf et al*, available at <http://scotusblog.com/wp-content/uploads/2010/01/08-1555_us-amicus-supporting-affirmance.pdf>, 4.

[208] See Secretariat of the United Nations (Legal Opinions), 'Note to the Secretary-General of the United Nations' [2003] UNJYB 531, 532, §5. On the apparent reluctance to recognize this claimant, see also UNSC res 1500 (14 August 2003) UN Doc S/RES/1500, §1. But see UNSC res 1511 (16 October 2003) UN Doc S/RES/1511, §4.

[209] See chapter 4, n 171.

[210] See further section 3.4.2.

[211] On the distinction between non-recognition of governmental status and denial of governmental status, recall section 3.2.3.

[212] See further sections 3.4.2–3.4.3.

3.4.2 Recognition, Non-Recognition, and Denial of Governmental Status and the Prohibition on Intervention

It is sometimes said that a state's recognition of governmental status in respect of a 'wrong' government of another state[213] amounts to unlawful intervention by the recognizing state in that other state's affairs.[214] The suggestion has also been made that the refusal of recognition of governmental status of the 'right' government is an unlawful intervention.[215] But, in the absence of any clear distinction drawn in this literature between the refusal of recognition of the 'right' government' and the denial of governmental status of the 'right' government,[216] such suggestions arguably concern only the latter. Indeed, one of the commentators who posits that '[t]o refuse recognition solely because of antipathy to a government's internal practices . . . constitutes intervention' acknowledges that a state is not obliged under international law to recognize the governmental status of an ostensible government which as a matter of customary international law qualifies as another state's government.[217] In any event, the non-recognition by a state of governmental status is not per se unlawful.[218] A claim to the contrary is in substance no different from the claim that there is an obligation under customary international law to recognize the governmental status of the 'right' government, which is not the case.[219] But this does not answer the question whether the denial of governmental status of the 'right' government is also lawful.

For the recognition of a 'wrong' government or the denial of governmental status to the 'right' government to amount to an unlawful intervention in the affairs of another state, two requirements must be met. First, the act must concern a matter that another state 'is permitted, by the principle of state sovereignty, to

[213] This practice is sometimes termed 'premature' recognition, a term which the present work avoids, given that an ostensible government may no longer satisfy the international legal criterion or criteria for governmental status, in which case the term 'prolonged' recognition may be more accurate. See also Peterson (n 3) 35, who mentions both 'premature recognition and prolonged recognition'.

[214] See eg 'Records of the Eighteenth Ordinary Session of the Assembly: Meetings of the Committees, 9th Meeting of the Sixth Committee' (1937) 175 LNOJ Supp 58, 63 (USSR); UNGA, 'Official Records, 20th Session, 877th Meeting of the Sixth Committee' (17 November 1965) UN Doc A/C.6/SR.877, §10 (Spain); Jennings and Watts (n 137) 143–4, §41 n 3. See also Lauterpacht (n 3) 95; Peterson (n 3) 35; Talmon, 'Who Is a Legitimate Government in Exile? Towards Normative Criteria for Governmental Legitimacy in International Law' in Goodwin-Gill and Talmon (eds), *The Reality of International Law: Essays in Honour of Ian Brownlie* (OUP 1999) 499, 521. See also nn 228 and 230 below and accompanying text.

[215] See eg Wright, 'The Chinese Recognition Problem' (1955) 49 AJIL 320, 335; Marek, *Identity and Continuity of States in Public International Law* (Librarie Droz 1954) 56.

[216] On the distinction between the non-recognition and the denial of governmental status, recall section 3.2.3.

[217] Wright (n 215) 335, 336, §3.

[218] See also Jennings and Watts (n 137) 432, §129 n 11: 'excessive delay in according recognition may in certain circumstances amount to overt encouragement to the former regime to reassert its control, but is unlikely in itself to constitute intervention'.

[219] Recall section 3.4.1.

decide freely'.[220] Secondly, the act must be coercive, in the sense that it deprives, or is calculated to deprive, another state of control over the matter. It is unclear, however, whether specifically a coercive intent or specifically a coercive effect is required, or whether either a coercive effect or coercive intent will suffice.[221]

As regards the first requirement, the recognition of the 'wrong' government and the denial of governmental status of the 'right' government both pertain to the identity of another state's government. Since the identity of a state's government is a matter that international law leaves to the sovereign discretion of that state,[222] each of these positions of a state as regards the identity of another state's government satisfy the first element of prohibited intervention.

In what concerns the second requirement for a prohibited intervention, the mere expression by a state of the view that the 'wrong' government qualifies for governmental status or that the 'right' government does not qualify for governmental status might not invariably be coercive.[223]

Insofar as a coercive effect is necessary for an act to amount to a prohibited intervention, regard might be had to any consequence that follows from the act of recognition or denial of governmental status. Relevant consequences might arise from express or implied recognition or denial of governmental status. Indeed, acts of implied recognition and denial of governmental status generally occur in a context that has some practical consequence, which may involve a coercive effect.[224] It nevertheless remains unclear whether all acts of recognition or of denial of governmental status do indeed have a coercive effect so as to amount to a prohibited intervention.

Insofar as the intention to coerce a state is relevant to the legality of an act of intervention in that state's affairs, it is arguable that the mere expression by a state of the view that the 'wrong' government qualifies for governmental status or that the 'right' government does not qualify for governmental status is, in certain circumstances, coercive. This is so not least because of the municipal legal consequences that frequently follow from recognition.[225] In ascertaining the existence of

[220] *Military and Paramilitary Activities in and against Nicaragua (Nicaragua v USA), Merits, Judgment* [1986] ICJ Rep 14 ('*Nicaragua v USA*'), 107–8, §205.

[221] Jennings and Watts (n 137) 432, §129 speak of acts that 'in effect' deprive a state of its choice over a matter, while, at ibid, 430, §129, they speak of acts that are 'calculated to impose certain conduct or consequences'; Jamnejad and Wood, 'The Principle of Non-Intervention' (2009) 22 LJIL 345, 348, 371 focus on a coercive 'intention'. For what it is worth, both Nicaragua and the ICJ appear to have treated as important the ostensible intention of the USA in determining whether or not the latter has violated the prohibition on intervention. See *Nicaragua v USA* (n 220) 123–4, §§240–1. That said, the ICJ speaks also of 'methods of coercion' in stipulating when intervention is wrongful (*Nicaragua v USA* (n 220) 108, §205). Further on the different positions in this regard, see Milanovic, 'Revisiting Coercion as an Element of Prohibited Intervention in International Law' (2023) 117 AJIL 601, 617–20.

[222] Recall section 2.4.

[223] *Maduro v Guaido* (Court of Appeal) (n 49) §§34–6.

[224] See the text accompanying nn 233–9 below.

[225] On the effects of non-recognition and denial of governmental status, see n 305 below and accompanying text. On the effects of recognition, see the text accompanying nn 236–9.

a coercive intent, it may be relevant that the ostensible government which is recognized has a plausible claim to governmental status as a matter of customary international law or that there is reasonable doubt as to the governmental status of the government which is denied governmental status.[226] It may then be arguable that the state which denies the governmental status of the 'right' government or accords recognition to the 'wrong' government does not intend to subordinate the will of the state whose ostensible government it is recognizing or denying as the government of that latter state. On the contrary, an act of recognition or denial of governmental status that expressly seeks to influence the policy or conduct of a specific state[227] might demonstrate a coercive intent. A question relevant to the qualification of such recognition or denial as unlawful intervention would be whether the policy or conduct in question concerns a matter that international law leaves to the sovereign discretion of the affected state.

As regards other possible bases for distinguishing whether recognition of the 'wrong' government or denial of governmental status to the 'right' government amounts to a prohibited intervention, Mexico suggested, in the proclamation of the so-called 'Estrada doctrine', that the express recognition of governmental status 'offends the sovereignty of other nations', while Mexico's 'maintenance or withdrawal . . . of its diplomatic agents' and its 'continued acceptance . . . of such similarly accredited diplomatic agents as the respective nations may have in Mexico' as Mexico 'may deem advisable' may be done without 'pronounc[ing] judgment . . . regarding the right of foreign nations to accept, maintain or replace their governments or authorities'.[228] Since then, Spain has claimed that the Estrada doctrine, which other states have adopted,[229] 'might constitute an important safeguard against unjustified intervention'.[230] In contrast to what these statements might suggest, however, it cannot be said that the express recognition of the 'wrong' government constitutes unlawful intervention and that certain forms of implied recognition of the 'wrong' government in the context of diplomatic relations do not constitute unlawful recognition. There is no basis to support such a position, whether it is a coercive intent or coercive effect that is relevant. To conclude otherwise is to oversimplify the legal position concerning 'the maintenance' by one state of another state's diplomatic agents on the territory of the former state. Indeed, a state may, in a sense and to an extent, 'maintain' a diplomatic presence abroad and not object to the presence of diplomatic agents previously operating in its territory without recognition of governmental status.[231]

[226] See also Blix (n 8) 679, who draws a distinction between 'early' and 'premature' recognition, given '[t]he difficulty, in practice, to indicate the moment when recognition is appropriate'.

[227] On such practice, see eg Peterson, 'Political Use of Recognition: The Influence of the International System' (1982) 34 World Politics 324, 336–40.

[228] Estrada doctrine (n 112).

[229] Recall n 113 above.

[230] UNGA, 'Official Records, 20th Session, 877th Meeting of the Sixth Committee' (n 214) 214–15, §11.

[231] Recall nn 134 and 147 above, including the accompanying text.

In what depends principally on whether there exists only a requirement of coercive intent, only of coercive effect, or of either coercive intent or coercive effect, at least certain acts of recognition of the 'wrong' government and of denial of governmental status to the 'right' government might not amount to unlawful intervention. Such acts may nevertheless result in unlawful intervention. Non-recognition of the 'right' government, which in itself does not amount to unlawful intervention, might also result in unlawful intervention. Such intervention arises where the state recognizing, refusing to recognize, or denying governmental status relies on its position as regards the qualification for governmental status by a particular ostensible government as the basis of some other decision that has the effect or purpose of depriving the state whose government's identity is in question of control over the identity of its government or over some other matter that international law leaves to the sovereign discretion of each state.[232]

Indeed, recognition, non-recognition or denial of governmental status might comprise the basis for a number of acts which have a coercive effect or purpose in respect of a matter that international law leaves to the sovereign discretion of each state.[233] This is so not least because it is generally only through whomever a state considers to comprise the government of another state that the former state will accept as effective the ostensible representation of the latter state, including on matters that international law leaves to the sovereign discretion to each state.[234] Judicial deference to executive recognition, which is not uncommon within a number of a states, might also contribute to a coercive act subsequent to recognition, non-recognition, or denial of governmental status.[235]

To illustrate the point, the recognition by a state of a 'wrong' government may result in that state providing military support to the ostensible government in question in violation of the obligation of non-intervention.[236] Conversely, the denial by a state of the governmental status of the 'right' government of another state may result in the former state not respecting the withdrawal of the latter state's consent to the military presence of the former state in the territory of the latter state. Further, it might be that the grant by a state of control over foreign state property

[232] See also Brownlie (n 5) 209; Crawford (n 8) 144 on 'non-recognition as a source of interference'; Blix (n 8) 678–9, 697.

[233] The conduct of a state resulting from its recognition of the 'wrong' government or from its refusal to recognize or its denial of governmental status of the 'right' government might also give rise to a violation of one or more other international legal obligations of that state. See section 3.4.3.

[234] Recall section 2.3. See also section 5.3.2.

[235] On possible consequences of such deference, see eg *Panama v Republic National Bank of New York* (USA, District Court, Southern District of New York, 15 March 1988) (1991) 86 ILR 1, 5–6; *British Arab Bank v NTC* (n 106) §25; *Rusoro Mining Ltd, Gold Fields Ltd v Bolivarian Republic of Venezuela, Case 1:16-cv-02020-RJL, Order filed on 1 May 2019* (USA, Court of Appeals for the District of Columbia Circuit), available at <http://italaw.com/sites/default/files/case-documents/italaw10521.pdf>; *Maduro v Guaido* (n 8) §§69–70; *In Re: Terrorist Attacks* (n 7) 26. See also Chen (n 5) 238–9.

[236] On such support as a violation of the prohibition on intervention, albeit not on the basis of the recognition of the 'wrong' government, see eg *Nicaragua v USA* (n 220) 126, §246; Jennings and Watts (n 137) 431, §129; Jamnejad and Wood (n 221) 368.

to the 'wrong' government, which may occur on the basis of the recognition of the 'wrong' government, amounts to unlawful intervention by the former state in the latter state's affairs.[237] The same goes for the refusal to grant such control to the 'right' government of the latter state on the basis of the refusal to recognize or the denial of governmental status to the 'right' government. In terms of possible examples of coercive situations which follow from the position of a state as to the identity of another state's government, regardless of whether or not these in fact concern the 'wrong' government, Egypt's willingness to provide armed support to the Tobruk-based ostensible government of Libya and the decision by UK courts to grant the board appointed by Juan Guaidó access to Venezuela's gold in the Bank of England have already been mentioned.[238] These situations resulted from executive practice concerning recognition of governmental status, as did the blocking by the USA's Federal Reserve of an attempted transfer of funds in the name of the Central Bank of Myanmar by one of the two ostensible governments of Myanmar.[239] At the same time, as with the lawfulness of the recognition of the 'wrong' government and the denial of governmental status of the 'right' government, the existence of a plausible claim to governmental status as a matter of international law of a 'wrong' government that is recognized, or of reasonable doubt as to the governmental status of the 'right' government which goes unrecognized, or which is denied governmental status might preclude an act of intervention that results from an act of recognition, non-recognition, or denial of governmental status from being unlawful, at least insofar as a coercive intent is necessary for an act of intervention to be unlawful.

The suggestion that there is more support for the view that recognition of the 'wrong' government constitutes unlawful intervention than for the position that 'delayed recognition' to the 'right' government constitutes unlawful intervention[240] is not necessarily accurate or relevant in assessing the lawfulness of recognition of the 'wrong' government or the lawfulness of denial of governmental status of the 'right' government. Insofar as 'delayed recognition' refers to the non-recognition of the 'right' government, the relative lack of support for the position that 'delayed recognition' is per se unlawful indicates nothing about the lawfulness of the recognition of the 'wrong' government or of the denial of governmental status of the 'right' government. But if 'delayed recognition' refers to the denial of governmental status of the 'right' government, then the difference in views as regards the lawfulness of 'delayed recognition' of the 'right' government and recognition of the 'wrong' government might support the view that neither of these acts constitute

[237] See also Talmon (n 3) 199 and n 451 thereof, with intervention being perhaps unlawful even if the granting of access to state property does not give one ostensible government 'a decisive advantage over [any other claimant] for effective control of the government'.

[238] See section 1.1.

[239] 'Remarks by President Biden on the Administration's Response to the Coup in Burma' (10 February 2021), available at <http://whitehouse.gov/briefing-room/speeches-remarks/2021/02/10/remarks-by-president-biden-on-the-administrations-response-to-the-coup-in-burma>.

[240] Blix (n 8) 678.

a prohibited intervention, at least absent any reason why the recognition of the 'wrong' government has the effect or intention of affecting to a greater extent the choice of a state over the identity of its government than the denial of the governmental status of the 'right' government.

In short, the recognition of the 'wrong' government and the denial of governmental status to the 'right' government may, at least in certain contexts, amount to or result in the violation by that state of the obligation of non-intervention. Non-recognition of the 'right' government may also result in unlawful intervention. Any subsisting uncertainty as regards the legal position in this regard does not relate to the question whether the identity of the government of a state is a matter in respect of which other states are prohibited from intervening but to what might satisfy the requirement of coercion.

3.4.3 Recognition, Non-Recognition, and Denial of Governmental Status and Other Violations of International Law

Certain international legal obligations require a state to treat a specific way the government or some members of the government of another state. For example, each state is entitled to see the person or at least some of the persons comprising its government benefit from immunity *ratione personae* in respect of criminal proceedings taking place in a foreign domestic court.[241] As a further example, every state is entitled to see itself and its organs benefit from immunity *ratione materiae* in respect of at least certain acts in the context of civil proceedings before a foreign municipal court. This entitlement extends to claims against a state's government *eo nomine*.[242]

In accordance with the objective international legal existence of the government of each state, the application of the rules of international law concerned with the treatment owed by states in respect of foreign governments is not generally dependent on the recognition by a state of the government of another state. Insofar as it results in the denial of such treatment,[243] the non-recognition or the denial by a state of governmental status of the 'right' government contributes to the violation by that state of an obligation owed by it under international law.[244] It may be for

[241] See eg O'Keefe, *International Criminal Law* (OUP 2015) 419. See also the ILC's ongoing consideration of this topic, including 'Text of the Draft Articles on Immunity of State Officials from Foreign Criminal Jurisdiction Adopted by the Commission on First Reading' in *ILC Report* (2022) UN Doc A/77/10, 189, 190 (arts 3–4).

[242] See eg ILC, 'Draft Articles on Jurisdictional Immunities of States and Their Property and Commentaries Thereto' in Ybk ILC [1991] vol II(1), 13, 15 (art 2, comment 9).

[243] Note that a state may deny according a foreign ostensible government the treatment ordinarily required under international law without this amounting to a denial of governmental status. Recall section 3.3.1.

[244] See also Brownlie (n 5) 209; *Halsbury's Laws of England* (n 2) §49. See also eg *In Re: Terrorist Attacks* (n 7) 26 for a recent pronouncement by a municipal court on a related point.

this reason that municipal courts of a state sometimes opt not to defer to executive policy on recognition of governments even if they ordinarily do so.[245]

At the same time, since international law does not generally prohibit states from according substantially-similar treatment to persons not belonging to the government of another state, a state may treat the 'wrong' government of another state in a manner identical or approximate to the treatment that international law requires in respect of foreign governments without violating international law.[246]

Given the distinctive function of a state's government in representing that state,[247] the recognition by another state of the 'wrong' government or the denial or non-recognition of the governmental status of the 'right' government may result in the commission of an internationally wrongful act by that other state in cases where the lawfulness or other unwrongfulness of its conduct depends on the effective representation of the first state.[248] As regards a state that has recognized the 'wrong' government, the wrongfulness of its conduct may arise from its mistaken reliance, in asserting the lawfulness or other unwrongfulness of its conduct, on the ostensible consent, waiver, or other representation of the state whose 'wrong' government it has recognized.[249] In relation to a state that does not recognize or that denies the governmental status of the 'right' government of another state, the wrongful conduct of the former state may arise from its mistaken view that the latter state has not withdrawn the consent that is necessary to render lawful or unwrongful the conduct of the former state.[250] The wrongful conduct of the former state may instead arise from the view that the latter state does not enjoy a particular right, for example where the former state denies that the latter state has consented to be bound by a treaty.[251]

As a separate matter, it is sometimes suggested that the recognition by a state of the 'wrong' government or the denial of the governmental status of the 'right'

[245] See eg *Wulfsohn v RSFSR* (n 7). For examples of such deference, see n 235 above.

[246] Recall nn 68 and 166–8, including the accompanying text.

[247] Recall section 2.2.2.

[248] See also Chen (n 5) 129; Henkin (n 197) 989. On the violation of the prohibition on intervention as a result of recognition of the 'wrong' government or of non-recognition or denial of governmental status of the 'right' government, see section 3.4.2.

[249] On consent and waiver, see eg ARSIWA (n 16) 72 and 121 (arts 20 and 45(*a*), respectively), although in this context, waiver results in a loss of the right to invoke responsibility, not in the unwrongfulness of conduct. For waiver of a right, see eg 'Third Report on Immunity of State Officials from Foreign Criminal Jurisdiction, by Mr. Roman Anatolevich Kolodkin, Special Rapporteur' (24 May 2011) UN Doc A/CN.4/646, §32. For another example where the representation of a state is relevant to the determination of the lawfulness of the conduct of another state, recall chapter 1, n 7 on the relevance of the consent of a state to the use of foreign force on its territory. See also the argument made by Talmon (n 3) 198–9 on unlawful expropriation.

[250] The example of withdrawal of consent for foreign military presence has already been mentioned. See section 3.4.2.

[251] An exception in this regard exists to the extent that a statement refusing recognition has had the effect of excluding the applicability of the treaty between the non-recognizing state and the state whose government is unrecognized. See chapter 2, n 102 and accompanying text.

government of another state amounts to a violation of the right of the latter state's population to self-determination in the capacity of that population as a 'people'.[252] Practice which suggests that the government of a state is at least the presumptive representative of that state's population in the latter's quality as a 'people' may not be irrelevant in this regard.[253] This is so even if the government of a state may be displaced from its status as the representative of a people, as appears to be the case where a state is violating certain international legal obligations owed in respect of its population, notably the right to self-determination of its people,[254] or where a people has its own representative which predates and retains a separate political existence from the government of the state whose population comprises that people.[255]

Regardless of the position under customary international law, states may have an obligation to recognize, not to recognize, or to deny governmental status to one or more specific claimants to governmental status as a matter of treaty law. Any such obligation may be found expressly within a treaty provision, as is the case with

[252] See eg UNGA, 'Official Records, 29th Session, 2299th Plenary Meeting' (26 November 1974) UN Doc A/PV.2299, §91 (Japan); UNGA, 'Official Records, 29th Session, 2301st Plenary Meeting' (27 November 1974) UN Doc A/PV.2301, §47 (Australia). On recognition of governmental status in the context of international organizations, see section 5.4. See also eg UNGA, 'Official Records, 20th Session, 877th Meeting of the Sixth Committee' (n 214), in which Spain appears to suggest that the non-recognition of the 'right' government involves the violation of a people's right to self-determination. But recall section 3.4.1 on the absence of a general obligation to recognize the 'right' government.

[253] This includes statements to the effect that the government of a state is 'the only authentic representative' of that state and its people (UNGA, 'Credentials of Representatives to the Twenty-Ninth Session of the General Assembly: Second Report of the Credentials Committee' (13 December 1974) UN Doc A/9779/Add.1, §8 (China)) and those which posit that the government of a state enjoys 'the capacity to express the aspirations, the interests and the will' of that state's people (UNGA, 'Official Records, 29th Session, 2299th Plenary Meeting' (n 252) §152 (Romania)). See also UNGA, 'Official Records, 29th Session, 2320th Plenary Meeting' (16 December 1974) UN Doc A/PV.2320, §40 (Albania); UNGA, 'Official Records, 35th Session, 35th Plenary Meeting' (13 October 1980) UN Doc A/35/PV.35, §112 (Angola); Crawford (n 236) 56; Talmon (n 17) 238.

[254] See eg UNGA res 3151 G (XXVIII) (14 December 1973) UN Doc A/RES/3151(XXVIII) §11. See also Protocol additional to the Geneva Conventions of 12 August 1949, and relating to the protection of victims of international armed conflicts (Protocol I) (adopted 8 June 1977, entered into force 7 December 1978) 1125 UNTS 3, art 96(3), which, in situations involving a violation of the right to self-determination, presupposes the existence of an 'authority representing a people' distinct from the 'High Contracting Party' that, in at least some of the relevant situations, has sovereignty over the territory in which that people resides. Some states appear to consider that the case of Syria since 2011 is another example of the government of a state not being the representative of the people of that state. At least some states have recognized an opposition group as one or the legitimate representative of the Syrian people, apparently in response to the ongoing violations by Syria of certain international legal obligations of a humanitarian character. See further Talmon (n 17) 219–39. Additionally, see UNGA res 39 (I) (n 177) on the UNGA's conviction 'that the Franco Fascist Government of Spain . . . does not represent the Spanish people', although this may refer to representation in a looser and less legally-significant sense, not least because the right of peoples to self-determination might not, at that time, have had a basis in positive customary international law in a way that it would have been implicated in that situation.

[255] See eg UNGA res 67/19 (4 December 2012) UN Doc A/RES/67/19, §2 as regards the distinction between the Palestine Liberation Organization and the State of Palestine.

Article I of the Additional Convention to the General Treaty of Peace and Amity of 1907. According to this provision,

> [t]he Governments of the High Contracting Parties shall not recognize any other Government which may come into power in any of the five Republics as a consequence of a *coup d'etat*, or of a revolution against the recognized Government, so long as the freely elected representatives of the people thereof have not constitutionally reorganized the country.[256]

A further example might be Article 5 of the Agreement on a Comprehensive Political Settlement of the Cambodia Conflict, which provides that '[t]he SNC shall, throughout the transitional period, represent Cambodia externally'.[257] Alternatively, such an obligation may arise from the decision of an organ of an international organization which its members have undertaken 'to accept'.[258] The decision of the Peace and Security Council of the African Union (AUPSC) that AU 'Member States [are] to challenge the participation of the representatives of [certain] de facto authorities in the activities of non-African international organizations, including the United Nations' might be a relevant example in this regard, as regards at least one form of recognition.[259] Another possible example in this regard is the UNSC's determination that the GCI 'embodies the sovereignty of the State of Iraq', an apparent decision on the governmental status of the GCI,[260] which might preclude UN member states from lawfully denying the governmental status of the GCI or lawfully recognizing the governmental status of any other ostensible government of Iraq at that time.[261]

[256] Adopted 20 December 1907, reproduced in (1908) 2 AJIL Supp 229, 229–30. See also the Troppau Protocol (signed 19 November 1820) art 2, reproduced in Lauterpacht (n 3) 419; General Treaty of Peace and Amity (concluded 7 February 1923, entered into force 24 November 1924) art II, reproduced in (1923) 17 AJIL Supp 117.

[257] Agreement Concerning Cambodia (n 79).

[258] See Charter of the United Nations (signed 26 June 1945, entered into force 24 October 1945, last amended 24 September 1973) ('UN Charter'), available at <http://un.org/en/about-us/un-charter/full-text>, art 25; Protocol Relating to the Establishment of the Peace and Security Council (adopted 8 July 2002, entered into force 26 December 2003) UN Registration No 55339, available at <https://au.int/en/treaties/protocol-relating-establishment-peace-and-security-council-african-union>, art 7(3).

[259] AUPSC, 'Communiqué, 216th Meeting' (19 February 2010) AU Doc PSC/PR/COMM.1(CCXVI) §8(iii). On recognition by states of governmental status through their acceptance of individuals as state representatives in the activities of international organizations, see section 5.4.3.

[260] UNSC res 1511 (n 208) §4. For other possible examples, see UNSC res 668 (20 September 1990) UN Doc S/RES/668, §4; UNSC res 1453 (24 December 2002) UN Doc S/RES/1453, third preambular para; UNSC res 1546 (8 June 2004) UN Doc S/RES/1546, §1; UNSC res 2259 (23 December 2015) UN Doc S/RES/2259, §3.

[261] UN Charter (n 258) art 25. For a related argument in another context, see UNSC, 'Official Records, 8588th Meeting' (29 July 2019) UN Doc S/PV.8588 (provisional) 19 (Libya).

3.4.4 An Obligation of Non-Recognition on Grounds Relating to Peremptory Norms?

It is often said that states are obliged under customary international law not to recognize as lawful a situation created by a serious breach of an obligation arising under a peremptory norm of general international law.[262] A number of states expressly support the customary status of this obligation.[263] At the same time, as the ILC's Special Rapporteur on State Responsibility put it, such an obligation may even in 2001 have been '*de lege ferenda*'.[264] Indeed, as recently as 2021, some states expressed doubts as to whether such an obligation comprises part of positive international law.[265]

Insofar as such an obligation exists and applies in respect of a putative state whose claim to statehood is consequent upon a serious breach of a peremptory norm (a position for which there is more express support than in respect of ostensible governments of existing states[266]), this obligation would also preclude the lawful recognition of any ostensible government of that entity as the government of that putative state. This might be the case in respect of the so-called 'Turkish Republic of Northern Cyprus'.[267] Any such obligation as might exist is capable in principle of encompassing an obligation not to recognize as the government of an existing state an ostensible government whose claim to power is in consequence of a serious breach of an obligation arising under a peremptory norm. At the same

[262] See ARSIWA (n 16) 114 (art 41(2)); Dawidowicz, 'The Obligation of Non-Recognition of an Unlawful Situation' in Crawford, Pellet, and Olleson (eds), *The Law of International Responsibility* (OUP 2010) 677, 684; Costelloe, *Legal Consequences of Peremptory Norms in International Law* (CUP 2017) 193; ILC, 'Draft Conclusions on Identification and Legal Consequences of Peremptory Norms of General International Law (*jus cogens*), with Commentaries' in *ILC Report* (2022) UN Doc A/77/10, 70 (ILC, 'Draft Conclusions on Peremptory Norms'), 76–8 (conclusion 19(2) and comments 13–14). For an overview of the views expressed by governments in the context of the ILC's work on this matter, see 'Fifth Report on Peremptory Norms of General International Law (*jus cogens*) by Dire Tladi, Special Rapporteur' (24 January 2022) UN Doc A/CN.4/747, §§174–7. See also ILC, 'State Responsibility: Comments and Observations Received from Governments' (28 June 2001) UN Doc A/CN.4/515 and Add.1–3, 64–72.

[263] See also UNGA, 'Official Records, 74th Session, 23rd Meeting of the Sixth Committee' (13 November 2019) UN Doc A/C.6/74/SR.23, §13 (Nicaragua); UNGA, '25th Meeting of the Sixth Committee' (20 November 2019) UN Doc A/C.6/74/SR.25, §21 (Cuba); UNGA, '26th Meeting of the Sixth Committee' (18 November 2019) UN Doc A/C.6/74/SR.26, §4 (Egypt), §15 (Spain), §28 (Togo).

[264] See 'Fourth Report on State Responsibility by James Crawford, Special Rapporteur' (2 April 2001) UN Doc A/CN.4/517, 12–13. See also ibid, 14 (that, in 2001, the obligation of non-recognition posited 'arguably reflect[ed]' customary international law, and that arts 40–1 of the draft ARSIWA comprised 'a framework for the progressive development . . . of a concept which is or ought to be broadly acceptable'); Crawford (n 8) 583.

[265] See eg ILC, 'Peremptory Norms of General International Law (*jus cogens*): Comments and Observations Received from Governments' (9 March 2022) UN Doc A/CN.4/748 (ILC, 'Peremptory Norms: Comments from Governments') 89 (UK, USA).

[266] See eg *Accordance with International Law of the Unilateral Declaration of Independence in Respect of Kosovo, Advisory Opinion* [2010] ICJ Rep 403 ('*Kosovo*'), 437, §81; Nicholson, *Statehood and the State-Like in International Law* (OUP 2019) 162.

[267] See eg Raič, *Statehood and the Law of Self-Determination* (Kluwer 2002) 122–7; Crawford (n 9) 160–1; Nicholson (n 266) 161.

time, there is little unambivalent practice to suggest or confirm that such a specific obligation currently exists under customary international law.[268]

The scarcity of practice in this regard is compounded by the factual and legal uncertainties concerning the determination whether or not a claim to governmental status is indeed created by a serious breach of a peremptory obligation. While most practice of possible relevance in this regard suggests that at least historically there has existed no such obligation, both the peremptory character of a rule and its serious breach might be questioned at the time of at least some of this practice. In this way, the existing practice holds some, if limited, probative value as regards the existence or otherwise of an obligation under present-day customary international law not to recognize a claimant to governmental status which is consequent upon a serious breach of a peremptory norm.

For example, while the prohibition on aggression already comprised part of positive international law, whether Tanzania engaged in a serious breach of a peremptory norm in its use of force in Uganda in 1979 is not beyond doubt.[269] Whatever light the apparent acceptance of the governmental status of the Yusuf Lule government[270] sheds on whether or not there exists an obligation of non-recognition under customary international law on grounds connected to the violation of a peremptory norm does not support the existence of such an obligation. The same goes for the recognition between 1979 and 1989 by some states of the governmental status of the Heng Samrin regime,[271] which was established subsequent to Vietnam's invasion of Cambodia. Nor does the practice of the states which appeared open to accepting the governmental status of that regime, subsequent to a change in circumstances, provide any indication in favour of the existence of the possible obligation in question.[272] The recognition by most states of each of the successive Nationalist governments in South Africa during the *apartheid* era

[268] See also Crawford (n 9) 107 n 38; Nicholson (n 266) 161–2.

[269] For the view that by 1979 the prohibition of aggression is of a peremptory character, see many of the materials cited in ARSIWA (n 16) 112 (art 40, comment 4) and in 'Fourth Report on Peremptory Norms of General International Law (*jus cogens*) by Dire Tladi, Special Rapporteur' (31 January 2019) UN Doc A/CN.4/727, §§62–8. See also ILC, 'Draft Articles on the Law of Treaties with Commentaries' in Ybk ILC [1966] vol II, 187, 247 (art 50, comment 1). At the same time, Tanzania's actions in Uganda in 1979 precede at least some of the practice on which reliance is had to support the peremptory status of the prohibition of aggression. While neither fact is decisive, it is worth noting that Tanzania justified its action on the basis of self-defence and that its action 'avoided condemnation by the Security Council or the General Assembly' (Gray, *International Law and the Use of Force* (4th edn, CUP 2018) 40).

[270] On the acceptance of the governmental status of this government, which came to power in Uganda subsequent to Tanzania's actions, see eg chapter 4, n 60.

[271] See eg UNGA, 'Official Records, 35th Session, 35th Plenary Meeting' (n 253) §6 (Czechoslovakia), §13 (USSR), §25 (German Democratic Republic), §39 (Poland), §42 (Mongolia), §83 (Ukrainian SSR), §112 (Angola), §157 (Bulgaria), §168 (Seychelles), §186 (Democratic Yemen), §193 (Byelorussian SSR).

[272] On the apparent willingness of certain states to recognize the governmental status of this regime in 1989, once its autonomy was seen to have been established, see European Parliament, 'Resolution on Cambodia' (23 November 1989) OJ C 323/101–102, recital C, §9. See also 'Australian Practice in International Law 1978–1980' (n 11) 274. On the criterion of autonomy for governmental status, see section 4.2.2.

as the government of South Africa[273] provides no further support for the existence of an obligation of non-recognition on grounds connected to a peremptory norm. The claim to power of each of these governments was in consequence of a racially-exclusory franchise that would today generally be considered to be in both gross and systematic breach[274] of the peremptory prohibition on systematic racial discrimination[275] and perhaps also of what is now frequently considered to be the peremptory right to self-determination.[276]

Perhaps the best direct support for the existence of an obligation not to recognize an ostensible government whose claim to power is in consequence of a serious breach of an obligation arising under a peremptory norm is the UNSC's call in 1990 'upon all States . . . [n]ot to recognize any regime set up [in Kuwait] by [Iraq]' consequent upon Iraq's aggression against Kuwait.[277] But even this might not provide much support for the existence of such an obligation. The UNSC's call may not have reflected any obligation under customary international law.[278] Even if the UNSC's call did reflect the *opinio juris* of at least some of the states that participated in the adoption of the resolution as regards an obligation of non-recognition under customary international law in respect of the FPGK,[279] this may have related to this claimant's manifest non-satisfaction of the customary international legal criteria for governmental status and especially to the unrebutted presumption of subordination applicable in respect of that clamant.[280] In any event, by reflecting at most the *opinio juris* of fifteen states, the state conduct involved in the adoption of the resolution is not of itself sufficient to demonstrate the existence of an obligation under customary international law not to recognize an ostensible government whose claim arises in consequence of the serious breach of a peremptory norm.[281] The non-recognition by states more generally of the FPGK[282] also provides little if

[273] See chapter 4, nn 280–1.

[274] On a breach of an obligation arising under a peremptory norm of international law being serious 'if it involves a gross or systematic failure by the responsible State to fulfil the obligation', see ARSIWA (n 16) 112 (art 40(2)).

[275] On the peremptory character of this prohibition, see ARSIWA (n 16) 85 (art 26, comment 5) and 112 (art 40, comment 4); 'Fourth Report on Peremptory Norms' (n 269) 42–5, §§91–100; ILC, 'Draft Conclusions on Peremptory Norms' (n 262) 89 (conclusion 23(*e*)).

[276] That the right to self-determination appears also to preclude the lawfulness of a government whose claim to power is in consequence of a racially-exclusory franchise, see chapter 4, n 278 and accompanying text. On the peremptory character of this prohibition, see ILC (n 269) 248 (art 50, comment 3); ARSIWA (n 16) 85 (art 26, comment 5) and 112 (art 40, comment 4); 'Fourth Report on Peremptory Norms' (n 269) 42–5, §§108–14; ILC, 'Draft Conclusions on Peremptory Norms' (n 262) 89 (conclusion 23(*h*)).

[277] See UNSC res 661 (6 August 1990) UN Doc S/RES/661, §9(*b*). On the peremptory character of the prohibition of aggression, recall n 269 above.

[278] For a similar argument in a different context, see Nicholson (n 266) 177.

[279] On this as a conceptual possibility, but not a certainty, see ILC (n 13) 122, 147 (conclusion 12, comments 1 and 3).

[280] On this presumption, see section 4.2.2.2. On the possible existence of an obligation under customary international law not to recognize the 'wrong' government, recall sections 3.4.2–3.4.3.

[281] See also ILC (n 13) 147 (conclusion 12, comment 2).

[282] See eg Talmon (n 3) 162, 315.

any support for the existence of such an obligation. This practice can again be explained by this claimant's manifest non-satisfaction of the customary international legal criteria for governmental status.[283]

A leading analysis of state practice up to the late 1990s supports the conclusion that international law does not oblige states not to recognize an ostensible government whose claim to power is in consequence of the violation of an obligation arising under a peremptory norm. Even though it observes that 'the international community, has, with considerable consistency, refused to recognize governments created by the illegal use of force'[284] (which may amount to creation by a serious breach of a peremptory norm[285]), it argues that 'recognition as the state's government should be denied to an effective government *in situ* on the grounds of its illegal creation only as long as the illegality lasts, that is, as long as it affects the government's . . . independence.'[286] In other words, the view appears to be that international law does not oblige states not to recognize a claim of an ostensible government to governmental status on the basis of its creation by a serious breach of a peremptory norm, although such illegality may affect that ostensible claimant's autonomy, which is necessary for the enjoyment of governmental status.[287]

More recent practice concerns the eventual apparent recognition of the GCI, which emerged subsequent to the US-led invasion of Iraq, as the government of Iraq in 2003.[288] This provides no further support that an obligation of non-recognition in respect of an ostensible government whose claim to power is in consequence of a serious breach of an obligation arising under a peremptory norm exists. Indeed, in the light of the greater general acceptance of the obligation of non-recognition in respect of certain claims which are consequent upon a serious breach of a peremptory norm, the acceptance of the GCI's claim to governmental status might suggest that no such obligation applies in respect of claims to governmental status. But it may instead be that other factors, such as the UN's involvement in the formation of the GCI,[289] removed the GCI from the scope of any such obligation. Perhaps an obligation of non-recognition applies in respect only of claims arising in direct or sole consequence of a serious breach of a peremptory norm.

A separate question exists as to whether or not an obligation of non-recognition exists in respect of an ostensible government whose enjoyment of governmental

[283] On the requirement of autonomy, see section 4.2.2.2. See also chapter 4 on the contemporary prioritization under international law, since at least 1991, of 'constitutional' claims, even in the presence of a rival autonomous claimant in effective control of the state's territory and population (section 4.2.2.3) and on the presumption in favour of incumbent governments (section 4.2.2.4.1).

[284] Talmon (n 214) 524.

[285] See eg ARSIWA (n 16) 85 (art 26, comment 5).

[286] Talmon (n 214) 528.

[287] On autonomy as a criterion for governmental status, see section 4.2.2.

[288] UNSC res 1511 (n 208) §4.

[289] See also chapter 4, n 62 and accompanying text.

status would amount to the violation of a peremptory norm.[290] But there is little practice to suggest that the success of a claim to governmental status in respect of an existing state[291] may amount to the violation of a peremptory norm and even less practice to indicate that an obligation of non-recognition applies in respect of such a claimant. Indeed, most of what practice does exist tends to suggest that there is no such obligation. Notably, each of the successive Nationalist governments in South Africa during the *apartheid* era was widely recognized as the government of South Africa.[292] This was so despite the success of the claim to governmental status by each of these claimants arguably amounting to a violation of what today is widely considered to be the peremptory right to self-determination.[293] The widespread acceptance of each of these governments may again be because the relevant international legal rules were not at that time of a peremptory character.[294] That said, there is evidence to suggest that the position under international law differed at that time in respect of a claim by a 'racist minority' to governmental status which was connected with a claim to statehood.[295]

In determining whether or not there exists in positive international law an obligation of non-recognition on grounds related to peremptory norms, it is perhaps worth noting that the existence of any such obligation is not necessarily determined by the position under international law as regards the enjoyment of governmental status by an ostensible government whose claim to power is in consequence of a serious breach of, or whose successful claim to power would amount to, a violation of an obligation arising under a peremptory norm. An obligation of non-recognition may be a function of a bar that international law imposes on the enjoyment of governmental status[296] or it may instead operate as 'an attempt to prevent [the] consolidation of a status' which international law does not otherwise definitively preclude.[297] Indeed, it has been suggested that the obligation of non-recognition operates in relation to situations that may otherwise produce legal

[290] For the distinction between creation in consequence of a breach of a peremptory norm and creation which would involve the violation of a peremptory norm, see eg Nicholson (n 266) 176–7 on the possibility that 'the customary duty of non-recognition does not always require a "serious breach" of a peremptory norm'.

[291] For such an obligation in other contexts, see eg Nicholson (n 266) 176–8. See also n 295 below and the accompanying text; *Kosovo* (n 266) 437, §81.

[292] See chapter 4, nn 280–1.

[293] On the obligation, pursuant to the right to self-determination, that each states possesses 'a government representing the whole people belong to the territory [of that state] without distinction as to race, creed or colour', see chapter 4, n 278.

[294] On the peremptory status of this right, recall n 276 above. But see ILC, 'Peremptory Norms: Comments from Governments' (n 265) 104 (Israel), 113 (USA); 'Fifth Report on Peremptory Norms' (n 262) 67, §218.

[295] See UNSC res 216 (12 November 1965) UN Doc S/RES/216, §2, in which the UNSC '[*d*]*ecide*[*d*] to call upon all states not to recognize [the] illegal racist minority régime in Southern Rhodesia'; and UNSC res 217 (20 November 1965) UN Doc S/RES/217, §6, in which the UNSC '[*c*]*all*[*ed*] *upon* all States not to recognize [the] illegal authority [in Southern Rhodesia]'.

[296] On whether international law imposes such a bar, see section 4.2.2.5.3.

[297] Crawford (n 9) 160 n 243.

effects[298] and that the obligation of non-recognition appears not to be co-extensive with the preclusion by international law of the success of the claim in respect of which the obligation of non-recognition applies.[299] Put differently, it might be possible for a claimant to satisfy the customary international legal criteria for governmental status while being the object of an obligation of non-recognition.

3.5 The Significance of Recognition and Denial of Governmental Status

3.5.1 Recognition and Denial of Governmental Status as 'Declaratory'

The evidence which suggests that to qualify as the government of a state is to enjoy an objective international legal status[300] supports the position that the identity of a state's government for the purposes of international law does not vary according to the view of each other state, and there is limited evidence to the contrary. Indeed, the recognition by another state of governmental status does not render the recognized claimant the government the state in question as a matter of international law.[301] Equally, neither the denial of recognition nor the non-recognition by a state of another state's government precludes the enjoyment by that claimant of governmental status as a matter of international law, including vis-à-vis the state denying or not recognizing governmental status.[302]

At the same time, the recognition of governmental status of the 'wrong' government by a state, especially through an organ which has the capacity to represent that state, may have international legal consequences, including the generation of international legal obligations in respect of the recognized ostensible government.[303] Moreover, a state may, in effect, lawfully refuse to treat the government of another state as such for certain if only limited purposes of international law without this undermining the objective international legal existence of a state's government.[304]

[298] See Talmon, 'The Constitutive versus the Declaratory Theory of Recognition: *Tertium non Datur?*' (2004) 75 BYIL 101, 136–9.

[299] See Nicholson (n 266) 165.

[300] Recall section 2.5.

[301] See eg Talmon (n 3) 29–30. See also *Cuculla v Mexico*, Mexico–US Claims Commission, reproduced in (1868) in Moore (ed), *History and Digest of the International Arbitrations to Which the United States Has Been a Party*, vol 3 (US Government Printing Office 1898) 2873, 2876–7.

[302] See eg *Wulfsohn v RSFSR* (n 7) 40; *Aguilar-Amory and Royal Bank of Canada Claims (Great Britain v Costa Rica)* (1923) I UNRIAA 375 ('*Tinoco*') 381; Hackworth (n 4) 161; Dinstein, *Non-International Armed Conflicts in International Law* (CUP 2014) 97, §301; Wright (n 3) 557.

[303] See, generally, 'Sixth Report on Unilateral Acts' (n 3) §§9, 49, 72; Saganek, *Unilateral Acts of States in Public International Law* (BRILL 2015) 477ff. Albeit principally in relation to putative states, see also n 9 above; Raič (n 267) 38, including n 81 thereof; Nicholson (n 266) 131–9.

[304] Recall eg chapter 2, n 102 and accompanying text.

That said, the suggestion that non-recognition of, and presumably *a fortiori* the denial of governmental status to, an ostensible government 'will affect [that ostensible government's] ability to perform those international acts which require action by governments' and that 'agents sent abroad by the non-recognized government will not have diplomatic, consular or other official status as regards a state withholding recognition'[305] is best understood as referring to the consequences that might follow from the perspective of the state not recognizing or denying the governmental status of the ostensible government in question rather than to the position under customary international law. Indeed, one state's non-recognition of or denial of governmental status to an ostensible government of another state which qualifies as a matter of international law as that other state's government may result in a breach of an obligation owed under international law by the former state to the state whose government's identity is in question.[306]

In short, governmental status is not dependent on recognition. In the terms of the two main theories concerning recognition in international law,[307] as a matter of customary international law the recognition of governmental status is 'declaratory', not 'constitutive'.[308]

3.5.2 Recognition and Denial of Governmental Status as Evidence of Governmental Status

Although the recognition by a state of a specific claimant as another state's government does not render that claimant the latter state's government as a matter of international law,[309] the recognition by states of governmental status provides evidence that the person who or collectivity of persons that is the object of recognition qualifies as a matter of customary international law as the latter state's government.[310] Conversely, the denial by a state of governmental status in respect of an ostensible government is evidence that that ostensible government does not qualify for governmental status as a matter of customary international law.[311] Non-recognition of governmental status in respect of an ostensible government

[305] See Jennings and Watts (n 137) 198, §56. For a similar view, see 'Sixth Report on Unilateral Acts' (n 3) §92.

[306] Recall sections 3.4.2–3.4.3.

[307] See eg 'Sixth Report on Unilateral Acts' (n 3) §§82–92. Albeit principally in relation to recognition of statehood, see Lauterpacht (n 3) chapter IV; Crawford (n 9) 19–26.

[308] See also Chen (n 5) 133; Wright (n 3) 557; Dinstein (n 302) §302. See, generally, Peterson (n 3) 23–6; Brownlie (n 5) 205–7.

[309] See section 3.5.1.

[310] See also *Georges Pinson (France) v United Mexican States (Decision No 1)* (1928) V UNRIAA 327, 423–4; *Tinoco* (n 302) 380; Kelsen (n 5) 606–7, who, in discussing recognition of governmental status, states that 'international law attaches to certain facts certain consequences' and that it leaves the determination of the existence of such facts 'to the interested parties'.

[311] *Tinoco* (n 302) 381.

provides no evidence as regards the qualification or otherwise by that ostensible government for governmental status as a matter of customary international law.

More specifically, the recognition or denial by a state of governmental status in respect of an ostensible government is state practice[312] that reflects the view of that state as to the identity of another state's government and that contributes to the ascertainment of any customary international legal criteria as might exist for governmental status.

Additionally, such practice might be presumed to reflect *opinio juris* on the part of the first state as to the criterion or criteria according to which the identity of a state's government is to be ascertained for the purposes of international law. In the applicability of such a presumption, it may be relevant that the international legal framework in this regard concerns the ascertainment of a juridical fact.[313] It has been said that the possibility of inferring *opinio juris* from state practice 'appears to depend on the character of the issues'[314] and, perhaps unlike in respect of rules which directly establish prohibitions on states, the presumption against limitations on state sovereignty does not preclude an inference of *opinio juris* from state practice in relation to rules concerning the establishment of a juridical fact.[315] Indeed, the presumption against limitations on state sovereignty may support the existence of a rebuttable presumption in favour of *opinio juris* in relation to the recognition and denial of governmental status as regards the customary international legal framework for the identification of a state's government. This may be because the retention by each state of its presumptive sovereign freedom to choose its government depends on the existence of an objective international legal framework for ascertaining the identity of the government of a state, and a presumption in favour of *opinio juris* enables the identification of such a framework. Put differently, the absence of *opinio juris*, which is necessary for an objective customary international legal framework for the identification of the government of a state, perhaps ought not to be readily inferred since this would ultimately limit the freedom of each state to choose its government.

Regardless of the applicability of a presumption in favour of inferring *opinio juris* from state practice, there is substantial state practice that supports the proposition that the practice concerning recognition of governmental status generally occurs by reference to an objective international legal framework and reflects the view of that state as to the content and application of this framework. In other words, there

[312] See ILC (n 13) 132 (conclusion 5 and commentary).

[313] Recall section 2.5. See also Wright (n 3) 556, §4: 'in principle recognition is a juridical act applying legal criteria to factual evidence'.

[314] Crawford (n 8) 27.

[315] See also eg *Question of the Delimitation of the Continental Shelf between Nicaragua and Colombia beyond 200 Nautical Miles from the Nicaraguan Coast (Nicaragua v Colombia), Judgment, 13 July 2023* (not yet reported) §77. Cf ILC (n 13) 129 (conclusion 3, comment 7, including n 687 thereof).

exist express indications of *opinio juris* in relation to practice concerning the recognition of governmental status.

Such practice can be found in general statements, such as in the view expressed by the UK Foreign Secretary that 'international law . . . defines the conditions under which a Government should be recognised . . . and it is a matter of judgment in each particular case whether a regime fulfils the conditions'.[316] Other general statements of possible relevance in this regard include that of Barbados, according to which there exist 'basic requirements in . . . international law for recognition [of governmental status]',[317] as well as the view of Spain that recognition of governments 'should be applied in a consistent manner without making use of double standards'.[318]

Further relevant practice can be seen in the context of specific decisions of states whether to recognize a specific ostensible government. For example, in 2011, Saint Vincent and the Grenadines appeared to refrain from recognizing the NTC as Libya's government on the ground that, in its view, the NTC either did not at that time qualify as a matter of international law as the government of Libya or that there were insufficient facts available to determine that the NTC did qualify as a matter of international law as Libya's government.[319] Moreover, in 1979, Australia explained that it did not recognize the Heng Samrin regime, which 'ha[d] not yet satisfied the internationally accepted criteria for recognition'.[320] A number of further practice concerning the recognition of a specific claimant's governmental status makes reference to certain objective facts and considerations.[321] Indeed, as one commentator has put it, it is generally the case that 'States attempt to relate their action in the matter of recognition of governments to some objective test for which they claim general validity'.[322]

Accordingly, there exist clear indications that practice concerning the recognition of governments generally reflects *opinio juris* as to the content of the customary international legal criterion or criteria by which governmental status is to be assessed as well as reflections of a view as to the application of that criterion or criteria to a specific context.

In this light, the occasional suggestion to the effect that recognition of governmental status is 'a matter of wholly subjective judgment and an expression of moral reaction . . . more than any reaction to the objective situation on the ground'[323] is

[316] HC Debs, 21 March 1951, vol 485, cols 2410–11.

[317] UNGA, 'Official Records, 20th Session, 877th Meeting of the Sixth Committee' (n 214) §11 (Spain).

[318] UNGA, 'Official Records, 28th Session, 2189th Plenary Meeting' (4 December 1973) UN Doc A/PV.2189, §109.

[319] UNGA, 'Official Records, 66th Session, 2nd Plenary Meeting' (n 203) 14.

[320] 'Australian Practice in International Law 1978–1980' (n 11) 274.

[321] For a number of examples of recognition of governmental status, see section 4.2.2.

[322] Lauterpacht (n 3) 159.

[323] 'Statement of 20 August 1991 by Australia's Minister for Foreign Affairs and Trade', reproduced in Brown, 'Australian Practice in International Law 1990 and 1991' (n 108) 231–2. See, not dissimilarly, FRUS [1948] vol V(2), 1051, 1052, §4.

best understood as referring to 'recognition' in a narrower sense that concerns only certain forms of acceptance of governmental status.[324]

Perhaps evidence of *opinio juris* exists also in the recognition or denial of governmental status by a state for some purpose of municipal law, for example, in a determination by a municipal court as to whether or not an ostensible government may represent or invoke a right of a state in that forum or whether a particular person is to be accorded the treatment due under the municipal law of a state in relation only to certain members of the government of another state.

This is so at least insofar as there exists a presumption in favour of *opinio juris*[325] which has not been rebutted in the circumstances of the instance of state practice in question or insofar as it is otherwise clear that the specific practice of recognition or denial of governmental status in question or the municipal law to which that practice relates is understood to reflect the position under customary international law.[326] For example, where judicial recognition or denial of governmental status occurs in deference to executive practice,[327] the view of a court on the identity of a state's government does not in itself manifest the *opinio juris* of a state. That said, the executive practice to which that court is deferring may reflect *opinio juris*.

The recognition or denial by a state of governmental status does not reflect the view of that state as regards the qualification of the claimant as the government of another state for the purposes of international law where it is clear that considerations of international law are irrelevant to the determination of governmental status, for example where a municipal court states that it is determining the governmental status of an ostensible government for a contract between parties who, in entering into the contract, were unconcerned with 'the niceties of international law'.[328]

While evidence of *opinio juris* as to the content of the international legal criterion or criteria by which governmental status is to be assessed may arise in relation to recognition and denial of governmental status by executive, judicial, and other organs of state, the weight accorded to the recognition or denial of governmental status may depend on the constitutional authority of the organ in question and its capacity as a matter of international law to represent a state in its international relations[329] as well as on whether the conduct of the state organ is ultra vires.[330] The weight accorded to the recognition or denial of governmental status by a state agent may also vary.

[324] On the different uses of the term 'recognition', recall section 3.2.1.

[325] Recall section 3.5.1.

[326] See also ILC (n 13) 140 (conclusion 10(2)) on national judicial decisions as a possible source of *opinio juris*.

[327] On such deference, n 245 above.

[328] *Luigi Monta of Genoa v Cechofracht Co Ltd* [1956] 2 QB 552, 568.

[329] See eg ILC (n 13) 135 (conclusion 7, comment 5).

[330] Dinstein, 'The Interaction between Customary International Law and Treaties' (2006) 322 Hague *Recueil* 243, 271, §20(c).

The general recognition by states of a specific claim to governmental status is, in effect, conclusive as regards the enjoyment by that claimant of governmental status as a matter of customary international law.[331] Conversely, the general denial by states that a specific claimant comprises the government of another state makes it virtually certain that that claimant does not comprise the government of that state. Moreover, despite recognition of governmental status not being constitutive of that status, the widespread reluctance to accept an ostensible government as the government of a specific state might raise doubts as to whether that claimant qualifies for governmental status under customary international law, especially if there is also doubt as to the satisfaction by that ostensible government of the accepted customary international legal criteria for governmental status. For example, this appears to be the case with the Taliban since its 2021 offensive in Afghanistan.[332]

Although inconsistent views as to the identity of a specific state's government may not provide clear guidance as to the identity of that state's government, such practice may nevertheless provide evidence as regards one or more aspects of the framework for the enjoyment of governmental status as a matter of customary international law, especially if the divergence in states' views results from disagreement on the application of one or more pertinent considerations, rather than on which considerations are pertinent. A contemporary example in this regard is the difference of views over the identity of the President of Venezuela, an office which, between 2019 and 2023, has been claimed by both Nicolás Maduro and Juan Guaidó, particularly since it is not uncommon for states supporting either of these claims to mention the perceived 'constitutionality' of whichever claimant they support.[333] Even isolated instances of recognition or denial of governmental status may have some probative value as regards both the identity of a state's government and at least part of the customary international legal framework against which claims to governmental status are to be assessed. The precise evidential weight attached to any specific instance of recognition or denial of governmental status depends on various factors, including, for example, the extent to which it accords with both the recognizing or denying state's practice and the practice of other states concerning the recognition of governments.[334]

[331] See also Wright (n 3) 557, §7.

[332] On non-recognition of the Taliban as the government of Afghanistan, recall n 126 above. See also *In Re: Terrorist Attacks* (n 7) 5; and recall nn 29–33 above. On challenges to the attainment by the Taliban of the requisite control over Afghanistan's territory and population, see chapter 4, n 167. But see also section 4.2.2.5.2 for other reasons of the non-recognition of the Taliban.

[333] See eg UNSC, 'Official Records, 8452nd Meeting' (26 January 2019) UN Doc S/PV.8452 (provisional) 7 (UK), 8 (Peru), 15 (Poland) in respect of support for Juan Guaidó and 27 (Nicaragua), 28 (Cuba), and 29 (Saint Vincent and the Grenadines) on support of Nicolás Maduro's claim to be President of Venezuela. On the relevance of 'constitutionality' to governmental status as a matter of customary international law, see chapter 4.

[334] See also ILC (n 13) 134–8 (conclusions 7–8).

3.6 Conclusion

A state can recognize or deny governmental status in various ways. One way is for it to make a statement expressly recognizing or denying a claimant's governmental status. Other ways include the conduct of a state that implies its acceptance or denial of the occupation by a specific person or collectivity of persons of an office or post within another state that may be occupied only by or through a state's government. Further possibilities in this regard include the conduct through which a state accepts the capacity of a person or collectivity of persons to represent the state for the purposes of customary international law. Whether a state has recognized or denied the governmental status of a specific ostensible government may not always be clear.

States are not obliged as a general rule to make known their view on the identity of another state's government. Nor does a state enjoy unfettered discretion to reject or accept whomever it wishes as the government of another state. The prohibition on intervention appears to limit the extent to which a state can lawfully recognize or deny governmental status to a specific claimant to governmental status. Any subsisting uncertainty as to when recognition of the 'wrong' government or denial of governmental status of the 'right' government might amount to prohibited intervention exists because of considerations other than doubt as to either the objective customary international legal identity of the government of a state or the subsistence of the presumptive sovereign freedom of each state to choose its government. In any event, international legal obligations concerning state representation and the treatment owed in respect of foreign governments limit how far a state may go in treating the 'wrong' government or in refusing to treat the 'right' government as the government of another state. Whether states are prohibited from recognizing an ostensible government which arises in consequence of or the attainment by which of governmental status would amount to the violation of a peremptory norm is unclear.

The recognition by a state of a person or collectivity of persons as the government of another state does not make that person or collectivity of persons the government of the other state as a matter of international law. Nor does the view by a state that an ostensible government does not qualify as the government of another state preclude that ostensible government from enjoying governmental status as a matter of international law. At the same time, recognition and denial of governmental status by states provides valuable evidence relevant to ascertaining both the international legal criterion or criteria for enjoyment of governmental status under international law and the identity of a specific state's government at a specific moment in time.

4
The International Legal Criteria for Governmental Status

4.1 Introduction

This chapter concerns itself with the criteria under customary international law for the identification of a state's government. More specifically, it seeks to ascertain the objective customary international legal framework for the enjoyment of governmental status by examining state practice concerning the recognition of governments in the light of the conceptual international legal aspects relating to the governments of states. Ascertaining this framework is important for assessing the compliance by states and possibly other actors with certain international legal rules. The existence and content of such a framework informs whether or not, at least in certain circumstances, the recognition or denial of the governmental status of a specific ostensible government is or may result in a violation of international law. Additionally, the application of at least certain international legal rules concerning the representation of states and the treatment owed in respect of certain persons requires the customary international legal identity of the government of a state to be known.[1] An analysis of relevant practice demonstrates the following.

As a general matter, the constitution of a state, while reflecting the identity of a state's government, is insufficient for the identification of a state's government. Moreover, the presumption against limitations on state sovereignty weighs against both the absence of an objective customary international legal framework for the identification of a state's government and the existence of any customary international legal criterion for governmental status that would limit the presumptive sovereign freedom of each state to choose its government, its political system, or its constitution. Accordingly, a plausible explanation of state practice on the recognition or denial of governmental status which does not reflect a limitation on any of these freedoms ought to be preferred over an alternative explanation which would reflect such a limitation.

[1] Recall sections 3.4.2–3.4.3. See also sections 5.5.1–5.5.2.

The Identity of Governments in International Law. Niko Pavlopoulos, Oxford University Press. © Niko Pavlopoulos 2024.
DOI: 10.1093/9780191991509.003.0004

Indeed, there exists an objective customary international legal framework for identifying the government of a state that preserves the presumptive sovereign freedom of each state to choose its government, its constitution, and its political system. There is no clear acceptance of a limitation on any of these presumptive sovereign freedoms in the customary international legal criteria for governmental status. Indeed, this framework has developed since the 1990s in a way that further privileges what is perhaps the most direct way by which a state can be taken to express its choice of government, namely its constitution. International law now has regard to alternative, less direct means for ascertaining the state's choice of government only where there is no claimant to governmental status that can be taken to reflect the state's more direct choice of government.

Under the contemporary customary international legal framework for the assessment of governmental status, a person or collectivity of persons need not have a valid claim to governmental status under the existing constitution of that state in order to qualify for governmental status as a matter of customary international law. If it is autonomous and if it exercises effective control over the territory and population of the state, an 'unconstitutional' ostensible government can attain governmental status as a matter of customary international law in the absence of a rival 'constitutional' claim. An autonomous 'unconstitutional' claimant can retain governmental status in the event that it loses effective control over the state's territory and population as long as there is neither a rival autonomous 'unconstitutional' claimant with effective control over that state's territory and population nor an autonomous 'constitutional' claimant to governmental status. An autonomous 'constitutional' ostensible government will invariably enjoy governmental status as a matter of customary international law as long as it maintains its claim to governmental status. This is so regardless of whether it exercises or has ever exercised effective control over the territory and population of the state. Whether 'constitutional' or otherwise, an ostensible government need not be democratically representative or otherwise 'legitimate' in order to qualify as the government of a state as a matter of customary international law. It is also unnecessary for an ostensible government of a state to be willing to ensure the state's compliance with the latter's international legal obligations in order for that claimant to enjoy governmental status as a matter of customary international law. It appears, moreover, that an ostensible government can enjoy governmental status as a matter of customary international law even if it is established in consequence of, or if its enjoyment of governmental status would amount to, the violation of an obligation arising under a peremptory norm of general international law.

4.2 The Criteria for Governmental Status

4.2.1 In General

While the constitution of a state invariably reflects the configuration of a state's government,[2] the constitution of a state does not suffice for the identification of a state's government as a matter of customary international law. This is clear from both the possibility that a state fundamentally changes its constitution through the success of a claim to governmental status by an 'unconstitutional' government[3] and from the practice by states concerning recognition of governments, which involves the reliance on additional considerations in determining whether they consider a specific ostensible government to enjoy governmental status as a matter of customary international law. Ultimately, the existence and content of the objective customary international legal framework for the assessment of governmental status derives from the general[4] practice of states, as accompanied by *opinio juris*, concerning the recognition of governments.

In assessing relevant state practice to ascertain which specific criteria comprise the objective framework for the identification of a state's government under customary international law, two points concerning the presumption against limitations on state sovereignty are noteworthy, in addition to the possible presumption in favour of *opinio juris* in state practice concerning recognition of governments.[5]

First, the presumption against limitations on state sovereignty militates against readily inferring the existence of a customary international legal criterion for governmental status that would limit the freedom of each state to choose its government, its constitution, or its political system. At least an equally-plausible understanding of relevant practice which does not in effect result in such a limitation is to be preferred over an alternative plausible understanding which would in effect result in such a limitation,[6] as, for example, would be the case with the limitation on the freedom of each state to choose its political system that would arise from a requirement of democratic representativity for the enjoyment of governmental status.[7] In what relates to the possible presumption in favour of *opinio juris* being reflected in state practice concerning recognition of governments, the

[2] Recall section 2.2.1.
[3] Recall chapter 2, n 8 and accompanying text.
[4] On what comprises 'general' practice, see ILC, 'Draft Conclusions on Identification of Customary International Law, with Commentaries' in *ILC Report* (2018) UN Doc A/73/10, 122, 135–8 (conclusion 8 and commentary thereto).
[5] Recall also section 3.5.2 on *opinio juris* generally accompanying state practice concerning recognition of governmental status, regardless of such a presumption.
[6] Recall section 2.4.
[7] On this, see section 4.2.2.5.1.2.

absence of an objective framework for the identification of a state's government under customary international ought also not to be presumed.[8]

Secondly, the presumptive sovereign freedom of each state to choose its government is in principle capable of providing the basis for the rationalization of the customary international legal framework for the identification of the government of a state. This framework may—indeed, is presumed to—operate as a means of ascertaining whom the state has chosen as its government.[9] That the customary international legal framework for the identification of a state's government may give effect to the state's choice of government can be seen in the traditional framework for the enjoyment by an 'unconstitutional' ostensible government of governmental status as a matter of customary international law. This framework was largely 'based on the principle of effectiveness'[10] and in practice often resulted in an 'unconstitutional' claimant enjoying governmental status insofar as that claimant exercised effective control over the state's territory and population.[11] As Taft CJ put it, as sole arbitrator in the so-called '*Tinoco Case*', governmental status for an 'unconstitutional' claimant generally followed from its attainment of 'independence and control'.[12] This can be understood as having comprised a generic means for the ascertainment of a state's choice fundamentally to change its constitution and, consequently, also to possess the 'unconstitutional' government in question.[13]

Before considering specific possible criteria for governmental status as a matter of customary international law, it is perhaps worth clarifying that the existence of a customary international legal framework for the identification of the government of a state does not preclude the possibility that occasionally the identity of a state's government is uncertain. As with virtually any legal standard, there may exist evidential or other difficulties in the application of one or more aspects of this framework.[14] Nor does such difficulty undermine the presumptive sovereign freedom

[8] Recall section 2.5.

[9] Recall section 2.4.

[10] Lauterpacht, *Recognition in International Law* (CUP 1947, repr 2013) 98, 115; Jennings and Watts (eds), *Oppenheim's International Law*, vol 1 (Wildy 1992) §45, 151; Roth, *Governmental Illegitimacy in International Law* (OUP 2000) 136–42; Talmon, 'Who Is a Legitimate Government in Exile? Towards Normative Criteria for Governmental Legitimacy in International Law' in Goodwin-Gill and Talmon (eds), *The Reality of International Law: Essays in Honour of Ian Brownlie* (OUP 1999) 499, 509.

[11] Further on effective control, see section 4.2.2.4. There also existed a general requirement of autonomy for any ostensible government to enjoy governmental status as a matter of customary international law, a criterion which in practice was often readily satisfied. See further section 4.2.2.2.

[12] *Aguilar-Amory and Royal Bank of Canada Claims (Great Britain v Costa Rica)* (1923) I UNRIAA 375 ('*Tinoco*') 381. Further on autonomy being labelled as 'independence', see n 36 below and accompanying text.

[13] Recall chapter 2, n 8 and accompanying text.

[14] See eg UNSC, 'Official Records, 900th Meeting' (14 September 1960) UN Doc S/PV.900, §67 (China): '[i]t is honestly impossible for my delegation to determine who constitutes the Government of the Republic of the Congo now, whether *de facto* or *de jure*'; UNGA, 'Official Records, 66th Session, 2nd Plenary Meeting' (16 September 2011) UN Doc A/66/PV.2, 14: '[Saint Vincent and the Grenadines] has not considered itself to be in a position—or in possession of sufficient factual data—to extend recognition to the National Transitional Council at this point in time'.

that each state enjoys to choose its government. The will of a state for one or more purposes of international law may be unclear,[15] including its choice of government.

4.2.2 Specific Criteria for Governmental Status

4.2.2.1 A Claim to Governmental Status

Most fundamentally, a person or collectivity of persons must claim or purport to be the government of that state in order to comprise the government of a state as a matter of customary international law.[16] This requirement applies in respect of ostensible governments which do not already enjoy governmental status and continues to apply in respect of ostensible governments which have already attained governmental status.

This criterion can readily be satisfied in a number of ways and, as such, does not often pose an obstacle to the ascertainment of the customary international legal identity of a state's government. Nor can this criterion readily be understood as a restriction on a state's freedom to choose its government.

Two of the ways in which the criterion of a claim to governmental status may be satisfied is through a public declaration or the issuance of an instrument purporting to have the force of municipal law. While any ostensible government may claim governmental status in these ways, it is common for ostensible governments not previously enjoying governmental status under customary international law to claim governmental status in these ways. For example, the declaration by the *Comité français de liberation nationale* (CFLN) in 1943 that it comprised 'the central power of France' exercising 'French sovereignty' and the *ordonnance* issued by the CFLN purporting to give legal effect to similarly-worded stipulations involve claims to governmental status.[17] Further possible examples of claims to governmental status through a public declaration concern the joint statement by the Allied Powers as to their assumption of 'supreme authority with respect to Germany, including all the powers possessed by the German Government'[18] and, more recently, the statement by the NTC in 2011 that 'it is the sole representative of all Libya'.[19] One further example of a claim to governmental status through the

[15] Recall section 2.3.1.

[16] See also O'Connell, 'The Status of Formosa and the Chinese Recognition Problem' (1956) 50 AJIL 405, 415; Brownlie, 'Recognition in Theory and Practice' (1982) 53 BYIL 197, 202.

[17] See *Declaration du 3 juin 1943* and *Ordonnance du 3 juin 1943 portant institution du Comité français de la libération nationale*, both available at <http://mjp.univ-perp.fr/france/co1943cfln.htm>.

[18] 'Declaration Regarding the Defeat of Germany and the Assumption of Supreme Authority with Respect to Germany by the Governments of the United States of America, the Union of Soviet Socialist Republics, the United Kingdom and the Provisional Government of the French Republic' (5 June 1945), available at <http://avalon.law.yale.edu/wwii/ger01.asp>. On the recognition of the quadripartite authority as the government of Germany, see n 55 below.

[19] See 'Founding Statement of the Interim Transitional National Council' (5 March 2011), available at <http://oxcon.ouplaw.com/display/10.1093/law:ocw/law-ocw-rd118.regGroup.1/law-ocw-rd118>.

promulgation of an instrument purporting to have the force of municipal law concerns the Transitional Military Council and the Forces for Freedom and Change, both of which signed the Draft Constitutional Charter for the 2019 Transitional Period. Article 9 of this designates certain specific collective bodies as 'the head of state' and as 'the supreme, executive authority of the state'.[20]

A person or groups of persons may additionally or alternatively claim governmental status by purporting to exercise one or more functions reserved for the occupant of one or more governmental offices. Again, a claim may be made in this way by an ostensible government regardless of whether or not it has previously enjoyed governmental status. For example, by commanding the armed forces of Libya, Muammar Qadhafi retained a claim to governmental status, despite his apparent renouncement of governmental functions.[21]

In what principally concerns the retention of a claim to governmental status, a person who or a collectivity of persons that is designated by the municipal law of a state as the occupant of one or more governmental offices may maintain a claim to governmental status simply by not resigning from the office or all of the offices in question. This enables an existing government to retain its governmental status whilst neither continuously making an express claim to governmental status nor regularly exercising specific functions.

In the absence of an express claim to governmental status or of any purported exercise of functions reserved for the occupants of governmental offices, however, a person who or collectivity of persons that has occupied de facto a governmental office may be considered not to maintain a claim to governmental status as a matter of customary international law.[22] The general recognition by states of the NTC as Libya's government before Muammar Qadhafi's death[23] may be explained in part on this basis. One commentator, in asserting that the continued enjoyment of governmental status by a claimant to governmental status 'that . . . is itself a progeny of a revolution or a *coup d'État* occurring at some juncture in the past' may be fatally undercut',[24] appears to make a similar point. That said, being 'a progeny of a revolution or a *coup*' does not alone 'undercut' a claimant's enjoyment of governmental status. What might be relevant is the combination of occupying no governmental office under the municipal law of the state and neither making an express claim to governmental status nor in fact exercising any relevant authority. At the very least,

[20] Draft Constitutional Charter for the 2019 Transitional Period (2019), available at <http://constitutionnet.org/sites/default/files/2019-08/Sudan%20Constitutional%20Declaration%20%28English%29.pdf>, art 9(1)–(2).

[21] See *Keesing's* [1979] 29665A. On the functions exercised by the occupants of governmental offices, recall section 2.2.1.

[22] On de facto state organs, recall chapter 2, n 5.

[23] See UNGA, 'Official Records, 66th Session, 2nd Plenary Meeting' (n 14) 15 (114-17-15). On the relevance to governmental status of the acceptance of an ostensible state representative's credentials, see sections 5.4.1.2 and 5.4.3.

[24] Dinstein, *Non-International Armed Conflicts in International Law* (CUP 2014) 104.

an express claim by such a person or collectivity of persons to not occupying a governmental office appears tantamount to resignation.[25]

When the person or collectivity of persons comprising an ostensible government occupies one or more governmental offices under the municipal law of a state, the person or collectivity of persons in question may terminate their claim to governmental status by resigning from the governmental office or offices in question, at least where the resignation concerns the office or offices whose occupant or occupants lead or appoint any other person as a member of the same ostensible government. In practice, this often means that the resignation of a head of state or head of government amounts to the termination of a claim to governmental status, while the resignation of a minister of a state does not amount to the termination of the claim to governmental status by the government to which that minister belongs.

The effectiveness as a matter of customary international law of a purported resignation from a governmental office may be questioned where the purported resignation is ineffective under that state's constitution. There is, however, little practice from which to draw a definitive conclusion on this point. For example, the continued acceptance by virtually all states of Abdrabbuh Mansur Hadi as the President of Yemen after he retracted his resignation in February 2015[26] until April 2022[27] does not provide much evidence as to the effectiveness of a constitutionally ineffective resignation.[28] Although the continued recognition by states of Abdrabbuh Mansur Hadi as the President of Yemen may have related to the view that his resignation had not been effective as a matter of international law, it may instead have been that Mr Hadi was able successfully to reclaim governmental status[29] in the presence of no rival autonomous 'constitutional' claimant or rival autonomous 'unconstitutional' ostensible government that exercised

[25] Not only did Muammar Qadhafi appear not to hold any governmental office under the municipal law of Libya (recall *Keesing's* (n 21)), but he also reportedly stated that there is no governmental office from which he can resign, with '[t]he people [being] free to choose the authority they see fit'. See 'Gaddafi: Libya Dignity under Attack' (*Al Jazeera*, 2 March 2011), available at <http://aljazeera.com/news/2011/3/2/gaddafi-libya-dignity-under-attack>. See also section 4.2.2.4.2 on the possibility that a lower threshold applies for 'effective control' where an 'unconstitutional' claimant to governmental status faces no rival claim.

[26] See eg UNSC res 2216 (14 April 2015) UN Doc S/RES/2216, eighth unnumbered preambular paragraph.

[27] By presidential decree of 7 April 2022, Mr Hadi established the Presidential Leadership Council, led by Rashad al-Alimi, to which Mr Hadi ceded his powers. See 'Hadi Out, Presidential Council Takes Over' (*Sana'a Center for Strategic Studies*, 8 April 2022), available at <http://sanaacenter.org/publications/analysis/17378>.

[28] The constitutional ineffectiveness of his resignation is reflected in the fact that the parliament of Yemen had not accepted his resignation and the fact that the constitution of Yemen required parliamentary consent for the first attempted resignation by the President of Yemen to be constitutionally effective. See Constitution of Yemen (2001, as amended by the 2011 Agreement on the Implementation Mechanism for the Transition Process in Yemen in accordance with the Initiative of the Gulf Cooperation Council) art 115.

[29] On the possible subsistence of a state's existing constitution in such circumstances, see also section 4.2.2.3.

sufficiently-effective control over Yemen's territory and population so as to qualify as the new government of Yemen.[30]

It is unclear, moreover, whether duress affects the effectiveness as a matter of international law of resignation from a governmental office. In seemingly all of the cases in which a claim of resignation under duress appears at least arguable, there had been no attempt by the resigning government to reclaim governmental status once the possible duress had ended. Examples in this regard involve the resignation of President Jean-Bertrand Aristide in Haiti in 2004 and of President Robert Mugabe in Zimbabwe in 2017.[31]

4.2.2.2 Autonomy

It is a general requirement for the enjoyment of governmental status as a matter of customary international law that an ostensible government be autonomous. A claimant to governmental status cannot qualify as the government of a state as a matter of customary international law if it is subordinate to a foreign entity.[32] In precluding the possibility of a state possessing a government which is subordinate to another state, the requirement of autonomy cannot readily be conceptualized as a restriction on a state's freedom to choose its government. Indeed, it serves to protect a state's freedom of action more generally since it is generally through its government that a state is represented for the purposes of international law.[33]

An ostensible government which lacks the requisite autonomy for the enjoyment of governmental status is sometimes referred to as a 'puppet' government. Examples of 'puppet' governments include the collaborationist regimes established in Greece during its occupation by the Axis powers during the Second World War[34] and the Heng Samrin regime established during Vietnam's occupation of Cambodia between 1979 and 1989.[35]

[30] On the enjoyment of governmental status by a claimant to governmental status in either such situation, see sections 4.2.2.2–4.2.2.4.

[31] For other ostensible changes of government in such circumstances, see Peterson, 'Recognition of Governments Should Not Be Abolished' (1983) 77 AJIL 31, 40.

[32] See eg *Tinoco* (n 12); HL Debs, 21 November 1956, vol 200, col 423; *Aksionairnoye Obschestvo Dlia Mechanicheskoyi Obrabotky Diereva (1) AM Luther (Company for Mechanical Woodworking AM Luther) v James Sagor and Company* [1921] 3 KB 532 ('*Luther v Sagor*') 548: 'an independent sovereign Government'; HL Debs, 28 April 1980, vol 408, col 1121–2WA; Blix, 'Contemporary Aspects of Recognition' (1970) 130 Hague *Recueil* 587, 642; Marek, *Identity and Continuity of States in Public International Law* (Librarie Droz 1954) 64–70; Talmon, *Recognition of Governments in International Law with Particular Reference to Governments in Exile* (OUP 1998) 173; Talmon (n 10) 517–20; Magiera, 'Governments' (2007) MPEPIL, available at <http://opil.ouplaw.com/home/mpil>, §16; Dinstein (n 24) 97.

[33] Recall section 2.3.

[34] See *In Re G* (Greece, Criminal Court of Heraklion, 1 January 1945) (1951) 12 ILR 437, 438–9.

[35] See eg UNGA, 'Credentials of Representatives to the Thirty-Fifth Session of the General Assembly: First Report of the Credentials Committee' (29 September 1980) UN Doc A/35/484, §13 (Singapore); HC Debs, 6 December 1979, vol 975, col 760. For other examples of 'puppet' governments, see Crawford, *The Creation of States in International Law* (2nd edn, CUP 2006) 81 n 199.

When it is considered in state practice or elsewhere, the criterion of autonomy is sometimes stated to be a criterion of 'independence'.[36] The present work uses an alternative term to avoid conflating the independence of a state and the autonomy of a government since the two criteria are distinct, each applicable in respect of a different entity. That said, they overlap in part. Actual independence, which is one of the two aspects of independence that a putative state must satisfy in order to attain statehood, reflects the requirement of autonomy for the enjoyment of governmental status as a matter of customary international law. Put differently, a putative state will attain statehood only if the authorities in which the powers of the putative state vest possess a sufficient 'degree of real governmental power at the[ir] disposal'—that is, if the government of the putative state is autonomous.[37]

There is a general presumption that a claimant to governmental status is autonomous, including with respect to a 'constitutional' claimant to governmental status that comes to power during belligerent occupation of the state whose government the claimant purports to be or in consequence of the unlawful use of force against that state.[38] An example in this regard is the change to the composition of the government of France after its occupation by Germany. The existing French government granted Philippe Pétain '*tout pouvoir au gouvernement de la République . . . à l'effet de promulguer par un ou plusieurs actes une nouvelle constitution de l'État français*',[39] on the basis of which Pétain established the 'Vichy government' in a non-occupied part of France, an ostensible government which was widely accepted, at least for some time thereafter, as France's government.[40] Other examples include the change to the government of Iran after the Anglo-Soviet invasion of 1941[41] and perhaps also the change to the government of Hungary following the forced abdication of Hungary's Regent in October 1944 during German occupation.[42] The requirement of autonomy may well have informed also the reluctance of states to recognize the regime in Hungary in 1956[43] and the ostensible government of Babrak Karmal that came to power in Afghanistan in 1979.[44]

An exception to this presumption applies in respect of an 'unconstitutional' claimant to governmental status of a state that comes to power either during the

[36] See eg *Tinoco* (n 12); *Luther v Sagor* (n 32); Talmon (n 10) 517.

[37] See Crawford (n 35) 72. See also ibid, 76, in which the requirement of actual independence of states is discussed as relevant also to a putative government of a state.

[38] See also Marek (n 32) 112–13; Roberts, 'What Is a Military Occupation?' (1984) 55 BYIL 249, 284; Crawford (n 35) 81 n 198; Talmon (n 10) 526; Foakes, *The Position of Heads of State and Senior Officials in International Law* (OUP 2014) 51–2.

[39] *Loi constitutionelle du 10 juillet 1940.*

[40] On the rival French national movement led by Charles de Gaulle, see chapter 3, n 88.

[41] See eg FRUS [1941] vol III, 461–2: 'the British Government had decided to support the new Shah and recognize his government because of the wishes express with regard thereto by the Iranian Government itself'; ibid, 461 on recognition of the new Shah by the USSR.

[42] See Crawford (n 35) 87–8.

[43] See chapter 5, n 84 and the text accompanying nn 89–90.

[44] See the text accompanying chapter 5, nn 129–33.

belligerent occupation of that state or in consequence of the unlawful use of force against that state.[45] A presumption of subordination instead applies in respect of any such claimant. The applicability of the presumption of subordination in the context of the lawful use of force is less clear,[46] at least as regards ostensible governments of existing states. For example, the NTC was generally accepted as the government of Libya subsequent to the military intervention in Libya. There were only isolated assertions that the NTC was a 'puppet' government,[47] although it may have been that the presumption of subordination was rebutted in that case.[48] In any event, the assertion by one commentator that 'foreign intervention . . ., even where lawful, vitiates the significance of effective control'[49] accords too much weight to intervention in relation to the enjoyment of governmental status. It is simply that a rebuttable presumption of subordination applies in respect of 'unconstitutional' ostensible governments which come to power in consequence of the use of force and perhaps only if the use of force is unlawful. An 'unconstitutional' ostensible government is not precluded from enjoying governmental status as a result of its having come to power in consequence of foreign intervention.[50]

As for the claim that the presumption of subordination 'may apply' to an ostensible government which is established pursuant to the threat of force,[51] there is little practice to indicate whether or not the presumption of subordination applies to an ostensible government which is established in consequence of a threat of the use of force.

Perhaps distinct from a claimant coming to power during belligerent occupation is a claimant which has 'good title to supreme authority, by subjugation'.[52] In such a case, 'substantial external domination may not be regarded as "foreign"'.[53] A notable example in this regard may be the claim by the Allied Powers with respect to Germany at the end of the Second World War.[54] The 'unconditional surrender' by Germany to the Allied Powers might have removed the Allied Control Council from the scope of application of the presumption of subordination of certain ostensible governments. In any event, this ostensible government was not deemed to be a 'puppet' government of Germany.[55]

[45] See also Brownlie (n 16) 210; Crawford (n 35) 132 (on the use by Crawford of the term 'entities' to refer to both ostensible states and governments, see ibid, 80); Marek (n 32) 65–6; Foakes (n 38) 51.

[46] But see eg Crawford (n 35) 80.

[47] UNGA, 'Official Records, 66th Session, 2nd Plenary Meeting' (n 14) 7.

[48] On the rebuttal of this presumption, see nn 59–63 and the accompanying text.

[49] Roth (n 10) 415. See also Talmon (n 32) 228.

[50] But see section 4.2.2.5.3 on the distinct possibility concerning claims to governmental status which arise in consequence of the breach of an obligation arising under a peremptory norm of general international law.

[51] See Crawford (n 35) 80.

[52] See Jennings, 'Government in Commission' (1946) 23 BYIL 112, 135.

[53] Crawford (n 35) 76. See also Kelsen, 'The Legal Status of Germany According to the Declaration of Berlin' (1945) 39 AJIL 518, 518–20.

[54] Recall n 18 above.

[55] On acceptance of the governmental status of the quadripartite authority, see eg *Rex v Bottrill, ex parte Kuechenmeister* (UK, Court of Appeal of England and Wales, 30 July 1946) (1951) 13 ILR 312,

The presumption in favour of the autonomy of a claimant to governmental status is said to be rebutted where there exists '[systematic] foreign control overbearing the decision-making of the [claimant] concerned on a wide range of matters . . . on a permanent basis'.[56]

To establish the subordination of an ostensible government in respect of which the presumption of autonomy applies, it is necessary 'to overcome a formidable burden of proof, though the fact that an entity is a puppet may be self-evident. Perhaps the most difficult situation is where an existing [*viz* 'constitutional'] government remains in power during a period of foreign occupation in time of war.'[57] That said, the absence of autonomy was the basis of the eventual derecognition of the Vichy government as the government of France. In Canada's view, for example,

> [t]he fact that the men who have been in nominal control of the Government of France have ordered the armed forces of France to offer resistance to military forces of the United Nations set to assist in the liberation of France from Nazi domination makes it perfectly clear that there no longer exists in France a government that has any effective independence existence—in other words, that there no longer exists in France a legal or constitutional government . . . but only a German puppet government. In these circumstances the Canadian Government has ceased to recognize the present Government at Vichy as being the *de jure* Government of France.[58]

The autonomy of an ostensible government in respect of which the presumption of subordination applies is perhaps most readily apparent where that ostensible government directs the exercise of authority over a state's territory and population after the force pursuant to which or the occupation under which it came to power has ended. For example, 'having regard to the completion of the withdrawal of Vietnamese forces from Cambodia', the European Parliament 'call[ed] upon all EEC Member States to recognise the *de facto* Government of Cambodia'.[59]

313–14. See further 'Exchange of Notes between the Government of the United Kingdom and the Spanish Government for the Recognition of the Assumption by the Allied Control Council of Powers of Disposal in regard to German Enemy Assets in Spain' (letters exchanged and agreement entered into force 28 October 1946) 147 BFSP 1058; *Clement v Agent Judiciaire du Trésor Public* (France, Court of Appeal of Paris, 10 February 1961) (1970) 41 ILR 478, 479–80.

[56] Crawford (n 35) 85–6 (emphasis removed, quoting Brownlie, *Principles of Public International Law* (2nd edn, OUP 1973) 76).

[57] Crawford (n 35) 86 (footnote omitted).

[58] See DCER [1943] vol IX, 19, 20–1.

[59] European Parliament, 'Resolution on Cambodia', 23 November 1989, OJ C 323/101–102, recital C, §9. See also 'Australian Practice in International Law 1978–1980' (1983) 8 AYIL 253, 273, 274. See, more generally, *Charles J Jansen v Mexico* (1868) in Moore (ed), *History and Digest of the International Arbitrations to Which the United States Has Been a Party*, vol 3 (US Government Printing Office, 1898) 2902, 2927; Warbrick, 'Kampuchea: Representation and Recognition' (1981) 30 ICLQ 234, 245; Talmon (n 32) 182, n 363; Marek (n 32) 113.

It appears that the autonomy of an ostensible government may be established sooner, especially where that claimant is able to maintain its authority over the state's territory and population without reliance on foreign military assistance. Notable in this regard is the distinction in treatment between the ostensible government of Uganda, which came to power subsequent to Tanzania's intervention, and the Heng Samrin regime, which came to power subsequent to Vietnam's intervention. Only the former was generally considered to enjoy governmental status, apparently on the basis that only the latter 'would not . . . survive without the support of [foreign] armed forces'.[60]

A claimant in respect of which the presumption of subordination applies may be autonomous even without establishing that that claimant can itself maintain its authority over the state's territory and population. The UNSC's apparent determination that the GCI comprised the government of Iraq[61] despite having been established during the occupation of Iraq by the Coalition Provisional Authority is a possible example. The establishment of the GCI pursuant to an internationally-facilitated political process[62] might have been relevant to the GCI's apparent satisfaction of the requirement of autonomy.

Where the presumption of subordination applies in respect of a specific claimant, the existence of that claimant as an autochthonous political movement prior to the occupation under which or the force subsequent to which it claimed governmental status might not be sufficient to rebut the presumption of subordination. The non-recognition and denial of governmental status to the ostensible government acting under Heng Samrin's leadership demonstrates this point.[63]

Whether an ostensible government is autonomous is ultimately a question of 'political fact'.[64] As such, there might not always be a clear answer to this question.[65]

[60] See HR Debs, 22 November 1979, vol 116, 3506 (question No 4917) (Australia). For a similar approach in respect of other ostensible governments, see eg UNGA, 'Official Records, 36th Session, 103rd Plenary Meeting' (17 December 1981) UN Doc A/36/PV.103, §99 (Germany); Marston (ed), 'UKMIL' (1985) 56 BYIL 363, 387, 389; UNSC, 'Official Records, 1974th Meeting' (22 November 1976) UN Doc S/PV.1974, §205 (USA). See further Brownlie (n 16) 210–11; Peterson, *Recognition of Governments: Legal Doctrine and State Practice, 1815–1995* (Macmillan 1997) 77–80; Jennings and Watts (n 10) 151–2, §45, including the references contained therein. On the denial of governmental status to the Heng Samrin regime, see n 63 below.

[61] UNSC res 1511 (16 October 2003) UN Doc S/RES/1511, §4. On the possible evidential value of the UNSC's practice to the identification of customary international law, see chapter 3, n 279.

[62] See eg UNSC res 1483 (22 May 2003) UN Doc S/RES/1483, §8(c). See also 'Report of the Secretary-General Pursuant to Paragraph 24 of Security Council Resolution 1483 (2003)' (17 July 2003) UN Doc S/2003/715, §24.

[63] On denial of the governmental status of this claimant, recall n 35 above. See also UNGA, 'Official Records, 35th Session, 35th Plenary Meeting' (13 October 1980) UN Doc A/35/PV.35, §33 (Nepal), §§70–1 (Japan), §90 (Pakistan), §§101–2 (Thailand), §107 (Indonesia), §120 (Senegal), §130 (Zaire), §143 (China), §§205–6 (Philippines), §240 (Canada), §253 (USA).

[64] Crawford (n 35) 72. On the importance of considering each case on its merits, see also Marek (n 32) 66.

[65] See also Talmon (n 10) 519. For the possibility that the autonomy of a particular claimant is unclear, see eg UNGA, 'Credentials of Representatives to the Eleventh Session of the General Assembly: Report of the Credentials Committee' (13 February 1957) UN Doc A/3536, §9 (Netherlands).

A list of factors have been said to be 'taken into account' in determining whether or not an ostensible government is a 'puppet'.[66] But one of these factors, namely that the claimant in question is 'in important matters . . . subject to foreign direction or control', is the basis on which the subordination of an ostensible government is established. The other factors, namely that the claimant 'was established unlawfully, by the . . . use of external armed force', 'that it was imposed on, and rejected by the vast majority of the population it claimed to govern', and 'that it was staffed, especially in more important positions, by nationals of the dominant State', may be indicative of the subordinate character of an ostensible government,[67] although the presence or absence of any of these appears not to be determinative of the 'puppet' status of an ostensible government. For example, the Heng Samrin regime in Cambodia was a 'puppet' government even though it was not 'staffed, especially in more important positions, by nationals of the dominant State'. In any event, mere foreign influence over the decisions of an ostensible government does not amount to the subordination of that claimant.[68] Foreign influence over the composition of an ostensible government appears insufficient, in at least circumstances, to preclude the autonomy of that claimant.[69] Additionally, a 'parent' state (that is, a state part of whose territory a nascent state claims as its own) may influence the identity of a nascent state's government, not least because the influence is not 'foreign'. At the same time, special arrangements, such as a mandate agreement, or other factors, such as the right of the nascent state's population to self-determination, may limit the 'parent' state's discretion in this regard.[70]

4.2.2.3 'Constitutionality': Significant But Not Indispensable

Since the person who or collectivity of persons that comprises the government of a state as a matter of customary international law invariably occupies certain offices under the constitution of a state, the configuration of a state's government reflects at least part of the constitution of a state. This does not mean that only a 'constitutional'[71] claimant to governmental status may enjoy governmental status as a matter of customary international law.[72] The presumptive sovereign freedom that each state enjoys under international law to change its constitution[73] militates

[66] Crawford (n 35) 80–1.

[67] See also eg UNGA, 'Official Records, 29th Session, 2301st Plenary Meeting' (27 November 1974) UN Doc A/PV.2301, §269 (Equatorial Guinea); UNGA, 'Official Records, 36th Session, 103rd Plenary Meeting (n 60) §98 (Belgium); UNGA, 'Credentials of Representatives to the Thirty-Sixth Session of the General Assembly: First Report of the Credentials Committee' (17 September 1981) UN Doc A/36/517, §7 (China), §12 (Papua New Guinea); UNGA, 'Credentials of Representatives to the Thirty-Eighth Session of the General Assembly: First Report of the Credentials Committee' (17 October 1983) UN Doc A/38/508, §11 (USA), §14 (Indonesia).

[68] See also Crawford (n 35) 76; Talmon (n 10) 519.

[69] Recall n 62 above.

[70] See, generally, Crawford (n 35) 333–4.

[71] On the use of the term 'constitutional' within the present work, recall section 1.3.

[72] Recall section 2.2.1.

[73] Recall chapter 2, n 115.

against readily inferring any requirement that an ostensible government have a valid claim to power under the state's existing constitution in order to qualify as the government of that state as a matter of international law. This is because it is precisely by opting for an 'unconstitutional' claimant to governmental status that a state may fundamentally change its constitution.[74] Put differently, a requirement of 'constitutionality' for the enjoyment of governmental status under customary international law would restrict the presumptive sovereign freedom of each state to choose its constitution, and the existence of such a restriction ought not readily to be inferred.

Indeed, despite the occasional, usually historical indication to the contrary,[75] the continued success of certain 'unconstitutional' claims to governmental status in receiving general recognition by other states as the government of a state demonstrates that 'constitutionality' is not a requirement for the enjoyment of governmental status under customary international law.[76] Put differently, an ostensible government need not have a 'constitutional' claim to power in order to qualify as the government of a state as a matter of customary international law. Relevant examples include the government that came to power as a result of the 1994 *coup* in The Gambia and the government formed after the 1997 *coup* in the Republic of the Congo.[77] More recent examples include the change to the identity of the government of Libya in 2011, of Egypt in 2013, and of Sudan in 2019.

Customary international law has nevertheless privileged 'constitutional' claimants in excluding them from having to satisfy the requirement of effective control, an exception which historically was of practical relevance for an autonomous 'constitutional' claimant only insofar as it faced no rival claim by an autonomous 'unconstitutional' ostensible government in effective control.[78] State practice since the early 1990s demonstrates that customary international law now privileges the claim of a state's autonomous 'constitutional' ostensible government over that of any 'unconstitutional' claimant to governmental status, even one that exercises effective control, whether the 'constitutional' claimant seeks to attain or retain governmental status. Indeed, an autonomous 'constitutional' claimant to governmental status will now generally enjoy governmental status as a matter of customary international law even where there exists a rival autonomous claimant in effective control over the state's territory and population. Examples of the attainment by a 'constitutional' claimant of governmental status as a matter of customary international law in the

[74] See chapter 2, n 8 and accompanying text.

[75] See Lauterpacht (n 10) 102–3; Brown, 'The Legal Effects of Recognition' (1950) 44 AJIL 617, 621.

[76] See also UNSC, 'Official Records, 899th Meeting' (14 September 1960) UN Doc S/PV.899, §37 (Argentina); UNGA, 'Official Records, 20th Session, 877th Meeting of the Sixth Committee' (17 November 1965) UN Doc A/C.6/SR.877, §10 (Spain); Marston (ed), 'UKMIL' (1999) 70 BYIL 517, 584. See further Moore, *Digest of International Law*, vol 1 (US Government Printing Office 1906) 250; *Tinoco* (n 12) and the various sources cited in 377–8.

[77] On these and other examples, see eg Talmon (n 10) 534.

[78] See further section 4.2.2.4.1.

presence of a rival autonomous claimant which was in effective control over the state's territory and population include the attainment of governmental status by Alassane Ouattara in respect of Côte d'Ivoire and by Adama Barrow in respect of The Gambia, subsequent to the constitutionally mandated presidential election of Côte d'Ivoire in 2010 and of The Gambia in 2016, respectively.[79] One example of the retention by a 'constitutional' government of its governmental status as a matter of customary international law where there is a rival autonomous claimant in effective control over the state's territory and population is the continued acceptance of Manuel Zelaya as President of Honduras after the 2009 '*coup*'.[80] An earlier example, which, in fact, concerns the first time there was consensus as to the enjoyment of governmental status as a matter of customary international law by a state's 'constitutional' claimant after an autonomous 'unconstitutional' claimant secured effective control over that state's territory and population, relates to the identity of the government of Haiti between 1991 and 1994.[81]

The privileging of 'constitutional' claims to governmental status in this way does not undermine the presumptive sovereign freedom of each state to choose its government. Indeed, absent a fundamental change to its constitution, a state can be said to have expressed its choice of government through its existing constitution[82] and, by privileging the claim of an autonomous 'constitutional' ostensible government over the claim of an autonomous 'unconstitutional' ostensible government, customary international law privileges what is perhaps the most direct means by which a state can be deemed to have expressed its choice of government. This is one important reason—in addition to all the practice that best lends itself to a conclusion that customary international law privileges 'constitutional' claimants[83]—to favour the plausible explanation of contemporary state practice concerning the recognition of governments which reflects the preferential treatment accorded to 'constitutional' claimants over an alternative understanding of practice, for example one which suggests that there exists no objective customary international legal framework for the assessment of governmental status or that such a framework includes a requirement of representativity. These alternative understandings

[79] In respect of Côte d'Ivoire, see eg UNGA, 'Credentials of Representatives to the Sixty-Fifth Session of the General Assembly: Report of the Credentials Committee' (22 December 2010) UN Doc A/65/583/Rev.1, §7, which was approved by the UNGA res 65/237 (23 December 2010) UN Doc A/RES/65/237. On The Gambia, see eg UNSC res 2337 (19 January 2017) UN Doc S/RES/2337, §2.

[80] UNGA res 63/301 (30 June 2009) UN Doc A/RES/63/301, §§1–3.

[81] See UNGA res 46/7 (11 October 1991) UN Doc A/RES/46/7, §§1–2; UNGA res 47/20 A (24 November 1992) UN Doc A/RES/47/20, §§1–2; UNGA res 48/27 A (6 December 1993) UN Doc A/RES/48/27, §§1–3. See also UNSC res 841 (16 June 1993) UN Doc S/RES/841, §8.

[82] Cf Research Services of the German Bundestag, 'Legal Questions Concerning Recognition of the Interim President in Venezuela' (15 February 2019), available at <http://bundestag.de/resource/blob/827466/f4de0cf7eb1e74f552fb711f7d07fb76/WD-2-017-19_EN-pdf-data.pdf>, 11 for the view that the reliance on a contested interpretation of a state's constitution to recognize a specific ostensible government is 'questionable' in the light of 'the principle of non-interference'.

[83] See further 4.2.2.5.1.2.

would undermine, among other things, the presumptive sovereign freedom of each state to choose its government.[84]

The preferential treatment accorded by international law to 'constitutional' claimants does not undermine the freedoms of each state to express anew its choice of government, constitution, and political system. An 'unconstitutional' claimant to governmental status may, albeit in limited circumstances,[85] enjoy governmental status, and it is precisely by opting for an 'unconstitutional' government that a state may fundamentally change its constitution and its political system.[86]

While the privileging of an autonomous 'constitutional' claim to governmental status over any 'unconstitutional' claim to governmental status is now apparent with the existence of no clear example to the contrary since the mid-1990s,[87] it may be noteworthy that, as is not infrequently the case,[88] practice was not entirely consistent, nor was the precise nature of the change in the law clear when the change to the scope of the privilege accorded to 'constitutional' claimants first gained traction. For example, in 1992, subsequent to his assertion of authority on an 'unconstitutional' basis,[89] Alberto Fujimori of Peru continued to be recognized as President of Peru even though the Congress he sought to dissolve impeached him and elected a new head of state, as it was constitutionally permitted to do to where the president attempted improperly to dissolve Congress. The uncertainty and inconsistency in practice in the early 1990s may have contributed to the proliferation of alternative accounts of the customary international legal framework for the assessment of governmental status[90] which are less convincing in the light of both the presumption against limitations on state sovereignty and further state practice on the recognition of governments.

In what concerns the identification of a 'constitutional' claimant to governmental status, the constitution of a state may take different forms. Although it typically takes the form of a municipal 'basic law', the constitution of a state may instead, for example, take the form of an agreement between warring factions within the state. Illustratively, the Peshawar Accord of 26 April 1992 comprised at least part of the constitution of Afghanistan at that time.[91] The same can be said of the Libreville Political Agreement of 11 January 2013 as regards the constitutions of the

[84] Recall section 4.2.1. See further section 4.2.2.5.1.2.

[85] An autonomous 'unconstitutional' ostensible government may enjoy governmental status as a matter of customary international law where there exists no rival autonomous 'constitutional' claimant.

[86] See chapter 2, n 8 and accompanying text.

[87] Note that, in 2011, the political authority operating under Qadhafi's leadership may, at some point prior to the recognition of the NTC as the government of Libya, be deemed no longer to have been a claimant to governmental status. Recall section 4.2.2.1.

[88] See also Crawford, 'Chance, Order, Change: The Course of International Law' (2013) 365 Hague *Recueil* 9, 66, §80.

[89] See Decree Law No 25418 of 6 April 1992.

[90] See eg Roth (n 10) 404.

[91] Available at <https://peacemaker.un.org/sites/default/files/document/files/2024/05/af920424peshawar20accord.pdf>.

Central African Republic.[92] As another example, the Libyan Political Agreement of 17 December 2015 'was in essence a new constitutional settlement' of Libya.[93] Other forms that a state's constitution may take include an agreement between that state and one or more other states. This was the case with the General Framework Agreement for Peace in Bosnia and Herzegovina of 14 December 1995, Annex 4 of which comprised the constitution of Bosnia and Herzegovina,[94] and the Agreement on a Comprehensive Political Settlement of the Cambodia Conflict of 1991, which reflected the constitution of Cambodia at that time.[95] The constitution of a state may also, or instead, take the form of the established practice of a state's organs.[96]

It may not always be clear whether an ostensible government qualifies as the 'constitutional' claimant to governmental status, especially where two or more rival claimants purport to be the 'constitutional' government.

Where only one claimant purports to be the 'constitutional' government of a state, a barely-plausible 'constitutional' claim that is uncontested by central organs of that state may be considered 'constitutional'. The invocation by Edvard Beneš of the 1920 Constitution of Czechoslovakia as the municipal legal basis of his authority appears to be an example in this regard. Although other authors take the view that his claim was not 'constitutional',[97] the acceptance by many states of his attainment of governmental status from 'exile', alongside the otherwise-clear difference in treatment between 'unconstitutional' and 'constitutional' ostensible 'governments-in-exile' as regards their prospect for the attainment of governmental status from 'exile',[98] suggests that many states did consider Edvard Beneš's claim to be 'constitutional'. More recent practice in respect of Mr Hadi's claim to governmental status in respect of Yemen might also be taken to suggest that a state's existing constitution may subsist in the absence of a 'constitutional' government[99] until the state fundamentally changes it. In any event, the acceptance by states of

[92] Available at <http://peaceagreements.org/viewmasterdocument/809>. See also eg UNSC res 2127 (5 December 2013) UN Doc S/RES/2127, §2.

[93] *Dr Ali Mahmoud Hassan Mohamed v Mr Abdulmagid Breish and others* [2020] EWCA Civ 637 ('*Mohamed v Breish*') §3.

[94] Attached to 'Letter Dated 29 November 1995 from the Permanent Representative of the United States of America to the United Nations Addressed to the Secretary-General' (30 November 1995) UN Doc A/50/790–S/1995/999.

[95] Agreement on a Comprehensive Political Settlement of the Cambodia Conflict, annexed to 'Letter Dated 30 October 1991 from the Permanent Representatives of France and Indonesia to the United Nations Addressed to the Secretary-General' (30 October 1991) UN Doc A/46/608–S/23177 ('Agreement Concerning Cambodia').

[96] Kelsen, *Pure Theory of Law* (Max Knight tr, 2nd edn, University of California Press 1967) 222; Roth (n 10) 51–2. Recall also, eg chapter 2, n 22 on the finding by the Court of Appeal of Paris that Muammar Qadhafi comprised Libya's head of state on the basis that he 'effectively and continuously' exercised certain functions.

[97] See both Marek (n 32) 313 and Oppenheimer, 'Governments and Authorities in Exile' (1942) 36 AJIL 568, 581.

[98] See n 147 below and accompanying text.

[99] Recall n 26 above and the accompanying text.

the transfer of power to Mr Pétain in respect of France in 1940[100] and to Rashad al-Alimi in respect of Yemen in 2022[101] suggests that there may be some flexibility in the treatment of the sole claimant purporting to be 'constitutional' as indeed being 'constitutional'. The acceptance of the governmental status of the Coalition Government of Democratic Kampuchea (CGDK) is a further possible example in this regard.[102]

That said, it is not necessarily the case that the only claimant purporting to have a valid claim to power under the state's existing constitution will invariably be considered 'constitutional', perhaps especially if the constitutionality of the claim is contested by one or more central organs of the state. Even without or before such contestation, the only ostensibly-'constitutional' claimant to governmental status may be 'unconstitutional'. A possible example in this regard involves the states comprising the so-called 'Lima Group', who considered 'that the electoral process that took place in Venezuela on May 20, 2018, lacked legitimacy' and therefore did 'not recognize the legitimacy of the new presidential term of Nicolas Maduro'.[103] This preceded the declaration by the National Assembly of Venezuela that Mr Maduro had 'usurped' power and the purported assumption of the presidency of Venezuela by Juan Guaidó.[104] The apparent reluctance of states to accept the governmental status of Amrullah Saleh—who, in August 2021, claimed to be 'caretaker' President of Afghanistan—might be another example.[105]

Where two or more rival claimants purport to be the 'constitutional' government on the basis of a contested election, an international mechanism for the verification or certification of the electoral results may prove useful, as was the case

[100] Recall n 38 above and the accompanying text.

[101] Recall n 27 above. On the apparent recognition of Mr al-Alimi's governmental status, see eg 'EU Ambassadors Meet President Rashad al-Alimi' (5 September 2022), available at <http://eeas.europa.eu/delegations/yemen/eu-ambassadors-meet-president-rashad-al-alimi_en?s=211>.

[102] On the formation of the CGDK, see 'Declaration of the Formation of the Coalition Government of Democratic Kampuchea' (1982) 4 CSEA 410. See also 'Letter Dated 11 September 1981 from the Permanent Representative of Democratic Kampuchea to the United Nations Addressed to the Secretary-General' (14 September 1981) UN Doc A/36/498–S/14687, Annex. On recognition of the CGDK, see eg UNGA, 'Official Records, 37th Session, 45th Plenary Meeting' (26 October 1982) UN Doc A/37/PV.45, §21 (Belgium), §27 (Federal Republic of Germany), §137 (Egypt). See also UNGA res 37/6 (28 October 1982) UN Doc A/RES/37/6, fourth unnumbered preambular paragraph, adopted by 105 votes to 23, with 20 abstentions. On recognition of governmental status by and in the context of international organizations, see section 5.4.

[103] 'Lima Group Declaration' (4 January 2019), available at <http://international.gc.ca/world-monde/international_relations-relations_internationales/latin_america-amerique_latine/2019-01-04-lima_group-groupe_lima.aspx>, §1. But recall section 2.2.1 on the different meanings of recognition, and see section 4.2.2.5.1 on the different senses in which the term 'legitimate' is used.

[104] See n 113 below.

[105] See also Paddeu and Pavlopoulos, 'Between Legitimacy and Control: The Taliban's Pursuit of Governmental Status' (*Just Security*, 7 September 2021), available at <http://justsecurity.org/78051/between-legitimacy-and-control-the-talibans-pursuit-of-governmental-status> and chapter 5, n 86 (on 'provisional' representation as not involving recognition of governmental status, see section 5.4.1.2).

in respect of the 2010 presidential election in Côte d'Ivoire.[106] Other situations, particularly those calling for complex constitutional legal analysis or an assessment of disputed incidents, may prove more difficult. Four examples further demonstrate the significance of 'constitutionality' to governmental status as a matter of customary international law while indicating that the 'constitutionality' of a claim may be unclear or contested or at least require an assessment of complex factual or legal issues.

The first example relates to the situation in Honduras when, in 2009, the incumbent president, Manuel Zelaya, was purportedly replaced by way of parliament's acceptance of a letter of resignation of disputed authenticity, following his forcible expatriation. Although there was no clear basis in the text of the Constitution of Honduras on which to find that any of these actions were 'unconstitutional', there was consensus on the 'constitutionality' of Manuel Zelaya's claim and on his governmental status from 'exile'.[107]

The second example concerns the apparent acceptance of the Ukrainian parliament's constitutional authority to declare that President Yanukovych 'has in the non-constitutional manner withdrawn from performing constitutional powers', to appoint Oleksandr Turchynov as interim President, and to resolve that presidential elections were to be held,[108] despite the absence of an explicit municipal legal basis for any such action and although neither the procedural nor the substantive constitutional conditions for the impeachment of the president were satisfied. The member states of the Council of Europe accepted the victor of the 2014 presidential election as the President of Ukraine, seemingly on the basis that the Ukrainian parliament had, in its conduct resulting in this election, acted with 'due consideration for constitutional principles',[109] although by that point, Viktor Yanukovych no longer claimed to be the President of Ukraine. Perhaps more notable is the acceptance by Lithuania and the UK of Oleksandr Turchynov's transitional government as the government of Ukraine at a time when Viktor Yanukovych still claimed to be President of Ukraine. Lithuania stated that Oleksandr Turchynov's government had been '[appointed by] the Ukrainian Rada, whose legitimacy have never and cannot be challenged . . . in accordance with the Ukrainian Constitution'.[110] According to the UK, 'an attempt to cast doubt on the legitimacy of the transitional Government in Ukraine . . . is entirely unwarranted'.[111] It was nevertheless Russia's

[106] See Special Representative of the Secretary-General for Côte d'Ivoire, 'Statement on the Certification of the Result of the Second Round of the Presidential Election Held on 28 November 2010', available at <http://peacekeeping.un.org/sites/default/files/past/unoci/documents/unoci_srsg_certification_en_03122010.pdf>.

[107] For the UNGA's response, see n 80 above.

[108] 'Plenary Meeting of the Fourth Session of the Verkhovna Rada' (22 February 2014), available at <https://www.rada.gov.ua/en/news/88480.html>.

[109] Council of Europe res 1988 (9 April 2014), available at <http://assembly.coe.int/nw/xml/xref/xref-xml2html-en.asp?fileid=20873&lang=en>, §3.

[110] UNSC, 'Official Records, 7134th Meeting' (13 March 2014) UN Doc S/PV.7134 (provisional) 16.

[111] Ibid, 7.

view that 'the legitimate legal President was overthrown and forced to leave Kyiv under the threat of physical violence'.[112]

The third example pertains to the ongoing situation in Venezuela. Nicolás Maduro retained a claim as President of Venezuela following the 2018 presidential election, even though the National Assembly rejected the result of this election with its then-President, Juan Guaidó, subsequently claiming to be interim President of Venezuela on the basis of a plausible reading of the Constitution of Venezuela.[113] The matter was complicated by the fact that the Supreme Tribunal of Justice had already declared the National Assembly to be unconstitutional, although the court itself faced a rival claim from the Supreme Tribunal of Justice 'in exile'. The situation became no less complex with the apparent end in 2020 of the constitutional term of the National Assembly over which Mr Guaidó presided and the subsequent emergence of a rival claim to the presidency of the National Assembly. Nicolás Maduro and Juan Guaidó nevertheless each enjoyed recognition by some states as President of Venezuela, seemingly on the view that the claimant being recognized is the 'constitutional' President.[114] In January 2023, the situation developed further, when the pre-2021 National Assembly dissolved Mr Guaidó's government, extended its own mandate, and conferred certain executive powers on itself, its Delegated Commission (*Comisión Delegada de la Asamblea Nacional*), and the Council of Administration and Protection of Assets (*Consejo de Administración y Protección de Activos*) it established.[115]

The fourth example relates to the rival ostensible governments of Myanmar since February 2021. Pursuant to a claim of fraud in relation to the November 2020 general election, the military proclaimed the electoral result invalid, declared a state of emergency, and purported to vest executive power in the commander-in-chief in reliance on certain provisions of the 2008 Constitution.[116] The military then formed the State Administration Council (SAC), which purports to be the government of Myanmar. By that time, hours before the electoral victors took oath

[112] Ibid, 15.

[113] See National Assembly of Venezuela, 'Acuerdo sobre la declaratoria de usurpación de la presidencia de la república por parte de Nicolas Maduro Moros y el restablecimiento de la vigencia de la constitución' (15 January 2019) 2 *Gaceta Legislativa* 4, on the basis of which Mr Guaidó subsequently claimed to be President of Venezuela. See eg 'Venezuela Opposition Leader Swears Himself in as Interim President' (*Reuters*, 23 January 2019), available at <http://reuters.com/article/us-venezuela-politics-guaido-idUSKCN1PH2AN>.

[114] See eg UNSC, 'Official Records, 8452nd Meeting' (26 January 2019) UN Doc S/PV.8452 (provisional) 27–9 for the views of Nicaragua, Cuba, and Saint Vincent and the Grenadines, on the one hand, and 32–3, 36 for the views of Paraguay, Argentina, and Chile on the other; and UNSC, 'Official Records, 8476th Meeting' (28 February 2019) UN Doc S/PV.8476 (provisional) 2, 6 for the views of South Africa and Russia, on the one hand, and the UK on the other.

[115] National Assembly of Venezuela, 'Ley de reforma del estatuto que rige la transición a la democracia para restablecer la vigencia de la constitución de la repúbica bolivariana de Venezuela' (3 January 2023) 66 *Gaceta Legislativa* 2, 6–8 (arts 7–9, 11).

[116] See eg 'Statement from Myanmar Military on State of Emergency' (*Reuters*, 1 February 2021), available at <http://reuters.com/article/us-myanmar-politics-military-text-idUSKBN2A11A2>.

as members of parliament, the military had arrested a number of individuals belonging to the NLD, the then-ruling party which had won enough seats to form also the post-2020 government. In response, a group of the elected individuals formed the Committee Representing Pyidaungsu Hluttaw (CRPH). The CRPH first reportedly claimed to have extended the term of the State Counsellor for five years, before ostensibly replacing the 2008 Constitution with an Interim Constitutional Arrangement,[117] on the basis of which the National Unity Government (NUG) was formed 'with the authority bestowed by the people's mandate resultant of all parties' democratic election held in 2020'.[118] With the military's actions considered 'unconstitutional' by a number of states,[119] and the NUG not claiming power on the basis of the existing constitution of the state, there is no apparent 'constitutional' claimant. The limited recognition by states of either ostensible government as the government of Myanmar[120] is thus unsurprising, given also that neither claimant appears to exercise effective control, as is necessary for the attainment of governmental status by an 'unconstitutional' ostensible government.[121]

4.2.2.4 Effective Control, Sometimes

4.2.2.4.1 Applicability and significance of effective control

An 'unconstitutional' claimant to governmental status in respect of an existing state[122] must exercise effective control over the territory and population of that state in order to attain governmental status.[123]

[117] See Part II of the Federal Democracy Charter (2021), available at <http://crphmyanmar.org/wp-content/uploads/2021/04/Federal-Democracy-Charter-English.pdf>.

[118] The announcement is available at CRPH, 'Announcement Number 23/2021: Formation of the National Unity Government' (16 April 2021), available at <http://burmakommitten.org/wp-content/uploads/2021/04/CRPH-Formation-of-National-Unity-Government.pdf>.

[119] See eg UNGA, 'Official Records, 75th Session, 83rd Plenary Meeting' (18 June 2021) UN Doc A/75/PV.83, 7 (Bangladesh), 14 (Costa Rica), 15 (Ukraine).

[120] On the avoidance of recognition of any claimant as the government of Myanmar, see chapter 3, n 128 and chapter 5, nn 21 and 86, including the accompanying text. See also European Parliament, 'Resolution on Myanmar, One Year after the Coup', 10 March 2022, OJ C 347/191, 195, §2 on the call upon 'the Tatmadaw to fully respect the outcome of the democratic elections of November 2020 [and to] reinstate the civilian government' and on the support for 'the CRPH, the NUG and the National Unity Consultative Council (NUCC) as the only legitimate representatives of the democratic wishes of the people of Myanmar'. (On the distinction between recognition as a government and recognition in other capacities, recall section 2.2.2.)

[121] See further section 4.2.2.4.1.

[122] As for an emerging state, the requirement of 'effective control' for governmental status is varied in accordance with the criterion of 'effective government' applicable in respect of statehood (on this latter criterion, see Crawford (n 35) 55–61). For example, where the 'parent' state has conferred independence on the local authorities of the nascent state, the requirement of 'government' for the purposes of statehood is applied more loosely, in which case the criterion of effective control for governmental status is satisfied more readily.

[123] See also Marek (n 32) 57–9; *Tinoco* (n 12); Lauterpacht (n 10) 88; Blix (n 32) 639–43; HL Debs, 28 April 1980, vol 408, col 1121–2WA; Marston (ed), 'UKMIL' (2000) 70 BYIL 517, 584. See also UNSC, 'Official Records, 899th Meeting' (n 76) §37 (Argentina); Siekmann, 'Netherlands State Practice for the Parliamentary Year 1989–1990' (1991) 22 NYIL 237, 237–8; Jimenez de Aréchaga, *Derecho Internacional Publico*, vol II (Fundación de Cultura Universitaria 1995) 57.

Whether 'constitutional' or 'unconstitutional', no ostensible government of an existing state must exercise effective control in order to retain governmental status as a matter of customary international law. An ostensible government that already enjoys governmental status as a matter of customary international law may retain this status without exercising any control over the territory and population of the state whose government it comprises and without retaining a physical presence in the territory of that state. In other words, a presumption operates in favour of incumbent governments.[124] For example, during the Spanish Civil War, most states continued to recognize the republican claimant as the government of Spain, even when nationalist forces controlled the greater part of Spain's territory and population, before the latter secured effective control over the territory and population of Spain.[125] Also, it is at least in part on the basis of this presumption that the possession by a state of a so-called 'government-in-exile' has historically been a not-infrequent phenomenon.[126]

Moreover, the criterion of effective control does not apply in respect of 'constitutional' claimants. This appears to have been the case long before the 1990s,[127] given changes to the composition of several 'constitutional' 'governments-in-exile' and other 'constitutional' governments not in effective control.[128] In other words, it appears to have been historically possible for a 'constitutional' ostensible government to attain governmental status as a matter of customary international law without first securing effective control over the state's territory and population, including from 'exile'.

The suggestion that, at least historically, the governmental status as a matter of customary international law of a 'government-in-exile' has depended instead on the 'international illegality of the government *in situ*' and on the 'representative character' of the 'government-in-exile'[129] does not withstand scrutiny. At least five points may be made in this regard.

First, the application of certain customary international legal criteria for governmental status to specific factual contexts might mistakenly be seen to reflect a requirement concerning the 'international illegality of the government *in situ*' for

[124] See, generally, Lauterpacht (n 10) 93–7. See also Siekmann (n 123) 238.

[125] See also Lauterpacht (n 10) 93–4.

[126] See the examples mentioned in Lauterpacht (n 10) 91 n I; Oppenheimer (n 97). See, generally, Talmon (n 32).

[127] This aspect of the customary international legal framework appears frequently to have been overlooked in the literature. See eg Crawford (n 35) 86, Talmon (n 10) 526, and n 147 below on the treatment of a 'constitutional' government as an incumbent government. See also Chen, *The International Law of Recognition, With Special Reference to the Practice in Great Britain and the United States* (Praeger 1951) 273. But see Blix (n 32) 641, who may be seen as acknowledging that the requirement of effective control applies only to 'revolutionary régime[s]' (*viz* 'unconstitutional' ostensible governments).

[128] See eg the changes to the composition of various governments-in-exile during the Second World War, including those of Belgium, Poland, Yugoslavia, and Greece. On some of these 'governments-in-exile' and others, see eg Oppenheimer (n 97) 569–70. See also Lauterpacht (n 10) 91 n I.

[129] Talmon (n 10) 523, 536. See also Redaelli, *Intervention in Civil Wars: Effectiveness, Legitimacy, and Human Rights* (Hart 2021) 137–8.

the enjoyment of governmental status by an ostensible 'government-in-exile'. More specifically, this misconception might arise from the application of the presumption of subordination in respect of an 'unconstitutional' ostensible government established during the belligerent occupation of or subsequent to the unlawful use of force against a state,[130] coupled with the fact that in such circumstances an incumbent government or a 'constitutional' claimant to governmental status may enjoy governmental status from 'exile', at least insofar as there was no rival autonomous claimant exercising effective control over the state's territory and population. The acknowledgement that the 'recognition as the state's government should be denied to an effective government *in situ* on the grounds of its illegal creation only as long as the illegality lasts, that is, as long as it affects the government's . . . independence'[131] further supports the view that the enjoyment of governmental status by an ostensible 'government-in-exile' historically resulted from the subordinate character of the ostensible government '*in situ*', not its 'international illegality'.[132]

Secondly, that it is not the 'illegality of the government *in situ*' that allows an ostensible 'government-in-exile' to enjoy governmental status as a matter of customary international law is apparent from those cases in which a state possessed a 'government-in-exile' as a matter of customary international law at a time when the conduct that led to the 'exile' or prevented the return from that 'exile' of the 'government-in-exile' was not internationally unlawful. Examples in this regard include the government of Belgium (1914–18) and the government of Serbia (1915–18).[133] This contributes *a fortiori* in dismissing any significance that has been accorded to the peremptory character of the obligation whose violation is apparently necessary for an ostensible 'government-in-exile' to enjoy governmental status as a matter of customary international law.[134] The emergence of peremptory norms as a part of positive international law postdates the prohibition on the conduct which has been considered relevant to the success of certain claims to governmental status by 'governments-in-exile'.

Thirdly, the existence of a requirement of a 'representative character' for the enjoyment of governmental status by an ostensible 'government-in-exile' does not necessarily follow from the references by states, in the context of decisions to recognize or deny governmental status, to whether an ostensible government had a representative character. Such references may instead relate to the view that the government of a state is the presumptive representative of the people of that state[135]

[130] Recall section 4.2.2.2.
[131] Talmon (n 10) 528.
[132] On the broader range of circumstances in which a 'government-in-exile' may enjoy governmental status as a matter of present-day customary international law, all unrelated to the 'international illegality of the government *in situ*', recall section 4.2.2.3.
[133] See eg Talmon (n 32) 286–7.
[134] Talmon (n 10) 522–3.
[135] See chapter 3, n 253 and accompanying text. Accordingly, a reference to an ostensible government having or not having a representative character might indicate whether or not that claimant is deemed to enjoy governmental status.

or to the 'constitutionality' of a claim to governmental status. Such plausible understanding of practice is to be preferred in the light of the presumptive sovereign freedoms of each state to choose its government and its political system.[136] Indeed, the author who suggests that representativity of an ostensible 'government-in-exile' is relevant to its enjoyment of governmental status accepts that the 'legal [*viz* 'constitutional'] successor of the last recognized government *in situ*' benefits from a presumption of representativity[137] and that 'Governments have been reluctant to confer the title of government in exile on an exile group . . . that lacks governmental authority'.[138] This accords with the view that the requirement of effective control does not and has not historically applied to 'constitutional' claimants.[139]

Fourthly, the fact that no 'unconstitutional' ostensible government has attained governmental status from 'exile', at least not without directing armed forces present in the territory of the state, further suggests that it is only on the basis of either the presumption in favour of incumbent governments or the exception to the requirement of effective control in respect of 'constitutional' ostensible governments that an ostensible government has enjoyed governmental status from 'exile'. Edvard Beneš's claim to governmental status in 1940, to which regard has been had in support of the possibility that an 'unconstitutional' ostensible government may attain governmental status from 'exile',[140] appears to have been 'constitutional'.[141] As for the examples involving the recognition of 'unconstitutional' ostensible 'governments-in-exile' of Algeria, of Angola, and of the Saharan Arab Democratic Republic (SADR),[142] the group of persons purporting to be the government of each putative state directed armed forces present in the territory of the respective putative state. It may also be relevant that each of those claims to governmental status was connected with a claim to statehood, as a result of which the application of the requirement of effective control may have varied.[143] Moreover, the statehood of the SADR and, consequently, the governmental status of its ostensible government remains unsettled.[144] Neither the mere existence of 'plans to establish in exile and to recognize governments'[145] nor the recognition by only a very small number of states of the attainment of governmental status by an ostensible 'government-in-exile'[146] provides much evidence that an 'unconstitutional' government may attain

[136] See further section 4.2.2.5.1.2.
[137] Talmon (n 10) 512, 515.
[138] Ibid, 516, quoting from Shain, *The Frontier of Loyalty: Political Exiles in the Age of the Nation-State* (Wesleyan University Press 1989) 116.
[139] See the text accompanying n 127 above.
[140] Talmon (n 10) 515–16.
[141] See n 98 above and accompanying text.
[142] See Talmon (n 10) 515.
[143] See n 122 above.
[144] See eg UNGA res 77/133 (16 December 2022) UN Doc A/RES/77/133.
[145] Talmon (n 10) 515–16.
[146] Ibid, 516 in respect of the 'Afghan Interim Government'.

governmental status as a matter of customary international law from 'exile'. As another commentator has noted, the

> difference between the continuing [or 'constitutional'] exiled governments which merely transferred their seat abroad . . . and the governments newly formed in exile after a period of complete break in governmental continuity . . . is clearly illustrated by the uncontested standing of the exiled constitutional governments of the Second World War, as contrasted with the precarious position of the Czechoslovak Government in exile and, to a much stronger degree, the French National Committee.[147]

Fifthly, situations which have been suggested to involve derecognition of a 'government-in-exile' on the grounds of '[t]he presumption of representativeness [being] refuted'[148] can be explained on other grounds, such as the existence of an autonomous claimant in effective control that rivalled the existing government operating from 'exile', which would historically have resulted in the enjoyment of governmental status by the autonomous claimant in effective control.[149] This may well have been the case with respect to both Montenegro in 1918 and Poland in 1945.

Regardless of the historical position, state practice concerning the recognition of governments since the early 1990s makes clear the present-day inapplicability of the requirement of effective control in respect of 'constitutional' claimants under customary international law. Such a claimant may attain governmental status without ever having exercised effective control over the state's territory and population.[150] The main difference between the historical position and present-day customary international law as regards the criterion of effective control appears to be the weight accorded to it for a successful claim to governmental status.

On account of either the presumption in favour of incumbent governments or the exception to the requirement of effective control in respect of 'constitutional' claimants, an autonomous ostensible government not in effective control of the state's territory and population could historically enjoy governmental status as a matter of customary international law only insofar as there was no rival autonomous claimant exercising effective control over the territory and population of the

[147] Marek (n 32) 99 (reference omitted).

[148] Talmon (n 10) 514.

[149] On this possibility more generally, see eg n 151 below and accompanying text.

[150] On the privilege accorded to 'constitutional' governments as a matter of present-day customary international law, recall section 4.2.2.3. For the occasional view to the contrary, see eg ICC, 'The Determination of the Office of the Prosecutor on the Communication Received in Relation to Egypt' (Press release, 8 May 2014) (ICC-OTP-20130508-PR1003), available at <http://icc-cpi.int/Pages/item.aspx?name=pr1003>, §4; *Valores Mundiales, SL and Consorcio Andino SL v Bolivarian Republic of Venezuela* (ICSID Case No ARB/13/11), *Annulment Proceeding, Procedural Resolution No 2* (29 August 2019) §42; OASPC (Permanent Council of the Organization of American States), 'Acta de la Sesión Extraordinaria celebrada el 9 de abril de 2019' (9 April 2019) OEA/Ser.G CP/ACTA 2217/19, 18 (Antigua and Barbuda).

state. Once a rival autonomous claimant secured effective control over the state's territory and population, it would attain governmental status. For example, once nationalist forces were in effective control of Spain's territory and population, most states treated the ostensible government operating under Francisco Franco's leadership, not the republican ostensible 'government-in-exile', as the government of Spain.[151] While there is little practice directly on this point, the same would appear to be true where a rival 'puppet' claimant in effective control established its autonomy. Although the situation in Cambodia was resolved through the establishment of a transitional government formed on an inclusive basis,[152] it may be relevant that once Vietnam withdrew its troops from Cambodia, the European Parliament 'call[ed] upon all EEC Member States to recognize the *de facto* Government of Cambodia',[153] an ostensible government which, having been a 'puppet' government, did not previously enjoy governmental status. Additionally, in an earlier situation involving the contested identity of Cambodia's government, the states which supported the claim to governmental status by the Royal Government of the National Union of Kampuchea (GRUNK) asserted that the Lon Nol regime was a 'puppet' government, dependent on foreign support.[154] This could be taken to suggest that the Lon Nol regime, in the view of those states, might otherwise have qualified for governmental status as a matter of customary international law.

In contrast, as a matter of present-day customary international law an 'unconstitutional' ostensible government will not enjoy governmental status, even if it exercises effective control, as long as a rival 'constitutional' claimant to governmental status exists.[155] Put differently, the contemporary privilege accorded by international law to autonomous 'constitutional' ostensible governments limits the sufficiency of autonomous effective control for a successful claim to governmental status.[156] An autonomous 'constitutional' claimant to governmental status will now

[151] Cf Talmon (n 32) 298.

[152] See Framework for a Comprehensive Political Settlement of the Cambodia Conflict in 'Letter Dated 30 August 1990 from the Permanent Representatives of China, France, the Union of Soviet Socialist Republics, the United Kingdom of Great Britain and Northern Ireland and the United States of America to the United Nations Addressed to the Secretary-General' (31 August 1990) UN Doc A/45/472, Appendix, section 1, §§1–4, 7.

[153] European Parliament (n 59).

[154] See eg UNGA, 'Official Records, 29th Session, 2244th Plenary Meeting' (26 September 1974) UN Doc A/PV.2244, §56 (Equatorial Guinea); UNGA, 'Official Records, 29th Session, 2298th Plenary Meeting' (26 November 1974) UN Doc A/PV.2298, §27 (Somalia), §§53–4 (Dahomey); UNGA, 'Official Records, 29th Session, 2301st Plenary Meeting' (n 67) §37 (Somalia). But see also n 177 below and the accompanying text.

[155] On the privilege accorded to 'constitutional' governments as a matter of present-day customary international law, recall section 4.2.2.3.

[156] For the sake of comprehensiveness, the privilege accorded to 'constitutional' claimants limits also the extent to which the presumption in favour of incumbent governments may apply. Recall eg n 79 above on the practice in relation to Côte d'Ivoire in 2010 and The Gambia in 2016.

enjoy governmental status as a matter of customary international law even where an autonomous rival claimant exercises effective control over the state.

4.2.2.4.2 Assessing effective control

In accordance with the presumptive sovereign freedom of each state to choose its political system and its constitution,[157] effective control—that is, it the effective direction of the exercise of public authority—can in principle be established and maintained through any form of government and any institutional arrangement. In order to demonstrate the exercise of such control, regard can nevertheless be had to the existence and effective functioning of those organs of state through which a government typically directs the exercise of public authority over a state's territory and population.[158] Regard can be had also to the existence and effective functioning of other common central organs of state (for example, a legislature and municipal courts) in a manner that demonstrates the acceptance of the assertion by the ostensible government of executive authority.[159]

To be effective, the exercise of public authority must, at least where there is more than one claimant to governmental status in respect of the same state, extend over a substantial majority of the territory and population of that state.[160] Although formally unnecessary in order to be 'effective', the direction by an ostensible government of the exercise of public authority over the territory and population of a state's capital may enable that claimant to exercise sufficiently-effective control for the attainment of governmental status as a matter of customary international law since the capital is where the central organs of state are usually located and since a significant portion of a state's population often resides there. Control over the capital alone, however, is unlikely to be sufficiently effective for the attainment of governmental status as a matter of customary international law by an 'unconstitutional' claimant.[161]

To be effective, at least where there is more than one claimant to governmental status, control must be consolidated. Ephemeral control will not suffice.[162] In other words, for an ostensible government to satisfy the requirement of effective control, its exercise of public authority must, at least where there are two or more

[157] Recall chapter 2, nn 114–15. On the criterion of effective control not undermining these freedoms, see section 4.2.2.4.3.

[158] Note that, '[b]eyond a certain limit, what is regarded as [an exercise of public authority] depends on the particular society [*viz* state], its history and traditions' (ILC, 'Articles on the Responsibility of States for Internationally Wrongful Acts' in Ybk ILC [2001] vol II(2), 31, 43 (art 5, comment 6)).

[159] See also *Tinoco* (n 12) 379; *Government of the Republic of Spain v SS 'Arantzazu Mendi'*, 264–5.

[160] See also *George W Hopkins (USA) v United Mexican States* (1926) IV UNRIAA 41, 45; UNGA, 'Official Records, 29th Session, 2301st Plenary Meeting' (n 67) §205 (Barbados); Lauterpacht (n 10) 88; Blix (n 32) 641.

[161] Compare Blix (n 32) 641–2; Talmon, 'Recognition of Opposition Groups as the Legitimate Representative of a People' (2013) 12 CJIL 219, 232–3.

[162] See *Cuculla v Mexico*, Mexico–US Claims Commission, reproduced in (1868) in Moore (n 59) 2873, 2877; Blix (n 32) 642.

rival claimants to governmental status, have a 'reasonable prospect of permanence and stability',[163] it being understood that a government can never guarantee its permanence.

The extent to which the state's population habitually obeys the assertion of authority by an ostensible government might be indicative of that claimant's prospects of permanence and stability.[164] Widespread opposition to a claimant's assertion of public authority may raise doubt as to the prospect of the latter's permanence and stability, even though the exercise of effective control does not require the popular approval of the ostensible government's claim to authority.[165] This might be at least part[166] of the reason why, since 2021, neither the Taliban in Afghanistan nor the SAC in Myanmar have received widespread acceptance of their respective claims to governmental status.[167]

Perhaps because of the evidential value that the habitual obedience of the state's population might have in relation to the effectiveness of an ostensible government's control, the allegiance of a state's population to an ostensible government might be indicative of the effectiveness of control by that claimant.[168] Not entirely dissimilarly, the requirement of effective control may be applied more loosely in respect of an ostensible government which is composed on an inclusive basis, as might be the case, for example, with an ostensible government that is composed by agreement of the main, if not all, persons or political movements previously competing for governmental status. The habitual obedience of a state's population to the assertion of authority by such a government might be presumed and its prospect of permanence and stability might be inferred from its inclusive character. Relevant examples in this regard might include the recognition of the Supreme National Council as Cambodia's government,[169] of the government of Afghanistan that was formed in accordance with the Peshawar Accord in 1992,[170] and of the GNA as the government of Libya, which was formed under the Libyan Political Agreement of 2015.[171]

[163] Jennings and Watts (n 10) 150. See also HL Debs, 28 April 1980, vol 408, col 1121–2WA; *Tinoco* (n 12) 378–80; Lauterpacht (n 10) 99.

[164] See Blix (n 32) 642–3; Roth (n 10) 138–41 and citations therein. See also Aréchaga (n 123); Lauterpacht (n 10) 88.

[165] See also Lauterpacht (n 10) 115. See further section 4.2.2.5.1.2. Recall also section 4.2.2.4.1.

[166] As regards other possible reasons for the reluctance to accept the governmental status of certain ostensible governments, recall section 3.4.1.

[167] In relation to Afghanistan, notable in this regard are the groups actively opposing Taliban rule, including the National Resistance Front, the Afghanistan Freedom Front, and the Afghanistan Islamic National and Liberation Movement. As for Myanmar, the SAC, for its part, faces widespread opposition to its rule.

[168] See also UNGA, 'Official Records, 29th Session, 2301st Plenary Meeting' (n 67) §40 (Somalia); *Western Sahara, Advisory Opinion* [1975] ICJ Rep 12, 44, §95, albeit in a different context.

[169] See eg Agreement Concerning Cambodia (n 95) art 3.

[170] See eg UNGA, 'Credentials of Representatives to the Forty-Ninth Session of the General Assembly: Second Report of the Credentials Committee' (9 December 1994) UN Doc A/49/517/Add.1, §§4–7.

[171] See 'Ministerial Meeting in Paris (France + Germany + United Kingdom + Italy + USA + EU): Statement on Libya' (13 March 2016), available at <https://www.diplomatie.gouv.fr/IMG/pdf/statement_on_libya_13th_march_cle82f4c6.pdf>.

Alternatively or additionally, the recognition of the governmental status of some inclusive ostensible governments might indicate that less extensive and less consolidated control may satisfy the requirement of effective control where there is only one claimant to governmental status in respect of a state. Perhaps the state's choice of its government can more readily be inferred in such circumstances. For example, the NTC was widely recognized as Libya's government at a time when 'a number of cities remain[ed] outside of the control of the NTC, and military action continue[d]'.[172] It is nevertheless unclear whether, in each of these cases the recognition of governmental status related only to the absence of any rival claim to governmental status rather than also or instead to the inclusive character of the ostensible governments in question. Indeed, in recognizing the governmental status of the NTC, at least certain states apparently took note of the fact that the NTC was operating 'through an inclusive political process'.[173]

In any event, neither the existence of only one claimant nor the existence of a claimant composed on an inclusive basis suggests that the qualification by an ostensible government for governmental status as a matter of customary international law may be based 'on the aspirations of the international community that effective control and free and fair elections will result from a negotiated government that includes all or most parties to the conflict'.[174] Indeed, 'free and fair elections' are in themselves of no relevance to the enjoyment of governmental status.[175]

As a separate consideration, effective control might be more readily satisfied where an ostensible government usurps control of the existing institutional machinery of a state as compared to where a claimant seeks to establish entirely novel institutions.[176] That said, the satisfaction of the requirement of effective control is ultimately dependent on the facts of each situation. The precise degree of control exercised by a claimant to governmental status or whether such control is sufficiently effective may be unclear. For example, at least part of the disagreement over the identity of the government of the Khmer Republic/Kampuchea arose from a difference in views over the extent of control exercised by the Lon Nol regime, on the one hand, and the GRUNK on the other.[177] More recently, Saint Vincent and the Grenadines raised a question as to both the effectiveness of the control exercised by the NTC and the information available in this regard.[178] As one commentator has

[172] UNGA, 'Official Records, 66th Session, 2nd Plenary Meeting' (n 14) 14. On recognition of the NTC, see n 23 above.

[173] See eg the UK Foreign Secretary's statement of 27 July 2011 in Hartmann, Shah, and Warbrick (eds), 'UKMIL' (2012) 82 BYIL 676, 742.

[174] Cf De Wet, *Military Assistance on Request and the Use of Force* (OUP 2020) 67–8.

[175] See section 4.2.2.5.1.2.

[176] *Georges Pinson (France) v United Mexican States* (1928) V UNRIAA 327, 422–4.

[177] See eg UNGA, 'Official Records, 29th Session, 2301st Plenary Meeting' (n 67) §108 (Mali), §213 (Zambia), §244 (Sudan). Cf ibid, §48 (Australia), §172 (UK), §§190–1 (Barbados), §§281–2 (Indonesia). But see also n 154 above and the accompanying text.

[178] UNGA, 'Official Records, 66th Session, 2nd Plenary Meeting' (n 14) 14 (Saint Vincent and the Grenadines).

put it, it is 'hard to quantify' stability.[179] The case of the Interim Government of Somalia, which was established in 1991 and which received some but not general recognition as the government of Somalia[180] may suggest the existence of uncertainty as regards the extent to which the threshold for effective control is lowered in respect of an ostensible government which is formed on an inclusive basis or in respect of the sole claimant to governmental status of a state.

4.2.2.4.3 Relevance of effective control to the state's freedom to choose its government

It has been suggested that the requirement of effective control operates as a 'presumptive guide' to ascertaining the 'popular will' of the population of a state.[181] While the exercise of effective control might indeed reflect the population's submission to the claimant's direction of the exercise of public authority within the state,[182] the presumption against limitations on state sovereignty favours an understanding of effective control as a means of ascertaining the state's choice of government, not of ascertaining the 'popular will' of a state's population.[183]

Indeed, the criterion of effective control is to be understood as comprising part of a generic basis for determining that a state has chosen a specific political system, a particular disposal of public power as its constitution, and an 'unconstitutional' claimant to governmental status as its government.[184] This explains why customary international law does not require and appears historically not to have required the exercise of effective control for the attainment, let alone the retention, of governmental status by a 'constitutional' claimant.[185] The generic criterion of effective control is relevant only in respect of an ostensible government which cannot be taken to reflect the state's choice of government as expressed in a more direct way, namely through its constitution.

The change in the customary international legal framework for the enjoyment of governmental status since the early 1990s—pursuant to which autonomous effective control no longer suffices for a successful claim to governmental status where there exists a rival autonomous 'constitutional' claim[186]—reflects the further prioritization by international law of what is perhaps the most direct means by which a state may express its choice of government. Since the early 1990s, customary international law defers to the generic criterion of effective control only

[179] Blix (n 32) 642.

[180] For the apparent recognition of this ostensible government, see eg UNSC, 'Official Records, 3060th Meeting' (17 March 1992) UN Doc S/PV.3060, 2. (On the recognition of governmental status by international organizations, see sections 5.4.1–5.4.2.) But see also eg *Republic of Somalia v Woodhouse Drake & Carey (Suisse) SA and others* [1993] QB 54, 67–8.

[181] Roth (n 10) 419.

[182] See n 164 above and accompanying text.

[183] See further 4.2.2.5.1.2 on the absence of a clear indication to the contrary, including in the light of state practice and the right of peoples to self-determination.

[184] See also section 4.2.1.

[185] Recall section 4.2.2.4.1.

[186] Ibid.

in the absence of an autonomous 'constitutional' claimant; a claimant would reflect the state's choice as expressed more directly by it. Historically, the exercise of effective control by an autonomous 'unconstitutional' claimant was taken as an indication that a state had chosen fundamentally to change its constitution and to have an 'unconstitutional' government, even in the presence of a rival autonomous 'constitutional' claim.[187] In the presence of an autonomous 'constitutional' claimant, a state is no longer deemed to have opted for a fundamental change to its constitution and for an 'unconstitutional' government. As a matter of present-day customary international law, a state is taken to have opted for such changes only where an autonomous 'unconstitutional' claimant exercises effective control in the absence of a rival autonomous 'constitutional' claim.[188]

4.2.2.5 Other Considerations?

4.2.2.5.1 A 'legitimate' basis

The term 'legitimate' in characterizing an ostensible government has been, and continues to be, used in several different senses. It may be used to refer to an ostensible government that enjoys or that is seen by the person or entity using the term to enjoy governmental status as a matter of customary international law.[189] The term may instead be used to refer to the 'constitutionality' of a claim to governmental status.[190] The term 'legitimate' and its antonym are sometimes also used in relation to an ostensible government as a means of expressing approval or disapproval of the basis of its claim to power or of its conduct without this necessarily encompassing a view as to the 'constitutionality' of, or the qualification for governmental status by, the claimant in question.[191] Given the different senses in which the term 'legitimate' is used, care must be taken as regards the evidential value assigned to practice that refers to the 'legitimacy' or 'illegitimacy' of an ostensible

[187] Recall chapter 2, n 8 and section 4.2.2.3.

[188] Recall section 4.2.2.4.1.

[189] See eg UNGA, 'Official Records, 28th Session, 2189th Plenary Meeting' (4 December 1973) UN Doc A/PV.2189, §76 (Mauritania); UNGA, 'Official Records, 29th Session, 2320th Plenary Meeting' (16 December 1974) UN Doc A/PV.2320, §41 (Albania); UNGA, 'Official Records, 24th Session, 1805th Plenary Meeting' (10 November 1969) UN Doc A/PV.1805, §88 (Mali); UNSC res 661 (6 August 1990) UN Doc S/RES/661, §9; UNGA res 63/301 (1 July 2009) UN Doc A/RES/63/301, §2; Guymon (ed), *Digest of United States Practice in International Law* [2019], available at <https://www.state.gov/wp-content/uploads/2020/09/2019-Digest-Complete.pdf>, 241. See also Talmon (n 10) 537; Crawford, *Brownlie's Principles of Public International Law* (OUP 2019) 135; Regulations concerning the Laws and Customs of War on Land, art 43 (annexed to Convention (IV) respecting the Laws and Customs of War on Land (adopted 18 October 1907, entered into force 26 January 1910), available at <http://ihl-databases.icrc.org/assets/treaties/195-IHL-19-EN.pdf>); *Legal Consequences for States of the Continued Presence of South Africa in Namibia (South West Africa) notwithstanding Security Council Resolution 276 (1970), Advisory Opinion* [1971] ICJ Rep 16, 218 (Separate Opinion of Judge de Castro); *Mohamed v Breish* (n 93) §35(2).

[190] To avoid confusion, the present work avoids using the term 'legitimacy' as a synonym for '"constitutionality"'.

[191] See eg Talmon (n 161) 238–9.

government in ascertaining the criteria for governmental status under customary international law.

It has been said that an ostensible government must, at least in certain circumstances, have a 'legitimate' claim to governmental status—by which is meant a claim founded on some specific source from which the claimant derives its authority—in order to qualify for governmental status as a matter of customary international law.[192] While certain instances of state practice can be taken to support the position that the claim of an ostensible government must be 'legitimate' in this sense in order for it to qualify for governmental status as a matter customary international law, the existence of such a criterion is not to be readily inferred since it would impose a limitation on the presumptive sovereign freedoms of each state to choose its constitution and its political system.[193] In any event, the bases of authority suggested as necessary for the enjoyment of governmental status have varied over time, and there is ultimately too little evidence in favour of, and a substantial amount of evidence against, any requirement that an ostensible government have some 'legitimate' claim to governmental status in order to qualify as a matter of customary international law as the government of a state.[194] Two of the more prominently-alleged bases of the 'legitimacy' of a government of a state have been some specific socio-political affiliation and, more recently, democratic representativity.

4.2.2.5.1.1 An affiliation with a specific family or political party

The need for an ostensible government to have a 'legitimate' basis in order to qualify as a state's government was invoked by the European hereditary monarchies at a time when the concepts of state and government were not as distinct as they are today.[195] In the early nineteenth century, the view 'that a dynasty enjoyed historical rights to rule a state and, thus, the prince continued to be sovereign even if in fact displaced from his throne' informed relevant practice,[196] although this practice may have simply reflected the presumption in favour of incumbent governments or an exception to the requirement of effective control in respect of 'constitutional' claimants to governmental status.[197] In any event, it eventually became

[192] See eg D'Aspremont, 'Legitimacy of Governments in the Age of Democracy' (2006) 38 NYUJILP 877, 910; Redaelli (n 129) 131, 151; Weller, 'Myanmar: Testing the Democratic Norm in International Law' (*EJIL:Talk!*, 30 March 2021), available at <http://ejiltalk.org/myanmar-testing-the-democratic-norm-in-international-law>.

[193] Recall section 4.2.1.

[194] See also Talmon (n 10) 536–7.

[195] On the distinction between a state and its government, see chapter 1, n 2. On the earlier character of the relationship between a state and its government under international law, see Watts, 'The Legal Position in International Law of Heads of States, Heads of Governments and Foreign Ministers' (1994) 247 Hague *Recueil* 9, 35; O'Connell, *State Succession in Municipal Law and International Law*, vol 1 (CUP 1967) 5–6.

[196] Grant, 'Defining Statehood: The Montevideo Convention and Its Discontents' (1999) 37 CJTL 403, 419. See, generally, ibid, 418–20; Lauterpacht (n 10) 99–106.

[197] Recall section 4.2.2.4.1.

clear, especially once the distinction between state and government was more definitively established, that as a matter of customary international law a claim to governmental status could be successful without a basis in an established monarchical system, hereditary or otherwise. Monarchical legitimacy eventually ceased to be a basis on which states withheld recognition from ostensible governments of other states.[198]

While it remains common for the government of a state to be comprised of persons that share a political or social connection (for example, a common affiliation to a specific political party or family), there is virtually nothing to suggest that such a connection is necessary for the enjoyment of governmental status as a matter of international law. A state remains free as a matter of international law to have a 'coalition' government (that is, a government composed of persons affiliated with different political parties) or a government whose constituent members share no political or social affiliation with its predecessor. The existence of such governments is uncontroversial as a matter of customary international law. Given, however, the significance of the 'constitutionality' of a claim for the enjoyment of governmental status under international law,[199] the political or social affiliation of an ostensible government will be relevant to assessing its claim to governmental status where the constitution of the state requires that its government has some affiliation with a specific political party or family.

4.2.2.5.1.2 Democratic representativity

Considerations of the 'legitimacy' of a claim to governmental status took a different form in the early twentieth century.[200] In 1907, in apparent furtherance of the so-called 'Tobar doctrine', five Central American states concluded a treaty under which they were obliged not to recognize an 'unconstitutional' government of any 'of the five Republics . . . so long as the freely elected representatives of the people thereof have not constitutionally reorganized the country'.[201] In other words, these states undertook not to accept in respect of any other state party the governmental status of any claimant whose claim had no basis in either the existing constitution or any novel constitution agreed by democratically-elected representatives. In 1923, the same states concluded a treaty in which they undertook the same obligation as in the 1907 treaty, alongside some additional obligations concerning the recognition of certain other 'unconstitutional' claims to governmental status.[202]

[198] See also Peterson (n 31) 37.

[199] Recall section 4.2.2.3.

[200] Isolated earlier instances of relevant practice also exist. See Peterson (n 31) 37 and the references therein.

[201] Additional Convention to the General Treaty of Peace and Amity of 1907 (adopted 20 December 1907) reproduced in (1908) 2 AJIL Supp 229, art I.

[202] The states undertook 'not to acknowledge the recognition' of an 'unconstitutional' claimant to governmental status even if 'the freely elected representatives of the people have . . . constitutionally reorganized the country' insofar as the situation of a person elected to one of a number of specified posts fell within one of the specific categories of situations, including but not limited to having been involved

These provisions provided for considerations of democratic representativity as informing what the states parties to the treaties in question may have recognized as a successful change to a state's constitution and consequently also as the possession by a state of an 'unconstitutional' government.[203] They did not generally require that a claimant be democratically representative in order to enjoy governmental status. In any event, the states parties did not generally adopt an approach consistent with these treaties when it came to claimants to governmental status in respect of non-party states or states parties. As it was, by 1934, the states parties had either denounced these treaties or no longer supported the approach of these treaties on the question of recognition of governmental status.[204] As for the practice of non-party states on the recognition of governments, this was not generally consistent with these treaties.[205] Indeed, throughout the first half of the twentieth century, any practice to suggest that either of these treaties reflected customary international law was far from general.[206]

Some relevant practice nevertheless emerged in the subsequent decades that might be taken to support the relevance of democratic representativity to the recognition and enjoyment of governmental status.[207] More recently, especially since the end of the Cold War, it has occasionally been suggested that an ostensible government of a state may enjoy governmental status as a matter of customary international law simply because it is democratically representative[208]—that is, because its claim to governmental status is based on a genuine electoral process in which the vast majority of adult citizens or residents of that state have had the opportunity to participate.[209]

in one or more specified ways in the emergence of the 'unconstitutional' claim. They also undertook not to recognize 'a government which arises from election to power of a citizen expressly and unquestionably disqualified by the Constitution of his country as eligible to election as President, Vice-President or Chief of State designate'. See General Treaty of Peace and Amity (adopted 7 February 1923, entered into force 24 November 1924) art II, reproduced in (1923) 17 AJIL Supp 117.

[203] Recall chapter 2, n 8 and accompanying text.

[204] See, generally, Woolsely, 'The Recognition of the Government of El Salvador' (1934) 28 AJIL 325; Stansifer, 'Application of the Tobar Doctrine to Central America' (1967) 23 The Americas 251.

[205] Some states, most notably the USA, did occasionally refuse recognition on such grounds. See Peterson (n 60) 60–1; Menon, *The Law of Recognition in International Law: Basic Principles* (Edwin Mellen Press 1994) 76; Woolsely (n 204) 328.

[206] See also *Affaire du Guano (Chili/France)* (1901) XV UNRIAA 77, 350; *Tinoco* (n 12) 381. See, generally, Menon (n 205) 91–2; Ben Achour, 'Changements anticonstitutionnels de gouvernement et droit international' (2015) 379 Hague *Recueil* 397, 439–41, §§73–9.

[207] See eg Peterson, 'Political Use of Recognition: The Influence of the International System' (1981–1982) 34 World Politics 324, 336 on the Betancourt doctrine and related practice.

[208] For some of the proponents of this position, see nn 216, 219, and 221 below.

[209] As one commentator has noted, 'there is no unitary definition of democracy in the scholarly debate' in relation to the criteria for governmental status as a matter of customary international law, but 'a procedural definition that focuses on a free and fair electoral process seems to constitute the smallest common denominator. References to democracy in the international legal discourse tend to regard free and fair elections as a minimum requirement for democratic governance': De Wet, 'The Modern Practice of Intervention by Invitation in Africa and Its Implications for the Prohibition of the Use of Force' (2015) 26 EJIL 979, 984–5. See also Vidmar, *Democratic Statehood in International Law: The Emergence of New States in Post-Cold War Practice* (Hart Publishing 2013) 15–19.

In terms of state practice, there have indeed been situations in which a democratically-representative ostensible government has received general recognition as a state's government over an autonomous rival claimant, including where the latter exercised effective control over the territory and population of the state. This was the case with the claim of Alassane Ouattara in respect of Côte d'Ivoire in 2010 and of Adama Barrow in respect of The Gambia in 2016, as well as with the claim of Jean-Bertrand Aristide in respect of Haiti between 1991 and 1994 and of Manuel Zelaya in respect of Honduras in 2009.[210] At the same time, there has continued to exist a number of claimants to governmental status which have lacked a plausible claim to democratic representativity but which states have generally accepted as enjoying governmental status, sometimes after overthrowing a democratically-elected government. Examples include the government of The Gambia in 1994 and of the Republic of the Congo in 1997,[211] as well as the transitional authority established in Sudan in 2019. A claimant may continue to be recognized, moreover, as the government of a state where a democratic election has demonstrated overwhelming support for a rival claimant. Albeit only in 1990, the 'National Coalition Government of Union of Burma', comprised of members of the National Legal for Democracy, received virtually no international support for its claim to governmental status despite the latter's electoral victory.[212] Instead, the military authority then known as the State Law and Order Restoration Council (SLORC) continued to be recognized as Myanmar's government. All of this strongly suggests that democratic representativity is unnecessary for the enjoyment of governmental status as a matter of customary international law. It suggests, moreover, that democratic representativity is insufficient for the enjoyment of governmental status.[213]

Even those who nevertheless claim that 'democratic representativity' is at least in certain circumstances relevant to the enjoyment of governmental status as a matter of customary international law seem unable to ascertain or at least agree on the conditions that would satisfy this requirement and the broader legal framework in which this requirement ostensibly operates.

For example, in 2010, one author, who acknowledges that '[n]othing has yet happened to demonstrate that the international community posits democracy, however defined, as a *sine qua non* of governmental legitimacy',[214] expressed

[210] For details, recall nn 79–81 above. For the view that such practice demonstrates the application of 'democratic criteria', see eg Fox, 'Intervention by Invitation' in Weller (ed), *The Oxford Handbook of the Use of Force in International Law* (OUP 2015) 816, 835–7. See also Crawford, 'Democracy and the Body of International Law' in Fox and Roth (eds), *Democratic Governance and International Law* (CUP 2000) 91, 117.

[211] See n 77 above.

[212] See Talmon (n 32) 315.

[213] See also UNGA, 'Official Records, 29th Session, 2281st Plenary Meeting' (12 November 1974) UN Doc A/PV.2281, §166 (US); Talmon (n 10) 533–4; Crawford (n 35) 150–5; Marks, 'What Has Become of the Emerging Right to Democratic Governance?' (2011) 22 EJIL 507, 511–13; De Wet (n 209) 984–90; Crawford (n 88) 282, §506.

[214] Roth (n 10) 417.

the view that '*at least some electoral results*—whether because of the presence of officially-invited international monitors or the magnitude of the electoral mandate, or both—[may be relevant to the assessment of governmental status]'.[215] The same author suggests that the results of democratic elections may comprise 'unambiguous manifestations of popular repudiation of the ruling apparatus', in which case these election are said to be relevant to the identification of the government of a state as a matter of customary international law.[216] But this author accepts the existence of 'limitations' to this view since practice does not generally support it.[217] In 2010, the same commentator posited that 'effective control . . . continues to play a crucial role [in relation to governmental status]', with democratic legitimacy being 'destined to have an ad hoc quality'.[218]

As a further example, in 2006, another commentator expressed the view that 'democratic origins can usually overcome a government's ineffectiveness',[219] while in 2011, this same commentator suggested that 'the emphasis put on the democratic origin of governments during the 1989–2010 period is ebbing away'.[220] In 2021, one other author posited that, '[w]hile the universal reach of the democratic principle can no longer be doubted, it has to be admitted that there are significant limitations to its application'.[221] Other authors accept that democratic representativity is not generally decisive, if at all relevant, to the enjoyment of governmental status as a matter of customary international law.[222] The acknowledgement of such variation in practice as regards the relevance of democratic representativity to governmental status has contributed to the suggestion that customary international law possesses no objective framework for the assessment of governmental status.[223]

A distinct attempt to explain the divergence in practice as regards the significance of democratic representativity to governmental status as a matter of customary international law has taken the form of a suggestion that democratic representativity may be acquiring significance as a matter of regional customary international law.[224] One issue with this suggestion is that there is no specific region within which democratic representativity has been consistently relevant. The

215 Ibid, 384 (emphasis in the original).

216 Ibid, 416.

217 Ibid, 416, 418.

218 Roth, 'Secessions, Coups and the International Rule of Law: Assessing the Decline of the Effective Control Doctrine' (2010) 11 MJIL 393, 396.

219 D'Aspremont (n 192).

220 D'Aspremont, 'The Rise and Fall of Democracy Governance in International Law: A Reply to Susan Marks' (2011) 22 EJIL 549, 561.

221 Weller (n 192). See also Redaelli (n 129) 131, 151.

222 See eg Murphy, 'Democratic Legitimacy and the Recognition of States and Governments' in Fox and Roth (n 210) 123, 143–51; Vidmar, 'Abusive Governments as a Threat' in Footer and others (eds), *Security in International Law* (Hart Publishing 2016) 249, 254; De Wet, 'The Role of Democratic Legitimacy in the Recognition of Governments in Africa since the End of the Cold War' (2019) 17 IJCL 470, 470; De Wet (n 174) 72–3.

223 Recall chapter 1, n 27.

224 See Wippman, 'Pro-Democratic Intervention', in Weller (ed) (n 210) 797, 801.

inconsistency in state practice concerning the recognition of governmental status as it relates to democratic representativity extends throughout the world.

Ultimately, both the practice that appears to accord weight to the democratic representativity of an ostensible government in assessing its claim to governmental status and the practice which suggests that democratic representativity is irrelevant to the enjoyment of governmental status can generally be explained on the basis of the traditional international legal criteria for governmental status alongside the enhanced privilege accorded to 'constitutional' claimants since the early 1990s.[225] Indeed, the result of a democratic election has been relevant to the 'constitutionality' of every ostensible government whose democratic representativity appears to have been relevant to its enjoyment of governmental status as a matter of customary international law.[226]

Even if it were equally plausible that democratic representativity is of direct relevance to the enjoyment of governmental status as a matter of customary international law in certain circumstances (for example, only if there are rival claimants of which only one is democratically elected[227]), the presumptive sovereign freedom of each state to choose its political system would militate in favour of the explanation that is based on the enhanced privilege accorded to 'constitutional' governments rather than on an 'application of the democratic norm'. In contrast to the privilege accorded to 'constitutional' claimants, the direct relevance of democratic representativity to the enjoyment of governmental status as a matter of customary international law would limit the freedom of each state to choose its political system.[228]

That said, democratic representativity as a criterion for governmental status does not even appear to be equally plausible to the alternative explanation of relevant practice which concerns the traditional international legal criteria alongside the enhanced privilege accorded by international law to 'constitutional' claimants. For example, some states accepted Mr Turchynov as President of Ukraine before Victor Yanukovych resigned and despite not having been democratically elected, apparently on the ground that his appointment was 'constitutional', even though Mr Yanukovych had been democratically elected.[229] Moreover, the disagreement

[225] This does not preclude the existence of the occasional instance of state practice which appears not to be explained on this basis. See eg 'Canada Will Not Recognize Taliban as Afghan Gov't—PM Trudeau' (*Reuters*, 17 August 2021), available at <http://reuters.com/world/asia-pacific/canada-will-not-recognize-taliban-afghan-govt-pm-trudeau-2021-08-17>. But even this can be explained on alternative grounds, specifically on the different meanings of the term 'recognition'. Recall section 3.2.1.

[226] See also Weller (n 192) on the circumstances in which he has said 'the democratic principle' applies, which can be seen to coincide with the situations in which democratic representativity is relevant to the 'constitutionality' of an ostensible government.

[227] For such a suggestion, see Redaelli (n 129) 131, 138–9, who nevertheless accepts (at ibid, 146) the existence of practice that does not fit her approach. See also ibid, 151. She ultimately considers that 'international law does not offer objective criteria to determine whom the government of a particular state is'. See ibid, 119.

[228] Recall section 4.2.1.

[229] See section 4.2.2.3.

among states as to the identity of Venezuela's governments since 2019 centres not directly on the democratic representativity but on the 'constitutionality' of each claimant.[230] Also, the NUG—which claims power not on the basis of the existing constitution of Myanmar but on 'the authority bestowed by the people's mandate resultant of all parties' democratic election held in 2020'[231]—has not generally been accepted as the government of Myanmar.[232]

The significance of democratic representativity to the identity of a state's government as a matter of present-day customary international law is thus indirect and restricted to situations where there is a 'constitutional' claim and where the 'constitutionality' of a claimant is assessed at least in part on the basis of the democratic representativity of that claimant. In other words, a democratic election is relevant to the enjoyment of governmental status under customary international law only insofar as such an election comprises the basis of a 'constitutional' claim to governmental status. For this reason, it is worth noting that the result of an election might not provide a basis for a 'constitutional' claim to governmental status. The 1990 election in Myanmar might be an example in this regard. At least in the post-election view of the incumbent government, the election was held solely to elect a committee tasked with drafting a new constitution and not a political party that would be constitutionally empowered to direct the exercise of public authority on Myanmar's behalf.[233] Another possible example concerns the 2020 election in Myanmar, the result of which was to determine the composition of its central legislature and which did not, in itself, provide a direct basis for a constitutionally-valid claim to power. The new government was to be elected by the national legislature subsequent to the commencement of its new term. It may be for this reason that the NUG—which is composed of persons who were elected in the legislative elections 2020, rather than persons who were elected to government by the legislature, with the legislature not having had an opportunity to commence its new term—does not claim to be the 'constitutional' government of Myanmar.[234]

The occasional suggestion in state practice that the identity of a state's government depends on the choice of that state's population in the latter's quality as a

[230] Recall eg chapter 3, n 333.

[231] See n 118 above and accompanying text.

[232] See chapter 5, nn 21 and 86.

[233] See SLORC, Declaration 1/90 of 27 July 1990, available at <https://natlex.ilo.org/dyn/natlex2/r/natlex/fe/details?p3_isn=79571>, §15. See also ibid, §§2, 11–14. That said, the continued recognition of Myanmar's incumbent government after this election preceded the first time there was consensus on the enhanced significance of the 'constitutionality' of a claim to governmental status to the enjoyment of governmental status as a matter of customary international law. The practice concerning the identity of Myanmar's government at that time may instead be explained by reference to the traditional customary international legal framework for the enjoyment of governmental status, according to which an autonomous claimant in effective control over the state's territory and population enjoyed governmental status, regardless of a subsisting claim by a 'constitutional' claimant. Recall section 4.2.2.4.1.

[234] Recall section 4.2.2.3.

people[235] appears to be a result of the not-uncommon use of the terms 'state' and 'people' as interchangeable.[236] A notable example in this regard is in the first preambular sentence of the UN Charter, which records the determination of 'the peoples of the United Nations' and the agreement of '[their] respective Governments', although the Charter was formally concluded by states through their respective governments. As another example, it has been said that preventing a state's government from representing that state in a particular context 'would constitute interference in the domestic affairs of the people, whose exclusive right it is to choose their own political regime or system of government',[237] even though it is uncontroversial that, at that time, it was the state that enjoyed the presumptive sovereign freedom to choose its political regime and system of government.[238]

As a formal legal matter, however, a people is distinct from a state. Accordingly, despite what has been said,[239] the right of a people to self-determination does not necessarily support the notion that the identification of the government of a state as a matter of customary international law involves the ascertainment of the will of the population of that state. Nor does the possibility that at least in certain circumstances the government of a state is the representative of that state's people[240] necessarily support the position that governmental status as a matter of customary international law is ascertained at least in part by the views of the population of a state. There is no clear indication that the right of a people to self-determination encompasses a right of a people to choose its representative in such a way.[241]

While there is no inherent reason why international law may not develop otherwise, the identity of a state's government under customary international law is not at present dependent on the expression by the population of a state of its support, through democratic elections, for some ostensible government.

That democratic representativity is unnecessary for the enjoyment of governmental status as a matter of customary international law does not preclude the possibility that a state consents to the limitation of one or more of its rights when it is possessed of a government which has not been democratically elected.[242]

[235] See eg UNGA, 'Official Records, 29th Session, 2301st Plenary Meeting' (n 67) §34 (Somalia), §166 (Grenada), §283 (Indonesia).

[236] See also Crawford, 'The Rights of Peoples: "Peoples" or "Governments"?' in Crawford (ed), *The Rights of Peoples* (Clarendon Press 1988) 55, 67, who suggests that the reiteration of certain international legal rules that substitute 'people' for 'state' 'are merely affirmative reformulations' of existing rules.

[237] UNGA, 'Official Records, 29th Session, 2301st Plenary Meeting' (n 67) §34 (Somalia). For another possible example of the use of the term 'people' as interchangeable with 'state' in a different context, see O'Keefe, 'The Meaning of "Cultural Property" under the 1954 Hague Convention' (1999) 46 NILR 26, 53.

[238] Recall chapter 2, nn 114–15.

[239] Roth (n 10) 414–15.

[240] Recall chapter 3, n 253 and accompanying text.

[241] Cf eg Human Rights Committee, 'General Comment No. 25' (1996) UN Doc CCPR/C/21/Rev.1/Add.7, §2.

[242] See eg sections 5.6.2.1.1–5.6.2.1.2.

4.2.2.5.2 Willingness or ability to ensure compliance with international law

There is some state practice that might or in any event has been taken to suggest that the willingness of an ostensible government to ensure compliance with some or all of the international legal obligations of the state of which it claims to be the government is necessary for the enjoyment of governmental status as a matter of customary international law.[243] Two of the more prominent recent examples[244] in this regard concern the identity of the government of Afghanistan between 1996 and 2001 and of Libya in 2011.[245] Another possible example relates to Afghanistan since the Taliban offensive in 2021. A closer look at the practice concerning these situations demonstrates, however, that there is little clear support for a customary international legal requirement according to which an ostensible government of a state must be willing to ensure that state's compliance with international law in order for that claimant to enjoy governmental status.

For example, much of the state practice on the identity of Afghanistan's government between 1996 and 2001 arose in relation to the credentials of ostensible representatives of Afghanistan to the UNGA.[246] During this time, the Taliban was not generally recognized as the government of Afghanistan. Indeed, some states denied its governmental status. More specifically, in 1996, when the Taliban—which controlled most of Afghanistan's territory and population, including the territory and population of Kabul—first presented credentials to the UN ostensibly in Afghanistan's name, some states expressed the view that the rival authority operating under Burhanuddin Rabbani's leadership was still the government of Afghanistan.[247] In subsequent years, until the 2001 peace process, Burhanuddin Rabbani's government continued to represent Afghanistan at the UN, albeit without acceptance of the credentials presented by his government,[248] perhaps because of a reluctance to recognize this transitional government.[249] For what it is

[243] See eg Siekmann (n 123) 237–8; Vidmar (n 222) 255–60; d'Aspremont (n 192) 910–11.

[244] For another recent example of practice where the willingness of an ostensible government of a state to ensure compliance with the latter's international legal obligations appears relevant to the derecognition of governmental status, see *The 'Maduro Board' of the Central Bank of Venezuela v The 'Guaidó Board' of the Central Bank of Venezuela* [2021] UKSC 57, §18.

[245] See eg Wolfrum and Philipp, 'The Status of the Taliban: Their Obligations and Rights under International Law' (2002) 6 MPUNYB 559, 573, 575; Vidmar, 'International Community and Abuses of Sovereign Power' (2014) 35 LLR 193, 196.

[246] On the evidential value of this practice, see section 5.4.2.

[247] UNGA, 'Credentials of Representatives to the Fifty-First Session of the General Assembly: First Report of the Credentials Committee' (23 October 1996) UN Doc A/51/548, §§6, 10–11.

[248] See chapter 5, n 88.

[249] On the possible reluctance to recognize certain transitional governments, see the text accompanying chapter 3, n 206. On the transitional character of Burhanuddin Rabbani's government, see Peshawar Accord, 24 April 1992 (n 91); Islamabad Accord of 7 March 1993, reproduced in 'Letter Dated 17 March 1993 from the Charges d'Affaires A.I. of the Permanent Mission of Afghanistan to the United Nations Addressed to the Secretary-General' (19 March 1993) UN Doc S/25435, Annex I, §§1, 3.

worth, prominent Afghan political figures eventually acknowledged Burhanuddin Rabbani's position of authority during this time.[250]

While it is apparent that between 1996 and 2001 the Taliban was not generally recognized as the government of Afghanistan, it is far from clear, in contrast to what has been suggested,[251] that the Taliban's disregard for certain international legal obligations was the reason for which states did not consider the Taliban to comprise the government of Afghanistan. Both the presumption in favour of incumbent governments[252] and the preferential treatment accorded by international law to 'constitutional' claimants[253] can explain the widespread non-recognition of the governmental status of the Taliban between 1996 and 2001[254] and the continued if limited express acceptance of the governmental status of the ostensible government of Burhanuddin Rabbani.

As for Libya, there is some—yet only limited—practice directly linking the continued enjoyment of governmental status by the authority acting under Muammar Qadhafi's leadership to respect for certain international legal obligations.[255] Again, the general acceptance of the NTC as the government of Libya and the implicit concomitant derecognition of the Qadhafi regime is explicable by reference to the existing customary international legal framework for the enjoyment of governmental status.[256]

As regards Afghanistan since 2021, some states indicated that '[t]he legitimacy of any future government depends on the approach it now takes to uphold its international obligations and commitments to ensure a stable Afghanistan',[257] but this does not necessarily involve a denial of governmental status.[258] Not dissimilarly, statements along the lines that the Taliban 'cannot expect to enjoy any legitimacy' if it 'continues to abuse basic human rights'[259] need not be understood as concerning the denial of the Taliban's governmental status under customary international law. Additionally, while some states have expressed their unwillingness to recognize a

250 See the Agreement on Provisional Arrangements in Afghanistan Pending the Re-Establishment of Permanent Government Institutions of 2001, UN Doc S/2001/1154, fifth recital, which acknowledges Burhanuddin Rabbani's 'readiness to transfer power'.

251 Recall n 245 above.

252 See n 124 above and accompanying text.

253 Recall section 4.2.2.3.

254 On the limited recognition of the Taliban's governmental status, see eg Wolfrum and Philipp (n 245) 566.

255 See eg 'Libya/National Transitional Council—Statement by Alain Juppé, Ministre d'Etat, Minister of Foreign and European Affairs' (7 June 2011), available at <http://in.ambafrance.org/Libya-National-Transitional> and, in respect of the conduct of the claimant in question more generally, Hartmann, Shah, and Warbrick (n 173) 741, 742.

256 See n 25 above and accompanying text.

257 See eg 'G7 Leaders Statement on Afghanistan' (24 August 2021), available at <http://gov.uk/government/news/g7-leaders-statement-on-afghanistan-24-august-2021>.

258 On the different uses of the word 'legitimacy', recall section 4.2.2.5.1.

259 UNSC, 'Official Records, 8834th Meeting' (16 August 2021) UN Doc S/PV.8834 (provisional) 7 (UK).

government 'that harbors terrorist groups',[260] the term 'recognition' may have been used in a narrower sense that does not concern non-acceptance of governmental status.[261] The doubt as to whether the statements invoking certain international legal obligations do indeed express views on the qualification for governmental status, coupled with uncertainty as to the Taliban's enjoyment of sufficiently-effective control[262] and the apparent recognition by some states of the Taliban as the government of Afghanistan,[263] suggests the development of no requirement of willingness to ensure compliance with international legal obligations for the enjoyment of governmental status under customary international law.

In light of the above, the assessment of one commentator, writing in relation to practice until the late 1940s, that the willingness of an ostensible government of a state to ensure the state's compliance with its international legal obligations did not appear to have 'gained wide acceptance' in state practice on the recognition of governments[264] remains accurate as regards contemporary state practice on the recognition of governments.[265]

In addition to the limited practice which might be taken to support the relevance of a claimant's willingness to ensure compliance with international law, the existence of alternative and no-less-plausible explanations for this practice which would not limit the presumptive sovereign freedom of each state to choose its government ought to be preferred.[266] Weight must be given also to the practice of states which expressly distinguishes the conduct of an ostensible government as regards flagrant non-compliance with certain international legal obligations from the question of governmental status.[267]

As for the occasional reference to a requirement that a claimant is able to comply with the international legal obligations of the state in order to qualify

[260] See eg Iqbal, 'US to Recognize Taliban Only If They Respect Basic Rights, Says Blinken' (*Dawn*, 16 August 2021), available at <http://dawn.com/news/1640919>.

[261] On the use of the term 'recognition' in different ways, recall section 3.2.1.

[262] Recall n 167 above.

[263] For possible instances of recognition of the Taliban's governmental status, see UNSC, 'Official Records, 9137th Meeting' (27 September 2022) UN Doc S/PV.9137 (provisional) 19 (China); 'Joint Statement of the Participants in the Moscow Format Consultations on Afghanistan' (20 October 2021), available at <http://archive.mid.ru/en/foreign_policy/news/-/asset_publisher/cKNonkJE02Bw/content/id/4913908>, §7; 'First Diplomat of Taliban-Led Afghanistan Accredited in Moscow' (*RFEL*, 31 March 2022), available at <http://rferl.org/a/moscow-accredits-afghan-taliban-diplomat/31779443.html>. (On recognition of governmental status by the receiving state's acceptance of a person as a diplomatic agent of the sending state, recall section 3.3.2.2.1.2.) Recall also chapter 3, nn 29–33 and the accompanying text.

[264] Lauterpacht (n 10) 110. See, generally, ibid, 109–14.

[265] For the view that this criterion is invoked inconsistently and by only a few states, see also Jennings and Watts (n 10) 153. Note chapter 3, n 254 on the distinct possibility that the government of a state may, on such grounds, no longer qualify as the representative of the people of that state.

[266] Recall section 4.2.1.

[267] See eg UNGA, 'Official Records, 35th Session, 35th Plenary Meeting' (n 63) §90 (Pakistan), §133 (Zaire), §163 (New Zealand), §209 (Philippines), §236 (Haiti), §240 (Canada), §245 (Federal Republic of Germany); UNGA, 'Credentials of Representatives to the Thirty-Sixth Session of the General Assembly' (n 67) §12 (USA).

for governmental status,[268] this is best seen as concerning effective control,[269] although the requisite degree of control does not vary according to the international legal obligations incumbent on the state whose government's identity is under consideration.

4.2.2.5.3 Not being in consequence of or amounting to the violation of a peremptory norm

International law might preclude the success of certain claims consequent upon a violation of an obligation arising under a peremptory norm of general international law. This appears to be the case for claims to statehood which are consequent upon the violation of at least certain peremptory norms.[270] As a separate matter, and as again appears to be the case in respect of claims to statehood, international law may preclude the success of a claim which, if accepted, would amount to the violation of a peremptory norm.[271] In either of these circumstances, international law would consequently also preclude the enjoyment of governmental status by an ostensible government of a putative state in precluding the putative state from attaining statehood on account of the claim to statehood resulting in, or being consequent upon, the violation of a peremptory norm. Possible examples in this regard concern the 'illegal racist minority régime' in Southern Rhodesia and the executive authority of the Turkish Republic of Northern Cyprus, respectively.[272]

As the above rules might be taken to suggest, customary international law may preclude the enjoyment by an ostensible government of governmental status in respect of an existing state where the claim of that ostensible government is consequent upon—or where, if accepted, it would amount to the violation of—an obligation arising under a peremptory norm. But each of these possibilities merits separate assessment on the basis of relevant practice. At the same time, as a general matter concerning both of these possible rules, the limitations imposed by international law on the success of certain claims on account of their being in consequence of or amounting to a violation of an obligation arising under a peremptory norm need not extend to a claim to governmental status in respect of an existing

[268] See eg Hackworth, *Digest of International Law*, vol 1 (US Government Printing Office 1940) 17; UNSC, 'Official Records, 899th Meeting' (n 76) §37 (Argentina); UNGA, 'Official Records, 22nd Session, 1602nd Plenary Meeting' (21 November 1967) UN Doc A/PV.1602, §5 (Iraq).

[269] See also Marek (n 32) 58; Lauterpacht (n 10) 109; Moore (n 76) 250, that to qualify as the government of a state, an 'unconstitutional' claimant to governmental status ought to be 'sufficiently established . . . to discharge [the state's] external obligations'.

[270] See, generally, Crawford (n 35) 128–48, 341–5; Nicholson, *Statehood and the State-Like in International Law* (OUP 2019) 165–70; *Accordance with International Law of the Unilateral Declaration of Independence in Respect of Kosovo, Advisory Opinion* [2010] ICJ Rep 403 ('*Kosovo*') 437, §81.

[271] See eg Nicholson (n 270) 175–80. See also *Kosovo* (n 270).

[272] On Southern Rhodesia, see eg Crawford (n 35) 129–31; Nicholson (n 270) 175–80; Talmon (n 10) 530–2. On the Turkish Republic of Northern Cyprus, see eg Crawford (n 35) 133–4, 146–7; Nicholson (n 270) 165–7.

state.[273] Nor does the existence or otherwise of an obligation under customary international law not to recognize the governmental status of an ostensible government on grounds related to peremptory norms necessarily provide guidance on whether such a claimant qualifies for governmental status as a matter of customary international law,[274] although relevant practice overlaps.

In terms of relevant practice,[275] notable examples concern the successive Nationalist governments in South Africa during the *apartheid* era, the claim to governmental status of each of which was in consequence of the violation of what today is generally considered to be the peremptory prohibition on systematic racial discrimination.[276] Moreover, the enjoyment of governmental status by each of these ostensible governments arguably comprised in itself a violation by South Africa of what may have been the peremptory right of the people of South Africa to self-determination,[277] at least insofar as at that time this right encompassed an obligation on each state to be 'possessed of a government representing the whole people belonging to the territory [of a state] without distinction as to race, creed or colour'.[278]

While there is some practice that might be taken to reflect doubt as to whether the Nationalist government in South Africa qualified as the government of South Africa for the purposes of customary international law at least in part because it 'was not representative of the people of South Africa',[279] a significant number of states accepted that this claimant did indeed qualify as South Africa's government.[280] Its capacity to express South Africa's consent to be bound by a treaty was

[273] See also Costelloe, *Legal Consequences of Peremptory Norms in International Law* (CUP 2017) 286; Nicholson (n 270) 147. But see Orakhelashvili, *Peremptory Norms in International Law* (OUP 2008) 216–17.

[274] Recall chapter 3, nn 296–7, including the accompanying text.

[275] Recall also chapter 3, nn 270–2 and the accompanying text in relation to the respective ostensible governments of Tanzania in 1979 and of Cambodia between 1979 and 1989.

[276] On the peremptory status of this prohibition, recall chapter 3, n 275.

[277] On the peremptory status of this right, recall chapter 3, n 276.

[278] UNGA res 2625 (XXV) (24 October 1970) UN Doc A/RES/2625(XXV) Annex, §1.

[279] See eg UNGA, 'Credentials of Representatives to the Eighteenth Session of the General Assembly: Report of the Credentials Committee' (14 December 1963) UN Doc A/5676/Rev.1, §16 (Algeria, the USSR, and Liberia); UNGA, 'Credentials of Representatives to the Nineteenth and Twentieth Sessions of the General Assembly' (20 December 1965) UN Doc A/6208, §18 (USSR, as well as Madagascar, Syria, and the United Arab Emirates); UNGA, 'Official Records, 25th Session, 1882nd Plenary Meeting' (23 October 1970) UN Doc A/PV.1882, §259; UNGA, 'Credentials of Representatives to the Twenty-Fifth Session of the General Assembly: Report of the Credentials Committee' (28 October 1970) UN Doc A/8142, §12; UNGA, 'Credentials of Representatives to the Twenty-Seventh Session of the General Assembly' (1 December 1972) UN Doc A/8921, §5. See also chapter 5, nn 93, 316, and 343 on the non-acceptance of credentials issued ostensibly in South Africa's name. On the possible relevance of such practice, see section 5.4.3.

[280] See eg UNGA, 'Credentials of Representatives to the Nineteenth and Twentieth Sessions of the General Assembly'(n 279) §19 (Australia, Costa Rica, Guatemala, Iceland, and the USA); UNGA, 'Official Records, 25th Session, 1900th Plenary Meeting' (11 November 1970) UN Doc A/PV.1900, §82 (USA); UNGA, 'Credentials of Representatives to the Twenty-Sixth Session of the General Assembly: Report of the Credentials Committee' (17 December 1971) UN Doc A/8625, §16 (Colombia); UNGA, 'Official Records, 36th Session, 103rd Plenary Meeting' (n 60) §§16–18 (Netherlands, speaking on behalf of the then 10 member states of the European Community), §19 (Canada), §23 (Austria),

also accepted[281] after the constitution on which its claim to power was based had been declared by both the UNGA and the UNSC to be 'null and void'.[282] Moreover, both the UNSC and the UNGA regularly referred to the Nationalist government in South Africa as 'the Government of South Africa'.[283] This practice does not support the view that there exists a criterion for governmental status that relates to peremptory norms.

A later example of an ostensible government whose claim to governmental status was consequent upon the violation of an obligation arising under a peremptory norm is that of the FPGK, which was established in consequence of Iraq's aggression against Kuwait.[284] In this regard, it is noteworthy that, unlike in respect of Iraq's subsequent annexation of Kuwait,[285] the UNSC did not decide that the proclamation of the FPGK lacked legal effect.[286] The UNSC did nevertheless call upon states '[n]ot to recognize any régime set up by the occupying Power',[287] which may be an indicator that international law precludes the attainment of governmental status by a claimant whose claim is in consequence of the breach of an obligation arising under a peremptory norm. Even if this call does reflect the *opinio juris* on the part of the states which voted in favour of it as to some pertinent rule of customary international law,[288] and although virtually all states denied the governmental status of the FPGK and accepted the governmental status of Kuwait's 'government-in-exile',[289] this does not lend clear support to the existence of a rule

§34 (USA), §37 (Iceland, on behalf of the Nordic countries), §40 (UK), §48 (New Zealand), §§58–9 (Australia), §60 (Samoa), §61 (Portugal), §63 (Costa Rica); UNGA, 'Credentials of Representatives to the Twenty-Seventh Session of the General Assembly' (n 280) §8 (Belgium, Costa Rica, Japan, USA, and Uruguay). On the acceptability to a state of another state's ostensible credentials as involving recognition of governmental status, see section 5.4.3. For what it is worth, see also UNSC res 311 (4 February 1972) UN Doc S/RES/311 for references in the fourth unnumbered preambular paragraph and in §1 to 'the Government of South Africa'.

[281] See Agreement among the People's Republic of Angola, the Republic of Cuba and the Republic of South Africa of 22 December 1988, annexed to 'Note verbale Dated 22 December 1988 from the Permanent Representative of the United States of America to the United Nations Addressed to the Secretary-General' (22 December 1988) UN Doc A/43/989.

[282] UNSC res 554 (17 August 1984) UN Doc S/RES/554, §2; UNGA res 39/2 (28 September 1984) UN Doc A/RES/39/2, §1.

[283] See eg UNSC res 276 (30 January 1970) UN Doc S/RES/276, §2; UNSC res 282 (23 July 1970) UN Doc S/RES/282, first preambular para; UNSC res 311 (n 280) first preambular para. See also the titles of the following UNGA resolutions: 3324 (XXIX) (16 December 1974) UN Doc A/RES/3324(XXIX); 3411 (XXX) (28 November 1975) UN Doc A/RES/3411(XXX); 31/6 (26 October 1976) UN Doc A/RES/31/6; 41/35 (10 November 1986) UN Doc A/RES/41/35. On the evidential value of this practice and of the practice of states in adopting these resolutions, see sections 5.4.2–5.4.3.

[284] On the peremptory status of this prohibition, recall chapter 3, n 269.

[285] See UNSC res 662 (9 August 1990) UN Doc S/RES/662, §1 (emphasis omitted), where the UNSC '[*d*]*ecide*[*d*] that the annexation of Kuwait by Iraq . . . has no legal validity, and is considered null and void'.

[286] On the UNSC's response to Iraq's aggression against Kuwait prior to the former's annexation of the latter, see UNSC res 661 (n 189).

[287] Ibid, §9(*b*).

[288] On the possibility, but not the certainty, that this resolution reflected the *opinio juris* of the states in favour of its adoption, recall chapter 3, n 279.

[289] Talmon (n 32) 315.

of customary international law that precludes the success of a claim to governmental status which is consequent upon the violation of an obligation arising under a peremptory norm. The call not to recognize 'any régime set up by the occupying Power' and the views of states on the identity of Kuwait's government can both be explained by the presumption of subordination applicable in respect of any such regime, including the FPGK.[290]

By way of a more recent situation, the UNSC's determination that the GCI, which claimed governmental status in consequence of the US-led invasion of Iraq, comprised the government of Iraq[291] provides no further support for the existence of a rule of customary international law precluding the success of an ostensible government whose claim to power is in consequence of the violation of an obligation arising under a peremptory norm. Indeed, the recognition of the GCI's claim to governmental status may suggest that no such rule exists. That said, the UN's support for the formation of the GCI[292] may have served to break the chain of causation, as it were, between the violation of the peremptory prohibition on aggression and the GCI's claim to governmental status. It may be that any relevant customary rule applies only in respect of ostensible governments established in direct or sole consequence of the violation of an obligation arising under a peremptory norm.

Ultimately, the limited practice does not suggest that customary international law precludes the enjoyment of governmental status by an ostensible government whose claim, if accepted, would amount to the violation of an obligation arising under a peremptory norm. Nor does the practice concerning an ostensible government whose claim to power is consequent upon the violation of an obligation arising under a peremptory norm conclusively demonstrate existence of a criterion for governmental status which precludes the enjoyment of governmental status by an ostensible government whose claim to power is consequent upon the violation of an obligation arising under a peremptory norm, even if there are indications in recent practice which are suggestive as to the existence of such a rule. Relatedly, the presumptive sovereign freedom of each state to choose its government militates against readily inferring the existence of such a limitation on who can comprise the government of a state for the purposes of customary international law, although peremptory norms do limit the freedom of states in respect of other matters, including in relation to a state's political system.[293]

[290] Recall section 4.2.2.2. Recall also n 274 above and accompanying text on the possibility that an obligation of non-recognition applies in respect of an ostensible government whose governmental status international law does not definitively preclude.

[291] Recall n 61 above and the accompanying text.

[292] Ibid.

[293] See eg UNSC res 554 (n 282) §§1–2.

4.3 Conclusion

The presumption against limitations on state sovereignty weighs against the existence of any customary international legal criterion for governmental status which would limit the presumptive sovereign freedom of each state to choose its government, its political system, or its constitution. This includes considerations such as democratic representativity and a willingness to ensure the state's compliance with its international legal obligations. At the same time, this presumption suggests that the absence of an objective customary international legal framework for identifying the government of a state ought not to be readily inferred. Indeed, there does exist an objective framework for identifying the government of a state for the purposes of customary international law which preserves the presumptive sovereign freedoms of each state to choose its political system, its constitution, and its government. Put differently, the objective framework by reference to which the identity of the government of a state is to be ascertained for the purposes of customary international law gives effect to the presumptive sovereign freedom of each state to choose its government, its political system, and its constitution. There is no clear acceptance of a limitation on any of these freedoms in the customary international legal criteria for governmental status.

Rather than changing in a way that has imposed a limitation on the presumptive sovereign freedom of each state to choose its government, the law in this regard has developed since the early 1990s so as to further privilege what is perhaps the most direct way by which a state can be taken to express its choice of government, namely its constitution. International law now has regard to alternative, less direct means for ascertaining the state's choice of government only where there is no claimant to governmental status that can be taken to reflect the state's more direct choice of government—that is, where there is no autonomous 'constitutional' claimant. An autonomous 'constitutional' claimant to governmental status will invariably enjoy governmental status as a matter of customary international law as long as it maintains its claim, regardless of whether it exercises or has ever exercised effective control over the territory and population of the state. An 'unconstitutional' ostensible government may attain governmental status as a matter of customary international law only in the absence of a rival 'constitutional' claim and only if it is autonomous and if it exercises effective control over the territory and population of the state. What satisfies the requirement of effective control may vary depending on the circumstances.

A claimant to governmental status need not be democratically representative or otherwise 'legitimate' in order to qualify as the government of a state as a matter of customary international law. It is also unnecessary for an ostensible government to be willing to ensure that the state complies with its international legal obligations in order for it to enjoy governmental status as a matter of customary international law. It appears, moreover, that an ostensible government can enjoy governmental status as a matter of customary international law even if it is established in consequence of, or if its enjoyment of governmental status would amount to, the violation of an obligation arising under a peremptory norm of general international law.

5
Questions Concerning Governments in International Organizations

5.1 Introduction

The present chapter focuses on questions concerning international organizations[1] that relate to the international legal regulation of governmental status and the identity of governments.[2] This includes an examination of the role of the customary international legal identity of a state's government to the representation of a state in the context of international organizations. It encompasses also an assessment of the existence and legal value of practice concerning the recognition of governmental status by and in the context of the work of international organizations. It extends to consideration of the powers of international organizations to take action, on grounds that are directly connected to a particular claim to governmental status, to limit aspects of that state's participation within the organization. An understanding of these matters may inform the understanding of the concept of the government of a state in international law, including in relation to the presumptive sovereign freedom of each state to choose its government, the objective international legal identity of a state's government, and the distinctive representative capacity of that government to represent the state. Analysis of some of these issues may shed light also on the content or relevance of the customary international

[1] The present work uses the term 'international organization' in accordance with the definition provided by the ILC in the context of its work on the responsibility of international organizations. See UNGA res 66/100 (9 December 2011) UN Doc A/RES/66/100, Annex, art 2(*a*).

[2] The chapter does not consider other matters related to governments of states, such as the power of international organizations to adopt sanctions or undertake other coercive measures in response to a situation concerning the identity of a state's government. On the not-infrequent exercise of such powers, see eg UNSC res 917 (6 May 1994) UN Doc S/RES/917, §3 and UNSC res 940 (31 July 1994) UN Doc S/RES/940, §4 (in relation to the situation in Haiti); UNSC res 1132 (8 October 1997) UN Doc S/RES/1132, §5 (in relation to the situation in Sierra Leone); UNSC res 2048 (18 May 2012) UN Doc S/RES/2048, §§4, 6 (in relation to the situation in Guinea-Bissau); and UNSC res 2134 (28 January 2014) UN Doc S/RES/2134, §§30, 32, 36, 37(g) (in relation to the situation in the Central African Republic). For a more recent example of the readiness to use such powers, see 'Extraordinary Session of the ECOWAS [Economic Community of West African States] Authority of Heads of State and Government on the Political Situation in Niger, Final Communique' (30 July 2023), available at <http://ecowas.int/final-communique-fifty-first-extraordinary-summit-of-the-ecowas-authority-of-heads-of-state-and-government-on-the-political-situation-in-niger>, §10(f). For relevant powers, see eg Protocol relating to the Mechanism for Conflict Prevention, Management, Resolution, Peacekeeping and Security (adopted 10 December 1999, immediate provisional entry into force) ECOWAS Doc A/P.10/12/99, arts 25(e), 26.

The Identity of Governments in International Law. Niko Pavlopoulos, Oxford University Press.
DOI: 10.1093/9780191991509.003.0005

legal criteria for governmental status. In considering the above matters, the following findings present themselves.

International organizations tend to accept as effective for their respective purposes the ostensible representation of a state which occurs through the ostensible government that qualifies as a matter of customary international law as that state's government. This accords with the objective international legal identity of the government of a state and its plenary or near-plenary capacity to represent the state for the purposes of international law. At the same time, an international organization may possess the power to accept as effective for one or more of its purposes the ostensible representation of a state by the 'wrong' government. Any such power, insofar as it extends only to circumstances that do not involve the recognition by the organization of the 'wrong' government, undermines neither the objective international legal existence of a state's government nor the presumptive sovereign freedom of each state to choose its government. To the extent that the decision of an international organization to allow the representation of a state by the 'wrong' government may involve recognition of that ostensible government and have legal effect, there would be limitations on the freedom of each state to choose its government and on the objective international legal existence of a state's government. But there is no clear acceptance of such a possibility. In any event, the apparent power of at least certain international organizations to accept as effective the ostensible representation of a state by the 'wrong' government nuances the distinctive representative capacity of the 'right' government. The exercise of such a power will result in an international organization accepting as effective the ostensible representation of a state by the 'wrong' government and in that organization treating as ineffective the ostensible representation of that state by the 'right' government. It is noteworthy that an international organization may exercise its power in this regard in response to matters related directly to the ostensible identity of a state's government that do not form part of the customary international legal framework for the identification of a state's government, including on the apparent unwillingness of a state's government to ensure the state's compliance with certain international legal obligations.

As a separate matter, it is not uncommon for an international organization to have the power under its constituent instrument to take action on grounds related in some direct way to a specific claim to governmental status to limit that state's participation in the work of one or more of its organs. Although it may take different forms, such action most often takes the form of the suspension of a member state or a measure to comparable effect. Certain international organizations have and exercise an express power to suspend their respective members on grounds relating to the existence of an ostensible 'unconstitutional' government which is not democratically representative. Further, certain international organizations have sometimes exercised an apparent power to suspend their respective members on other grounds that relate to the identity of the government of a state but that do not comprise part of the customary international legal framework for the identification of a state's government. An example of a relevant consideration in this regard is the apparent unwillingness by the government of a state to ensure the state's compliance with the latter's international legal obligations. Accordingly, considerations beyond those that are relevant to its enjoyment of governmental status under customary international law might contribute to the government of a state being unable to represent the state for certain purposes of international law.

5.2 A Selection of International Organizations

The chapter does not undertake the impracticable task of surveying the approach of every international organization to the issues in question. For reasons explained below, it concentrates instead on the UN, the African Union (AU), and the OAS as a basis to form certain conclusions, while also having regard to other international organizations to support or nuance these conclusions.

As regards the rules and practice of international organizations concerning the acceptance of a person as a state representative, the rules and practice of the UN have informed or are otherwise reflected in the rules and practice of a number of other international organizations as well as other multilateral settings.[3] A focus on the rules and practice of the UN as regards the representation of states thus provides insights into the approach of other international forums to this matter. Certain differences among international organizations are nonetheless commonplace. An analysis of the approaches of some other international organizations to questions of state representation thus provides some insight into the possible dissimilarities of approach between international organizations to these questions.

[3] See eg 'Fifth Report on Relations between States and International Organizations, by Mr. Abdullah El-Erian, Special Rapporteur' (1 April 1970) Ybk ILC [1970] vol II, 1, 20 (art 66, comment 1) for the influence that the UNGA's rules on credentials of state representatives have had on such rules in international conferences. (On state representation at international conferences more generally, see Sabel, *Rules of Procedure at the UN and at Inter-Governmental Conferences* (3rd edn, CUP 2017) 61–70.) On the influence of the UNGA's practice concerning the approach to credentials of state representatives, see eg 'Report of the Credentials Committee, 12 April 1961', §§5–6, in United Nations Conference on Diplomatic Intercourse and Immunities (2 March–14 April 1961), 'Official Records, vol II' (1962) UN Doc A/CONF.20/14/Add.1, 75, which was adopted by the plenary ('Eighth Plenary Meeting 12 April 1961', §65, in United Nations Conference on Diplomatic Intercourse and Immunities (2 March–14 April 1961), 'Official Records, vol I' (1962) UN Doc A/CONF.20/14, 28, 29). See, similarly, 'Report of the Credentials Committee at the First Session of the Conference, 21 May 1968', §§10–11 in United Nations Conference on the Law of Treaties, First and Second Sessions (26 March–24 May 1968; 9 April–22 May 1969), 'Official Records, Documents of the Conference' (1969) UN Doc A/CONF.39/11/Add.2, 4, which was accepted by the plenary ('Fifth Plenary Meeting, 24 May 1968', §17, in United Nations Conference on the Law of Treaties, First Session (26 March–24 May 1968), 'Official Records, Summary Records of the Plenary Meetings and of the Committee of the Whole' (1969) UN Doc A/CONF.39/11, 9, 10).

As regards limitations on state participation, a focus on the rules and practice of the AU and the OAS arises from the fact that these two organizations are among the most notable international organizations which possess and which have exercised express powers to limit state participation in their respective work on grounds that relate specifically to the existence of a particular type of claim to governmental status, even though other international organizations possess similar powers.[4] In contrast, the UN, with its broad political functions and virtually-universal membership,[5] is an important example of the ways in which an international organization may otherwise limit state participation in its work on grounds relating to a particular claim to governmental status.

5.3 The Representation of a State and the Identity of Its Government

After outlining the different aspects of state representation in the context of international organizations, this section looks at the extent to which international organizations have adopted for their own purposes the position under customary international law according to which a state may be represented only through whoever qualifies as a matter of customary international law as that state's government.

5.3.1 The Different Aspects of State Representation

There are two broad situations in which an international organization may be faced with whether or not to accept as effective for its purposes the ostensible representation of a state. This question may arise, first, in the ostensible participation of a state

[4] Other international organizations with relevant powers include but are not limited to the Commonwealth and the ECOWAS. On the Commonwealth, see eg Magliveras, *Exclusion from Participation in International Organizations: The Law and Practice behind Member States' Expulsion and Suspension of Membership* (Kluwer 1999) 185–94; Duxbury, *The Participation of States in International Organisations: The Role of Human Rights and Democracy* (CUP 2010) 204–11. On the ECOWAS, see Supplementary Protocol on Democracy and Good Governance Supplementary to the Protocol relating to the Mechanism for Conflict Prevention, Management, Resolution, Peacekeeping and Security (adopted 21 December 2001, entered into force 8 December 2005) ECOWAS Doc A/SP.1/12/1, art 45(1)–(2); *Organisation Internationale de la francophonie*, 'Déclaration de Bamako' (3 November 2000), available at <https://www.francophonie.org/sites/default/files/2019-09/Declaration_Bamako_2000_modif_02122011.pdf>.

[5] See also Vienna Convention on the Representation of States in their Relations with International Organizations of a Universal Character (adopted 14 March 1975, not in force) reproduced in (1975) 69 AJIL 730 ('VCRSIO') art 1(1)(2).

in the work of one or more organs of the organization or, secondly, in the state's ostensible interactions vis-à-vis the organization.[6]

This chapter refers to the first category of state representation, when accepted by the international organization in question as effective, as the 'representation of a state in an international organization'. The conduct that comprises state representation in this context depends on, inter alia, the nature of the organ in which the state is represented. For example, in a deliberative political organ of an international organization, the representation of a state may include speaking, submitting draft resolutions, and voting or abstaining from voting on particular resolutions or other decisions by that organ. Before an adjudicative body, the representation of a state principally includes submissions in respect of factual and legal questions. The persons by whom the ostensible representation of a state in one or more organs of an international organization is accepted by the organization as effective include persons designated in certain organs as 'state delegates', even if international organizations do not themselves consistently use this term.[7]

'The representation of a state vis-à-vis an international organization' refers within the present work to the expression by a state of its intention or any other manifestation of its authoritative position on general aspects of its relationship and dealings with that organization. This includes, for example, its communication to the organization of its intention to become a member, or to terminate its membership, or to change its name. Such representation may also include the accreditation of an individual as a state delegate to one or more organs of the organization.[8] As regards at least certain international organizations, each state ordinarily, though not necessarily, has a diplomatic mission dedicated to the coordination of its interaction with the organization on such matters, the head of which is often referred to as the state's 'permanent representative' to the organization.[9] A state may have persons additional or alternative to a 'permanent representative' to represent it vis-à-vis an international organization.

The circumstances in which an international organization accepts as effective the ostensible representation of a state in respect of each type of representation are

[6] On this distinction, see also VCRSIO (n 5) arts 1(1)(7), 1(1)(9), 1(1)(18), and 1(1)(22); Magiera, 'Article 9' in Simma and others (eds), *The Charter of the United Nations: A Commentary*, vol 1 (3rd edn, OUP 2012) 445, 451, §9.

[7] Cf UNSC, Provisional Rules of Procedure (adopted 17 January 1946, last amended 21 December 1982) UN Doc S/96/Rev.7 ('UNSC Provisional Rules of Procedure') Rule 13 and UNGA, Rules of Procedure of the General Assembly (as amended on 13 March 2003) UN Doc A/520/Rev.18 ('UNGA Rules of Procedure') Rule 27, both of which refer to an individual representing a state in the work of the UNSC and the UNGA, respectively, as a 'representative', on the hand, and Statute of the International Court of Justice (signed 26 June 1945, entered into force 24 October 1945) ('ICJ Statute') art 42(1), according to which a person representing a state before the Court is an 'agent' of the state, on the other. Note also ICJ Statute, art 42(2) as regards 'counsel' and 'advocates', who in fact often provide considerable assistance to the agent of a state.

[8] For relevant rules, see n 28 below. The representation of the state by the accredited person in an organ of the organization amounts to representation in an international organization.

[9] On permanent representatives, see eg VCRSIO (n 5) arts 1(1)(7), (1)(18), and 6.

not necessarily uniform. That said, an international organization may accept the same person as a state representative both in and vis-à-vis that organization. This may be pursuant to separate decisions by different organs of the organization,[10] or it may be that acceptance in one context is taken to amount to acceptance in another context.[11] Equally, however, an international organization may respond differently for different purposes to the ostensible representation of a state by the same person or by different persons acting under the authority of the same ostensible government. For example, since May 2021, Myanmar's representative at the UNGA claimed to act under the authority of the National Unity Government (NUG),[12] while the State Administration Council (SAC) represented Myanmar in proceedings before the ICJ.[13] Either way, the conceptual distinction between the representation of a state in an international organization and the representation of a state vis-à-vis an international organization may be relevant to one or more questions concerning the representation of states in the context of international organizations. Where the analysis does not turn on the distinction, the chapter uses the term 'representation of a state in the context of an international organization' to refer to one or more situations in which an international organization accepts as effective for one or more of its purposes the ostensible representation of a state by a particular individual or collectivity of individuals. The term 'state representative' is used in the present chapter[14] to refer, unless otherwise specified, to any person or collectivity of persons whose ostensible representation of a state in the context of an international organization is accepted as effective by the organization.

5.3.2 The Function of a State's Government in the Representation of a State

Each international organization decides for itself whether or not to accept as effective for its purposes the ostensible representation of a state in any particular instance. The process by which an international organization does so and the

[10] See also ILC, 'Draft Articles on the Representation of States in Their Relations with International Organizations' Ybk ILC [1971] vol II(1), 284, 294 (art 11, comment 6).

[11] See eg the Constitutive Act of the African Union (adopted 7 November 2000, entered into force 26 May 2001) 2158 UNTS 3 ('AU Constitutive Act') art 21(1).

[12] See eg 'Letter from Ambassador Kyaw Moe Tun to Secretary-General Antonio Guterres' (14 May 2021), available at <http://myanmarmissionnewyork.org/post/letter-ambassador-kyaw-moe-tun>; 'Statement by Ambassador Kyaw Moe Tun at the UN General Assembly Plenary Meeting Agenda Item 135' (16 May 2021), available at <http://myanmarmissionnewyork.org/post/statement-by-ambassador-kyaw-moe-tun-at-the-un-general-assembly-plenary-meetingagenda-item-135>. On the formation of the Committee Representing Pyidaungsu Hluttaw and the NUG, recall section 4.2.2.3. On the representation of Myanmar during this time on a 'provisional' basis, see n 88 below.

[13] *Application of the Convention on the Prevention and Punishment of the Crime of Genocide (The Gambia v Myanmar), Judgment, 22 July 2022* (not yet reported) 5.

[14] In other parts of this work, the term 'state representative' is used in a broader sense. Recall section 1.1.

substantive considerations that inform any such decision may vary among and within international organizations. This may depend on whether a person seeks to represent a state in or vis-à-vis that international organization and, as specifically regards the representation of a state in an international organization, perhaps also on the organ of the international organization in which the person purports to represent the state.[15]

Attempts have been made to harmonize decisions of different organs of the same international organization and as between international organizations on questions concerning the ostensible representation of states. For its part, the UNGA recommended in 1950 that 'the attitude adopted by it [on] any such question should be taken into account in other organs of the United Nations and in the specialized agencies'.[16] It has been said to have 'invariably been the case since 1950' that 'the General Assembly's decisions on representation are followed by the organizations of the United Nations system'.[17] But there are cases suggesting otherwise. For example, the International Labour Organization (ILO) rejected as Hungary's representatives the persons ostensibly representing Hungary in 1958 and 1959,[18] although the UNGA had allowed persons appointed by the same ostensible government to represent Hungary at the UNGA, albeit without positively accepting their credentials.[19] In certain cases, it may not be possible for the UNGA's recommendation to be followed, even if only for practical reasons concerning the timing of any possible decision by the UNGA on credentials issued by the ostensible government in question.[20] That said, the absence of guidance by the UNGA might lead another UN organ or specialized agency to defer its own decision on the question of a specific state's representation 'pending guidance from the United Nations General Assembly' on the understanding that no one would represent that state in some specific context. This was the approach recently adopted by the World Health Assembly in respect of Myanmar, subsequent to the emergence of the rival claims to governmental status by the SAC and the NUG.[21] The UNGA's approach

[15] See also Secretariat of the United Nations (Legal Opinions), 'Practice of the General Assembly with Regard to the Examination of Credentials Submitted by Member States—Replies to a Questionnaire Concerning the Practice of the General Assembly with Regard to the Examination of Credentials' [1985] UNJYB 128, 129, §8.

[16] UNGA res 396 (V) (14 December 1950) UN Doc A/RES/396(V) §3.

[17] Secretariat of the United Nations (Legal Opinions), 'Note to the Secretary-General of the United Nations' [2003] UNJYB 531, 531, §2. See also Secretariat of the United Nations (n 15) 129, §8.

[18] See eg Lauterpacht, 'The Contemporary Practice of the United Kingdom in the Field of International Law—Survey and Comment, VI' (1958) 7 ICLQ 514, 574.

[19] See nn 89–90 below.

[20] See Schermers and Blokker, *International Institutional Law* (6th rev edn, BRILL 2018) 218, §261.

[21] Seventy-Fourth World Health Assembly, 'Committee on Credentials: Report' (26 May 2021) UN Doc A74/56, §7, accepted in substance by the plenary ('5th plenary meeting, 26 May 2021', reproduced in World Health Organization, 'Seventy-Fourth World Health Assembly (24 May–1 June 2021), Resolutions and Decisions, Annexes', UN Doc WHA74/2021/REC/1, 73–4).

is nevertheless often followed or at least 'taken into account' by other organs and specialized agencies of the UN.[22]

The decision of an international organization to accept as effective the ostensible representation of a state may pertain only to a specific act (that is, may be taken on a strict *ad hoc* basis) or it may be of wider scope, covering the ostensible representation of the state through a specific ostensible government for one or more purposes with respect to a specific situation or period or even generally and indefinitely, at least until the international organization decides otherwise.[23]

Regardless, it is generally the case that an international organization may and does accept as effective for its purposes the ostensible representation of a state through the claimant that, in the organization's view, qualifies as a matter of customary international law as the government of the state.[24] This is apparent from the following three points.

First, the representative capacity for the purposes of an international organization of one or more of three office-holders who possess *ex officio* plenary or near-plenary capacity to represent the state for other purposes of international law[25] is reflected in the practice,[26] if not the written rules,[27] of international organizations.

Secondly, pursuant to its rules, each international organization ordinarily accepts as effective, for its purposes, the ostensible representation of a state by a person that the organization positively accepts as having been appointed or as

[22] For another example, see Food and Agriculture Organization of the United Nations (FAO) res 33/71 (adopted by the FAO Conference on 25 November 1971, reproduced in [1971] UNJYB 107). But recall nn 12–13 above, as well as the accompanying text, on the representation of Myanmar at the UNGA and before the ICJ.

[23] See eg Magiera (n 6) 454, §20.

[24] See also Talmon, *Recognition of Governments in International Law with Particular Reference to Governments in Exile* (OUP 1998) 183.

[25] For the position under customary international law, recall section 2.2.1.

[26] As regards representation at the UNGA, see eg Secretariat of the United Nations (Legal Opinions), 'Letter to the Permanent Representative of a Member State to the United Nations Regarding Credentials and Composition of Delegations for the Sessions of the General Assembly' [2005] UNJYB 460, 460; ILC, 'The Practice of the United Nations, the Specialized Agencies and the International Atomic Energy Agency Concerning Their Status, Privileges and Immunities: Study Prepared by the Secretariat' Ybk ILC [1967] vol II, 154, 166, §19; Magiera (n 6) 453, §19. As for representation before the ICJ, see the representation of Iran at the ICJ by Iran's head of government, without any indication that he was designated as 'agent', 'counsel', or 'advocate', ICJ Statute (n 7) art 42(1)–(2) notwithstanding: *Anglo-Iranian Oil Co Case (Jurisdiction), Judgment of July 22nd, 1952* [1952] ICJ Rep 93, 94. See also, more recently, the representation of Myanmar at the ICJ by Aung San Suu Kyi (eg 'Application of the Convention on the Prevention and Punishment of the Crime of Genocide (*The Gambia v. Myanmar*) Verbatim Record' (11 December 2019) CR 2019/19, 12 (Myanmar)).

[27] See eg UNSC Provisional Rules of Procedure (n 7) Rule 13; AU Constitutive Act (n 11) art 10(1); AU, 'Rules of Procedure of the Peace and Security Council' (adopted by the AU Executive Council in 'Decision on the Operationalization of the Peace and Security Council', fourth ordinary session (12–16 March 2004) AU Doc EX/CL/Dec.79 (IV) §5 and approved by the AU Assembly in 'Decision on the Operationalization of the Protocol Relating to the Peace and Security Council of the African Union', AU Doc Assembly/AU/Dec.34 (III) Rev 1, §2) ('AUPSC Rules of Procedure') Rule 18; Assembly of the African Union (AU Assembly), 'Rules of Procedure of the Assembly of the Union' (adopted at the First Ordinary Session of the Assembly of the African Union, 'Decision on the Interim Period' (9–10 July 2002) AU Doc Ass/AU/Dec.1 (I) §2 ('AU Assembly Rules of Procedure') Rule 3.

otherwise acting under the authority of the person or one or more of the persons that the international organization considers to comprise the government of that state.[28]

The variation in the express terms of rules on the representation of states both between and within international organizations does not affect either of these two points. For example, one set of rules may mention that the representation or the authorization of representation of a state is to take place by one or more of the three office-holders who possess *ex officio* plenary or near-plenary capacity as a matter of customary international law to represent the state.[29] A set of rules may also or instead expressly provide that 'the government' of a state may represent or appoint state representatives.[30] Pertinent rules might provide that a state may be represented by a 'duly accredited' or 'specially designated' representative or by a person who has been authorized to represent a state by a 'competent authority', each of which formulations refers to a person who acts under the authority of the government of a state.[31] The rules of an international organization may instead use different words to similar effect.

Thirdly, references within the rules of international organizations to 'the government' of, and to office-holders within, a state have generally been interpreted and applied consistently with the customary international legal understanding of these terms.[32] References to a 'competent authority' or to a 'duly accredited representative' are generally understood, moreover, to refer to one or more persons comprising at least part of or acting under the authority of the government or to a person appointed as a state representative through the government of that state, respectively. Other relevant phrases are generally understood in a similar way. All this is apparent from the practice of states, which, in general, when deciding whether or not to vote in favour of accepting a specific person as the representative of another state for one or more purposes of an international organization, defer to their position as to whether or not they accept the customary international legal

[28] See eg UNGA Rules of Procedure (n 7) Rule 27; UNSC Provisional Rules of Procedure (n 7) Rule 13; AU Constitutive Act (n 11) art 10(1); AUPSC Rules of Procedure (n 27) Rule 18; AU Assembly Rules of Procedure (n 27) Rule 3; OASGA, 'Rules of Procedure of the General Assembly' (as amended on 5 June 2000) OEA/Ser.P/1.1/rev.13 ('OASGA Rules of Procedure') art 1; OASPC, 'Amendments to the Rules of Procedure of the Permanent Council of the Organization of American States' (26 June 2003) OEA/Ser.G, CP/RES.847 (1373/03) ('OASPC Rules of Procedure') art 1. See also Higgins and others, *Oppenheim's International Law: United Nations* (OUP 2017) 308.

[29] See n 27 above. Albeit as a recommendation, see also UNGA res 257 A (III) (3 December 1948) UN Doc A/RES/257(III) §1 on permanent representatives of states to the UN, and see the discussion in ILC (n 26) 168, §30, which notes that '[t]he procedure outlined in resolution 257 A (III) has been observed since 1949'.

[30] See eg OASGA Rules of Procedure (n 28) art 1; OASPC Rules of Procedure (n 28) art 1; AU Constitutive Act (n 11) art 10(1).

[31] See eg UN Charter of the United Nations (signed 26 June 1945, entered into force 24 October 1945, last amended 24 September 1973) ('UN Charter'), available at <http://un.org/en/about-us/un-charter/full-text>, art 28(2); AUPSC Rules of Procedure (n 27) Rule 18; AU Assembly Rules of Procedure (n 27) Rule 3.

[32] On the customary international legal understanding of relevant terms, recall section 2.2.1.

governmental status of the claimant comprised at least in part by the ostensible representative of the latter state or under whose authority the ostensible representative acts.[33] The practice involving the purported disclaimer by a state against recognition of governmental status in the context of a decision by an international organization to accept an individual as the representative of another state which the former state does not in some sense recognize as the government of the latter state provides further support in this regard.[34]

Indeed, the rules of customary international law providing that a state may have no more than one government,[35] that each state is presumed free to choose its government,[36] and that there exists an objective framework by reference to which the identity of a state's government is to be ascertained[37] may be relevant to whom an international organization has the power to accept as the representative of a state. This is because these rules may inform the construction of treaty-based rules concerning the representation of states in the context of an international organization.[38] In any event, the non-possession by international organizations of inherently-plenary powers,[39] coupled with the presumption against limitations on state sovereignty, suggests that, as a rebuttable[40] presumption, each state remains free to choose its representatives and that international organizations have not been conferred the power to make this choice for a state. According to such a presumption, the role of the international organization is to ascertain the state's choice of representative, as expressed through the 'right' government.[41] This is

[33] See eg UNGA, 'Credentials of Representatives to the Seventh Session of the General Assembly: First Report of the Credentials Committee' (22 October 1952) UN Doc A/2234, §10 (Burma); UNGA, 'Official Records, 7th Session, 389th Plenary Meeting' (25 October 1952) UN Doc A/PV.389, §36 (UK); UNGA, 'Credentials of Representatives to the Eleventh Session of the General Assembly: Report of the Credentials Committee' (13 February 1957) UN Doc A/3536, §6 (Spain); UNGA, 'Official Records, 17th Session, 1201st Plenary Meeting' (20 December 1962) UN Doc A/PV.1201, §92 (Jordan); UNGA, 'Official Records, 17th Session, 1202nd Plenary Meeting (20 December 1962) UN Doc A/PV.1202, §§1–2 (Burma), §54 (Cuba), §§56–7 (Sudan), §§99–101 (Somalia); UNGA, 'Credentials of Representatives to the Thirty-Sixth Session of the General Assembly: First Report of the Credentials Committee' (17 September 1981) UN Doc A/36/517, §7 (China), §12 (Papua New Guinea); UNSC, 'Official Records, 900th Meeting' (14 September 1960) UN Doc S/PV.900, §67 (China). See also Secretariat of the United Nations (n 17) 532, §5: '[i]n the absence of a sovereign government in Iraq, there is no recognized authority to issue such credentials'; Fitzmaurice, 'Chinese Representation in the United Nations' (1952) 6 Ybk World Aff 36, 39, who notes that, when voting on matters concerning the representation of China at the UN, states vote 'in the light of their view as to the status of [the authority issuing credentials] and its right to act on behalf of the State concerned'; Talmon (n 24) 175–6. On non-acceptance of credentials as not necessarily involving denial of governmental status, see section 5.4.3, including the text accompanying n 128.

[34] On such practice, see section 5.4.3.

[35] See chapter 2, n 130 and accompanying text.

[36] See chapter 2, n 109 and accompanying text.

[37] See sections 2.5 and 4.2.2.

[38] See eg Vienna Convention on the Law of Treaties (adopted 23 May 1969, entered into force 27 January 1980) 1155 UNTS 331, art 31(3)(*c*).

[39] See eg *Legality of the Use by a State of Nuclear Weapons in an Armed Conflict, Advisory Opinion* [1996] ICJ Rep 66 ('*Nuclear Weapons*') 77, §25.

[40] See also Lauterpacht (n 18) 576, who suggests that 'the term a "Government" [need not refer] to an absolute and inflexible concept', and UNGA res 396 (n 16) §1, which does not preclude such flexibility.

[41] Recall section 1.3 on the use of the term 'right' government in the present work.

corroborated by practice which expressly supports the existence of the freedom of each state to choose its representatives in the context of an international organization.[42] The same goes for practice which suggests that the representation by a state in the work of an international organization through the 'wrong' government is incompatible with a limitation on the organization's powers in respect of matters that international law leaves to the sovereign discretion of each state or amounts to interference in the affairs of that state.[43]

All of this might be taken to suggest that it is only through whomever qualifies for governmental status as a matter of customary international law that a state may and will be represented in the context of an international organization. Such a position would not be incompatible with the UNGA's recommendation that 'whenever more than one authority claims to be the government entitled to represent a member State . . . becomes the question of controversy [that] the question should be considered in the light of the Purposes and Principles of the [UN] Charter',[44] especially since these Principles include the non-interference by the UN 'in matters which are essentially within the domestic jurisdiction of any state'.[45] The view of its Secretariat that the UN cannot 'consider [the] constitutionality' of the claim of an ostensible government in determining whether or not to accept an ostensible government as such[46] can be explained as being based on a misunderstanding of the criteria for governmental status under customary international law.

At the same time, there may be a misrepresentation' of a state—a term which in the present context serves as no more than convenient shorthand for the situation in which a state is represented by a 'wrong' government—as a result of at least three distinct possibilities.

First, international organizations typically determine for themselves whether or not a specific person qualifies as a state representative, regardless of whether there are rival ostensible representatives of a state. In so doing, they might incorrectly identify or apply the relevant international legal considerations as regards the identity of a state's government. This would result in the organization accepting as effective the ostensible representation of a state by a 'wrong' government.

[42] See eg UNGA, 'Official Records, 5th Session, 277th Plenary Meeting' (19 September 1950) UN Doc A/PV.277, §§18–19 (USSR); UNGA, 'Official Records, 52nd Session, 76th Plenary Meeting' (18 December 1997) UN Doc A/52/PV.76, §15 (Pakistan); *Walid Ahmed Al-Juffali v Christina Estrada* [2016] EWCA Civ 176, §15; World Trade Organization (Appellate Body), 'European Communities—Regime for the Importation, Sale and Distribution of Bananas' (9 September 1997) WTO Doc WT/DS27/AB/R, §§5–6, 10. See also Shaw, *Rosenne's Law and Practice of the International Court: 1920–2015*, vol 3 (5th edn, BRILL 2016) 1332.

[43] See nn 161–2 below.

[44] UNGA res 396 (n 16).

[45] UN Charter (n 31) art 2(7).

[46] Secretariat of the United Nations (Legal Opinions), 'Practice of the United Nations in Cases of Challenged Representation of a Member State—General Assembly Resolution 396 (V) of 14 December 1950: Memorandum to the Under-Secretary-General for Political Affairs' [1997] UNJYB 465, 468, §4.

Secondly, at least some international organizations are empowered to accept as effective for one or more of their respective purposes the ostensible representation of a state on a 'provisional' basis—that is, pending a determination as to the acceptance or rejection of the credentials ostensibly issued by that state and thus without a determination on the qualification for governmental status by the ostensible government through which those credentials were issued.[47] On this basis also, an international organization might allow the 'misrepresentation' of a state.

Thirdly, certain adjudicative organs of international organizations appear not to consider themselves as having to determine the identity of a state representative for proceedings before them based on the customary international legal identity of a state's government, at least insofar as there is no specific rule requiring this. For example, one such organ took a decision as to who may represent a state on the basis of considerations such as 'procedural fairness and efficiency', which were expressly treated as being 'different from those [criteria] relevant to the recognition of . . . governments'.[48] This might result in the adjudicative organ accepting as effective the ostensible representation of a state by a 'wrong' government.

The 'misrepresentation' of a state might be questioned in terms of both its legal effect and its compatibility with the international legal rights of the state in question. Moreover, at least insofar as such a decision has full legal effect, such a decision informs at least certain conceptual aspects of the government of a state in international law.[49] But before considering each of these matters, it pays to assess the extent to which decisions concerning the representation of a state in the context of an international organization involve the recognition of governmental status.

[47] See eg UNGA Rules of Procedure (n 7) Rule 28; UNSC Provisional Rules of Procedure (n 7) Rule 16; AUPSC Rules of Procedure (n 27) Rule 20. But there is not always an apparent express provision for representation on such a basis. See eg the rules on representation at the OAS. Further on representation in the context of an international organization without recognition by that organization, see section 5.4.1.2.

[48] *Mobil Cerro Negro Holding, Ltd and others v Venezuela* (ICSID Case No ARB/07/27), *Resubmission Proceeding, Decision on the Respondent's Representation in this Proceeding* (1 March 2021) ('*Mobil Cerro Negro v Venezuela*') §45. For additional examples of such decisions not based on the customary international legal identity of a state's government, see *ConocoPhillips Petrozuata BV, ConocoPhillips Hamaca BV and ConocoPhillips Gulf of Paria BV v Venezuela* (ICSID Case No ARB/07/30), *Annulment Proceeding, Order on the Applicant's Representation* (3 April 2020) ('*ConocoPhilips v Venezuela*, 3 April 2020) §§29–31, 35–7; ibid, *Order on the Applicant's Request for Reconsideration dated 3 August 2020 on the Issue of Venezuela's Legal Representation* (2 November 2020) ('*ConocoPhilips v Venezuela*, 2 November 2020') §§35–40; ibid, *Order on the Applicant's Third Request for Reconsideration of 21 September 2021 on the Issue of Venezuela's Legal Representation* (15 February 2023) ('*ConocoPhilips v Venezuela*, 15 February 2023') §24.

[49] See section 5.5.3.

5.4 Practice Concerning the Recognition of Governmental Status

The present section considers the ways in which international organizations may recognize[50] or deny the governmental status of an ostensible government as well as the evidential value of such practice as regards the identification of a state's government as a matter of customary international law. Further, it considers the ways in which a state that participates in the decision-making process of an international organization may recognize or deny the governmental status of an ostensible government in the context of such a process.

5.4.1 Modes of Recognition and Denial of Governmental Status by International Organizations

5.4.1.1 In General

In principle, an international organization may recognize or deny the qualification by a specific ostensible government for governmental status through any of its organs and in the performance of any functions.[51]

An international organization may recognize the governmental status of a specific ostensible government through an official statement to that effect. One apparent example in this regard is the reference by the UNGA to 'the legitimate and Constitutional Government of the President of the Republic of Honduras, Mr. José Manuel Zelaya Rosales'.[52] This stands in contrast with a reference to a claimant which the organization seeks not to recognize, if not to deny its governmental status, such as the description by the UNSC of 'the Afghan faction known as the Taliban, which also calls itself the Islamic Emirate of Afghanistan'.[53] As for recognition by other organs of an international organization, in addition to the possible recognition of governmental status by an adjudicative organ, there may also be judicial affirmation of recognition of governmental status.[54]

[50] In the present chapter, the 'recognition' of governmental status refers, unless otherwise specified, to the acceptance by an international organization of a specific ostensible government as the government of a state.

[51] See also Schermers and Blokker (n 20) 1236, §1851. As a matter internal to an international organization, one or more organs may defer to the decision of one or more other organs. See eg Annex I to the 'Transmission of Communications Submitted by the United Nations and the Bureau of the Assembly of States Parties Pursuant to Pre-Trial Chamber II's Decision ICC-02/17-165 of 8 October 2021' (5 November 2021) ICC-02/17-169 ('Letter from the Under-Secretary-General for Legal Affairs and United Nations Legal Counsel to the Registrar of the International Criminal Court' (18 October 2021), available at <http://icc-cpi.int/sites/default/files/RelatedRecords/CR2021_10229.PDF>).

[52] UNGA res 63/301 (30 June 2009) UN Doc A/RES/63/301, §§1–2. For further examples, see UNGA res 46/7 (11 October 1991) UN Doc A/RES/46/7, §2; UNSC res 1453 (24 December 2002) UN Doc S/RES/1453, third unnumbered preambular paragraph.

[53] UNSC res 1267 (15 October 1999) UN Doc S/RES/1267, §1.

[54] See eg ECommHR, 'Decision of 26 May 1975 on the admissibility of the applications (App Nos 6780/74 and 6950/75)', *Decisions and Reports*, vol 2, 125, 135; *Application of the Convention*

More frequently, recognition of governmental status arises from the acceptance of a person as a state representative, including by the acceptance as effective of the ostensible representation of a state.[55] Indeed, the decision by an international organization to accept as effective the ostensible representation of a state typically implies the organization's recognition of a particular person or collectivity of persons as the government of that state under customary international law. This is because the acceptance by an international organization of a person as a state representative often amounts to its acceptance that that person comprises at least a part of, or acts under the authority of, the ostensible government that qualifies, in the organization's view, as the state's government and because the organization generally defers to the customary international legal position in identifying the state's government.[56] The occasional suggestion that an international organization does not as a general matter engage in recognition of governments or that one of more of its organs lack 'the capacity to recognize a government'[57] appear to be premised on a narrower understanding of the term 'recognition' which does not exclude acceptance of governmental status.[58] That said, an international organization may accept a person as a state representative without according recognition of governmental status.[59]

on the Prevention and Punishment of the Crime of Genocide (Bosnia and Herzegovina v Yugoslavia), Preliminary Objections [1996] ICJ Rep 595 ('*Bosnia and Herzegovina v Yugoslavia*') 622, §44; *Beijing Urban Construction Group Co Ltd v Yemen* (ICSID Case No ARB/14/30) *Procedural Order No 2* (8 November 2016) §§5–6 and *Yemen Company for Mobile Telephony-Sabafon v Yemen* (PCA Case No 2010-03) *Procedural Order No 11* (2 May 2018) §§88–9, as covered in Mohtashami, 'Protecting the Legitimacy of the Arbitral Process: Jurisdictional and Procedural Challenges in Public–Private Disputes' in Kalicki and Raouf (eds), *Evolution and Adaptation: The Future of International Arbitration* (Kluwer 2019) 619, 625–7.

[55] See eg Secretariat of the United Nations (n 17) 532, §5; UNGA, 'Official Records, 26th Session, 1973rd Plenary Meeting' (21 October 1971) UN Doc A/PV.1973, §52 (Romania); OASPC, 'Acta de la Sesión Extraordinaria celebrada el 9 de abril de 2019' (9 April 2019) OEA/Ser.G, CP/ACTA 2217/19, 23 (Dominica). The view to the contrary (eg 'Letter Dated 8 March 1950 from the Secretary-General to the President of the Security Council Transmitting a Memorandum on the Legal Aspects of the Problem of Representation in the United Nations' (9 March 1950) UN Doc S/1466, 2–3 ('Letter Dated 8 March 1950')) appears to be based on the mistaken view that recognition of governmental status by an international organization precludes the possibility of separate recognition, non-recognition, or denial of governmental status by states. See also Kleczkowskwa, '"Recognition" of Governments by International Organizations—The Example of the UN General Assembly and Asian States' (2017) 35 CYILA 136, 148–55; Barber, 'The Role of the General Assembly in Determining the Legitimacy of Governments' (2022) 71 ICLQ 627, 644–5. On the distinction between recognition of governmental status by an international organization from recognition of governmental status by states, see section 5.4.3.

[56] Recall section 5.3.2.

[57] See eg 'Letter Dated 8 March 1950' (n 55) 2–3; Secretariat of the United Nations (Legal Opinions), 'Scope of Credentials in Rule 27 of the Rules of Procedure of the General Assembly: Statement by the Legal Counsel Submitted to the President of the General Assembly at Its Request' [1970] UNJYB 169, 170, §3; *Mobil Cerro Negro v Venezuela* (n 48) §45; 'Daily Press Briefing by the Office of the Spokesperson for the Secretary-General' (7 September 2021), available at <http://press.un.org/en/2021/db210907.doc.htm>.

[58] On the various meanings of the term 'recognition', recall section 3.2.1.

[59] See further section 5.4.1.2.

As distinct from the mere non-recognition of governmental status,[60] an international organization may deny the governmental status of a specific ostensible government. It may do so through an official statement to that effect, including in the context of a decision concerning the ostensible representation or an ostensible representative of a state. An example in this regard is the determination by the Office of the Prosecutor of the International Criminal Court that 'on both the date that [a] purported declaration was signed and the date it was submitted, ... Dr Morsi was no longer the governmental authority with the legal capacity to incur new international legal obligations on behalf of the State of Egypt'.[61]

The decision of an international organization to treat as ineffective for one or more of its purposes the ostensible representation of a state may, but does not necessarily, reflect the view by that organization that a specific claimant does not qualify for governmental status as a matter of customary international law. The same is true in respect of the decision of an international organization that a person does not qualify as a state representative. Whether or not the view by an international organization that a person is not a state representative or that the ostensible representation of a state is ineffective amounts to denial by that organization of governmental status depends on the reason for which the organization took the view in question.[62]

5.4.1.2 State Representation and Recognition of Governmental Status

In accordance with the general position that the acceptance of a person as a state representative involves recognition of governmental status,[63] an act of recognition of governmental status by an international organization that occurs on a regular basis is the decision to accept as effective the ostensible appointment by a state of its representatives in or vis-à-vis that organization. This typically occurs in the form of the acceptance of credentials.[64] The occasional suggestion that a decision whether or not to accept the credentials of a state's ostensible representative is

[60] On the distinction between non-recognition of governmental status and denial of governmental status, recall chapter 3, n 36 and accompanying text.

[61] ICC, 'The Determination of the Office of the Prosecutor on the Communication Received in Relation to Egypt' (Press release, 8 May 2014) (ICC-OTP-20130508-PR1003), available at <http://icc-cpi.int/Pages/item.aspx?name=pr1003>, §4.

[62] Recall section 3.3.1 on the analogous situation concerning the denial by states of the effectiveness of the ostensible representation of a state.

[63] Recall section 5.4.1.1.

[64] See eg UNSC (n 33) §67 (China); OASGA, 'Cuadragésimo Noveno Período Ordinario de Sesiones' (26–28 June 2019) Actas y Documentos, vol II, OEA/Ser.P/XLIX-O.2, 39 (Uruguay). See also Wright, 'Some Thoughts about Recognition' (1950) 44 AJIL 548, 558, §11; Kelsen, *Principles of International Law* (2nd edn, Rinehart & Winston 1966) 406; Ciobanu, 'Credentials of Delegations and Representation of Member States at the United Nations' (1976) 25 ICLQ 351, especially 360–8; Halberstam, 'Excluding Israel from the General Assembly by a Rejection of Its Credentials' (1984) 78 AJIL 179, 183; Talmon (n 24); Schermers and Blokker (n 20) 215, §260 and 1236, §1851; Conforti and Focarelli, *The Law and Practice of the United Nations* (5th rev edn, BRILL 2016) 70–1; Magiera (n 6) 455–60, §§25–39. But see eg Secretariat of the United Nations (n 57) 170, §3.

only a 'technical' matter which concerns only the authenticity of the credentials in question—that is, whether or not the credentials are indeed issued by the person or collectivity of persons by whom they purport to be issued[65]—does not carry much weight. Indeed, the UNGA 'physically examine[s] credentials . . . only . . . exceptionally in individual cases if the need arises'.[66] As one state has put it, '[a]n examination of the credentials . . . can only mean a verification that these credentials are in fact issued by the true and lawful Government of the Member State'.[67] Even some of the occasional suggestions that the acceptance of the credentials of an ostensible state representative 'is not an act of recognition'[68] acknowledge that it is the 'criteria for recognition which would justify receiving [the ostensible] representatives [of a state] at the United Nations'.[69] Such statements[70] may thus be taken to refer to 'recognition' in some narrower sense, which does not preclude the acceptance of a specific ostensible government as the government of a state.[71]

Other ways by which an international organization may recognize governmental status in the context of the acceptance of a person as a state representative include its invitation to have a person represent a state in the work of that organization or perhaps even its mere circulation of documents submitted by an ostensible state representative as documents of that state.[72]

The acceptance of a person as a state representative is to be distinguished from the acceptance of a person as a representative of some other entity or group of persons. For example, the UNSC may invite a person to participate in its work on the basis of Rule 39 of its Provisional Rules of Procedure, which allows for the limited participation in the UNSC's work by persons not as state representatives.[73] While the acceptance of a person as a representative of an entity other than a state does not necessarily involve recognition of governmental status, such acceptance does ordinarily imply recognition of governmental status when the representatives in question are to be appointed by a state. An example in this regard concerns the

[65] See eg UNGA, 'Official Records, 29th Session, 2320th Plenary Meeting' (16 December 1974) UN Doc A/PV.2320, §62 (Saudi Arabia) and Schermers and Blokker (n 20) 221–2, §263, albeit seemingly only in relation to the UNGA's Credentials Committee.

[66] Secretariat of the United Nations (n 15) 129, §5. See also UNGA, 'Official Records, 29th Session, 2248th Plenary Meeting' (30 September 1974) UN Doc A/PV.2248, §124 (India).

[67] UNGA, 'Official Records, 27th Session, 2104th Plenary Meeting' (8 December 1972) UN Doc A/PV.2104, §21 (Tanzania). See also UNGA, 'Credentials of Representatives to the Twenty-Eighth Session of the General Assembly: Second Report of the Credentials Committee' (12 December 1973) UN Doc A/9179/Add.1, §8 (Tanzania); Secretariat of the United Nations (n 17) 532, §6: 'the Credentials Committee . . . would . . . be compelled to reject any credentials which are not issued by a sovereign Iraqi government'.

[68] See eg HC Debs, 6 December 1979, vol 975, col 760.

[69] UNGA, 'Official Records, 29th Session, 2301st Plenary Meeting' (27 November 1974) UN Doc A/PV.2301, §175 (UK).

[70] For further examples, see n 123 below.

[71] Recall section 3.2.1.

[72] See *a contrario* Secretariat of the United Nations (n 46) 468, §6.

[73] UNSC Provisional Rules of Procedure (n 7) Rule 39.

'delegates representing . . . the employers and the workpeople of each of the members' in the ILO.[74]

Genuine doubt as to the identity of a state's government or other reasons may lead an international organization to refrain from expressing its view on a particular claim to governmental status, even if this results in a state being temporarily unrepresented for one or more purposes of the organization.[75] That said, restraint by an international organization from expressing its view on the governmental status of one or more ostensible governments does not invariably result in a state being unrepresented for any purpose of the organization.

There are different ways by which an international organization may avoid recognition of governmental status while allowing an ostensible state representative to participate in its work.

The possibility of allowing for limited participation, not as a state representative, in the work of the UNSC based on Rule 39 of its Provisional Rules of Procedure has already been mentioned. It was in this way that the UNSC had two persons, each acting under the authority of a different ostensible government of the Dominican Republic, participate in the UNSC's work without recognizing either claim to governmental status.[76] Not entirely dissimilarly, a person purporting to be the representative of a state may be invited to participate in the work of the UNSC without the UNSC indicating whether or not its invitation is based on Rule 37 of its Provisional Rules of Procedure, a rule which provides for the participation in the work of the UNSC by '[a]ny Member of the United Nations which is not a member of the Security Council'.[77] This was the case with the participation of the representative of the Federal Republic of Yugoslavia (Serbia and Montenegro) (FRY) in the UNSC's work in the 1990s, although the absence of a reference to a specific rule may have been motivated by the desire to avoid an inference of UN membership, not to avoid recognition of governmental status.[78] The Security Council may even confer 'the same rights of participation as those conferred on a Member State when invited to participate under rule 37' without, however, allowing an individual to participate under Rule 37.[79]

[74] Constitution of the International Labour Organization (adopted 28 June 1919, entered into force 10 January 1920, last amended 21 February 1973), available at <http://ilo.org/dyn/normlex/en/f?p=1000:62:0::NO:62:P62_LIST_ENTRIE_ID:2453907:NO>, art 3(1) and (5). On the persons appointed by states to participate in the work of the ILO in different capacities, see also *Competence of the International Labour Organization to Regulate, Incidentally, the Personal Work of the Employer, Advisory Opinion* (1926) PCIJ, Series B, No 13, 5, 16, in which the Court distinguishes between the two classes of so-called 'Representatives of the Members'. On the one hand are 'representatives' appointed by the members but who represent employers or employees, and, on the other hand, are representatives of 'the governments'—that is, 'representatives' in the sense of actually representing the views of the state.

[75] For examples of such action, which has sometimes left a state unrepresented, see Secretariat of the United Nations (n 46) 465–7, §§3, 6.

[76] See eg UNSC, 'Official Records, 1232nd Meeting' (26 July 1965) UN Doc S/PV.1232, §8.

[77] UNSC Provisional Rules of Procedure (n 7) Rule 37.

[78] See Wood, 'Participation of Former Yugoslav States in the United Nations and in Multilateral Treaties' (1997) 1 MPUNYB 231, 250.

[79] See UNSC, 'Official Records, 2221st Meeting' (8 May 1980) UN Doc S/PV.2221, §§5, 8.

An international organization might even have the power to allow an ostensible state representative to represent that state for one or more purposes of the organization without accepting governmental status.

One prominent example of the acceptance of a person as a state representative without recognition of governmental status is the acceptance of a person as a state representative on a 'provisional' basis.[80] Such acceptance, as well as the subsequent acceptance as effective of the ostensible representation of a state, on a 'provisional' basis is an act of mere non-recognition.[81] Perhaps for this reason, the acceptance as effective of the ostensible representation of a state on a 'provisional' basis is not uncommon where there is doubt as to the identity of the government of the state or where there is reluctance to recognize an ostensible government for some other reason.[82] The UNGA's approach to the ostensible representation of Hungary between 1957 and 1962[83] appears to be an example of a case that at least initially involved doubt as to whether its ostensible government qualified for governmental status as a matter of customary international law,[84] although it is possible that this was eventually a 'symbolic' gesture involving the disapproval of the circumstances that led to the emergence to power of that ostensible government.[85] More recent examples of 'provisional' representation which relate to doubt as to who, if anyone, qualifies for governmental status under customary international law appear to include the approach of the UNGA in respect of the representation, since 2021, of Myanmar and Afghanistan[86] and, in 2022, also of

[80] On the meaning and rules of international organizations pertaining to 'provisional' representation, recall n 47 above and accompanying text.

[81] On the distinction between non-recognition and denial of governmental status, see section 3.2.3. Cf Wilde, 'In the Matter of the Statute of the International Criminal Court and in the Matter of the Declaration Made by the National Unity Government as the Republic of the Union of Myanmar Accepting the Jurisdiction of the International Criminal Court under Article 12(3) of the Statute: Opinion' (15 August 2022), available at <http://the-world-is-watching.org/wp-content/uploads/2022/08/Wilde-Burma-ICC-opinion-15-Aug.pdf>, §§40–1.

[82] On the reluctance to recognize certain governments, recall section 3.4.1.

[83] On the apparent non-recognition of this ostensible government, see nn 89–90 below and the accompanying text.

[84] On that claimant's potential non-satisfaction of the requirement of autonomy, see eg UNGA res 1133 (XI) (14 September 1957) UN Doc A/RES/1133(XI) §4(*b*); UNGA, 'Official Records, 12th Session, 726th Plenary Meeting' (10 December 1957) UN Doc A/PV.726, §7 (USA). For doubt as to the enjoyment by that claimant of governmental status, see also eg UNGA, 'Credentials of Representatives to the Eleventh Session of the General Assembly: Report of the Credentials Committee' (n 33) §9 (Netherlands).

[85] Crawford, 'Democracy and the Body of International Law' in Fox and Roth (eds), *Democratic Governance and International Law* (CUP 2000) 91, 108. See also eg UNGA, 'Credentials of Representatives to the Seventeenth Session of the General Assembly: Report of the Credentials Committee' (20 December 1962) UN Doc A/5395, §§10–16.

[86] UNGA, 'Credentials of Representatives to the Seventy-Sixth Session of the General Assembly: Report of the Credentials Committee' (1 December 2021) UN Doc A/76/550, §§9, 15; UNGA res 76/15 (6 December 2021) UN Doc A/RES/76/15; UNGA, 'Credentials of Representatives to the Seventy-Seventh Session of the General Assembly: Report of the Credentials Committee' (12 December 2022) UN Doc A/77/600, §§11, 17; UNGA res 77/239 (16 December 2022) UN Doc A/RES/77/239. On doubt as to the identity of the respective governments of those states, recall section 4.2.2.3 and chapter 4, n 167.

Libya.[87] The UNGA's approach between 1996 and 2001 in allowing Burhanuddin Rabbani's government to represent Afghanistan on a 'provisional' basis might have been motivated by reluctance to recognize this 'transitional' government.[88]

The precise way by which the 'provisional' representation of a state arises in an international organization may vary, even as regards the practice of only one organ of an international organization. In respect of state delegates at the UNGA, for example, the UNGA may refrain from taking an affirmative or negative stance on the credentials of an ostensible state representative with, without, or against the recommendation of its Credentials Committee. An example in this regard includes the UNGA's approval of the Credentials Committee's report in 1957, which recorded the adoption of the motion to 'take no decision regarding the credentials submitted on behalf of the representatives of Hungary'.[89] This was the approach of the UNGA and its Credentials Committee in respect of the credentials submitted by the ostensible representatives of Hungary until 1962.[90] Further examples concern the ostensible representatives of South Africa in 1965 and between 1970 and 1972. In 1965, the UNGA decided 'to take no decision on the credentials submitted on behalf of the representatives of South Africa',[91] despite the Credentials Committee's recommendation that the UNGA approve the Committee's report, in

[87] UNGA, 'Credentials of Representatives to the Seventy-Seventh Session of the General Assembly' (n 86) §11.

[88] On the non-recognition of this government, see UNGA, 'Credentials of Representatives to the Fifty-First Session of the General Assembly: First Report of the Credentials Committee' (23 October 1996) UN Doc A/51/548, §14; UNGA res 51/9 (8 November 1996) UN Doc A/RES/51/9; UNGA, 'Credentials of Representatives to the Fifty-Second Session of the General Assembly: Report of the Credentials Committee' (11 December 1997) UN Doc A/52/719, §§10–11; UNGA res 52/178 (18 December 1997) UN Doc A/RES/52/178; UNGA, 'Credentials of Representatives to the Fifty-Third Session of the General Assembly: First Report of the Credentials Committee' (29 October 1998) UN Doc A/53/556, §§8–9; UNGA res 53/23 (10 November 1988) UN Doc A/RES/53/23; UNGA, 'Credentials of Representatives to the Fifty-Fourth Session of the General Assembly: First Report of the Credentials Committee' (18 October 1999) UN Doc A/54/475, §§9–10; UNGA res 54/6 (25 October 1999) UN Doc A/RES/54/6; UNGA, 'Credentials of Representatives to the Fifty-Fifth Session of the General Assembly: First Report of the Credentials Committee' (1 November 2000) UN Doc A/55/537, §§89; UNGA res 55/16 (6 November 2000) UN Doc A/RES/55/16.

[89] UNGA, 'Credentials of Representatives to the Eleventh Session of the General Assembly: Report of the Credentials Committee' (n 33) §§4, 10; UNGA res 1009 (XI) (21 February 1957) UN Doc A/RES/1009(XI).

[90] See UNGA, 'Credentials of Representatives to the Twelfth Session of the General Assembly: Report of the Credentials Committee' (9 December 1957) UN Doc A/3773, §§4, 12; UNGA res 1183 (XII) (10 December 1957) UN Doc A/RES/1183(XII); UNGA, 'Credentials of Representatives to the Thirteenth Session of the General Assembly: Report of the Credentials Committee' (12 December 1958) UN Doc A/4074, §§10, 13; UNGA res 1346 (XIII) (13 December 1958) UN Doc A/RES/1346(XIII); UNGA, 'Credentials of Representatives to the Fourteenth Session of the General Assembly: Report of the Credentials Committee' (9 December 1959) UN Doc A/4346, §§9, 11; UNGA res 1457 (XIV) (10 December 1959) UN Doc A/RES/1457(XIV); UNGA, 'Credentials of Representatives to the Fifteenth Session of the General Assembly: Report of the Credentials Committee' (20 April 1961) UN Doc A/4743, §§10, 12; UNGA res 1618 (XV) (21 April 1961) UN Doc A/RES/1618(XV); UNGA, 'Credentials of Representatives to the Sixteenth Session of the General Assembly: Report of the Credentials Committee' (18 December 1961) UN Doc A/5055, §§11, 14; UNGA res 1693 (XVI) (19 December 1961) UN Doc A/RES/1693(XVI); UNGA (n 85) §§10, 18; UNGA res 1871 (XVII) (20 December 1962) UN Doc A/RES/1871(XVII).

[91] UNGA res 2113 (XX) B (21 December 1965) UN Doc A/RES/2113(XX).

which all credentials were found to be in order, including those of South Africa.[92] Between 1970 and 1972, the UNGA approved the report of the Credentials Committee under consideration in each case, 'except with regard to the credentials of the representatives of the Government of South Africa'.[93] This was so despite the Credentials Committee having recommended the acceptance of South Africa's credentials, at least in 1971 and 1972.[94] The more recent decisions by the UNGA to 'defer' its decision on the credentials of Afghanistan (1996–2001, 2021),[95] Guinea and Madagascar (2009),[96] Guinea-Bissau (2012),[97] Myanmar (2021–),[98] and Libya (2022–)[99] resemble the UNGA's approach in the 1950s and in 1960 to 'postpone . . . consideration of all proposals to exclude the representatives of the Government of the Republic of China and to seat representatives of the Central People's Government of the People's Republic of China'.[100]

The UNGA may also decide that any proposal to change the claimant to governmental status under whose authority a state is represented is an 'important question'. This raises the requisite majority for the recognition by the UNGA of any other ostensible government of that state.[101] To date, this has been done only in respect

[92] See UNGA, 'Credentials of Representatives to the Nineteenth and Twentieth Sessions of the General Assembly: Report of the Credentials Committee' (20 December 1965) UN Doc A/6208, §§23–7.

[93] UNGA res 2636 (XXV) A (13 November 1970) UN Doc A/RES/2636(XXV); UNGA res 2862 (XXVI) (20 December 1971) UN Doc A/RES/2862(XXVI); UNGA res 2948 (XXVII) (8 December 1972) UN Doc A/RES/2948(XXVII). On a different interpretation of a similarly-worded decision of the UNGA, also in respect of the credentials concerning South Africa, see n 316 below and accompanying text.

[94] See UNGA, 'Credentials of Representatives to the Twenty-Fifth Session of the General Assembly: Report of the Credentials Committee' (28 October 1970) UN Doc A/8142, §§16, 18; UNGA, 'Credentials of Representatives to the Twenty-Sixth Session of the General Assembly: Report of the Credentials Committee' (17 December 1971) UN Doc A/8625, §§16–22; UNGA, 'Credentials of Representatives to the Twenty-Seventh Session of the General Assembly: Report of the Credentials Committee' (1 December 1972) UN Doc A/8921, §§17–18, 22.

[95] Recall nn 86, 88 above.

[96] UNGA, 'Credentials of Representatives to the Sixty-Fourth Session of the General Assembly: Report of the Credentials Committee' (17 December 2009) UN Doc A/64/571, §§10, 12, 16; UNGA res 64/126 (16 December 2009) UN Doc A/RES/64/126.

[97] UNGA, 'Credentials of Representatives to the Sixty-Seventh Session of the General Assembly: Report of the Credentials Committee' (4 December 2012) UN Doc A/67/611, §§10–12, 16; UNGA res 67/103 (12 December 2012) UN Doc A/RES/67/103.

[98] Recall n 86 above.

[99] Recall n 87 above.

[100] UNGA res 609 A (VII) (21 December 1952) UN Doc A/RES/609(VII) §2. For identical or similar decisions in subsequent years, see UNGA res 800 (VIII) (15 September 1953) UN Doc A/RES/800(VIII); UNGA res 903 (IX) (21 September 1954) UN Doc A/RES/903(IX); UNGA res 990 (X) (20 September 1955) UN Doc A/RES/990(X); UNGA res 1108 (XI) (16 November 1956) UN Doc A/RES/1108(XI); UNGA res 1135 (XII) (24 September 1957) UN Doc A/RES/1135(XII); UNGA res 1239 (XIII) (23 September 1958) UN Doc A/RES/1239(XIII); UNGA res 1351 (XIV) (22 September 1959) UN Doc A/RES/1351(XIV); UNGA res 1493 (XV) (8 October 1960) UN Doc A/RES/1493(XV). For earlier UNGA practice to similar effect, see UNGA, 'Report of the General Committee' (10 November 1951) UN Doc A/1950, §6; UNGA, 'Official Records, 6th Session, 342nd Plenary Meeting' (13 November 1951) UN Doc A/PV.342, §155. See also UNGA res 490 (V) (19 September 1950) UN Doc A/RES/490(V) second unnumbered operative paragraph.

[101] UN Charter (n 31) art 18(2).

of the representation of China at the UN during the later years of its continued representation by its nationalist claimant[102] between 1961 and 1970.[103] During this time, none of the attempts at the UNGA to have the communist claimant represent China at the UN were successful.[104] Indeed, until at least 1965, the Credentials Committee understood the UNGA's decision to preclude the Committee from rejecting the credentials of the ostensible government already representing China at the UN.[105]

Beyond 'provisional' representation, further possible examples of the acceptance of a person as a state representative without recognition of governmental status involve certain decisions of adjudicative bodies to accept specific individuals as state representatives for the purposes of proceedings before them on considerations that are expressly stated or are otherwise clearly distinct from the customary international legal framework for the enjoyment of governmental status. Illustratively, one annulment committee of the International Centre for Settlement of Investment Disputes (ICSID) found that, in its rejection of a request for reconsideration of an order concerning who may represent Venezuela, it 'has not identified the legitimate government of Venezuela' and, indeed, had not examined any criterion for governmental status or the recognition by states of either ostensible government.[106]

It may not always be clear whether or not the acceptance of a person as a state representative involves recognition of governmental status. The approach of an ICSID tribunal to decide who may represent Venezuela before it without

[102] See UNGA res 1668 (XVI) (15 December 1961) UN Doc A/RES/1668(XVI); UNGA res 2025 (XX) (17 November 1965) UN Doc A/RES/2025(XX); UNGA res 2159 (XXI) (29 November 1966) UN Doc A/RES/2159(XXI); UNGA res 2271 (XXII) (28 November 1967) UN Doc A/RES/2271(XXII); UNGA res 2389 (XXIII) (19 November 1968) UN Doc A/RES/2389(XXIII); UNGA res 2500 (XXIV) (11 November 1969) UN Doc A/RES/2500(XXIV); UNGA res 2642 (XXV) (20 November 1970) UN Doc A/RES/2642(XXV).

[103] In 1971, the UNGA '[*d*]*ecide*[*d*] . . . to recognize the representatives of [the] Government [of the People's Republic of China] as the only legitimate representatives of China to the United Nations, and to expel forthwith the representatives of Chiang Kai-shek from the place which they unlawfully occupy at the United Nations' (UNGA res 2758 (XXVI) (25 October 1971) UN Doc A/RES/2758(XXVI) sole unnumbered operative paragraph).

[104] See eg UNGA, 'Official Records, 17th Session, 1162nd Plenary Meeting' (30 October 1962) UN Doc A/PV.1162, §81.

[105] See eg UNGA (n 85) §§6–8; UNGA, 'Credentials of Representatives to the Eighteenth Session of the General Assembly: Report of the Credentials Committee' (14 December 1963) UN Doc A/5676/Rev.1, §§8–10; UNGA, 'Credentials of Representatives to the Nineteenth and Twentieth Sessions of the General Assembly: Report of the Credentials Committee' (20 December 1965) UN Doc A/6208, §§8–17. For a change to the approach of the Credentials Committee on this matter, see UNGA, 'Credentials of Representatives to the Twenty-First Session of the General Assembly: Report of the Credentials Committee' (17 December 1966) UN Doc A/6620, §§5–13. For subsequent consideration and acceptance of the credentials issued by the nationalist claimant, see eg UNGA, 'Credentials of Representatives to the Twenty-Fourth Session of the General Assembly: Report of the Credentials Committee' (15 December 1969) UN Doc A/7634, §§8–11; UNGA, 'Credentials of Representatives to the Twenty-Fifth Session of the General Assembly' (n 94) §§7–9.

[106] *ConocoPhilips v Venezuela*, 2 November 2020 (n 48) §40. See also ibid, §§35–7; *ConocoPhilips v Venezuela*, 15 February 2023 (n 48) §24.

'deciding on "the recognition of a Venezuelan government" or on the recognition of Venezuela's "legitimate Government"'[107] while nevertheless having regard to whether various 'consideration[s]' 'rebut[ted] the presumption in favour of the formal "representative of record"', including an examination of whether at least one of the ostensible governments exercised effective control, albeit as apparently distinct from considerations of international law, appears to illustrate this point.[108] Further possible examples also concern the not-infrequent reliance of certain adjudicative bodies on the status quo as the position against which the burden of proof lies,[109] an approach which bears resemblance to the presumption in favour of incumbent governments.[110] Decisions involving such reliance may be said to involve recognition of governmental status, depending perhaps on the reason or reasons for adopting this position[111] and on the considerations which are deemed relevant to satisfying the burden of proof for departing from the status quo. It is unclear, moreover, whether an international organization recognizes the governmental status of a specific claimant in requesting whomever happens to occupy the diplomatic premises in the international organization's host country to transmit certain materials 'to the competent . . . authorities' of a state.[112]

5.4.2 The Value of Recognition of Governmental Status by International Organizations

For at least the same reasons as the recognition or denial by states of governmental status,[113] the recognition or denial of governmental status by an international organization is not determinative of governmental status as a matter of

[107] *Mobil Cerro Negro v Venezuela* (n 48) §45.

[108] Ibid, §§53, 56–66.

[109] See ibid, §§53–4; *Valores Mundiales SL and Consorcio Andino SL v Bolivarian Republic of Venezuela* (ICSID Case No ARB/13/11), *Annulment Proceeding, Procedural Resolution No 2* (29 August 2019) ('*Valores v Venezuela*') §42.

[110] On this presumption, recall chapter 3, n 124 and accompanying text. On the adoption of 'the *status quo* approach' by a municipal court, see *Bank of China v Wells Fargo Bank & Union Trust Co* (1950) 92 F Supp 920 (cf *Bank of China v Wells Fargo Bank & Union Trust Co* (1952) 104 F Supp 59). But see eg *ConocoPhilips v Venezuela*, 3 April 2020 (n 48) §§31–7 on the adoption of 'the *status quo* approach' in a situation that resulted in the representation of a state by two rival ostensible governments.

[111] For example, there may be a difference between the adoption of a presumption in favour of the status quo because one ostensible representative already has 'the formal quality' of being representative and the adoption of this presumption because it 'provides continuity in the interest of orderly proceedings and the right of defence'. For both of these approaches, see *Mobil Cerro Negro v Venezuela* (n 48) §52.

[112] See eg *Decision Pursuant to Article 18(2) of the Statute Authorising the Prosecution to Resume Investigation*, Pre-Trial Chamber II (31 October 2022) ICC-02/17-196, §11. But see *Judgment on the Prosecutor's Appeal against the Decision of Pre-Trial Chamber II Entitled 'Decision Pursuant to Article 18(2) of the Statute Authorising the Prosecution to Resume Investigation'*, Appeals Chamber (4 April 2023) ICC-02/17 OA5, §15 for the subsequent treatment of the representation by the head of a state's diplomatic mission as the position of that state.

[113] Recall section 3.5.1.

customary international law. At the same time, such practice may have evidential value with respect to the content and application of the customary international legal framework by reference to which the identity of a state's government is to be established.[114] For example, the ICJ relied on his recognition as head of state by the UN in finding that Alija Izetbegović qualified as head of state of Bosnia and Herzegovina.[115] Similarly, the decision of the ECommHR on the representative capacity of a specific ostensible government was informed by the UN's recognition of that ostensible government as the government of Cyprus.[116] The domestic courts of a state may also have regard to the recognition of governmental status by an international organization in assessing the governmental status of a specific ostensible government of another state.[117] But any practice concerning the recognition of governments by international organizations is of relatively limited evidential value as compared to the decision of states to accord or deny governmental status to a specific person or collectivity of persons.[118]

5.4.3 State Practice Concerning Recognition of Governments in the Context of International Organizations

There are a number of contexts in which a state may recognize or deny the government status of a specific claimant as the government of another state, regardless of the decision of the organization. The decision of an international organization to recognize, not to recognize, or to deny the governmental status of an ostensible government does not ipso facto amount to the recognition or denial of governmental status by the member states of that organization.[119] The acceptance of governmental status by one or more states in the context of the work of an international organization nevertheless typically occurs in situations where the international organization itself recognizes the governmental status of one or more ostensible governments. In any event, an international organization may contribute to the identification of a state's government by serving as a forum for the recognition of governmental status by any number of states that are participating in the work of an international organization.[120]

[114] Recall chapter 3, n 279.
[115] *Bosnia and Herzegovina v Yugoslavia* (n 54) 622, §44.
[116] ECommHR (n 54) 135.
[117] *Republic of Somalia v Woodhouse Drake & Carey (Suisse) SA and others* [1993] QB 54, 67–8.
[118] See ILC, 'Draft Conclusions on Identification of Customary International Law, with Commentaries' in *ILC Report* (2018) UN Doc A/73/10, 122 (ILC, 'Draft Conclusions on Identification of Customary International Law'), 130–1 (conclusions 4(1)–(2) and comments 1–7).
[119] See also Talmon (n 24) 174–5; UNGA res 396 (n 16) §4: 'the attitude adopted by the General Assembly . . . shall not of itself affect the direct relations of individual Member States with the State concerned'.
[120] See also ILC, 'Draft Conclusions on Identification of Customary International Law' (n 118) 147–8 (conclusion 12, in particular conclusion 12(2) and comments 2–3 and 5–6).

For example, a state's vote in favour of the adoption of a resolution which includes a statement of recognition by the international organization amounts to recognition by the state of governmental status.[121] In what occurs with greater frequency, a positive indication by a state that it accepts as effective the appointment of an individual as another state's representative implies the former state's recognition of the claimant to governmental status through which the ostensible representative was appointed as at least part of the latter state's government. Accordingly, the expression by a state of the view that the credentials issued through a specific ostensible government are indeed credentials of a state generally involves acceptance of governmental status, even if the international organization does not accept those credentials as valid. Such acceptance may take the form of a state's vote in favour of adopting a resolution to accept the credentials in question, generally among credentials of the representatives of other states,[122] at least where the voting state makes no declaration to the contrary. The occasional suggestion by a state that, in general, its acceptance of another state's ostensible credentials as being in order 'should not necessarily be taken as implying recognition of the authorities by whom the credentials were issued'[123] is to be understood as referring to a narrower understanding of the term 'recognition' that does not exclude acceptance of governmental status.[124]

Through a disclaimer against recognition, a state may nevertheless refrain from recognizing or even deny the governmental status of an ostensible government of another state, even if the former state votes in favour of action by the international organization that would involve the organization's recognition of governmental status of the ostensible government in question.

As in other contexts,[125] whether or not a particular statement amounts to either the non-acceptance or the denial of governmental status may be unclear. This includes, for example, statements in which states reserved their position in respect of the credentials ostensibly submitted by South Africa or indicated that they could not recognize those credentials because the ostensible government that submitted those credentials was not representative of the people of South Africa.[126] Absent any further clarification,[127] such statements are ambivalent as to

[121] For examples of such statements, recall n 52 above.

[122] Recall n 33 above and accompanying text. Additionally, recall section 5.4.1.2 for the acceptance by an international organization of credentials as involving recognition by that organization of governmental status.

[123] UNGA, 'Official Records, 17th Session, 1202nd Plenary Meeting' (n 33) §106 (UK). See also eg UNGA, 'Official Records, 29th Session, 2320th Plenary Meeting' (n 65) §78 (Saudi Arabia). The same point has also been made by the UN. See 'Letter Dated 8 March' (n 55) 5.

[124] Recall, similarly, the text accompanying nn 68–71 above. On the different meanings of the term 'recognition', recall section 3.2.1.

[125] Recall section 3.3.2.1.

[126] See eg chapter 4, n 279 for such statements.

[127] The characterization in some such statements of the credentials as being 'of the representatives of the Government of South Africa' or even as being 'the credentials of the South African delegation' or

whether they reflect either non-recognition or denial of governmental status.[128] The same is true of the more recent statement that arose during the work of that Credentials Committee in which the USA 'dissociated [itself] from the adoption of the Committee's resolution . . . with respect to the acceptance of the credentials submitted by the Maduro representative on behalf of the Bolivarian Republic of Venezuela'.[129] One complicating factor in ascertaining the meaning of such statements is the different senses in which the term 'recognition' may be used. A statement purporting not to recognize a specific ostensible government might concern only 'recognition' in a sense that does not exclude acceptance of governmental status.[130] At the same time, a statement might reflect the non-recognition of governmental status without employing the term 'recognition'. For example, in 1981, the UK stated 'that the fact that [its] delegation has not objected to the credentials of Afghanistan does not mean that [its] Government regards the Babrak Karmal regime as a Government'.[131] The same can be said for the denial of governmental status.

One indication that a disclaimer concerns denial of governmental status might be the suggestion by the disclaiming state of its view that the ostensible government in question does not satisfy one or more of the customary international legal criteria of governmental status. For example, in what might be taken to concern the requirement of autonomy,[132] in 1981, Belgium sought 'to make it clear that the fact that [its] delegation did not raise any objection to the credentials of Afghanistan should not be interpreted as recognition by [it] of the present regime in Afghanistan, which was imposed from outside upon the Afghan people'.[133] But again, the different possible meanings of the term 'recognition' do not facilitate the ascertainment of whether or not this statement involves denial of governmental status. Similarly, the Federal Republic of Germany's explanation that its lack of protest against the Credentials Committee's report on the acceptance of 'the credentials

of 'the minority Government in South Africa' might indicate a different position from the reference to those credentials as being 'of the so-called South African delegation'.

[128] Recall chapter 3, nn 253–5 and accompanying text on the government of a state being the presumptive representative of the people of the state and on the possibility of this presumption being rebutted.

[129] UNGA, 'Credentials of Representatives to the Seventy-Fifth Session: Report of the Credentials Committee' (23 November 2020) UN Doc A/75/606, §9 (USA). See, similarly, UNGA, 'Credentials of Representatives to the Seventy-Sixth Session: Report of the Credentials Committee' (n 86) §12; UNGA, 'Credentials of Representatives to the Seventy-Seventh Session' (n 86) §14 (USA). See also UNGA, 'Official Records, 76th Session, 44th Plenary Meeting' (6 December 2021) UN Doc A/76/PV.44, 2 (Colombia, on behalf of a number of states).

[130] On the different meanings of 'recognition', recall section 3.2.1.

[131] UNGA, 'Official Records, 36th Session, 103rd Plenary Meeting' (17 December 1981) UN Doc A/36/PV.103, §97.

[132] See section 4.2.2.2.

[133] UNGA, 'Official Records, 36th Session, 103rd Plenary Meeting' (n 131) §98. On the relevance of such imposition to the requirement of autonomy, recall section 4.2.2.2.

of the Afghan delegation' 'does not mean that [it] recognize[s] the legitimacy of a regime installed and kept in power by foreign intervention' appears ambivalent, given the possible different meanings of the term 'legitimacy'.[134] Its clarification that its position was to be understood in the light of its 'view that that [Credentials] Committee has solely the technical task of examining whether the credentials of a delegation are formally in order' nevertheless indicates non-recognition of governmental status.[135]

A disclaimer against recognition might be coupled with the recognition of a rival ostensible government of the state whose government's identity is in question, in which case the disclaiming state would generally be taken to deny the governmental status of the ostensible government which the disclaimer concerns.[136] An example in this regard is the statement on behalf of the states comprising the so-called 'Lima Group' in which they provide that their approval of the Credentials Committee's report 'should not be interpreted as those countries' tacit recognition of Mr Nicolás Maduro Moros' regime'. They explained that they 'do not recognize Mr Maduro's illegitimate regime in Venezuela. Instead, they recognize Mr Juan Guaidó as Acting President of Venezuela.'[137] Earlier examples include 'reservations' made by delegates in expressing their support for a report of the Credentials Committee on the acceptance of certain credentials concerning their view that they consider only the communist ostensible government of China to be 'entitled to represent China in the United Nations'.[138]

A state's view on the identity of another state's government may be expressed in other contexts related to international organizations. For example, the view of a state on the identity of another state's government may manifest in relation to what might in practice, if not in law, be a bilateral issue between the two states. Illustrative in this regard is the situation in which the state in the territory of which an international organization has its headquarters has to decide whether to treat the ostensible premises of a diplomatic mission of another state to an international organization as inviolable.[139] As in other circumstances, the acceptance of a person as a state representative ordinarily implies recognition of governmental status, while the refusal to treat a specific individual as a state representative does not necessarily involve either denial or non-recognition of governmental status.[140]

[134] Recall section 4.2.2.5.1.

[135] UNGA, 'Official Records, 36th Session, 103rd Plenary Meeting' (n 131) §99.

[136] On the recognition of the governmental status of one ostensible government as the denial of governmental status of any other ostensible government of that state, recall section 3.2.3.

[137] UNGA, 'Official Records, 75th Session, 33rd Plenary Meeting' (1 December 2020) UN Doc A/75/PV.33, 17–18.

[138] See UNGA, 'Official Records, 17th Session, 1202nd Plenary Meeting' (n 33) §56 (Sudan). See also ibid, §§1, 3 (Burma), §56 (Sudan), §§99–100 (Somalia).

[139] See the example discussed in ILC (n 26) 202–3, §§52–6. But see eg Agreement regarding the Headquarters of the United Nations (adopted 26 June 1947, entered into force 21 November 1947) 11 UNTS 11, art V, s 15 for a treaty which makes express provision for the entitlement to privileges and immunities by 'Members whose governments are not recognized by the United States'.

[140] Recall section 3.3.1.

In the absence of any indication suggesting otherwise, a state's vote against a proposal which would involve the recognition by an international organization of governmental status is an example of non-recognition. At the same time, the acceptance by a state of a person as the representative of another state on a 'provisional' basis or on some other basis that does not involve the organization's acceptance of governmental status[141] does not amount to recognition by the state of governmental status.

5.5 The 'Misrepresentation' of a State

The exercise of a power to allow the 'provisional' representation or otherwise to accept an individual as a state representative without an assessment of governmental status or the mistaken acceptance of an individual as a member or authorized representative of that state's government are reasons why an international organization might accept as effective the ostensible representation of a state by or under the authority of the 'wrong' government.[142]

For example, China was represented at the UN between 1950 and 1971 by its nationalist ostensible government on a 'provisional' basis. This first involved the decision 'provisionally' to seat the nationalist claimant's representative before postponing consideration of all proposals to change China's representation, it eventually being decided that any such proposal is an 'important question'.[143] Some states appear to have supported this approach so as to preclude the representation of China by the communist claimant, which at the time qualified as a matter of customary international law as China's government but which was seen as disregarding certain international legal obligations of China.[144]

Another possible example concerns the representation—seemingly not on a 'provisional' basis and without otherwise excluding recognition of governmental status[145]—of Venezuela in the OAS since 2019 by a person acting under the authority of Juan Guaidó, whom the OAS considered, perhaps mistakenly,[146] to comprise part of Venezuela's government.[147] Having underscored 'the constitutional authority of the democratically elected National Assembly' and having resolved to 'not recognize the legitimacy of Nicolas Maduro's new term as of the 10th of

[141] Further on representation in an international organization without recognition of governmental status by that organization, recall section 5.4.1.

[142] Recall section 5.3.2.

[143] Recall nn 100 and 102, as well as the accompanying text.

[144] See eg UNGA, 'Official Records, 25th Session, 1911th Plenary Meeting' (19 November 1970) UN Doc A/PV.1911, §§45–6 (Thailand); UNGA, 'Official Records, 25th Session, 1913th Plenary Meeting' (20 November 1970) UN Doc A/PV.1913, §3 (Cambodia). See also UNGA res 396 (V) (n 16) §1.

[145] See eg OASGA (n 64) 39 (Uruguay).

[146] On uncertainty as to the identity of the government of Venezuela, recall chapter 4, n 114.

[147] On the earlier unsuccessful attempt to suspend Venezuela from the OAS on account of the alteration of the Constitutional order, see section 5.6.2.1.3.

January of 2019',[148] the Permanent Council of the Organization of American States (OASPC) accepted 'Mr. Gustavo Tarre as the [Venezuelan] National Assembly's designated Permanent Representative'.[149] This was after Juan Guaidó purported to 'annul the supposed denunciation of the OAS Charter'.[150] Later that year, the President of the OASGA was taken by the Secretary for Legal Affairs to have approved the Secretary-General's report on credentials.[151] This report included persons appointed by Juan Guaidó as the representative of Venezuela.[152] Mr Guaidó's appointees have, until 2022,[153] represented Venezuela at the OASGA, pursuant to the approval of the annual report of the Secretary-General.[154]

Further, the acceptance by an ICSID committee of an individual operating under the authority of the ostensible government of Mr Maduro and, simultaneously, of an individual operating under the authority of the rival ostensible government of Mr Guaidó as representatives of Venezuela will have involved the representation of Venezuela by at least one 'wrong' government. The committee, having considered itself to have 'the power and duty to conduct the process before it in such a way that the parties are treated fairly and with equality' deemed that the maintenance of these two representatives 'accords . . . with procedural fairness'.[155]

[148] OASPC, 'Resolution on the Situation in Venezuela' (10 January 2019) OEA/Ser.G, CP/RES.1117/19 (2200/19) fourth unnumbered preambular paragraph and §1.

[149] OASPC, 'Resolution on the Situation in Venezuela' (9 April 2019) OEA/Ser.G, CP/RES.1124 (2217/19) rev.2, §1. In this regard, the OASPC took note of a letter, dated 22 January 2019, sent from the National Assembly of Venezuela to the OAS Secretary-General. On 15 January 2019, the National Assembly had already declared that its President was to assume the functions of the presidency of Venezuela. On 23 January 2019, Juan Guaidó, the then-President of the National Assembly, claimed the presidency of Venezuela on a transitional basis. Recall chapter 4, n 113 and accompanying text.

[150] See 'Letter from Juan Guaidó to the Secretary General of the Organization of American States' (8 February 2019), available at <http://oas.org/en/sla/dil/docs/a-41_note_Juan_Guaido_03-7-2019.pdf>. For Venezuela's prior intention to withdraw from the OAS, see 'Note from the Permanent Mission of the Bolivarian Republic of Venezuela Enclosing a Copy of the Letter Denouncing the Charter of the Organization of American States (OAS) Pursuant to Article 143 and Initiating the Permanent Withdrawal of the Bolivarian Republic of Venezuela from the Organization. April 28, 2017' (29 April 2017) OEA/Ser.G, CP/INF.7707/17.

[151] See OASGA (n 64) 38. As a result of such apparent approval, and pursuant to the OASGA's rule on reconsideration of a decision taken by the plenary, a two-thirds majority of the delegations that are members was deemed necessary for the reassessment of Venezuela's ostensible credentials.

[152] 'Lista de participantes/List of Participants' (27 June 2019) OEA/Ser.P, AG/doc.5673/19/rev.2.

[153] It appears that at the 53rd regular session of the OASGA in 2023, no credentials were presented ostensibly in Venezuela's name or, at least, no such credentials were accepted by the Secretary-General as having been presented by Venezuela. See 'Lista de participantes/List of Participants' (19 July 2023) OEA/Ser.P, AG/doc.5801/23/rev.2. See also 'Report of the Secretary General on the Presentation of Credentials of the Delegations Taking Part in the Fifty-Third Regular Session of the General Assembly' (22 June 2023) OEA Ser./P, AG/doc.5799/23.

[154] OASGA, 'Quincuagésimo Período Ordinario De Sesiones' (20–21 October 2020) Actas y Documentos, vol II, OEA/Ser.P/L-O.2, 33; OASGA, 'Quincuagésimo Primer Período Ordinario De Sesiones' (10–12 November 2021) Actas y Documentos, vol II, OEA/Ser.P/LI-O.2, 37; OASGA, 'Quincuagésimo Segundo Período Ordinario De Sesiones' (5–7 October 2022) Actas y Documentos, vol II, OEA/Ser.P/LII-O.2, 35.

[155] See *ConocoPhilips v Venezuela*, 3 April 2020 (n 48) §§36–8. See also *ConocoPhilips v Venezuela*, 2 November 2020 (n 48) §41; *ConocoPhilips v Venezuela*, 15 February 2023 (n 48) §31.

A decision of an international organization which results in a state being 'misrepresented' might raise the following distinct questions.[156] First, there might be doubt as to the validity and legal effect of such a decision and of any subsequent decision adopted with the participation of the 'misrepresented' state. Secondly, it might be asked whether the 'misrepresentation' of a state involves any violations of any international legal rights of that state. Thirdly, at least insofar as it has legal effect, a question might arise as to the implications of the 'misrepresentation' of a state on the concept of the government of a state as a matter of international law, including on the freedom of each state to choose its government, the objective international legal existence of a state's government, and the distinctive capacity of the government of a state to represent that state. Each of these questions is examined below in turn.

5.5.1 Validity and Legal Effect of 'Misrepresentation' of a State

It is not inconceivable that a decision of an international organization to accept as effective the ostensible representation of a state through its 'wrong' government is ultra vires. Indeed, the identity of a state's government and the persons chosen as state representatives in the context of an international organization are prima facie matters which international law leaves to the sovereign discretion of each state[157] and at least certain international organizations lack the power 'to intervene in matters which are essentially within the domestic jurisdiction of any State'.[158] In terms of relevant practice,[159] the following points can be made.

On the one hand, member states, whose views are relevant to the interpretation of the constituent instrument of an international organization,[160] sometimes

[156] On the distinction between the question whether an international organization acts in excess of its powers and the question whether an international organization violates any international legal obligations incumbent on it, see Lauterpacht, 'The Legal Effect of Illegal Acts of International Organisations' in *Cambridge Essays in International Law: Essays in Honour of Lord McNair* (Stevens & Sons 1965) 88, 89; Amerasinghe, *Principles of the Institutional Law of International Organizations* (2nd edn, CUP 2009) 197.

[157] Recall section 5.3.2.

[158] See UN Charter (n 31) art 2(7). See, similarly, Charter of the Organization of American States (adopted 30 April 1948, entered into force 13 December 1951, last amended 10 June 1993) ('OAS Charter') (an up-to-date version of which is available at <http://oas.org/en/sla/dil/docs/inter_american_treaties_A-41_charter_OAS.pdf>), art 1. Such a limitation does not appear in the AU Constitutive Act, which refers only to 'non-interference by any member State in the internal affairs of another'. See AU Constitutive Act (n 11) art 4(g).

[159] As a separate matter, it might be argued that a decision concerning the representation of a state is being taken by an organ of an international organization that lacks the requisite power. See eg OASPC (n 55) 12 (Mexico), 14 (Uruguay), 19 (El Salvador), 20 (Bolivia), 20–1 (Nicaragua).

[160] See eg *Immunities and Criminal Proceedings (Equatorial Guinea v France), Judgment* [2020] ICJ Rep 300, 322, §69. See also *Legal Consequences for States of the Continued Presence of South Africa in Namibia (South West Africa) notwithstanding Security Council Resolution 276 (1970) Advisory Opinion* [1971] ICJ Rep 16 ('*Namibia*') 22, §22.

suggest that a decision of an international organization to accept as effective for its purposes the 'misrepresentation' of another member state is beyond the powers of the organization, especially when the organization expressly lacks the power 'to intervene in matters which are essentially within the domestic jurisdiction of any State'. Such a suggestion sometimes takes the form of an assertion that a decision of an international organization which, in the view of the reacting state, results in the 'misrepresentation' of another member state is incompatible with a provision in the constituent instrument of the international organization which limits the organization's powers in respect of matters that are left to the sovereign discretion of each state.[161] This suggestion is reflected also in the position of member states that an international organization's acceptance as effective of what they consider to be the 'misrepresentation' of another member state amounts to an interference in the affairs of that state, especially when the international organization is expressly precluded from interfering in such affairs.[162]

On the other hand, the practice of the international organization, including practice which results in the 'misrepresentation' of a state, is also relevant to the interpretation of the constituent instrument of that organization.[163] Further, even member states which expressly opposed a decision that in their view would result in the 'misrepresentation' of another member state sometimes question the legality of neither the decision, once adopted, to accept as effective the ostensible representation of the state through what those states consider to be the 'wrong' government nor of any subsequent decision adopted with the participation of the ostensibly-'misrepresented' state. For example, the states that considered China to be represented at the UN by the 'wrong' government[164] do not generally appear to have questioned the validity of decisions made by UN organs with China's participation.[165]

[161] See eg UNGA, 'Official Records, 24th Session, 1805th Plenary Meeting' (10 November 1969) UN Doc A/PV.1805, §46 (Yemen); UNGA, 'Official Records, 28th Session, 2189th Meeting' (4 December 1973) UN Doc A/PV.2189, §§93–4 (Barbados); OASGA (n 64) 39 (Uruguay), 40–1 (Mexico), 42 (Nicaragua, Grenada, and Antigua and Barbuda), 43 (Saint Vincent and the Grenadines, and Suriname), 44 (Dominica), 44–5 (Bolivia); OASGA res 2944 (28 June 2019) AG/RES.2944 (XLIX-O/19) n 11 (Saint Kitts and Nevis).

[162] See eg UNGA, 'Official Records, 22nd Session, 1602nd Plenary Meeting' (21 November 1967) UN Doc A/PV.1602, §81 (Albania); UNGA, 'Official Records, 24th Session, 1803rd Plenary Meeting' (7 November 1969) UN Doc A/PV.1803, §83 (Congo (Brazzaville)); UNGA, 'Official Records, 24th Session, 1804th Plenary Meeting' (7 November 1969) UN Doc A/PV.1804, §13 (Ceylon); UNGA, 'Official Records, 24th Session, 1805th Plenary Meeting' (n 161) §74 (Cuba); UNGA, 'Official Records, 28th Session, 2189th Meeting' (n 161) §123 (Romania); UNGA, 'Official Records, 29th Sessmion, 2301st Plenary Meeting' (n 69) §34 (Somalia, referring to the views of other states), §133 (Costa Rica), §158 (Grenada), §175 (UK); UNGA, 'Credentials of Representatives to the Twenty-Eighth Session of the General Assembly' (n 67) §11 (Uruguay); UNSC (n 33).

[163] *Nuclear Weapons* (n 39) 75, §19; *Voting Procedure on Questions relating to Reports and Petition concerning the Territory of South West Africa, Advisory Opinion* [1955] ICJ Rep 67, 106 (Separate Opinion of Judge Lauterpacht).

[164] This view is reflected in, inter alia, UNGA res 2758 (XXVI) (n 103).

[165] But see eg 'Cablegram Dated 29 June 1950 from the Deputy Minister of Foreign Affairs of the Union of Soviet Socialist Republics to the Secretary-General Concerning the Security Council

Ultimately, it may be that the presumption of the legality of a decision of an international organization taken in accordance with the rules of the organization applies as much in this situation as in any other[166] and in at least certain circumstances is not rebutted.[167] While it is unclear in what, if any, circumstances the decision of an international organization to accept as effective the ostensible 'misrepresentation' of a state is ultra vires, the following four points indicate circumstances on which the legality of such a decision may depend.

First, the refusal of states to accept the legality of a decision by the organization to allow the 'misrepresentation' of a state appears more common where such acceptance implies recognition of governmental status as compared to when it does not involve recognition of governmental status.[168]

This is reflected in the apparent difference in views between the states who considered Venezuela to be 'misrepresented' at the OASGA and the states who considered China to be 'misrepresented' at the UNGA. The member states of the OAS that considered Nicolás Maduro to be the President of Venezuela questioned the validity of the decision of the OAS to allow Venezuela to be represented in the OASGA by Juan Guaidó,[169] the rival ostensible President of Venezuela, while such questions were not raised by states who considered China to be 'misrepresented' at the UNGA. In contrast to the representation of China at the UNGA,[170] the OASGA's approach to Venezuela's representation appears to have involved recognition of governmental status.[171]

It may indeed be that the legality of a decision of an international organization which results in the 'misrepresentation' of one of its member states depends on whether or not the decision amounts to the organization's recognition of the governmental status of the 'wrong' government, perhaps because only the 'misrepresentation' of a state that involves the recognition of a 'wrong' government amounts to intervention 'in matters which are essentially within the domestic jurisdiction of any State'.

Support for the view that an international organization possesses the power to allow the 'misrepresentation' of a state insofar as this does not imply recognition of the 'wrong' government also appears elsewhere. For example, in 1952 the UK, which had already recognized the communist claimant as the government of

Resolution of 27 June 1950 (S/1511)' (29 June 1950) UN Doc S/1517 early on in the perceived 'misrepresentation' of China.

[166] *Certain Expenses of the United Nations (Article 17, Paragraph 2 of the Charter) Advisory Opinion* [1949] ICJ Rep 151 ('*Certain Expenses*') 151, 168; ibid, 203–5 (Separate Opinion of Judge Fitzmaurice); *Namibia* (n 160) 22, §20.

[167] See also Wright (n 64) 554.

[168] On whether or not representation of a state in the context of an international organization involves recognition by that organization of governmental status, recall section 5.4.1.2.

[169] See eg nn 188–92 below.

[170] Recall n 100 above.

[171] Recall n 145 above.

China, did not consider itself in a position to accept as valid the credentials submitted by the nationalist ostensible government of China, but it had no issue with the UN postponing 'any vote on the question of Chinese representation [at the UN]', which would allow the nationalist ostensible government to continue to represent China at the UN.[172] The decisions by adjudicative organs of international organizations to allow what might be perceived to be the 'misrepresentation' of a state without recognition of governmental status, as well as the limited challenge to such decisions,[173] provides no further support that 'misrepresentation' of a state without recognition of governmental status is ultra vires.

Secondly, it might also, or instead, be that an international organization enjoys the power to accept as effective the ostensible representation of a state by the 'wrong' government only in relation to certain matters, for example matters concerning the representation of a state in the work of that organization, not matters concerning the representation of a state vis-à-vis an international organization.[174] This may be because the presumptive sovereign freedom of each state to choose its government and its representatives remains unrestricted only as regards the representation of a state vis-à-vis an international organization, not the representation of a state in an international organization, perhaps especially where a state may accept as effective the ostensible representation of a state in an international organization without the recognition of governmental status. For example, the fact that the controversy concerning Venezuela's representation in the context of the OASGA pertained to the acceptance not only of a person as a representative of Venezuela at the OASGA but also of Venezuela's ostensible denunciation of its intention to withdraw from the OAS[175] may be a reason why the validity of the 'misrepresentation' of a state was more controversial in this context than it has been elsewhere. At least some of the states which challenged the validity of the ostensible representation of Venezuela in the OASGA—a challenge which has been sustained by at least some OAS member states—referred to Venezuela's denunciation of the OAS Charter or its non-member status.[176] Additionally, despite failing to reach the requisite two-thirds majority for adoption, most OAS member states voted in favour of a draft resolution providing for the 'withdraw[al by the OASGA] of its acceptance of a

[172] See UNGA, 'Official Records, 7th Session, 389th Plenary Meeting' (n 33) §36.
[173] See eg *ConocoPhilips v Venezuela*, 3 April 2020 (n 48) §40.
[174] On the different aspects of state representation, recall section 5.3.1.
[175] Recall n 150 above.
[176] See eg OASGA (n 64) 42 (Grenada; Antigua and Barbuda), 43 (Saint Vincent and the Grenadines; Suriname), 44–5 (Bolivia), 213–14 (Dominica); OASGA, 'Quincuagésimo Período Ordinario De Sesiones' (n 154) 30 (Antigua and Barbuda), 31 (Saint Vincent and the Grenadines); OASGA, 'Quincuagésimo Primer Período Ordinario De Sesiones' (n 154) 31 (Saint Vincent and the Grenadines), 32 (Mexico), 33 (Bolivia), 34 (Argentina), 35 (Dominica; Antigua and Barbuda), 36 (Belize). See also 'informe del Secretario General sobre la presentación de credenciales de las delegaciones participantes en el quincuagéstimo primer período ordinario de la sesiones de la asamblea general' (23 November 2021) OEA Ser./P, AG/doc.5744/21/rev.1, nn 1–6, 9 (Mexico, Bolivia, Saint Vincent and the Grenadines, Nicaragua, Argentina, Antigua and Barbuda, and Peru).

Permanent Representative to the OAS designated by [Mr Guaidó]',[177] indicating also that Venezuela had 'ceased to be a member of the OAS'.[178]

Thirdly, it may be relevant that the 'misrepresentation' of a state precludes that state from being represented by an ostensible government which is considered to be unwilling to ensure the state's compliance with certain international legal obligations that arise from that state's membership in the organization. This might relate to the possibility that action taken by an international organization in furtherance of its purposes affects the applicability or strength of the presumption in favour of the intra vires character of that action.[179] That said and although the 'right' government of China was indeed considered to be unwilling to comply with certain obligations arising under the UN Charter,[180] the invocation by the OASPC of 'the obligation' of OAS member states to promote and defend democracy under Article 1 of the Inter-American Democratic Charter (IADC)[181] did not suffice to preclude the controversy arising from what some states consider to be Venezuela's 'misrepresentation' at the OAS.

Fourthly, decisions of adjudicative bodies to allow what is perceived by at least some states to involve the 'misrepresentation' of a state appear not to be challenged, even where recognition of governmental status is not clearly excluded in such decisions.[182] The absence of such challenge is not in itself determinative as to the existence of a power of adjudicative bodies to allow the 'misrepresentation' of a state in circumstances that involve the recognition of the 'wrong' government's governmental status. Such inaction might nevertheless reflect an understanding that the specific express or implied powers of adjudicative organs, including the power to resolve procedural questions as necessary for the performance of their functions,[183] is relevant to the legality of their decisions to allow the 'misrepresentation' of a state.[184] While the possession by an adjudicative organ of a power to determine

[177] See 'Note from the Permanent Mission of Antigua and Barbuda' (3 October 2022) OEA Ser.P, AG/doc.5785/22, Attachment, §2. For the vote on this resolution, see OASGA, 'Quincuagésimo Segundo Período Ordinario De Sesiones' (n 154) 32.

[178] 'Note from the Permanent Mission of Antigua and Barbuda' (n 177) Attachment, §3.

[179] See eg *Certain Expenses* (n 166) 167–8. See also Akehurst, 'Enforcement Action by Regional Agencies, with Special Reference to the Organization of American States' (1967) 42 BYIL 175, 193–4.

[180] Recall n 144 above.

[181] OASPC (n 149) first unnumbered preambular paragraph.

[182] On such decisions, recall section 5.4.1.2, including the text accompanying n 106.

[183] For an express power on which adjudicative bodies have relied for determining whether an individual qualifies as a state representative, see Convention on the Settlement of Investment Disputes between States and Nationals of other States (adopted 18 March 1965, entered into force 14 October 1966) 575 UNTS 159, art 44. For reliance on this power for such purposes, see eg *Mobil Cerro Negro v Venezuela* (n 48) §43; *ConocoPhilips v Venezuela*, 3 April 2020 (n 48) §30. See also *Valores v Venezuela* (n 109) §33 for reasoning that supports a claim to an implied power to resolve questions of representation for the performance of their functions. In this regard, albeit in different contexts, see also *Reparation for Injuries Suffered in the Service of the United Nations, Advisory Opinion* [1949] ICJ Rep 174, 182; Osieke, '*Ultra Vires* Acts in International Organizations—The Experience of the International Labour Organization' (1976) 48 BYIL 259, 263–4.

[184] Note also that the 'misrepresentation' of a state before an adjudicative organ of an international organization might occur pursuant to a specific rule which, in effect, allows the organ to defer to the recognition by some other entity of a specific claimant's governmental status. See eg ICJ, 'Rules of Court'

questions of state representation for its purposes does not necessarily suggest that the exercise of such a power is unconstrained by the customary international legal identity of a state's government, the practice of relevant organs[185] suggests that this power allows for determinations on state representation based on grounds other than the enjoyment of governmental status under customary international law.[186]

If a decision of an international organization which results in the 'misrepresentation' of a state is ultra vires, it may in turn be that both the decision to allow the 'misrepresentation' of a state and any subsequent decision made with the participation of the 'misrepresented' state is invalid and, as such, void *ab initio*.

There is substantial support for the position that an ultra vires act of an international organization is, as such, void.[187] At the same time, the views of the OAS member states that objected to the participation of Venezuela's ostensible representative in the work of the OASGA since 2019 might be taken to suggest that the invalidity of an act is not generally accepted as necessarily following from the act being ultra vires. More specifically, while these states appear to have agreed that what they considered to be the ultra vires 'misrepresentation' of a state will have some consequence for the effectiveness of subsequent decisions of the OASGA that have been taken with Venezuela's participation, their views appear to diverge on the precise consequence in this regard.

For example, Nicaragua asserted that, '[b]y exceeding [the OAS'] authority, this action [of allowing for Venezuela's participation] is null and void and, as a consequence, no decision adopted on this basis has any validity or binding effect, sets any precedent, or may be imposed on other states',[188] Bolivia 'reserve[d] the

(adopted 14 April 1978, entered into force 7 July 1978, last amended 25 June 2020), available at <http://icj-cij.org/en/rules>, art 38(3), which appears to provide for the acceptance by the ICJ as effective of the submission of an application ostensibly in a state's name 'by the diplomatic representative of that [state] in the [Netherlands]'. In such a situation, there is no apparent basis for which to consider the 'misrepresentation' of a state to be ultra vires.

[185] Recall n 48 above.

[186] On the significance of the practice of an international organization to the ascertainment of the powers of that organization, see nn 163 and 166 above.

[187] See *Certain Expenses* (n 166) 212, §8 (Separate Opinion of Judge Morelli); 'Fragmentation of International Law: Difficulties Arising from the Diversification and Expansion of International Law: Report of the Study Group of the International Law Commission, Finalized by Martti Koskenniemi' (13 April 2006) UN Doc A/CN.4/L.682, 169; Akande, 'International Organizations' in Evans (ed), *International Law* (5th edn, OUP 2018) 227, 242–3; the view of India as reiterated in *Appeal Relating to the Jurisdiction of the ICAO Council (India v Pakistan), Judgment* [1972] ICJ Rep 46, 49; 'Observations by Professor Roger O'Keefe, Pursuant to Rule 103 of the Rules of Procedure and Evidence, on the Merits of the Legal Questions Presented in "The Hashemite Kingdom of Jordan's Appeal against the 'Decision under Article 87(7) of the Rome Statute on the Noncompliance by Jordan with the Request by the Court for the Arrest and Surrender [of] Omar Al-Bashir'" of 12 March 2018 (ICC-02/05-01/09-326)' (18 June 2018) ICC-02/05-01/09 OA2, available at <http://icc-cpi.int/CourtRecords/CR2018_03100.PDF>, §16. For the view that the international legal consequences of an ultra vires act are unclear, see Jennings, 'Nullity and Effectiveness in International Law' in *Cambridge Essays in International Law: Essays in Honour of Lord McNair* (Stevens & Sons 1965) 64, 81; Amerasinghe (n 156) 209; Schmalenbach, 'International Organizations or Institutions, General Aspects' (2014) MPEPIL, §52.

[188] See eg OASGA res 2944 (n 161) n 8.

right to recognize resolutions and declarations adopted with the participation of [Venezuela]',[189] and Trinidad and Tobago 'reserve[d] the right not to be bound by . . . any decision taken at the OAS which is based on, principally includes, or in any other manner involves the participation of the [ostensible] representative of . . . Venezuela'.[190] A range of other views along similar lines was also expressed.[191] Perhaps the most accurate view is that of Antigua and Barbuda, which did 'not consider itself bound by any declaration or resolution . . . that includes the participation of any person or entity purporting to speak for or act on behalf of . . . Venezuela and in which 18 votes are attained with the participation of a purported representative of . . . Venezuela'.[192]

The apparent differences within these statements as to the legal effect of an ultra vires decision may be explained, however, by the possibility that reliance on an ultra vires act, as distinct from the act as such, may produce legal effects. As for the member states of the OAS which expressed no view on the invalidity or absence of legal effect of Venezuela's participation in the OASGA, this may be explained by their view that Venezuela was not 'misrepresented'.

5.5.2 'Misrepresentation' of a State as a Violation of That State's Rights?

As for whether the 'misrepresentation' of a state involves the violation of an international legal right of that state, it may not be irrelevant that action taken in furtherance of having the 'right' government replace a 'wrong' government for the representation of a state in the political organ of an international organization is sometimes referred to as the 'restoration of the lawful rights' of that state.[193]

[189] Ibid, n 2. See also ibid, n 6 for Suriname's similar position.

[190] Ibid, n 3. See ibid, nn 9 and 11 for the similar position of Barbados and Saint Kitts and Nevis, respectively.

[191] In ibid, n 7, Grenada declared itself 'not obligated to adhere to any decisions pertaining to [the OAS's decision to accept as Venezuela's representative to the OAS a person appointed by Juan Guaidó] and reserve[d] its rights to not recognize and honor any mandates arising from its adoption'. See ibid, n 5 for the identical statement of Saint Vincent of the Grenadines. For another view, see ibid, n 10, on Dominica's position. See also 'Report of the Secretary General on the Presentation of Credentials of the Delegations Taking Part in the Forty-Ninth Regular Session of the General Assembly' (15 July 2019) OEA/Ser.P, AG/doc.5653/19/rev.2, nn 1 and 3 for statements by Mexico and Uruguay, in which they 'reserve[d] the right to question the validity of all . . . decisions derived from the [acceptance of Juan Guaidó's appointee as Venezuela's representative to the OAS]'; OASGA, 'Quincuagésimo Primer Período Ordinario De Sesiones' (n 154) 31 (Saint Vincent and the Grenadines), 32 (Mexico).

[192] OASGA res 2944 (n 161) n 4. See also eg OASGA, 'Quincuagésimo Período Ordinario De Sesiones' (n 154) 30 (Antigua and Barbuda).

[193] See eg UNGA res 2758 (XXVI) (n 103). (On China having, prior to this, been represented at the UNGA on a 'provisional' basis, recall n 100 above. On the representation of a state on a 'provisional' basis not amounting to recognition of governmental status, recall section 5.4.1.2.) See also the title of UNGA res 3238 (XXIX) (29 November 1974) UN Doc A/RES/3238(XXIX). See further UNGA, 'Official Records, 21st Session, 1478th Plenary Meeting' (25 November 1966) UN Doc A/PV.1478, §102 (Yemen), §§119 and 128 (Mali), §150 (United Arab Republic); UNGA, 'Official Records, 24th Session, 1807th Plenary Meeting' (11 November 1969) UN Doc A/PV.1807, §5 (Algeria).

Conversely, the 'misrepresentation' of a member state in a political organ of an international organization is sometimes referred to as an 'unlawful[] occup[ation]' of the state's place in the organization.[194] At the same time, there appears to be little, if any, suggestion by a plausibly-'misrepresented' state that it sustained international legal injury due to its 'misrepresentation' in the context of an international organization. In any event, it is perhaps worth noting that the plausible 'misrepresentation' of a state in a political organ of an international organization appears to have been said to involve a violation of that state's right more frequently than it has in relation to other aspects of the representation of a state in the context of an international organization.[195]

The examination of whether or not the 'misrepresentation' of a state involves a violation of one or more international legal rights of that state appears to arise principally in respect of the right against intervention and the right to participate in one or more specific organs of that organization. Separate consideration is to be given to each of these rights.

For the 'misrepresentation' of a state to involve a violation of the right against intervention, the decision to allow the 'misrepresentation' of a state must be coercive in respect of a matter that international law reserves for the sovereign discretion of that state.[196] Even if the 'misrepresentation' of a member state does not involve recognition of governmental status and thus does not concern the presumptive sovereign freedom of that state to choose its government,[197] it might still concern the apparent presumptive sovereign freedom of each state to choose its representatives[198] and thus satisfy the first requirement of a prohibited intervention. In at least some circumstances, moreover, action by the international organization to have a state be 'misrepresented' and conduct by other states in furtherance of such action might be said to be coercive in relation to the choice of the 'misrepresented' state to choose its government or at least its representatives.[199]

At the same time, it is unclear on what basis the right of a state against intervention might be opposable to an international organization. That international organizations are under an international legal obligation not to intervene in the affairs of a state is not beyond doubt. It is not necessarily the case that obligations incumbent on states under customary international law are opposable to international

[194] See eg UNGA res 2758 (XXVI) (n 103) sole unnumbered operative paragraph. See also eg UNGA, 'Official Records, 28th Session, 2189th Meeting' (n 161) §12 (Albania), §114, §127 (Romania). See also UNGA, 'Official Records, 29th Session, 2301st Plenary Meeting' (n 69) §135 (Costa Rica); Blix, 'Contemporary Aspects of Recognition' (1970) 130 Hague *Recueil* 587, 692.

[195] But see eg the position of one of Venezuela's ostensible representatives in *ConocoPhilips v Venezuela*, 2 November 2020 (n 48) §40.

[196] Recall chapter 3, nn 220–1.

[197] See also eg *ConocoPhilips v Venezuela*, 2 November 2020 (n 48) §40. See also *ConocoPhilips v Venezuela*, 15 February 2023 (n 48) §24. On the presumptive sovereign freedom of each state to choose its government, recall section 2.4.

[198] Recall section 5.3.2.

[199] Further on the requirement of coercion, recall section 3.4.2.

organizations vis-à-vis their member states.[200] Nor is it clear that a provision in the constituent instrument of an international organization which expressly limits the power of the organization from 'interven[ing] in matters which are essentially within the domestic jurisdiction of any State' amounts to an international legal obligation of the international organization.[201] For example, Article 2(7) of the UN Charter presents itself as a 'Principle' of the 'Organization and its Members' and is, in any event, on its face framed as a limitation on the powers of the UN, not as an international legal obligation incumbent on the UN.

In any event, at least as regards the intra vires decision of an international organization to allow the 'misrepresentation' of a member state, the member state in question can be taken to have consented to the possibility of its 'misrepresentation'.[202] Accordingly, insofar as a decision of an international organization to allow the 'misrepresentation' of a state is intra vires, the organization and any member state that supports such a decision might be considered not to be acting in respect of a matter that international law leaves to the sovereign discretion of the 'misrepresented' state or at least might be considered to be acting in accordance with how the latter state is taken to have exercised its discretion. Put differently, member states of an international organization can perhaps be taken to have consented to the possession by each other of discretion in the performance of acts involved in the decision to accept as effective, in accordance with the rules of the organization, their ostensible representation for one or more purposes of that organization. The position of non-member states may be more complex.

As a separate matter, the plausible right of member states to participate to the fullest extent in the work of one or more political organs of an international organization[203] is perhaps at least part of the reason why the suggestion that the 'misrepresentation' of a state involves a violation of that state's rights has arisen mainly in relation to political organs of international organizations. For its part, the UNGA eventually considered the Taiwan-based claimant to have 'unlawfully occup[ied]' a place in representing China at the UN.[204] On the other hand, it might be argued that any such right protects the participation of a state on the basis of whomever the international organization accepts as a representative of that state such that the 'misrepresentation' of a member state does not involve a violation of any participatory right of that state, either by the international organization or by member

[200] See, generally, Bordin, *The Analogy between States and International Organizations* (CUP 2018) 86, 195–9 for the view that, even if general international law is applicable to international organizations in certain contexts, the rules internal to the international organization exclusively govern the relationship between the international organization and its members.

[201] See also ILC, 'Draft Articles on the Responsibility of International Organizations, with Commentaries Thereto' in Ybk ILC [2011] vol II(2), 40, 64 (art 10, comment 7: '[b]reaches of obligations under the rules of the organization are not always breaches of obligations under international law').

[202] See eg *Nuclear Weapons* (n 39) 78–9, §25, quoting also from *Jurisdiction of the European Commission of the Danube, Advisory Opinion*, PCIJ, Series B, No 14, 5, 64.

[203] On the possible existence of such a right, see n 217 below.

[204] UNGA res 2758 (XXVI) (n 103) sole unnumbered operative paragraph.

states that participate in the decision which results in the 'misrepresentation' of the affected state.

As a possibility that is distinct from both the obligation of non-intervention and the apparent right of member states to participate in at least some aspects of the work of an international organization, states or international organizations might expressly undertake an obligation concerning the representation of a specific state in the work of one or more international organizations by a particular ostensible government. An example in this regard appears to be Article 5 of the Agreement on a Comprehensive Political Settlement of the Cambodia Conflict, which provides that '[t]he Supreme National Council shall . . . represent Cambodia externally and occupy the seat of Cambodia at the United Nations, in the United Nations specialized agencies, and in other international institutions and international conferences'.[205] The representation of that state in the work of the international organization or organizations in question by a rival ostensible government may involve a violation of this obligation, depending on the actors involved in that decision and the actors to whom that obligation is opposable.

5.5.3 'Misrepresentation' of a State and the Concept of 'the Government' of a State

Insofar as it does not involve recognition by the international organization of governmental status,[206] the 'misrepresentation' of a state in the context of an international organization undermines neither the objective international legal identity of a state's government nor the presumptive sovereign freedom of each state to choose its government. This is because the 'misrepresentation' in question will not involve a determination by the international organization of the identity of a state's government. To the extent that a decision of an international organization to allow the 'misrepresentation' of a state in circumstances that involve recognition of the 'wrong' government may have legal effect, it can be said that the possibility of such a decision limits the freedom of each state to choose its government[207] and the objective international legal existence of a state's government. This is because, for at least one or more purposes of an international organization, the identity of a state's government would not accord with the customary international legal identity of that state's government. But there is no general acceptance that a decision of

[205] Annexed to 'Letter Dated 30 October 1991 from the Permanent Representatives of France and Indonesia to the United Nations Addressed to the Secretary-General' (30 October 1991) UN Doc A/46/608–S/23177.

[206] On whether or not representation of a state in the context of an international organization involves recognition by that organization of governmental status, recall section 5.4.1.2.

[207] Not entirely unrelatedly, see also *Military and Paramilitary Activities in and against Nicaragua (Nicaragua v USA), Merits, Judgment* [1986] ICJ Rep 14, 131, §259.

an international organization to allow the 'misrepresentation' of a state in circumstances that involve recognition of the 'wrong' government has legal effect.[208]

At the same time, the possibility that an international organization allows the 'misrepresentation' of a member state, with or without recognition of governmental status, demonstrates that a state may be represented for one or more purposes of international law not through the 'right' government. While the intra vires character of such a decision necessarily results from the prior acceptance by the 'misrepresented' state of the possibility of such a decision,[209] the power to take such a decision nevertheless reflects a nuance to the distinctive capacity of the 'right' government. The 'right' government may be left unable to represent a state, and the 'wrong' government may represent the state for at least certain purposes of international law. It is notable that such a power may be exercised in situations such as when the government of that state is perceived to be unwilling to ensure the state's compliance with certain international legal obligations.[210]

5.6 Claims to Governmental Status and Limits on State Participation

The present section focuses on limitations imposed by international organizations on state participation in its work on grounds that, at least in part, relate directly to the existence of a particular ostensible government.[211] Possible grounds in this regard include matters concerning the basis of the claim to power of an ostensible government, the understanding that an ostensible government is not the 'right' government, and the perceived unwillingness of an ostensible government to ensure the state's compliance with the international legal obligations of the state. Perhaps needless to say, such decisions are to be distinguished from the choice of a state not to participate in the work of one or more organs of an international organization,[212] from the application of a rule which permits only certain specific member states of an international organization to participate in aspects of its work,[213] and from action to limit a state's participation in its work for reasons

[208] Recall section 5.5.1.

[209] This is because international organizations possess only the powers conferred on them by their member states. Recall n 202 above.

[210] Recall eg n 144 above and accompanying text.

[211] An international organization may take action to limit a state's participation for other reasons, including on grounds that relate to some policy or conduct of a state which are not taken to indicate tan ostensible government's unwillingness to comply with one or more international legal obligations of the state. Matters relating to such action are excluded from the scope of the present work.

[212] See eg the USSR's decision not to participate in the work of the UNSC, a decision coincidentally taken in response to the continued representation of China in the UNSC by the nationalist government: UNSC, 'Official Records, 459th Meeting' (10 January 1950) UN Doc S/PV.459, 3–4.

[213] See eg UN Charter (n 31) art 23(1) on the UNSC.

bearing no direct relation to a specific claimant to governmental status, as provided, for example, by Article 19 of the UN Charter.[214]

The main actions which international organizations may take and have taken to limit the extent to which a state may participate in the work of one or more of its organs include refusing to admit a state as a member of the organization, [215] suspending the exercise by a member state of one or more of the international legal rights pertaining to its participation in the work of the organization, and refusing to allow the only or every ostensible government seeking to represent a member state in an international organization to represent that state. Each of these actions, which may limit state participation to different extents and in different ways, is considered in turn below.

By considering the scope and exercise of the powers of international organizations to take such actions, this section provides insights into the concept of the government of a state in international law, most notably on the extent to which some matter relating specifically to a state's ostensible government may render the government of that state unable to represent the state.

5.6.1 Refusal of Membership

In general, a state need not be a member of an international organization in order to participate in the work of that organization.[216] Each international organization nevertheless typically has at least one plenary organ in the work of which all of its members are entitled under its constituent instrument to participate to the fullest extent,[217] while the participation of a non-member in the work of one or more

[214] See eg ibid, art 19.

[215] Since the admission of a state to membership of an international organization has a positive effect on the extent to which that state can participate in the work of that international organization, it follows that the expulsion of a state from an international organization is also liable to affect the extent to which that state can participate in the work of that organization. The present work does not consider, however, the expulsion of a state from an international organization since such action is not common in the contemporary practice of international organizations. See nevertheless, for example, the attempts to have South Africa expelled from the UN: eg 'Kenya, Mauritania and United Republic of Cameroon: draft resolution' (24 October 1974) UN Doc S/11543. For the UNSC's refusal to adopt the resolution, see UNSC, 'Official Records, 1808th Meeting' (30 October 1973) UN Doc S/PV.1808, §155. On earlier practice concerning the expulsion of states from international organizations, see eg Jenks, 'Expulsion from the League of Nations' (1935) 16 BYIL 155. On expulsion from international organizations generally, see Magliveras (n 4) 7–100; Amerasinghe (n 156) 121–4; Tams, 'Article 6' in Simma and others (n 6) 374; Schermers and Blokker (n 20) 120–8, §§137–48; Mathias and Trengrove, 'Membership and Representation' in Cogan, Hurd, and Johnstone (eds), *The Oxford Handbook of International Organizations* (OUP 2016) 962, 981–2.

[216] See also VCRSIO (n 5) arts 5(2), 11(3), 71.

[217] See eg OAS Charter (n 158) art 56. See also AU Constitutive Act (n 11) art 23(1), which refers to 'the right to speak at meetings [and] to vote'. A right to participate in one or more organs of an international organization may exist also where the text is less explicit. See eg UN Charter (n 31) art 9(1), according to which the UNGA 'shall consist of all the members' of the UN. In this regard, consider also: Grant, *Admission to the United Nations, Charter Article 4 and the Rise of Universal Organization* (Martinus Nijhoff 2009) 251; Blix (n 194) 692; Magiera (n 6) 452, §14, who speaks in passing of a 'right'

organs of the organization typically depends on an a priori[218] or *ad hoc*[219] decision of the organization. Even if an international organization permits a non-member state routinely to participate in the work of one more of its organs, that participation may be limited in comparison to the extent to which a member state may participate in the organ's proceedings. This is true especially in respect of organs whose decision-making process formally involves the participation of member states. For example, while an 'observer' state may voice its views during a meeting of an organ of an international organization, it may not be permitted to contribute formally to a decision of that organ by means of a vote. Another possible difference concerning the participation of a member state and a non-member state in the work of an organ of an international organization is that typically only the former enjoys treaty-based entitlements to see its representatives benefit from privileges and immunities 'necessary for the independent exercise of their functions in connection with the [o]rganization'.[220] A non-member state typically lacks such treaty-based entitlements, although it may enjoy similar or identical privileges and immunities on some other basis. In short, refusing to admit a state as a member of an international organization generally prevents that state from participating as readily or as fully in the work of the organization as the member states. Accordingly, the refusal of membership to a state is one way in which an international organization may limit state participation in the work of that organization.

The decision of an international organization to refuse to admit a state as a member may relate, among other possible considerations, to the existence of a particular claim to governmental status in respect of that state. More specifically, admission to membership of the organization may be conditioned by the organization's constituent instrument on the satisfaction by an applicant state of one or more criteria,[221] criteria which may require or permit the organization to take into account some matter directly connected to a particular claim to governmental status in respect of the applicant state. For example, even though the conditions of admission for membership in the UN do not expressly or directly relate to the existence or absence of some specific type of claimant to governmental status, their 'very wide and very elastic nature' 'allow[s] for a wide liberty of appreciation'

of UN member states to participate in the UNGA's work; and eg UNGA, 'Official Records, 29th Session, 2281st Plenary Meeting' (12 November 1974) UN Doc A/PV.2281, §§161, 168 (USA), §195 (Canada).

218 For example, such a decision may take the form of according a particular state 'observer State status'. See eg UNGA res 67/19 (4 December 2012) UN Doc A/67/19, §2 in respect of Palestine.

219 For example, such a decision may take the form of an invitation to a particular individual to participate as a state representative in one or more specific meetings of an organ of the organization. See eg UN Charter (n 31) art 32, which provides, in certain circumstances, for participation without a vote in the UNSC's proceedings by a state which is not a UN member.

220 See UN Charter (n 31) art 105(2). See, similarly, OAS Charter (n 158) art 134. On the less straightforward situation in respect of AU member states, see Magliveras (n 4) 219–22.

221 See eg UN Charter (n 31) art 4(1). Note the possibly-different position of 'original' members of an international organization, eg UN Charter (n 31) art 3; and cf AU Constitutive Act (n 11) arts 27 and 29.

in their application,[222] including by having regard to matters concerning a state's ostensible government of a state. For example, in 1945, the USA, the UK, and the USSR considered the government led by Francisco Franco in Spain 'not [to] possess the necessary qualifications to justify [Spain's] admission' to the UN.[223] If no express criteria govern the admission of a state to membership, or perhaps even where such criteria as do exist provide no basis for the organization to take account of the existence of a particular claim to governmental status when deciding whether to admit a state, the organization may nonetheless have the power, under its constituent instrument, to take into account some matter directly connected to a particular claim to governmental status when deciding whether to admit the state as a member.[224]

5.6.2 Suspension of Rights of Membership and Measures to Comparable Effect

Whether pursuant to a specific provision of the organization's constituent instrument or otherwise, a member state of an international organization may be temporarily barred by the organization from exercising some or all of the international legal rights and privileges that it enjoys as a consequence of its membership of the organization. Such rights and privileges typically include the opportunity to participate in the work of one or more organs of the organization.[225] In relation to such action, the present work distinguishes 'formal suspension' from 'de facto suspension'.

The 'suspension of a state from an international organization' or, synonymously, 'formal suspension' is used within the present work as shorthand for the imposition by an international organization of limits on the exercise by a member state of some or all of its rights of membership, even though such action generally affects neither the obligations incumbent on that state as a consequence of its membership of the organization nor the state's membership of the organization.[226]

[222] See also *Conditions of Admission of a State to Membership in the United Nations (Article 4 of the Charter) Advisory Opinion* [1948] ICJ Rep 57 ('*Conditions of Admission*') 62–4.

[223] UNGA res 32 (I) (9 February 1946) UN Doc A/RES/32(I) §2, recalling the joint statement of those states.

[224] See OAS Charter (n 158) art 6 and AU Constitutive Act (n 11) art 29(2), both of which appear to admit the existence of substantial discretion on each organization's part in deciding whether to admit a state to membership. See also *Conditions of Admission* (n 222) 90, §§17–18 (Dissenting Opinion of Judges Basdevant, Winiarski, Sir Arnold McNair, and Read), according to whom, contrary to the view of the Court, 'considerations foreign to the qualifications specified in [Article 4(1) of the UN Charter]' may be taken into account in a decision on admitting a state to membership in the UN.

[225] Recall n 217 above.

[226] See eg OAS Charter (n 158) art 9(e); AU Assembly Rules of Procedure (n 27) Rule 37(2)(d). This is also implicit in UN Charter (n 31) art 5, which speaks of the suspension only of 'the exercise of the rights and privileges of membership' and which assumes the suspended state's continued membership of the UN.

'De facto suspension from an international organization' or simply 'de facto suspension' serves, within the present work, as shorthand for the refusal of an international organization to allow the only or every claimant to governmental status to represent a state in the work of one or more organs of the organization. While the effects of de facto suspension of a state might be similar, if not identical, depending on the circumstances, to the formal suspension of a state from an international organization,[227] nevertheless, there exists at the least a conceptual distinction between the two actions.[228] But like formal suspension, the de facto suspension of a state affects neither the obligations incumbent on the state as a consequence of its membership of the organization nor its membership of the organization.

5.6.2.1 Formal Suspension

It is not uncommon for an international organization to possess the power formally to suspend one of its members. Since each international organization ultimately derives its powers from the consent of its member states,[229] the suspension of a state from an international organization in the circumstances discussed below cannot be said to limit the freedom that each state enjoys under international law to choose its government.[230] At the same time, the suspension of a state in effect restricts the representative capacity of the government of a state for one or more purposes of international law.

5.6.2.1.1 The United Nations

According to Article 5 of the Charter of the United Nations, '[a] Member of the United Nations against which preventive or enforcement action has been taken by the Security Council may be suspended from the exercise of the rights and privileges of membership by the General Assembly upon the recommendation of the Security Council'.[231] The 'rights and privileges of [UN] membership' include participating in and voting on the UNGA's work[232] as well as in the work of any other organ of the UN in which that state would otherwise have a right to participate. Article 5 thus provides a basis for the UN to suspend one of its members from participating in its work.

[227] For the acknowledgment that de facto suspension is analogous, at least in certain respects, to formal suspension, see Magliveras (n 4) 203–6; Duxbury (n 4) 20. See also Ciobanu (n 64) 358–9: 'the distinction between the State and its government is artificial when applied to representation in international relations, because the former cannot, strictly speaking, act as an international person except through an established form of government'.

[228] Further on potential differences between formal and de facto suspension, see section 5.6.2.2.2.

[229] Recall n 202 above.

[230] Recall n 209 above.

[231] See eg UN Charter (n 31) art 5. See also Tams, 'Article 5' in Simma and others (n 6) 362.

[232] See eg Tams (n 231) 368, §20; Secretariat of the United Nations (n 57) 171, §6; UNGA, 'Official Records, 29th Session, 2281st Plenary Meeting' (n 217) §61 (UK); Wood (n 78) 249. Recall n 217 above. See also Schermers and Blokker (n 20) 222, §263.

Given the terms of Article 5, a state may be suspended from participating in the work of the UN's organs on grounds entirely unrelated to the existence of a particular claim to governmental status. The existence of a particular claim to governmental status may nevertheless inform a decision of the UN to suspend a state under Article 5. More specifically, the only requirement on which Article 5 conditions the exercise by the UNSC and the UNGA of their respective discretions to suspend a state is that the UNSC has taken 'preventive or enforcement action' against that state. The UNSC may take and most frequently has taken 'preventive or enforcement action' not in specific relation to a particular ostensible government of a state. That said, the existence of a particular claimant to governmental status may relate and sometimes has directly related to the Security Council's decision to take 'preventive or enforcement' action against that state. For example, the UNSC took action against Haiti as a result of, inter alia, the 'illegal de facto regime' operating there and its non-compliance with certain international legal obligations.[233] More recently, the UNSC took action under Article 41 of the UN Charter subsequent to 'the continued refusal of the "Military Command"' to restore 'constitutional order' and to reinstate 'the legitimate democratic Government' of Guinea-Bissau.[234]

While this shows that a UN member state may be suspended from the UN on grounds related directly to a particular claim to governmental status, the UN is yet to suspend any of its members under Article 5 on grounds related to a particular claim to governmental status in respect of that state. Indeed, the UN appears never to have suspended a member pursuant to Article 5.[235]

As a separate matter, the UN may suspend a state from participating in the work of a subsidiary UN organ. On the few occasions when suspension from a subsidiary UN organ has happened, it has typically related to a state's conduct or policy[236] rather than to some matter directly connected to an ostensible government of that state, although a state's conduct or policy may indicate or arise from

233 See eg UNSC res 940 (n 2) third unnumbered preambular paragraph, §3.

234 UNSC res 2048 (n 2) eighth unnumbered preambular paragraph.

235 See eg Grant (n 217) 266. The decision by the UNGA, upon the recommendation of the UNSC, not to allow the FRY to participate in the work of the UNGA appears not to have been taken pursuant to Article 5 of the UN Charter because not only was this article not expressly invoked but also this decision was premised on the view 'that the Federal Republic of Yugoslavia (Serbia and Montenegro) cannot continue automatically the membership of the former Socialist Federal Republic of Yugoslavia in the United Nations' (UNGA res 47/1 (19 September 1992) UN Doc A/RES/47/1, §1). See also Tams (n 231) 372–3, §28; Wood (n 78) 248; 'Letter Dated 29 September 1992 from the Under-Secretary-General, the Legal Counsel, Addressed to the Permanent Representatives of Bosnia and Herzegovina and Croatia to the United Nations' (30 September 1992) UN Doc A/47/485, Annex; Schermers and Blokker (n 20) 222, §263.

236 See eg the suspension of Libya's and Russia's membership in the United Nations Human Rights Council (UNHRC) in 2011 and 2022, respectively (UNGA res 65/265 (3 March 2011) UN Doc A/RES/65/265, §1; UNGA res ES-11/3 (8 April 2022) UN Doc A/RES/ES-11/3, §1), on each occasion pursuant to the rules of the UNHRC. On the rules of the UNHRC, see UNGA res 60/251 (3 April 2006) UN Doc A/RES/60/251, §8.

the unwillingness of the government of a state to comply with the latter's international legal obligations.

5.6.2.1.2 The African Union

Since its establishment, it has not been uncommon for the AU to suspend a member state from participating in its activities on grounds directly connected to the existence of a particular claim to governmental status in respect of that state.

For the states that are party to it, the Protocol Relating to the Establishment of the Peace and Security Council (PSC Protocol)[237] provides a clear legal basis for such action. Article 7(1)(g) of the PSC Protocol provides that, '[i]n conjunction with the Chairperson of the Commission, the Peace and Security Council shall . . . institute sanctions whenever an unconstitutional change of Government takes place in a Member State, as provided for in the Lomé Declaration'. The Lomé Declaration, in turn, provides that 'the government [arising from an unconstitutional change of government] should be suspended from participating in the Policy Organs of the OAU'.[238]

The Lomé Declaration concerns itself with the non-participation of a specific ostensible government, and Article 30 of the Constitutive Act of the African Union (AU Constitutive Act) provides that 'Governments which shall come to power through unconstitutional means shall not be allowed to participate in the activities of the Union'. The AU's subsequent practice nevertheless makes clear that Article 7(1)(g) of the PSC Protocol is understood to provide, inter alia, for the suspension of a member state from participating in the political organs of the AU,[239] not just the preclusion of the participation of a member state through an ostensible government which comes to power 'through unconstitutional means'. As the suspension of Côte d'Ivoire in 2010 suggests,[240] the existence of a rival 'constitutional' ostensible government in respect of a state does not operate definitively to preclude the suspension of that state from the AU, nor does it appear to matter whether or not the 'unconstitutional' ostensible government of a state has sought to represent the state in or vis-à-vis the AU.

[237] Adopted 8 July 2002, entered into force 26 December 2003, UN Registration No 55339 ('PSC Protocol'), available at <https://au.int/en/treaties/protocol-relating-establishment-peace-and-security-council-african-union>.

[238] Assembly of the Organization of African Unity, 'Lomé Declaration of July 2000 on the Framework for an OAU Response to Unconstitutional Changes of Government', 36th Ordinary Session (10–12 July 2000) OAU Doc AHG/Decl.5 (XXXVI) ('Lomé Declaration'). On suspension as a sanction, according to the AU's understanding of the latter term, see also AU Constitutive Act (n 11) art 23(1); AU Assembly Rules of Procedure (n 27) Rule 37.

[239] See also AU Assembly Rules of Procedure (n 27) Rule 37(1); AU Assembly, Decision on Unconstitutional Changes of Government and the Strengthening of the Capacity of the AU to Manage such Situations', 14th Ordinary Session (2 February 2010) AU Doc Assembly/AU/4(XVI) ('Decision on Unconstitutional Changes of Government of 2010') §6(i)(b).

[240] Peace and Security Council of the African Union (AUPSC), 'Communiqué, 252nd Meeting' (9 December 2010) AU Doc PSC/PR/COMM.1(CCLII) §4.

The suspension by the AUPSC of AU member states that have undergone 'an unconstitutional change of Government' from participating in the AU's activities, even when those states were not, at the time of suspension, party to the PSC Protocol[241] suggests that the AUPSC possesses powers of suspension beyond those arising from the PSC Protocol.[242] Such powers may arise under Article 30 of the AU Constitutive Act, pursuant to a delegation of powers by the AU Assembly.[243] Indeed, on certain occasions the AUPSC has expressly invoked Article 30 in suspending an AU member state.[244]

As for its general practice, it is not uncommon for the AUPSC to suspend an AU member state as a result of an 'unconstitutional change of Government'. The action taken in response to situations in Mauritania (2005),[245] Guinea (2008),[246] Madagascar (2009),[247] Niger (2010, 2023),[248] Côte d'Ivoire (2010),[249] Guinea-Bissau (2012),[250] Mali (2012, 2020),[251] the Central African Republic (2013),[252] Egypt (2013),[253] Burkina Faso (2015, 2022),[254] Sudan (2019),[255] and Gabon (2023)[256] demonstrates this.

In taking action to suspend one of its members from participating in its activities,[257] the AU operates on the basis of its own understanding of what comprises an 'unconstitutional change of Government'. This understanding is reflected in a number of instruments adopted by and in the practice of AU organs.[258] In the

[241] See eg AUPSC, 'Statement, 36th Meeting' (4 August 2005) AU Doc PSC/PR/Stat.(XXXVI)-(ii) second unnumbered operative paragraph; AUPSC, 'Communiqué, 165th Meeting' (29 December 2008) AU Doc PSC/PR/COMM(CLXV) §3 on the suspension of Mauritania and Guinea, respectively.

[242] On the possible relevance of the practice of the AUPSC, recall n 163 above.

[243] AU Constitutive Act (n 11) art 9(2).

[244] See eg AUPSC, 'Statement, 36th Meeting' (n 241). See also AUPSC, 'Communiqué, 181st Meeting (20 March 2009) AU Doc PSC/PR/COMM(CLXXXI) §4.

[245] AUPSC, 'Statement, 36th Meeting' (n 241) second unnumbered operative paragraph.

[246] AUPSC, 'Communiqué, 165th Meeting' (n 241) §3.

[247] AUPSC, 'Communiqué, 181st Meeting' (n 244) §4.

[248] AUPSC, 'Communiqué, 216th Meeting' (19 February 2010) AU Doc PSC/PR/COMM.2(CCXVI) §5; AUPSC, 'Communiqué, 1168th Meeting' (14 August 2023) AU Doc PSC/PR/COMM.1168(2023) §7.

[249] AUPSC, 'Communiqué, 252nd Meeting' (n 240) §4.

[250] AUPSC, 'Communiqué, 318th Meeting' (17 April 2012) AU Doc PSC/PR/COMM(CCCXVIII) §6.

[251] AUPSC, 'Communiqué, 315th Meeting' (23 March 2012) AU Doc PSC/PR/Comm(CCCXV) §9; AUPSC, 'Communiqué, 941st Meeting' (19 August 2020) AU Doc PSC/PR/COMM(CMXLI) §2. See also AUPSC, 'Communiqué, 1001st Meeting (1 June 2021) AU Doc PSC/PR/COMM.1001(2021) §3.

[252] AUPSC, 'Communiqué, 363rd Meeting' (25 March 2013) AU Doc PSC/PR/COMM(XXXLCIII) §8.

[253] AUPSC, 'Communiqué, 384th Meeting' (5 July 2013) AU Doc PSC/PR/COMM(CCCLXXXIV) §6.

[254] AUPSC, 'Communiqué, 544th Meeting' (18 September 2015) AU Doc PSC/AHG/COMM.3(DXLIV) §11; AUPSC, 'Communiqué, 1062nd Meeting' (31 January 2022) AU Doc PSC/PR/COMM.1/062(2022) §5.

[255] AUPSC, 'Communiqué, 854th Meeting' (6 June 2019) AU Doc PSC/PR/COMM(DCCCXLIV) §12.

[256] AUPSC, 'Communiqué, 1172nd Meeting' (31 August 2023) AU Doc PSC/PR/COMM.1172(2023) §3.

[257] The situation concerning a state's so-called 'permanent representation' appears unaffected by measures taken pursuant to the AU's powers to respond to 'unconstitutional changes of Government'.

[258] On the relevance of the practice of an international organization to the interpretation of the terms of a treaty regulating the functioning of the organization, see n 163 above and accompanying text.

AUPSC's own words, the 'relevant AU instruments and provisions on unconstitutional changes of government [are] scattered in various instruments'.[259]

There is substantial overlap between situations in which there is an 'unconstitutional' claim to governmental status and situations that comprise 'an unconstitutional change of Government' for the AU's purposes. This is so especially where a democratic election is the basis of a constitutionally-valid claim to power, regardless of whether the 'unconstitutional' claim to governmental status is successful. An 'unconstitutional change of Government' for the AU's purposes covers, inter alia, a 'military coup d'etat against a democratically elected Government', the 'replacement of democratically elected Governments by armed dissident groups and rebel movements', and situations in which an incumbent government refuses 'to relinquish power to the winning party after free, fair and regular elections'.[260] An unconstitutional attempt to remove from power a government governing on the basis of a transitional constitution in the context of a transition towards the establishment of a constitution requiring the government to base its claim to power on democratic election also appears to comprise an 'unconstitutional change of Government' for the AU's purposes, as the suspension of Burkina Faso in 2015 suggests.[261]

An 'unconstitutional change of Government' for the AU's purposes appears to refer also to certain situations where there is no 'unconstitutional' claimant to governmental status but which nevertheless similarly concerns the protection or promotion of a democratically-representative government. It includes 'intervention by mercenaries to replace a democratically elected Government'[262] and '[a]ny amendment or revision of the constitution or legal instruments . . . which is an infringement on the principles of democratic change of government'.[263]

[259] See AUPSC, 'Press Statement, 791st Meeting' (22 August 2018) AU Doc PSC/PR/BR.(DCCXCI). The main relevant instruments and provisions include the following: the Lomé Declaration (n 238); Assembly of the Organization of African Unity, 'Decision on Unconstitutional Changes of Government in Africa-CM/2166(LXXII)', 36th Ordinary Session (10–12 July 2000) AHG/Dec.150(XXXVI); AU Constitutive Act (n 11) art 30; PSC Protocol (n 237) art 7(1)(g). See also AU Assembly Rules of Procedure (n 27) Rule 37; African Charter on Democracy, Elections and Governance (adopted 30 January 2007, entered into force 15 February 2012) UN Registration No 55377 ('Addis Ababa Charter'), available at <http://treaties.un.org/doc/Publication/UNTS/No%20Volume/55377/Part/I-55377-0800000280321cc6.pdf>, art 23; AUPSC Retreat, 'Ezulwini Framework for the Enhancement of the Implementation of Measures of the African Union in Situations of Unconstitutional Changes of Government in Africa' (17–19 December 2009), available at <http://peaceau.org/uploads/ezulwini-framework-english.pdf>. See also de Wet, 'The African Union's Struggle against "Unconstitutional Change of Government": From a Moral Prescription to a Requirement under International Law?' (2021) 32 EJIL 199, 202–4.

[260] Lomé Declaration (n 238). See also AU Assembly Rules of Procedure (n 27) Rules 37(2)(a), 37(2)(c)–(d); Addis Ababa Charter (n 259) arts 23(1), 23(3), and 23(4).

[261] AUPSC, 'Communiqué, 544th Meeting' (n 252) §§4, 7, 11.

[262] Lomé Declaration (n 238). See also AU Assembly Rules of Procedure (n 27) Rule 37(2)(b); Addis Ababa Charter (n 259) art 23(2).

[263] Addis Ababa Charter (n 259) art 23(5).

An assessment of the situations in which the AU has not suspended one of its members from participating in its activities might be relevant to ascertaining the scope of what comprises an 'unconstitutional change of Government' for the purposes of the AU, especially where there has emerged an 'unconstitutional' claim to governmental status in respect of that state. For example, in 2011, the AUPSC '[e]ncourage[d] the Libyan stakeholders to accelerate the process leading to the formation of an all-inclusive transitional Government that would be welcome to occupy the seat of Libya in the AU'.[264] It then '[d]ecide[d], . . . taking into account the uniqueness of the situation in Libya and the exceptional circumstances surrounding it, and without prejudice to the relevant AU instruments, to authorize the current authorities in Libya to occupy the seat of Libya in the AU and its organs'.[265]

In the light of such practice, it may be that certain situations involving an 'unconstitutional' claim to governmental status are, or come to be, excluded from the AU's understanding of what constitutes an 'unconstitutional change of Government'. For its part, the AUPSC has agreed to the taking of steps to develop 'a consolidated AU framework on how to respond to situations of unconstitutional changes and popular uprisings', including 'the appropriate refinement of the definition of unconstitutional changes of government, in light of the evolving challenges facing the continent, notably those related to popular uprisings against oppressive systems'.[266] Although recommendations for the 'elaboration of a guideline for determining the compatibility of popular uprisings with AU norms on unconstitutional changes of Government' have since been made,[267] the AUPSC has more recently 'stressed that the notion of "popular uprising" is complex, contested and controversial and [it] emphasized the absence of a universally accepted and applicable definition of what constitutes a "popular uprising" . . . [The notion of 'popular uprising'] is an invention that needs to be interrogated and reflected upon before it is embraced by the Union.'[268] That said, already in 2014 the AUPSC recalled 'the recognition of the right of peoples to rise up peacefully against oppressive political systems' in responding to the situation in Burkina Faso at that time, differentiating between 'a civilian-led and consensual transition', on the one hand, and 'a military-led transition', on the other hand.[269]

The AU's non-suspension of member states in respect of certain 'unconstitutional' claims to governmental status suggests that the AU possesses at least some

[264] AUPSC, 'Communiqué, 291st Meeting' (26 August 2011) AU Doc PSC/AHG/COMM(CCXCI) §6.

[265] AUPSC, 'Communiqué, 297th Meeting' (20 October 2011) AU Doc PSC/PR/COMM.2(XXCXVII) §4.

[266] AUPSC, 'Press Statement, 432nd Meeting' (29 April 2014) AU Doc PSC/PR/BR.(CDXXXII).

[267] AUPSC, 'Final Report of the African Union High-Level Egypt Panel, 442nd Meeting' (17 June 2014) AU Doc PSC/AHG/4(CDXVI) §83.

[268] See AUPSC, 'Press Statement, 871st Meeting' (22 August 2019) AU Doc PSC/PR/BR.(DCCCLXXI).

[269] AUPSC, 'Communiqué, 465th Meeting' (3 November 2014) AU Doc PSC/PR/COMM(CDLXV) §§2, 9(ii).

discretion in deciding whether or not to suspend a member state that has undergone an 'unconstitutional change of Government'. This is reflected in, among other places,[270] the AUPSC's '[a]ffirm[ation] that the overthrow of the democratically elected President [of Sudan] . . . falls under the definition of an unconstitutional change of Government as provided for in the AU instruments'[271] and in its 'demand[] that the Sudanese military . . . hand over power to a transitional civilian-led political authority, in accordance with the will of the people and constitutional order, within a maximum period of fifteen . . . days . . . failing which, Council will automatically apply Article 7[(1)](g) of its Protocol'.[272] The AUPSC then extended the deadline for the handing over of power 'for an additional period of up to sixty (60) days'.[273] The AUPSC eventually suspended Sudan on 6 June 2019.[274]

In the exercise of its apparent discretion in this regard, the AUPSC might not suspend a member state from participating in the AU's activities at least where, in its view, there exists a real possibility of the emergence of an inclusive ostensible government that is actively committed to the implementation of a constitutional order in which a valid claim to power requires a basis in a democratic electoral process, perhaps especially where this involves a 'popular uprising' 'against [an] oppressive political system'.[275] The AUPSC's response to the situation in Sudan (2019) and to that in Libya (2011) has already been mentioned.[276] As another possible example, in 2014, the AUPSC refrained from suspending Burkina Faso subsequent to 'a coup d'État', instead giving the Burkinabe military two weeks to transfer power to a civilian authority.[277]

As for the termination of the suspension of an AU member state, the AUPSC often expressly conditions this on the restoration of 'constitutional order' within that state.[278] The precise factual circumstances in which the AUPSC has terminated the suspension of an AU member state have varied, depending in part on the circumstances of each situation.

[270] See also eg AUPSC, 'Communiqué, 1164th Meeting' (28 July 2023) AU Doc PSC/PR/COMM.1164(2023) §3 and AUPSC, 'Communiqué, 1168th Meeting' (n 248) §7 for the non-immediate suspension of Niger in 2023.

[271] See eg AUPSC, 'Communiqué, 840th Meeting' (15 April 2019) AU Doc PSC/PR/COMM(DCCCXL) §3.

[272] Ibid, §5(c).

[273] AUPSC, 'Communiqué, 846th Meeting' (30 April 2019) AU Doc PSC/PR/COMM(DCCCXLVI) §5.

[274] See AUPSC, 'Communiqué, 854th Meeting' (n 255) §12.

[275] Recall nn 266 and 269 above and accompanying text.

[276] Recall nn 264 and 265 above and accompanying text in relation to Libya. Recall nn 271–74 above and accompanying text in relation to Sudan.

[277] AUPSC, 'Communiqué, 465th Meeting' (n 268) §§§9(iii) 14. See also AUPSC, 'Communiqué, 468th Meeting' (18 November 2014) AU Doc PSC/PR/COMM(CDLXVIII) §§5–6.

[278] See eg the following AUPSC Communiqués: '165th Meeting' (n 241) §3; '181st Meeting' (n 244) §4; '315th Meeting' (n 251) §9; '384th Meeting' (n 253) §6; and '941st Meeting' (n 251) §2. See also AUPSC, 'Communiqué, 216th Meeting' (n 248) §5; AUPSC, 'Communiqué, 252nd Meeting' (n 240) §4.

The AUPSC terminated the suspension of Côte d'Ivoire[279] and Niger in 2011,[280] Madagascar in 2014,[281] and the Central African Republic in 2016[282] after the assumption of power by the constitutional and democratically-elected government of each state. The AUPSC terminated the suspension of Mauritania in 2007[283] and 2009,[284] the Republic of Guinea in 2010,[285] and Guinea-Bissau in 2014[286] when an assumption of power by such a government was imminent. Burkina Faso's suspension was terminated in 2015, subsequent to the restoration to power of a claimant which was operating under transitional arrangements in furtherance of the establishment of a democratic form of government.[287] Similarly, the suspension of Mali and Sudan was terminated in 2012 and 2019, respectively, after the emergence to power of a claimant in respect of each state which was operating under a transitional constitution towards the re-establishment of democracy.[288]

The AU Assembly's Decision on the Prevention of Unconstitutional Changes of Government and Strengthening the Capacity of the African Union to Manage Such Situations provides, moreover, that the 'non-participation of the perpetrators of the unconstitutional change in the elections held to restore constitutional order' is among the measures that 'shall apply' 'in cases of unconstitutional changes of Government'.[289] Egypt nevertheless resumed its participation in the AU after the 2014 victory of Abdel Fattah el-Sisi—the leader of the 2013 *coup d'état*, which resulted in Egypt's suspension from the activities of the AU—in the 2014 presidential elections in Egypt. While the AUPSC's decision 'to lift the suspension of the participation of Egypt' was made 'on the understanding that this does not constitute a precedent in terms of adherence to the relevant provisions of [the aforementioned Decision of the AU Assembly]',[290] it is difficult to see how this case suggests

[279] AUPSC, 'Communiqué, 273rd Meeting' (21 April 2011) AU Doc PSC/PR/COMM.1(CCLXXIII) §§2–3.

[280] AUPSC, 'Communiqué, 266th Meeting' (16 March 2011) AU Doc PSC/PR/COMM(CCLXV) §6.

[281] AUPSC, 'Communiqué, 415th Meeting' (27 January 2014) AU Doc PSC/PR/COMM(CDXV) §§6–7.

[282] AUPSC, 'Communiqué, 586th Meeting' (31 March 2016) AU Doc PSC/PR/COMM(DLXXXVI) §6.

[283] AUPSC, 'Communiqué on the Situation in the Islamic Republic of Mauritania, 76th Meeting' (10 April 2007) AU Doc PSC/PR/Comm(LXXVI) §§4, 7.

[284] AUPSC, 'Communiqué, 196th Meeting' (29 June 2009) AU Doc PSC/MIN/COMM(CXCVI) §§2–3.

[285] AUPSC, 'Communiqué, 252nd Meeting' (n 240) §§1–2.

[286] AUPSC, 'Communiqué, 442nd Meeting' (17 June 2014) AU Doc PSC/PR/COMM(CDXLII) §8.

[287] AUPSC, 'Communiqué, 547th Meeting' (26 September 2015) AU Doc PSC/AHG/COMM.3(DXLVII) §§8–9.

[288] AUPSC, 'Communiqué, 339th Meeting' (24 October 2012) AU Doc PSC/MIN/COMM.2(CCCXXXIX) §6; AUPSC, 'Communiqué, 875th Meeting' (6 September 2019) AU Doc PSC/PR/COMM(DCCCLXXV) §4.

[289] 'Decision on Unconstitutional Changes of Government of 2010' (n 239) §6(i)(b)(a). See also Addis Ababa Charter (n 259) art 25(4).

[290] AUPSC, 'Communiqué, 442nd Meeting' (17 June 2014) AU Doc PSC/PR/COMM.2(CDXLII) §8.

anything other than that the participation by a perpetrator of an 'unconstitutional change of Government' in an election for the formation of a new government in a state does not necessarily preclude that state from resuming its participation in the AU's activities.

In apparent furtherance of the AU's objectives[291] and the principles in accordance with which it 'shall function',[292] the AU's legal framework on the suspension of its member states in response to 'unconstitutional change[s] of Government' enables, if not directs, the AU to support the emergence or subsistence of certain ostensible governments over others. More specifically, the AU framework permits, if not requires, the AU to suspend a member state whose constitution provides that a democratic election is to be the basis of its government's claim to power and in respect of which there exists an 'unconstitutional' claim to governmental status. At the same time, this framework excludes action, or at least permits inaction, in respect of a situation in a member state that involves the existence or likely emergence of an 'unconstitutional' inclusive ostensible government that is actively committed to the implementation of a constitutional order that requires a democratic electoral process for a valid claim to power and that is operating as a rival to what is seen to be an 'oppressive political system'.

While not beyond doubt, the AU appears to have the power to suspend one of its member states in circumstances that do not involve an 'unconstitutional change of Government'. This might include where there exists a claimant to governmental status in respect of an AU member state that has subverted the state's democratic process in circumstances that do not involve an 'unconstitutional change of Government' or where an AU member state possesses a government that is unwilling to comply with the obligations of AU member states 'to accept and implement the decisions of the [AUPSC]'.[293] This is because Article 23(2) of the AU Constitutive Act provides a legal basis for the imposition by the AU of sanctions, which may include the suspension of an AU member state from the AU[294] in response to that state's failure 'to comply with the decisions and policies of the [African] Union'. It is not unlikely that some such decisions and policies may reflect the AU's pursuit to maintain a democratic form of government within its member states. This is so especially since 'respect for democratic principles' and 'condemnation and rejection of unconstitutional changes of governments' are among the principles in accordance with which the AU 'shall function',[295] and since the

[291] See AU Constitutive Act (n 11) art 3(g).

[292] See ibid, art 4(m). Note also n 158 above on the absence within the AU Constitutive Act or other AU instruments of an express limitation on the powers of the AU in respect of the internal affairs of each of its members.

[293] PSC Protocol (n 237) art 7(3).

[294] See AU Constitutive Act (n 11) art 23(1); AU Assembly Rules of Procedure (n 27) Rule 37(1).

[295] AU Constitutive Act (n 11) art 4(m) and (p).

promotion of 'democratic principles and institutions, popular participation and good governance' is among the objectives of the AU.[296]

5.6.2.1.3 The Organization of American States

Among the contemporary purposes of the OAS is the 'promot[ion] and consolidat[ion of] representative democracy, with due respect for the principle of non[-]intervention'.[297] Pursuant to what is today Article 9 of the OAS Charter,[298]

> [a] Member of the Organization whose democratically constituted government has been overthrown by force may be suspended from the exercise of the right to participate in the sessions of the General Assembly, the Meeting of Consultation, the Councils of the Organization and the Specialized Conferences as well as in the commissions, working groups and any other bodies established.[299]

This power is to be exercised by the OASGA. It 'shall be exercised only when such diplomatic initiatives undertaken by the Organization for the purpose of promoting the restoration of representative democracy in the affected Member State have been unsuccessful'.[300] The OASGA has never taken action to suspend a member state in express pursuance of Article 9 of the OAS Charter.

An additional basis for suspension is reflected in Article 20 of the IADC,[301] adopted by the OASGA in 2001. This provides that, '[i]n the event of an unconstitutional alteration of the constitutional regime that seriously impairs the democratic order in a member state, any member state or the Secretary General may request the immediate convocation of the Permanent Council'. The OASPC, in turn, 'shall immediately convene a special session of the General Assembly' if 'diplomatic initiatives prove unsuccessful, or if the urgency of the situation so warrants'. Under Article 21 of the IADC,

> [w]hen the special session of the General Assembly determines that there has been an unconstitutional interruption of the democratic order of a member state, and that diplomatic initiatives have failed, the special session shall take the decision to suspend said member state from the exercise of its right to participate in the OAS.

296 Ibid, art 3(g).

297 OAS Charter (n 158) art 2(b).

298 This provision was introduced by the Protocol of Amendments to the Charter of the Organization of American States (adopted 14 December 1992, entered into force 25 September 1997), available at <http://refworld.org/docid/3de4a1f84.html>, art 1.

299 OAS Charter (n 158) art 9.

300 Ibid, art 9(a)–(b).

301 OASGA, Inter-American Democratic Charter (adopted 11 September 2001) ('IADC'), available at <http://www.oas.org/charter/docs/resolution1_en_p4.htm>.

According to Article 22 of the IADC, the OASGA may lift the suspension of a member state '[o]nce the situation that led to suspension has been resolved'.[302]

As for relevant practice under the IADC, in 2002, the OASPC 'condemn[ed] the alteration of the constitutional order in Venezuela' and agreed to convoke a special session of the OASGA following the attempted removal of democratically-elected President Hugo Chávez from office.[303] Mr Chávez returned to office very soon after his removal, before the OASGA might have taken any further action. The OASGA subsequently 'express[ed] satisfaction at the restoration of the constitutional order and the democratically elected government of President Hugo Chávez Frías in the Bolivarian Republic of Venezuela' and

> the determination of the member states to continue applying, without distinction, and in strict accordance with the letter and spirit of the Inter-American Democratic Charter, the mechanisms provided for therein for the preservation and defense of representative democracy, reiterating their rejection of the use of violence to replace any democratic government in the Hemisphere.[304]

Accordingly, the initial steps towards suspension had been taken, but the situation was resolved before a decision on suspension could be adopted.

The only time a member state of the OAS has been suspended pursuant to Article 21 of the IADC was in 2009. The OASGA suspended Honduras,[305] having found that 'the *coup d'état* staged against the constitutionally established Government of Honduras and the arbitrary detention and expulsion from the country of the constitutional president José Manuel Zelaya Rosales . . . produced an unconstitutional alteration of the democratic order' of Honduras.[306] The retention of a claim to governmental status by the 'constitutional' President of Honduras did not preclude Honduras's suspension. Honduras resumed its participation in the activities of the OAS following the reconciliation of the 'unconstitutional' and 'constitutional' claims to governmental status.[307]

[302] This decision requires 'the vote of two thirds of the [OAS] member states in accordance with the OAS Charter'. See IADC (n 301) art 22.

[303] OASPC, 'Situation in Venezuela' (13 April 2002) OEA/Ser.G/CP/RES.811(1315/02) §§1, 3.

[304] OASGA, 'Support for Democracy in Venezuela' (18 April 2002) OEA/Ser.P, AG/RES.1 (XXIX-E02) §§1–2.

[305] OASGA, 'Suspension of the Right of Honduras to Participate in the Organization of American States' (16 July 2009) OEA/Ser.P, AG/RES.2 (XXXVII-E/09) rev.1, §1.

[306] OASGA, 'Resolution on the Political Crisis in Honduras' (1 July 2009) OEA/Ser.P, AG/RES.1 (XXXVII-E/09) rev.1, §1. All of this resulted from the convocation of the OASGA by the OASPC in accordance with article 20 of the IADC (n 301). See OASGA, 'Resolution on the Political Crisis in Honduras', third preambular paragraph; OASPC, 'Current Situation in Honduras' (28 June 2009) OEA/Ser.G, CP/RES.953 (1700/09) §6. The OASPC had already found the situation in Honduras to have 'produced an unconstitutional alteration of the democratic order'. See ibid, §1.

[307] See OASGA, 'Participation of Honduras in the Organization of American States' (1 June 2011) OEA/Ser.P, AG/RES.1 (XLI-E/11) rev.1, fourth unnumbered preambular paragraph and §1.

In 2016, the OAS Secretary-General requested the convocation of the OASPC pursuant to Article 20 of the IADC 'to address the 'alteration of the Constitutional order' and how this affects 'the democratic order' of . . . Venezuela'.[308] While the OASPC did convene on the matter, this did not result in a special session of the OASGA, let alone in the suspension of Venezuela.[309]

The OAS's limited practice pursuant to Articles 20 and 21 of the IADC thus suggests the following. Both an 'unconstitutional alteration of the constitutional regime that seriously impairs the democratic order' under Article 20 and, to the extent that it differs, 'an unconstitutional interruption of the democratic order of [a] State' within the meaning of Article 21 encompass at least certain situations in which an 'unconstitutional' claimant to governmental status that is not democratically elected usurps power from a democratically-elected 'constitutional' government.[310]

5.6.2.2 De Facto Suspension

5.6.2.2.1 In general

An international organization may suspend de facto one of its member states on either an a priori or a more-or-less[311] *ad hoc* basis. An a priori decision to suspend de facto a member state refers to a decision taken before—or, at least, not specifically in respect of—any particular ostensible representation of a state. In contrast, an *ad hoc* decision to suspend de facto a member state refers to a decision taken in response to the ostensible representation of a state. De facto suspension may affect the member state's participation in the work of one or more organs of the organization.

An example of a priori de facto suspension is the decision of the OAS in respect of 'the present Government of Cuba' in 1962. The Consultation of Ministers

[308] 'Letter from the Secretary-General of the OAS to the Chairman of the Permanent Council' (30 May 2016) OSG/243-16, available at <http://oas.org/documents/eng/press/OSG-243.en.pdf>.

[309] For the outcome of the special meeting of the OASPC, see 'Declaration of the Permanent Council about the Situation in the Bolivarian Republic of Venezuela' (1 June 2016) OEA/Ser.G, CP/DEC.63 (2076/16). For the later acknowledgement by the OASPC of 'the unconstitutional alteration of the democratic order in the Bolivarian Republic of Venezuela', see OASPC, 'Resolution on the Recent Events in Venezuela' (3 April 2017) OEA/Ser.G, CP/RES.1078 (2108/17). On Venezuela's intention to withdraw from the OAS and on the purported annulment of the denunciation of the OAS Charter, recall n 150 above. On questions concerning Venezuela's participation and representation at the OAS since then, recall section 5.5.1.

[310] See also OASPC, 'Resolution on the Recent Events in Venezuela' (n 309) fourth unnumbered preambular paragraph and §1 for the apparent treatment of the Supreme Court of Venezuela's suspension and 'arrogat[ion]' of the powers of the National Assembly as an 'unconstitutional alteration of the democratic order in the Bolivarian Republic of Venezuela'.

[311] The hedging as to degree in respect of the *ad hoc* de facto suspension of a member state reflects the fact that an international organization may take either a separate decision in respect of each act of ostensible representation of a state or a decision which amounts to the rejection of this ostensible representation as effective for a particular period or indefinitely, at least absent a subsequent decision to the contrary. Recall n 23 above and accompanying text.

of Foreign Affairs resolved that 'the present Government of Cuba, which has officially identified itself as a Marxist-Leninist government, is incompatible with the principles and objectives of the inter-American system' and that 'this incompatibility excludes the present Government of Cuba from participation in the inter-American system'. It then declared that 'the present Government of Cuba has voluntarily placed itself outside the inter-American system'.[312]

An example of *ad hoc* de facto suspension of a state which prevented the state's participation in the proceedings of an annual session of an organ of an international organization is the exclusion of the delegation of South Africa from participating in the twenty-ninth ordinary session of the UNGA. This followed from the 'interpretation' by the President of the UNGA of the UNGA's decision in respect of the credentials presented for that session.[313] The UNGA decided to adopt the Credentials Committee's recommendation to accept the 'credentials of representatives . . . with the exception of the credentials of the representatives of South Africa'.[314] In the view of the President of the UNGA, a view that withstood challenge in the UNGA,[315] this was 'tantamount to saying in explicit terms that the General Assembly refuses to allow the South African delegation to participate in its work'.[316]

In each of the above examples, the de facto suspension of a state appears to have related to the unwillingness of the government of the state in question to comply with certain international legal obligations of that state.[317] The de facto suspension of a member state, which is not common[318] but which may result from some matter related directly to some specific ostensible government of a state, raises the following questions.

[312] Consultation of Ministers of Foreign Affairs of the OAS, Eighth Meeting, 'Final Act' (22–31 January 1962) Resolution VI, available at <http://oas.org/consejo/MEETINGS%20OF%20CONSULTATION/Actas/Acta%208.pdf>. For the termination of this de facto suspension, see OASGA res 2438 (3 June 2009) AG/RES.2438 (XXXIX-O/09) §1.

[313] UNGA, 'Official Records, 29th Session, 2281st Plenary Meeting' (n 217) §153.

[314] UNGA res 3206 (XXIX) (30 September 1974) UN Doc A/RES/3206(XXIX); UNGA, 'Credentials of Representatives to the Twenty-Ninth Session of the General Assembly: First Report of the Credentials Committee' (28 September 1974) UN Doc A/9779, §§14–15.

[315] See UNGA, 'Official Records, 29th Session, 2281st Plenary Meeting' (n 217) §185.

[316] Ibid, §159. The President's interpretation withstood challenge in the UNGA by a majority of 91 votes, with 22 votes against and 19 abstentions. See ibid, §185. The President's interpretation was not, however, the only one possible. For a similar phrase which had been understood differently, recall n 93 above. See also UNGA, 'Official Records, 29th Session, 2281st Plenary Meeting' (n 217) §155.

[317] In respect of Cuba, see the determination that the situation in Cuba 'violate[d] the obligation inherent in membership in the regional system [*viz* the OAS] and [was] incompatible with that system' (Resolution VI (n 312)). On South Africa, see eg UNGA, 'Official Records, 29th Session, 2281st Plenary Meeting' (n 217) §12 (Tanzania), §§30, 35 (Syria), §146 (Guatemala). See also §117 (USSR) and §146 (Iraq).

[318] See also Schermers and Blokker (n 20) 219, §262. Cf Higgins and others (n 28) 284–5. For another example of de facto suspension, see United Nations Economic and Social Council ('ECOSOC') res 947 D IV (XXXVI) §2, reproduced in ECOSOC), 'Official Records of the 36th Session (2 July–2 August 1963) "Resolutions, Supplement No. 1"' (1963) UN Doc E/3816, 4.

5.6.2.2.2 An ultra vires act?

There is little doubt that an international organization possesses the implied power to suspend de facto a member state to prevent that state from being represented in the work of the organization through the 'wrong' government, perhaps especially where to do otherwise would imply the organization's recognition of the governmental status of that claimant.[319] This is so even where the action taken precludes the member state from exercising an entitlement it enjoys under the organization's constituent instrument to participate in the proceedings of one or more organs of the organization,[320] including where there exists only one ostensible government of a state.

The occasional suggestion to the contrary, in specific relation to a situation in which there is only one ostensible government of a state, is unconvincing. For example, one commentator claims that the practice of the UNGA in rejecting the credentials issued by an ostensible government in situations involving rival ostensible credentials cannot provide a 'justification' for the rejection of credentials in situations where there is only one set of credentials for consideration since these are 'completely different situations'.[321] But a state may be precluded from participating in the work of one or more organs of the organization in either case. Moreover, it is unclear why, in contrast to the situation involving rival ostensible credentials, the situation involving only one set of ostensible credentials of a state 'does not require a decision by the [UN]GA on the authority of representation'.[322] The ostensible credentials in each of these situations may not be issued by an ostensible government that qualifies for governmental status as a matter of customary international law. The rejection of the credentials issued by the only ostensible government of a state is not invariably a decision that is taken for 'political reasons'.[323]

The question whether an international organization acts in excess of its powers in preventing a member state from participating in its work through the 'right' government of that state requires some further consideration. This is so not least because of the existence of some objection to such practice, an example of which appears to have been the preclusion in 1974 of South Africa's participation in the twenty-ninth ordinary session of the UNGA.[324]

[319] See also Secretariat of the United Nations (n 17) 532, §6. Indeed, at least insofar as it amounts to recognition of governmental status, an international organization may be acting ultra vires in accepting as effective the ostensible representation of a state by a 'wrong' government. Recall section 5.5.1.

[320] On such a right, recall n 217 above.

[321] Magiera (n 6) 459, §§36–7. See also Schermers and Blokker (n 20) 221–2, §263.

[322] Magiera (n 6) 459, §36. Recall also section 5.4.1.2.

[323] Cf Schermers and Blokker (n 20) 221, §263.

[324] Recall n 316 above and accompanying text. On the governmental status of the Nationalist claimant, recall chapter 4, nn 280–1, 283.

Where the legality of the de facto suspension has been challenged, it is usually on one of two grounds:[325] that de facto suspension has been undertaken in the absence of any rule on the suspension of a member state[326] or that the procedure for formal suspension for which the rules of the organization expressly provide has not been followed, despite the effects of de facto suspension being analogous to those of formal suspension.[327] For example, the Legal Counsel of the UN took the view that de facto suspension from the UNGA 'would not satisfy the . . . requirements [of Article 5 of the UN Charter] and would therefore be contrary to the Charter'.[328]

Although both formal suspension and de facto suspension typically prevents the affected state from participating in the work of the organization, the two actions do not necessarily have the exact same effects. De facto suspension might have more limited effects than formal suspension (for example, when the former involves a decision that affects the participation of a member state in only one organ of the organization), while the latter tends to affect the participation of the member state in several organs of the organization, among other rights and privileges of membership. On the contrary, a decision may be taken formally to suspend the exercise by a member state of only certain rights of membership,[329] while a decision to refuse the participation of a member state through a particular government may be of wider effect.[330] In short, the refusal by an international organization to permit the only, or every, claimant to governmental status in respect of a member state to participate in the proceedings of one or more organs of the organization is not necessarily the same as formally suspending a state from exercising its rights and privileges of membership of the organization. When the UNGA did not accept credentials submitted by the Nationalist government in South Africa, this affected only the representation of South Africa in the UNGA. South Africa was still able to exercise its other rights and privileges of UN membership.[331] As one state put it, 'in deciding not to admit the representatives of South Africa to this session of

[325] The power of an international organization to take such action is less frequently disputed on other, less plausible grounds. See eg Ciobanu (n 64) 357–8 for objections in respect of the UNGA's decision not to permit the ostensible representatives of South Africa to represent South Africa at the UNGA on the basis of the UNGA's past practice and, as a separate argument, on the ground that the Security Council was seized of the same matter.

[326] See eg UNSC, 'Official Records, 992nd Meeting' (14 March 1962) UN Doc S/PV.992, §81 (Ecuador) and §84 (Bolivia); UNSC, 'Official Records, 993rd Meeting' (15 March 1962) UN Doc S/PV.993, §52 (USSR).

[327] See eg UNGA, 'Official Records, 29th Session, 2281st Plenary Meeting' (n 217) §§60–3 (UK), §142 (Guatemala), §163 (USA), §187 (Finland), §190 (France), §198 (Canada), §200 (Federal Republic of Germany), §211 (Australia), §219 (Nicaragua), §221 (Austria). See also Schermers and Blokker (n 20) 222–3, §263; Magiera (n 6) 459–60, §38; Halberstam (n 64) 188–91; Ciobanu (n 64) 358, 371–80.

[328] Secretariat of the United Nations (n 57) 170–1, §6. See also Secretariat of the United Nations, 'Statement Submitted in Response to a Request Made at the 1236th Meeting of the Second Committee of the General Assembly' [1968] UNJYB 195, 198, §14.

[329] See Tams (n 231) 369, §21.

[330] See eg n 312 above on the OAS's decision in respect of Cuba in 1962, which ultimately precluded Cuba from participating in all of the OAS's activities.

[331] See Suttner, 'Has South Africa Been Illegally Excluded from the United Nations General Assembly?' (1984) 17 CILSA 279, 292–4. See also the statement by the President of the UNGA that

the General Assembly . . . we shall not be expelling or suspending South Africa'.[332] Accordingly, the view that de facto suspension is ultra vires because of such action having similar consequences as formal suspension without having followed the procedure for formal suspension carries little weight.

In any event, for the most part, relevant practice does not support the general view that either the existence or the absence of an express power of an international organization to suspend a member state necessarily implies that the organization lacks the implied power to take action that is similar to formal suspension.[333] In this regard, the following four points may be noted.

First, member states[334] have only infrequently and inconsistently contested the de facto suspension of another member state. For example, while the UK voted in favour of rejecting the credentials of the ostensible representative of Hungary within the context of the ILO,[335] it considered South Africa's exclusion from the UNGA to be a decision that was taken 'improperly, unconstitutionally and illegally'.[336] As another example, while Cuba considered the action taken against it by the OAS to have been ultra vires,[337] it was in favour of not accepting the credentials submitted by South Africa at the UNGA.[338] While at least some such apparent inconsistencies[339] might be explicable by reference to considerations that call for distinct treatment among the situations in question (in particular, the perceived preclusion in only one situation of a state's participation through the 'right' government[340] or the relatively-narrower powers of one organization), this does not appear generally to have been so. For instance, in voting to reject the credentials

'[his] interpretation [of the UNGA's decision in respect of the credentials submitted in South Africa's name] refers exclusively to the position of the South African delegation within . . . the General Assembly' (UNGA, 'Official Records, 29th Session, 2281st Plenary Meeting' (n 217) §160).

[332] UNGA, 'Official Records, 29th Session, 2281st Plenary Meeting' (n 217) §76 (India). See also ibid, §129 (Nigeria) (that, in respect of the question of whether or not to exclude the delegation of South Africa from participating in the UNGA's work, '[w]e are not discussing suspension and/or expulsion'); §218 Nepal ('the ruling just made by the President should not be construed as the suspension or expulsion of South Africa from the United Nations').

[333] For a range of scholarly views on the legality of decisions to suspend de facto a state, albeit all invariably with a focus on the UNGA's refusal to allow representatives of the Nationalist government in South Africa to represent South Africa at the UNGA, see eg the authors cited in Magliveras (n 4) 209–10 nn 38–9; Amerasinghe (n 156) 129–30, including ns 83–84, as well as Ciobanu (n 64) 374–80; Sohn, 'Expulsion or Forced Withdrawal from an International Organization' (1964) 776 Harvard LR 1381, 1418 1419–20 (though the case of Cuba at the OAS is not one of expulsion); Schermers and Blokker (n 20) 197–9, §233A.

[334] On the relevance of the practice of member states to the understanding of the constituent instrument, and thus also the powers of an international organization, recall n 160 above.

[335] Lauterpacht (n 18) 573.

[336] UNGA, 'Official Records, 29th Session, 2281st Plenary Meeting' (n 217) §62.

[337] UNSC, 'Official Records, 992nd Meeting' (n 326) §70.

[338] UNGA, 'Official Records, 29th Session, 2248th Meeting' (n 66) §105.

[339] For other apparent inconsistencies, see eg Ciobanu (n 64) 367–8.

[340] On the legality of de facto suspension that involves only the preclusion of a state's participation through one or more 'wrong' governments, recall n 319 above and the accompanying text.

of the ostensible representative of Hungary within the context of the ILO, the UK seemingly acknowledged that its action was taken in respect of a claimant that qualified for governmental status on grounds that 'transcended' 'established practice and constitutional forms'.[341]

Secondly, the absence of virtually any practice suggesting that the de facto suspension by an international organization of a member state lacks legal effect, even where doubts have been raised about the intra vires character of such suspension, provides no further evidence as to the illegality of the decisions taken by international organizations in this regard.

Thirdly, a number of states have made statements which, in addition to their votes in favour of the adoption of an act of de facto suspension, reflect an understanding that such acts are intra vires.[342]

Fourthly, it is not irrelevant that, more recently than 1974, the UNGA has again de facto suspended South Africa, with more states in favour of this decision than before.[343] Not entirely dissimilarly, in 1997, the UNGA accepted, by consensus,[344] the decision of the Credentials Committee 'to defer a decision on the credentials of Cambodia on the understanding that . . . no one would occupy the seat of that country at the fifty-second session'.[345] No legal question or challenge was raised in respect of this decision.

To the extent that the question of the legality of de facto suspension subsists, it is perhaps worth noting that the principles and purposes of the international organization are sometimes invoked in apparent support of a decision to suspend de facto a member state. This is especially so where the de facto suspension does not relate principally, if at all, to uncertainty over the customary international legal identity of the member state's government.

For example, the OAS considered that 'the present Government of Cuba . . . is incompatible with the principles and objectives of the inter-American system'.[346] As another example, during a debate related to whether the UNGA's decision in respect of the credentials of South Africa at the twenty-ninth session of the UNGA

[341] Lauterpacht (n 18) 574.

[342] See eg UNGA, 'Official Records, 29th Session, 2281st Plenary Meeting' (n 217) §74 (India), §136 (Nigeria), §148 (Iraq). See also UNGA, 'Credentials of Representatives to the Thirteenth Session of the General Assembly' (n 92) §18 (USSR, with '[s]imilar views' expressed by other states). On the vote in favour of the adoption of an act of de facto suspension, recall n 316 above.

[343] See UNGA, 'Official Records, 35th Session, 103rd Plenary Meeting' (2 March 1981) UN Doc A/35/PV.103, §12 on the approval (by 112 votes to 22, with 6 abstentions) of the Credentials Committee's report in which the Committee 'decided to reject the credentials of the delegation of South Africa for the thirty-fifth session of the General Assembly' (UNGA, 'Credentials of Representatives to the Thirty-Fifth Session of the General Assembly: Second Report of the Credentials Committee' (2 March 1981) UN Doc A/35/484/Add.2, §14).

[344] UNGA res 52/178 (n 88).

[345] UNGA, 'Credentials of Representatives to the Fifty-Second Session of the General Assembly' (n 88) §§4–5, 11.

[346] See n 317 above.

amounted to the de facto suspension of South Africa, Syria expressed the view that '[t]he very presence of the South African delegation in this General Assembly is in utter contravention of [certain UN] principles'; the Philippines stated that South Africa 'cannot [be] allow[ed] . . . to flout the principles of the Charter'; the USSR took the position that the 'policies and practices' of '[t]he racist regime of South Africa . . . are incompatible with the principles and purposes of the Charter of the United Nations'; and Iraq considered that '[t]he continued presence within the Organization of [South Africa], which has persistently flouted the principles of the Charter . . . , in no way contributes to safeguarding the Charter'.[347]

This might be relevant since action taken by an international organization in furtherance of its purposes may affect the applicability or strength of the presumption in favour of the intra vires character of that action.[348] Insofar as this is the case, the apparent flexibility in determining whether or not the de facto suspension furthers the international organization's purposes or principles, an international organization would appear to have a broad power to suspend de facto a member state.

5.6.2.2.3 *A violation of the suspended state's rights?*

It might be suggested that the de facto suspension of a member state from an international organization involves the violation of an international legal right of that state, not least because the representation of a state in one or more political organs of an international organization is often considered to be a 'basic' right[349] of its membership of the organization. Further, insofar as an international organization is obliged not to intervene in the affairs that international law leaves to the sovereign discretion of its member states,[350] the de facto suspension by an international organization of one of its member states on grounds directly connected to a particular claim to governmental status might also be thought to violate the prohibition on intervention. Such action might be seen as being coercive in respect of the identity of the state's government or representatives.[351] Regardless, moreover, of whether an international organization is prohibited from intervening in the sovereign affairs of a state, the conduct of one or more states that is associated with a decision of an international organization to suspend de facto one of its members may violate the prohibition on intervention that is without a doubt opposable to states.[352]

[347] UNGA, 'Official Records, 29th Session, 2281st Plenary Meeting' (n 217) §34 (Syria), §93 (Philippines), §120 (USSR), §146 (Iraq). See also UNGA, 'Credentials of Representatives to the Eighteenth Session of the General Assembly) (n 105) §16; Magliveras (n 4) 227–9 in respect of Israel at the UNGA.

[348] Recall n 179 above and accompanying text.

[349] See Schermers and Blokker (n 20) 222, §263. Recall n 217 above.

[350] On this, recall section 5.5.2.

[351] On the requirements of prohibited intervention and on the circumstances in which they might be satisfied, recall section 3.4.2. On the freedom of each state to choose its representatives, recall n 42 above.

[352] Recall, generally, section 3.4.2.

That said, the de facto suspension of a member state that precludes its participation only by a 'wrong' government appears unlikely to violate any rights of that state under international law. Neither any right to representation nor any right against intervention can readily be understood to entitle a state to participate in the work of an international organization through such an ostensible government. Indeed, a decision not to allow a member state to participate in the work of an international organization through a 'wrong' government might even be necessary in certain circumstances to ensure that the organization is acting intra vires and not in violation of any international legal rights of the state.[353]

Moreover, there is little to suggest that the de facto suspension of a member state violates any international legal right of that state, even when a state is precluded from participating in the work of an international organization through the 'right' government. The de facto suspension comprises practice of the organization. As such, it informs the interpretation and application of the constituent instrument under which the state enjoys any relevant treaty-based right,[354] supporting in this way, especially in the absence of compelling evidence to the contrary, the conclusion that any treaty-based right the enjoyment of which is implicated is not absolute and is not violated by the de facto suspension of a member state. There is also little practice to suggest that the de facto suspension of a state involves a violation of any other international legal obligation. It may be that the de facto suspension of a member state from an international organization is not deemed to be coercive as regards a matter that international law leaves to the sovereign discretion of that state.

5.6.3 Limitations on State Participation and the Concept of 'the Government' of a State

In general, limitations imposed by international organizations on state participation in their work do not undermine the presumptive sovereign freedom of each state to choose its government. Nor do they undermine the objective international legal existence of each state's government. At the same time, the power of international organizations to limit a state's participation in their work demonstrates the existence, in effect, of possible limitations on the representative capacity of a state's government.[355] The grounds on which such limitations have been imposed[356] highlight the possible significance in fact, if not in law, of certain characteristics of an ostensible government in this regard. Notably, these include the

[353] Recall sections 5.5.1–5.5.2.
[354] See n 163 above and accompanying text.
[355] Recall section 2.3.2.
[356] Recall section 5.6.2, in particular sections 5.6.2.1.2–5.6.2.1.3. Recall also section 5.6.2.2, especially the text accompanying n 317 as well the text accompanying nn 346–7.

apparent willingness of the state's government to ensure compliance with certain international legal obligations of the state and the existence of an ostensible government of a state status that is undermining a democratic form of government within that state.

5.7 Conclusion

The customary international legal identity of a state's government is generally relevant to the state's representation in and vis-à-vis an international organization. The decision of an international organization to accept as effective for its purposes the ostensible representation of a state tends to turn at least in part on the organization's acceptance of the claimant to governmental status through which the purported representation of the state occurs as the claimant that qualifies as a matter of customary international law as the government of that state. At least to this extent, the presumptive sovereign freedom of each state to choose its government, the objective customary international legal identity of a state's government, both the plenary, or near-plenary and distinctive representative capacity of a state's government remain intact.

An international organization may, nevertheless, possess the power to allow the 'misrepresentation' of one of its member states without it being clear that this involves a violation of any international legal right of that state. Insofar as such a power does not extend to circumstances that involve recognition of the 'wrong' government, it undermines neither the freedom of a state to choose its government nor the objective international legal existence of a state's government. To the extent that a decision of an international organization to allow the 'misrepresentation' of a state in circumstances that involve recognition of the 'wrong' government may have legal effect, the possibility of such a decision would limit the freedom of each state to choose its government and the objective international legal existence of a state's government. But there is no general acceptance of such a possibility. In any event, the power to allow the 'misrepresentation' of a state reflects a nuance as regards the distinctive representative capacity of the government of a state in the sense that the 'right' government may find itself unable to represent the state while a 'wrong' government may represent the state for at least certain purposes of international law, including because of some matter directly connected to the identity of that state's government.

As a separate matter, it is not uncommon for an international organization to have the power under its constituent instrument to take action on grounds related in some direct way to a specific claim to governmental status in order to limit that state's participation in the work of one or more of its organs. Such action, which appears not to violate any international legal rights of the affected state, may take the form of the refusal to admit a state to membership. It may instead and more commonly does take the form of the suspension of a member state or of a measure to comparable effect. While generally undermining neither the freedom of a state to choose its government nor the objective international legal existence of a state's government, the existence and exercise of such powers indicate that a state's government may find itself unable to represent a state for certain purposes of international law, including because of some matter directly connected to the identity of a state's government.

The situations in which a state's ability to participate in the work of an international organization may be limited, as well as the circumstances in which states may be and have arguably been 'misrepresented' in the context of an international organization, indicate that some specific characteristic of an ostensible government might preclude the government of a state from representing the state for certain purposes of international law. Notable considerations in this regard include the apparent unwillingness of the government of a state to ensure that state's compliance with certain international legal obligations and, as at least regards the limitations imposed by international organizations on state participation in their work, the undermining by a state's ostensible government of a democratic system of government within that state.

6
Conclusion

6.1 Ascertaining the Law

There is a wealth of practice, including conduct of states and international organizations, concerning the identity of the governments of states in international law. Such practice covers the recognition of and criteria for governmental status. It extends also to other matters, including, for example, questions arising from the representation of states in the context of international organizations as well as more general issues such as the foundational aspects of the concept of the government of a state.

Over the years, a number of doctrines emerged with an apparent view to guiding certain matters concerning the identity of governments. Still, none of these doctrines can account, in general, for existing practice on the matter. A prominent example in this regard is the Estrada doctrine, which was formulated in 1930 and eventually adopted by many states, pursuant to which they claimed not to recognize governments.[1] This doctrine gained some of its popularity during the Cold War as states sought to disentangle their acceptance of a claimant's governmental status from the perceived political approval of that claimant.[2] During that time, practice on recognition of governments nevertheless subsisted[3] and was often divided on political grounds, with controversies concerning the identity of governments sometimes being rather protracted.[4]

Similarly, the conduct of states and international organizations concerning the identity of governments might at times find itself in alignment with certain scholarly views as regards aspects of the law in this regard. Yet, none of these positions offers a comprehensive, let alone convincing, account of practice. For example, in seeking to ascertain the criteria for governmental status, practice over the past thirty or so years has been considered principally through the lens of whether effective control has been supplanted by democratic representativity as the basis for determination of governmental status,[5] frequently without regard to the possible

[1] Recall further chapter 3, nn 112–13 and the accompanying text.

[2] For the view that political approval accompanies at least certain forms of recognition, recall chapter 3, n 11.

[3] Recall chapter 3, n 115 and the accompanying text as well as section 3.3 more generally. Recall also chapter 4.

[4] Recall eg chapter 5, nn 100 and 102, including the accompanying text, on China's representation at the UN between 1950 and 1971.

[5] Recall section 1.1, especially n 25.

The Identity of Governments in International Law. Niko Pavlopoulos, Oxford University Press. © Niko Pavlopoulos 2024.
DOI: 10.1093/9780191991509.003.0006

relevance of autonomy or 'constitutionality' in this regard.[6] At the same time, as even proponents of the relevance of democratic representativity have come to accept, contemporary practice on recognition of governments cannot generally be explained on the basis of democratic representativity.[7] In this regard, it can be said that the tendency in the literature to focus on only some of the possible aspects of the international legal regulation of governmental status[8] has not facilitated the ascertainment, importance, and rationalization of such criteria.[9] On the contrary, it has enabled the recently-made and rather striking suggestion[10] that there exists no objective customary international legal framework for the identification of a state's government.[11]

The limited attention accorded by the literature to the regulation of the identity of governments in international law is notable also in its own right, given the contemporary complex and controversial questions that have arisen in practice in relation to such matters. A clear example in this regard concerns the 'misrepresentation' of states in the context of international organizations, including before adjudicative and political organs, plausible cases of which include the nationalist claimant's representation of China at the UN during the 1950s and 1960s as well as the representation of Venezuela by Juan Guaidó's appointee, starting in 2019. Such practice involves questions concerning the possible right of a state not to be 'misrepresented' and the powers of international organizations in relation to the 'misrepresentation' of a state as well as on the distinctive representative function of a state's government.[12]

More generally, various components of the international legal framework on the identity of governments do ultimately contribute to the ascertainment and better understanding of other elements of this framework. Perhaps the most notable absences resulting from the fragmented consideration of aspects of the international legal regulation of the identity of governments relate to certain aspects of the relationship between a state and its government.[13] The presumptive sovereign freedoms of each state to choose its government, its constitution, and its political system ultimately prove to have particular explanatory, analytical, and substantive value on the rules of international law concerning the identity of the governments

[6] Recall, generally, sections 4.2.2.2 and 4.2.2.3. See also section 6.2.4.

[7] Recall sections 1.1 and 4.2.2.5.1.2.

[8] Recall also section 1.1.

[9] Recall, generally, section 4.2.1. On other aspects of the law that are of particular relevance in relation to the customary international legal criteria for governmental status, recall sections 2.4, 2.5, 3.5.1, 3.5.2, 5.4.2, 5.4.3.

[10] This suggestion is striking, not least because of the far-reaching implications of the absence of an objective customary international legal framework for the identification of a state's government. Recall, in particular, sections 2.3.1, 2.4, 3.4.2, 3.4.3.

[11] Recall chapter 1, n 27.

[12] Recall section 5.5.

[13] Recall section 2.4.

of states, including, but not limited to, the customary international legal criteria for governmental status.[14]

6.2 Main Findings

Systematic analysis of state and organizational practice, coupled with sustained attention to conceptual aspects of the governments of states in international law, allows certain overarching conclusions to be drawn on the international legal identity of the governments of states. These findings pertain to the significance of the presumption against limitations on state sovereignty to the international legal framework on the identity of the governments of states; to the objective existence and distinctive representative capacity of a state's government in international law; to the relevance of democratic representativity and respect for international law to the enjoyment of governmental status and the representation of a state for the purposes of international law; and to the customary international legal criteria for governmental status, including the significance of 'constitutionality' in this regard.

6.2.1 The Significance of the Presumption against Limitations on State Sovereignty

In accordance with the general presumption against limitations on state sovereignty, a state enjoys certain presumptive sovereign freedoms. Three such freedoms are relevant, to say the least, to the international legal framework on the identity of the governments of states. This includes the freedom of each state to choose its government. Given the relationship between the government of a state, on the one hand, and the constitution and political system of a state, on the other hand, the freedoms of each state to choose its political system and its constitution are also pertinent to the international legal framework on the identity of the governments of states.[15]

Each of the presumptive sovereign freedoms of a state to choose its government, its political system, and its constitution has analytical value in the ascertainment of the customary international legal criteria for governmental status. These freedoms suggest that the absence of an objective legal framework in this regard ought not to be readily inferred.[16] At the same time, this and the two related freedoms weigh against the existence of certain customary international legal criteria for

[14] See further section 6.2.1.
[15] Recall section 2.4.
[16] Recall section 3.5.2.

governmental status, specifically any criterion that would limit the freedom of each state to choose its political system or its constitution.[17]

The presumptive sovereign freedom of each state to choose its government also has explanatory force in relation to the customary international framework for the identification of the government of a state. More specifically, the criteria under customary international law for determining the identity of a state's government can be—and, in the light of the presumptive sovereign freedom of each state to choose its government, ought, insofar as plausible, to be—conceptualized as means of ascertaining the state's choice of government.[18] None of the considerations which definitively comprise part of the framework for the identification of the government of a state as a matter of customary international law appear to limit the presumptive sovereign freedom of each state to choose its government.[19] At least to this extent, despite what has been said, the international legal framework on the identity of the governments of states does not 'disappoint . . . the adherents of traditional sovereign prerogative'.[20] Indeed, by according priority to an autonomous 'constitutional' claimant over any 'unconstitutional' rival, the contemporary customary international legal framework for the identification of a state's government privileges perhaps the most direct way in which a state may express, in the exercise of its sovereignty, its choice of government.[21]

Finally, the presumptive sovereign freedom of each state to choose its government is of substantive relevance to the rules of international law on the treatment by other states and international organizations of an ostensible government as the government of a state. The presumptive sovereign freedom of each state to choose its government suggests that states may not enjoy unfettered discretion as a matter of customary international law to recognize the 'wrong' government or to deny the governmental status of the 'right' government since international law prohibits the intervention by one state in the sovereign affairs of another state.[22] In relation to questions concerning governmental status in international organizations, the presumptive sovereign freedom of each state to choose its government might be relevant, in at least certain circumstances, to the validity and legal effect of a decision of an international organization to accept as effective the ostensible representation of a state through a 'wrong' government. This may be the case especially where such a decision implies the recognition by the organization of that ostensible government and where the organization lacks the power to interfere in matters which international law leaves to the sovereign discretion of each state.[23] In any event, the

[17] Recall section 4.2.1.
[18] Recall sections 2.4 and 4.2.1.
[19] See, generally, section 4.2.2.
[20] Roth, *Governmental Illegitimacy in International Law* (OUP 2000) 413.
[21] See, in particular, section 4.2.2.3.
[22] Recall section 3.4.2.
[23] Recall section 5.5.1.

presumptive sovereign freedom of each state to choose its government cannot definitively be said to be undermined by any matter concerning governmental status in international organizations.[24]

6.2.2 The Objective Existence and Distinctive Representative Capacity of a State's Government

There is a wealth of support for the position that to be the government of a state is to qualify for an objective international legal status, whether as a government '*in situ*' or as a government 'in exile'. This includes state practice in favour of the existence of objective requirements for the enjoyment of governmental status under customary international law; the understanding that a state's constitution reflects the identity of a state's government and that the constitution of a state has an objective international legal existence, including because each state enjoys a presumptive sovereign freedom to choose its constitution; the presumptive sovereign freedom of each state to choose its government; the view that each state can possess no more than one government; and the indications that recognition of governmental status is 'declaratory' of and has evidentiary value in respect of the identity of a state's government.[25]

While the practice of states on the recognition of governments is of principal importance in ascertaining the objective framework under customary international law for the identification of the government of a state,[26] the qualification for governmental status under customary international law is not dependent on the recognition of that status by one or more other states.[27] Although states are under no customary international legal obligation to recognize the government of every other state,[28] a state may not rely on its withholding of recognition to deny the governmental status under customary international law of an ostensible government of another state which qualifies for that status. Nor may a state successfully rely in all contexts on its recognition of an ostensible government of another state to support the lawfulness of its treatment of that ostensible government as the government of another state that does not enjoy governmental status as a matter of customary international law.[29] It is not doubt as to the objective customary international legal existence of the government of a state that accounts for any subsisting uncertainty over whether the recognition or denial of governmental status to an ostensible government amounts to prohibited intervention.[30]

24 Recall section 5.5.2.
25 See, principally, sections 2.5 and 3.5.
26 Recall section 3.5.2.
27 Recall section 3.5.1.
28 Recall section 3.4.1.
29 Recall sections 3.4.2–3.4.3.
30 Recall section 3.4.2.

The rules of international organizations and the practice by and within international organizations generally indicate that the objective international legal existence of the government of a state extends to matters concerning the identity of the government of a state in the context of international organizations. There is no general agreement that an international organization may, with legal effect, accept as the government of a state for one or more of its purposes a person who or collectivity of persons that does not qualify for governmental status as a matter of customary international law.[31]

The objective international legal existence of a state's government is significant not least because of the distinctive capacity of each state's government to represent that state for the purposes of international law, which, in contrast to what eminent commentators have suggested, does not vary according to whether or not it is operating from 'exile'.[32] It is generally only by or under the authority of its government that a state is represented for the purposes of international law, except to the extent that states opt to vary the application of these rules *inter se*, notably in the context of international organizations.[33]

While the representation of states in international organizations generally affirms the distinctive representative capacity of the government of a state, organizational rules and practice suggest that a state may be effectively represented for at least some purposes of at least certain international organizations by an ostensible government which does not enjoy governmental status as a matter of customary international law. This reflects a nuance in the distinctive representative capacity of a state's government and might not always be in conformity with the international legal rights of that state.[34] An international organization may have the power, moreover, to limit the extent to which a state may participate in its work on account of some matter concerning the identity or claim of an ostensible government of that state. Also in this way, an international organization may in effect limit the ability of a state's government to represent that state for certain purposes of international law.[35]

6.2.3 Democratic Representativity and Respect for International Law as Paramount?

In contrast to what has been said,[36] the customary international legal identity of the government of a state does not depend on the assumed or exercised 'popular

[31] Recall section 5.5.1.
[32] Recall section 2.3.2.
[33] Recall sections 2.3.2 and 5.3.2.
[34] Recall section 5.5.
[35] Recall section 5.6, in particular section 5.6.3.
[36] See eg Roth (n 20) 414–17.

will' of the population of a state. The oft-repeated assertion that the democratic representativity of an ostensible government is of direct relevance in at least certain circumstances to its qualification for governmental status as a matter of regional or general customary international law does not withstand scrutiny,[37] although the result of a democratic election may inform the identity of the government of a state as a matter of customary international law insofar as that result provides an ostensible government with a 'constitutional' claim to power.[38] The willingness of an ostensible government of a state to ensure that state's compliance with its obligations under international law is also unnecessary for the enjoyment of governmental status.[39] Further, it appears that an ostensible government may, at least in certain circumstances, enjoy governmental status and have its governmental status lawfully recognized under customary international law even if it is established in consequence of, or if its enjoyment of governmental status amounts to, a breach of an obligation arising under a peremptory norm of general international law.[40] The presumption against limitations on state sovereignty weighs against—and the state practice concerning recognition of governments does not convincingly weigh in favour of—any of these requirements.

The formal agnosticism of customary international law with respect to different types of governments notwithstanding, and despite the distinctive position of the ostensible government of a state which qualifies as a matter of customary international law as the government of that state to represent that state for the purposes of international law,[41] at least certain international organizations may exercise a power they appear to enjoy to accept as effective the ostensible representation of a state by a 'wrong' government,[42] including to prevent the representation of a state by a government that is deemed unwilling to ensure the state's compliance with certain international legal obligations of that state,[43] although it is not beyond doubt that this will accord with the international legal rights of that state.[44]

Certain international organizations, moreover, have powers to limit the participation of a state in their work on grounds relating specifically to an ostensible government of that state.[45] At least some such powers are not-uncommonly exercised on grounds connected to a challenge faced by a democratically-representative government.[46] Other matters, including the apparent disregard by an ostensible government of a state of certain international legal obligations owed by that state, may

[37] Recall section 4.2.2.5.1.2.
[38] Recall section 4.2.2.3.
[39] Recall section 4.2.2.5.2.
[40] Recall sections 3.4.4 and 4.2.2.5.3.
[41] See, generally, section 2.3.
[42] Recall sections 5.3.2 and 5.5.
[43] See eg chapter 5, n 144 and accompanying text.
[44] Recall section 5.5.2.
[45] See, generally, section 5.6.
[46] Recall section 5.6, especially 5.6.2.1.2.

also or instead inform the existence or exercise of the power of an international organization to prevent the participation of a state in its work.[47]

In these ways, international law permits international organizations to preclude an ostensible government of a state which is not democratically representative or which disregards the international legal obligations of the state from representing the state for certain purposes of international law and, in certain circumstances, permitting instead a rival ostensible government to represent the state. In so doing, international law may be seen to at least permit the preferential treatment of ostensible governments on grounds connected to democratic representativity and compliance with international legal obligations, despite the formal irrelevance of such considerations to the enjoyment of governmental status.

6.2.4 The Identification of a State's Choice of Government

To be the government of a state under customary international law, it is necessary but insufficient for a person or collectivity of persons to claim governmental status and to be autonomous. Additionally, to attain governmental status, an 'unconstitutional' claimant must exercise effective control over the state's territory and population in order to attain governmental status. Until the end of the Cold War, such a claimant could retain governmental status if it lost effective control, even if there existed a rival 'constitutional' claimant. Practice since the early 1990s indicates that an 'unconstitutional' claimant may only enjoy governmental status if there is no 'constitutional' claimant to governmental status in respect of the same state. An autonomous 'constitutional' claimant to governmental status may now attain and retain governmental status as long as it has a 'constitutional' claim, regardless of whether it exercises effective control and even if some other ostensible government exercises such control.

Given the unrebutted presumptive sovereign freedom of each state to choose its government,[48] the customary international legal criteria for governmental status comprise a means of identifying the state's own choice of its government. By privileging 'constitutional' claims in such a way that an autonomous 'constitutional' ostensible government will generally enjoy governmental status, customary international law can be said to defer to what is perhaps the most direct way in which a state can express its choice of government. Until the 1990s, international law deferred to this form of a state's expression of its choice to a more limited extent. By accepting the governmental status of an autonomous 'unconstitutional' claimant in effective control, even in the presence of a rival 'constitutional' claimant, it more readily accepted a state's willingness fundamentally to change its

[47] See chapter 5, especially nn 294 and 317, including the accompanying text.
[48] Recall section 6.2.1.

constitution and, concomitantly, to opt for an 'unconstitutional' government.[49] Customary international law now has regard to alternative, less direct means for ascertaining the state's choice of government only where there is no claimant to governmental status that can be taken to reflect the state's more direct choice of government. A state is treated as having opted to possess an 'unconstitutional' government and fundamentally to change its constitution only in the absence of an autonomous 'constitutional' claimant to governmental status.

[49] Recall chapter 2, n 8 and accompanying text. Recall also sections 4.2.2.3 and 4.2.2.4.3.

Bibliography

1. Articles, Books, Book Chapters, and Encyclopaedic Entries

Halsbury's Laws of England: International Law and Foreign Relations (LexisNexis 2018)
'México aplica la doctrina Estrada en el caso de Venezuela' (2003) 67–8 RMPA 191

Akande, Dapo, 'International Organizations' in Malcolm Evans (ed), *International Law* (5th edn, OUP 2018) 227
Akehurst, Michael, 'Enforcement Action by Regional Agencies, with Special Reference to the Organization of American States' (1967) 42 BYIL 175
Amerasinghe, CF, *Principles of the Institutional Law of International Organizations* (2nd edn, CUP 2009)
Ando, Nsiuke, 'The Recognition of Governments Reconsidered' (1985) 28 JAIL 29
Angelet, Nicolas, and Tamara Leidgens, 'Article 8' in Olivier Corten and Pierre Klein (eds), *The Vienna Convention on the Law of Treaties: A Commentary* (OUP 2011) 155
Barber, Rebecca, 'The Role of the General Assembly in Determining the Legitimacy of Governments' (2022) 71 ICLQ 627
Ben Achour, Rafâa, 'Changements anticonstitutionnels de gouvernement et droit international law' (2015) 379 Hague *Recueil* 397
Benvenisti, Eyal, *The International Law of Occupation* (2nd edn, OUP 2012)
Blix, HM, 'Contemporary Aspects of Recognition' (1970) 130 Hague *Recueil* 587
Bordin, Fernando Lusa, *The Analogy between States and International Organizations* (CUP 2018)
Brown, Philip Marshall, 'The Legal Effects of Recognition' (1950) 44 AJIL 617
Brownlie, Ian, *International Law and the Use of Force by States* (OUP 1963)
Brownlie, Ian, *Principles of Public International Law* (2nd edn, OUP 1973)
Brownlie, Ian, 'Recognition in Theory and Practice' (1982) 53 BYIL 197
Charpentier, Jean, *La Reconnaissance Internationale et l'Évolution du Droit des Gens* (Pedone 1956)
Chen, Ti-Chiang, *The International Law of Recognition with Special Reference to Practice in Great Britain and the United States* (Praeger 1951)
Ciobanu, Dan, 'Credentials of Delegations and Representation of Member States at the United Nations' (1976) 25 ICLQ 351
Conforti, Benedetto, and Carlo Focarelli, *The Law and Practice of the United Nations* (5th rev edn, BRILL 2016)
Corten, Olivier, *The Law against War* (2nd edn, Hart 2021)
Costelloe, Daniel, *Legal Consequences of Peremptory Norms in International Law* (CUP 2017)
Crawford, James 'The Rights of Peoples: "Peoples" or "Governments"?' in James Crawford (ed), *The Rights of Peoples* (Clarendon Press 1988) 55
Crawford, James 'Democracy and the Body of International Law' in Gregory H Fox and Brad R Roth (eds), *Democratic Governance and International Law* (CUP 2000) 91
Crawford, James, *The Creation of States in International Law* (2nd edn, CUP 2006)
Crawford, James, 'Sovereignty as a Legal Value' in James Crawford and Martti Koskenniemi (eds), *The Cambridge Companion to International Law* (CUP 2012) 117

Crawford, James, 'Change, Order, Change: The Course of International Law' (2013) 365 Hague *Recueil* 9

Crawford, James, *State Responsibility: The General Part* (CUP 2013)

Crawford, James, *Brownlie's Principles of Public International Law* (OUP 2019)

D'Aspremont, Jean, 'Legitimacy of Governments in the Age of Democracy' (2006) 38 NYUJILP 877

D'Aspremont, Jean, 'The Rise and Fall of Democracy Governance in International Law: A Reply to Susan Marks' (2011) 22 EJIL 549

Dai, Poeliu, 'Recognition of States and Governments under International Law with Special Reference to Canadian Postwar Practice and the Legal Status of Taiwan (Formosa)' (1965) 3 CYIL 290

Dawidowicz, Martin, 'The Obligation of Non-Recognition of an Unlawful Situation' in James Crawford, Alain Pellet, and Simon Olleson (eds), *The Law of International Responsibility* (OUP 2010) 677

De Wet, Erika, 'The Modern Practice of Intervention by Invitation in Africa and Its Implications for the Prohibition of the Use of Force' (2015) 26 EJIL 979

De Wet, Erika, 'The Role of Democratic Legitimacy in the Recognition of Governments in Africa since the End of the Cold War' (2019) 17 IJCL 470

De Wet, Erika, *Military Assistance on Request and the Use of Force* (OUP 2020)

De Wet, Erika, 'The African Union's Struggle against "Unconstitutional Change of Government": From a Moral Prescription to a Requirement under International Law?' (2021) 32 EJIL 199

Denza, Eileen, *Diplomatic Law: Commentary on the Vienna Convention on Diplomatic Relations* (4th edn, OUP 2016)

Dinstein, Yoram, 'The Interaction between Customary International Law and Treaties' (2006) 322 Hague *Recueil* 243

Dinstein, Yoram, *The International Law of Belligerent Occupation* (CUP 2009)

Dinstein, Yoram, *Non-International Armed Conflicts in International Law* (CUP 2014)

Doswald-Beck, Louise, 'The Legal Validity of Military Intervention by Invitation of the Government' (1985) 56 BYIL 189

Duxbury, Alison, *The Participation of States in International Organisations: The Role of Human Rights and Democracy* (CUP 2010)

Ferro, Luca, 'A Libyan Playground for Foreign Powers: Presenting the Case for "Negative Equality"' (*Opinio Juris*, 26 June 2020), available at <http://opiniojuris.org/2020/06/26/a-libyan-playground-for-foreign-powers-presenting-the-case-for-negative-equality>

Fitzmaurice, GG, 'Chinese Representation in the United Nations' (1952) 6 Ybk World Aff 36

Foakes, Joanne, *The Position of Heads of State and Senior Officials in International Law* (OUP 2014)

Foakes, Joanne, and Eileen Denza, 'The Appointment and Functions of Consuls' in Ivor Roberts (ed), *Satow's Diplomatic Practice* (7th edn, OUP 2017) 120

Foakes, Joanne, and Eileen Denza, 'The Diplomatic Mission, the Corps, Breach of Relations, and Protection of Interests' in Ivor Roberts (ed), *Satow's Diplomatic Practice* (7th edn, OUP 2017) 153

Fox, Gregory H, 'Intervention by Invitation' in Marc Weller (ed), *The Oxford Handbook of the Use of Force in International Law* (OUP 2015) 816

Franck, Thomas M, 'The Emerging Rights to Democratic Governance' (1992) 86 AJIL 46

Grant, Thomas D, 'Defining Statehood: The Montevideo Convention and Its Discontents' (1999) 37 CJTL 403

Grant, Thomas D, 'Current Developments: Afghanistan Recognizes Chechnya' (1999–2000) 15 AUILR 869

Grant, Thomas D, *Admission to the United Nations, Charter Article 4 and the Rise of Universal Organization* (Martinus Nijhoff 2009)
Gray, Christine, *International Law and the Use of Force* (4th edn, CUP 2018)
Halberstam, Malvina, 'Excluding Israel from the General Assembly by a Rejection of Its Credentials' (1984) 78 AJIL 179
Hart, HLA, *The Concept of Law* (OUP 1961)
Henkin, Louis, 'Restatement of the Foreign Relations Law of the United States (Revised): Tentative Draft No. 2' (1981) 75 AJIL 987
Higgins, Rosalyn, Philippa Webb, Dapo Akande, Sandesh Sivakumaran, and James Sloan, *Oppenheim's International Law: United Nations* (OUP 2017)
Jamnejad, Maziar, and Michael Wood, 'The Principle of Non-Intervention' (2009) 22 LJIL 345
Jenks, CW, 'Expulsion from the League of Nations' (1935) 16 BYIL 155
Jennings, Robert, 'Government in Commission' (1946) 23 BYIL 112
Jennings, Robert, 'Nullity and Effectiveness in International Law' in *Cambridge Essays in International Law: Essays in Honour of Lord McNair* (Stevens & Sons 1965) 64
Jennings, Robert, and Arthur Watts (eds), *Oppenheim's International Law*, vol 1 (Wildy 1992)
Jimenez de Aréchaga, Eduadro, *Derecho Internacional Publico*, vol II (Fundación de Cultura Universitaria 1995)
Kelsen, Hans, 'Recognition in International Law: Theoretical Observations' (1941) 35 AJIL 605
Kelsen, Hans, 'The Legal Status of Germany According to the Declaration of Berlin' (1945) 39 AJIL 518
Kelsen, Hans, *Principles of International Law* (2nd edn, Rinehart & Winston 1966)
Kelsen, Hans, *Pure Theory of Law* (Max Knight tr, 2nd edn, University of California Press 1967)
Kleczkowskwa, Agata, '"Recognition" of Governments by International Organizations—The Example of the UN General Assembly and Asian States' (2017) 35 CYILA 136
Lauterpacht, Elihu, 'The Contemporary Practice of the United Kingdom in the Field of International Law—Survey and Comment, III' (1957) 6 ICLQ 301
Lauterpacht, Elihu, 'The Contemporary Practice of the United Kingdom in the Field of International Law—Survey and Comment, IV' (1957) 6 ICLQ 506
Lauterpacht, Elihu, 'The Contemporary Practice of the United Kingdom in the Field of International Law—Survey and Comment, VI' (1958) 7 ICLQ 514
Lauterpacht, Elihu, 'The Contemporary Practice of the United Kingdom in the Field of International Law—Survey and Comment, VII' (1959) 8 ICLQ 146
Lauterpacht, Elihu, 'The Legal Effect of Illegal Acts of International Organisations' in *Cambridge Essays in International Law: Essays in Honour of Lord McNair* (Stevens & Sons 1965) 88
Lauterpacht, Hersch, *Recognition in International Law* (CUP 1947, repr 2013)
Lee, Luke T, and John Quigley, *Consular Law and Practice* (3rd edn, OUP 2008)
Magiera, Siegfried, 'Governments' (2007) MPEPIL, available at <http://opil.ouplaw.com/home/mpil>
Magiera, Siegfried, 'Article 9' in Bruno Simma, Daniel-Erasmus Khan, Georg Nolte, and Andreas Paulus (eds), *The Charter of the United Nations: A Commentary*, vol 1 (3rd edn, OUP 2012) 445
Magliveras, Konstantinos D, *Exclusion from Participation in International Organizations: The Law and Practice behind Member States' Expulsion and Suspension of Membership* (Kluwer 1999)

Marek, Krystyna, *Identity and Continuity of States in Public International Law* (Librairie Droz 1954) 24

Marks, Susan, 'What Has Become of the Emerging Right to Democratic Governance?' (2011) 22 EJIL 507

Mathias, Stephen and Stadler Trengrove, 'Membership and Representation' in Jacob Katz Cogan, Ian Hurd, and Ian Johnstone (eds), *The Oxford Handbook of International Organizations* (OUP 2016) 962

McLachlan, Campbell, *Foreign Relations Law* (CUP 2014)

McNair, Arnold, and Arthur Watts, *The Legal Effects of War* (4th edn, CUP 1966)

Menon, PK, *The Law of Recognition in International Law: Basic Principles* (Edwin Mellen Press 1994)

Milanovic, Marko, 'Revisiting Coercion as an Element of Prohibited Intervention in International Law' (2023) 117 AJIL 601

Mohtashami, Reza, 'Protecting the Legitimacy of the Arbitral Process: Jurisdictional and Procedural Challenges in Public–Private Disputes' in Jean Engelmayer Kalicki and Mohamed Abdel Raouf (eds), *Evolution and Adaptation: The Future of International Arbitration* (Kluwer 2019) 619

Momtaz, Djamchid, 'Attribution of Conduct to the State: State Organs and Entities Empowered to Exercise Elements of Governmental Authority' in James Crawford, Alain Pellet, and Simon Olleson (eds), *The Law of International Responsibility* (OUP 2010) 237

Murphy, Sean, 'Democratic Legitimacy and the Recognition of States and Governments' in Gregory H Fox and Brad R Roth (eds), *Democratic Governance and International Law* (CUP 2000) 123

Nicholson, Rowan, *Statehood and the State-Like in International Law* (OUP 2019)

Nomura, Issei, 'Recognition of Foreign Governments' (1982) 25 JAIL 67

O'Connell, DP, 'The Status of Formosa and the Chinese Recognition Problem' (1956) 50 AJIL 405

O'Connell, DP, *State Succession in Municipal Law and International Law*, vol 1 (CUP 1967)

O'Keefe, Roger, 'The Meaning of "Cultural Property" under the 1954 Hague Convention' (1999) 46 NILR 26

O'Keefe, Roger, *International Criminal Law* (OUP 2015)

Oppenheimer, FE, 'Governments and Authorities in Exile' (1942) 36 AJIL 568

Orakhelashvili, Alexander *Peremptory Norms in International Law* (OUP 2008)

Osieke, Ebere, '*Ultra Vires* Acts in International Organizations—The Experience of the International Labour Organization' (1976) 48 BYIL 259

Paddeu, Federica, and Niko Pavlopoulos, 'Between Legitimacy and Control: The Taliban's Pursuit of Governmental Status' (*Just Security*, 7 September 2021), available at <http://justsecurity.org/78051/between-legitimacy-and-control-the-talibans-pursuit-of-governmental-status>

Peterson, MJ 'Political Use of Recognition: The Influence of the International System' (1982) 34 World Politics 324

Peterson, MJ, 'Recognition of Governments Should Not Be Abolished' (1983) 77 AJIL 31

Peterson, MJ, *Recognition of Governments: Legal Doctrine and State Practice, 1815–1995* (Macmillan 1997)

Raič, David, *Statehood and the Law of Self-Determination* (Kluwer 2002)

Redaelli, Chiara, *Intervention in Civil Wars: Effectiveness, Legitimacy, and Human Rights* (Hart 2021)

Reisman, W Michael, 'International Law after the Cold War' (1990) 84 AJIL 859

Roberts, Adam, 'What Is a Military Occupation?' (1984) 55 BYIL 249Roberts, Ivor, 'Formal Aspects of Diplomatic Relations' in Ivor Roberts (ed), *Satow's Diplomatic Practice* (7th edn, OUP 2017) 110

Roberts, Ivor, 'Functions of Diplomatic Missions and Consulates' in Ivor Roberts (ed), *Satow's Diplomatic Practice* (7th edn, OUP 2017) 71

Roth, Brad R, *Governmental Illegitimacy in International Law* (OUP 2000)

Roth, Brad R, 'Secessions, Coups and the International Rule of Law: Assessing the Decline of the Effective Control Doctrine' (2010) 11 MJIL 393

Ruys, Tom, and Luca Ferro, 'Weathering the Storm: Legality and Legal Implications of the Saudi-Led Military Intervention in Yemen' (2016) 65 ICLQ 61

Sabel, Robbie, *Rules of Procedure at the UN and at Inter-Governmental Conferences* (3rd edn, CUP 2017)

Saganek, Przemyslaw, *Unilateral Acts of States in Public International Law* (BRILL 2015)

Salmon, Jean, 'Representatives of States in International Relations' (2007) MPEPIL, available at <http://opil.ouplaw.com/home/mpil>

Schermers, Henry G, and Niels M Blokker, *International Institutional Law* (6th rev edn, BRILL 2018)

Schmalenbach, Kirsten, 'International Organizations or Institutions, General Aspects' (2014) MPEPIL, available at <http://opil.ouplaw.com/home/mpil>

Sereni, Angelo Pieri, 'La représentation en droit international' (1948) 73 Hague *Recueil* 69

Shain, Yossi, *The Frontier of Loyalty: Political Exiles in the Age of the Nation-State* (Wesleyan UP 1989)

Shaw, Malcolm, *Rosenne's Law and Practice of the International Court: 1920–2015*, vol 3 (5th edn, BRILL 2016)

Sivakumaran, Sandesh, *The Law of Non-International Armed Conflict* (OUP 2012)

Sohn, Louis B, 'Expulsion or Forced Withdrawal from an International Organization' (1964) 776 Harvard LR 1381

Stahn, Carsten, *The Law and Practice of International Territorial Administration: Versailles to Iraq and Beyond* (CUP 2008)

Stansifer, Charles L, 'Application of the Tobar Doctrine to Central America' (1967) 23 The Americas 251

Suttner, Raymond, 'Has South Africa Been Illegally Excluded from the United Nations General Assembly?' (1984) 17 CILSA 279

Talmon, Stefan, 'Recognition of Governments: An Analysis of the New British Policy and Practice' (1992) 63 BYIL 231

Talmon, Stefan, *Recognition of Governments in International Law with Particular Reference to Governments in Exile* (OUP 1998)

Talmon, Stefan, 'Who Is a Legitimate Government in Exile? Towards Normative Criteria for Governmental Legitimacy in International Law' in Guy S Goodwin-Gill and Stefan Talmon (eds), *The Reality of International Law: Essays in Honour of Ian Brownlie* (OUP 1999) 499

Talmon, Stefan, 'The Constitutive versus the Declaratory Theory of Recognition: *Tertium non Datur?*' (2004) 75 BYIL 101

Talmon, Stefan, 'Recognition of the Libyan National Transitional Council' (*ASIL Insights*, 16 June 2011), available at <http://asil.org/insights/volume/15/issue/16/recognition-libyan-national-transitional-council>

Talmon, Stefan, 'Recognition of Opposition Groups as the Legitimate Representative of a People' (2013) 12 CJIL 219

Tams, Christian, 'Article 5' in Bruno Simma, Daniel-Erasmus Khan, Georg Nolte, and Andreas Paulus (eds), *The Charter of the United Nations: A Commentary*, vol 1 (3rd edn, OUP 2012) 362

Tams, Christian, 'Article 6' in Bruno Simma, Daniel-Erasmus Khan, Georg Nolte, and Andreas Paulus (eds), *The Charter of the United Nations: A Commentary*, vol 1 (3rd edn, OUP 2012) 374

Verhoeven, Joe, *La reconnaissance internationale dans la pratique contemporaine: Les relations publiques internationales* (Pedone 1975)

Vidmar, Jure, *Democratic Statehood in International Law: The Emergence of New States in Post-Cold War Practice* (Hart Publishing 2013)

Vidmar, Jure, 'International Community and Abuses of Sovereign Power (2014) 35 LLR 193

Vidmar, Jure, 'Abusive Governments as a Threat' in Mary E Footer, Julia Schmidt, Nigel D White, and Lydia Davies-Bright (eds), *Security in International Law* (Hart Publishing 2016) 249

Warbrick, Colin, 'Kampuchea: Representation and Recognition' (1981) 30 ICLQ 234

Warbrick, Colin, 'The New British Policy on Recognition of Governments' (1981) 30 ICLQ 568

Waseem, Mubarak, 'Introductory Note to *"Maduro Board" of the Central Bank of Venez. v "Guaidó Board" of the Central Bank of Venez* (UKSC)' (2022) 62 ILM 120

Watts, Arthur, 'The Legal Position in International Law of Heads of States, Heads of Governments and Foreign Ministers' (1994) 247 Hague *Recueil* 9

Weller, Marc, 'The Kuwait Crisis: A Survey of Some Legal Issues' (1991) 3 AfJIL 1

Weller, Marc, 'Myanmar: Testing the Democratic Norm in International Law' (*EJIL:Talk!*, 30 March 2021), available at <http://ejiltalk.org/myanmar-testing-the-democratic-norm-in-international-law>

Wilde, Ralph, *International Territorial Administration: How Trusteeship and the Civilizing Mission Never Went Away* (OUP 2008)

Wilde, Ralph, 'In the Matter of the Statute of the International Criminal Court and in the Matter of the Declaration Made by the National Unity Government as the Republic of the Union of Myanmar Accepting the Jurisdiction of the International Criminal Court under Article 12(3) of the Statute: Opinion' (15 August 2022), available at <http://the-world-is-watching.org/wp-content/uploads/2022/08/Wilde-Burma-ICC-opinion-15-Aug.pdf>

Wippman, David, 'Pro-Democratic Intervention' in Marc Weller (ed), *The Oxford Handbook of the Use of Force in International Law* (OUP 2015) 797

Wolfrum, Rüdiger, and Christiane E Philipp, 'The Status of the Taliban: Their Obligations and Rights under International Law' (2002) 6 MPUNYB 559

Wood, Michael, 'Participation of Former Yugoslav States in the United Nations and in Multilateral Treaties' (1997) 1 MPUNYB 231

Woodward, Ernest Llewellyn, *British Foreign Policy in the Second World War*, vol 2 (Her Majesty's Stationery Office 1962)

Woolsely, Lester, 'The Recognition of the Government of El Salvador' (1934) 28 AJIL 325

Wright, Quincy, 'Some Thoughts about Recognition' (1950) 44 AJIL 548

Wright, Quincy, 'The Chinese Recognition Problem' (1955) 49 AJIL 320

Wright, Quincy, 'United States Intervention in Lebanon' (1959) 53 AJIL 112

2. News Reports

'Canada Will Not Recognize Taliban as Afghan Gov't—PM Trudeau' (*Reuters*, 17 August 2021), available at <http://reuters.com/world/asia-pacific/canada-will-not-recognize-taliban-afghan-govt-pm-trudeau-2021-08-17>

'First Diplomat of Taliban-Led Afghanistan Accredited in Moscow' (*RFEL*, 31 March 2022), available at <http://rferl.org/a/moscow-accredits-afghan-taliban-diplomat/31779443.html>

'France Says Niger's Junta "Has No Authority" to Ask Ambassador to Leave' (*France 24*, 25 August 2023), available at <http://france24.com/en/live-news/20230825-%F0%9F%94%B4-niger-s-military-junta-gives-french-ambassador-48-hours-to-leave-country>

'Gaddafi: Libya Dignity under Attack' (*Al Jazeera*, 2 March 2011), available at <http://aljazeera.com/news/2011/3/2/gaddafi-libya-dignity-under-attack>

'Hadi Out, Presidential Council Takes Over' (*Sana'a Center for Strategic Studies*, 8 April 2022), available at <http://sanaacenter.org/publications/analysis/17378>

'Ministry of Foreign Affairs of Myanmar Responds to the Tweet by My. Peter Vowles' (*Eleven*, 15 July 2022), available at <http://elevenmyanmar.com/news/ministry-of-foreign-affairs-of-myanmar-responds-to-the-tweet-by-mr-peter-vowles>

'Statement from Myanmar Military on State of Emergency' (*Reuters*, 1 February 2021), available at <http://reuters.com/article/us-myanmar-politics-military-text-idUSKBN2A11A2>

'Venezuela Opposition Leader Swears Himself In as Interim President' (*Reuters*, 23 January 2019), available at <http://reuters.com/article/us-venezuela-politics-guaido-idUSKCN1PH2AN>

'Venezuela Says Wins Ruling to Recoup $1.5 Bln in Portugal Funds' (*Reuters*, 9 August 2023), available at <http://reuters.com/world/americas/venezuela-says-wins-ruling-recoup-15-bln-portugal-funds-2023-08-09>

Baddour, Dylan, 'Uruguay Walks Out of OAS Assembly over Guaido Envoy Inclusion' (*Al Jazeera*, 27 June 2019), available at <http://aljazeera.com/news/2019/06/uruguay-walks-oas-assembly-inclusion-guaido-envoy-190627191520096.html>

Iqbal, Anwar, 'US to Recognize Taliban Only If They Respect Basic Rights, Says Blinken' (*Dawn*, 16 August 2021), available at <http://dawn.com/news/1640919>

Laya, Patricia, and Alex Vazquez, 'IMF Won't Lend to Venezuela Because Maduro Lacks Recognition' (*Bloomberg*, 17 March 2020), available at <http://bloomberg.com/news/articles/2020-03-17/venezuela-requests-5-billion-from-imf-to-fight-coronavirus>

3. Records of State Practice

The following are listed in addition to the meeting records and certain other documents that are contained in the Table of Instruments.

3.1 Collections of State Practice

'Australian Practice in International Law 1978–1980' (1983) 8 AYIL 253
DCER [1941] vol VIII (Canada)
DCER [1943] vol IX (Canada)
FRUS [1918] Supp 1, vol I
FRUS [1920] vol III
FRUS [1941] vol III
FRUS [1943] vol II
FRUS [1948] vol V(2)
HC Debs, 14 November 1916, vol 87, col 55
HC Debs, 8 November 1937, vol 328, cols 1386–7

HC Debs, 4 April 1938, vol 334, col 4
HC Debs, 24 November 1938, vol 341, col 1970WA
HC Debs, 3 July 1940, vol 362, col 385
HC Debs, 27 May 1941, vol 371, col 1713
HC Debs, 21 March 1951, vol 485, cols 2410–11
HC Debs, 6 December 1979, vol 975, col 760
HC Debs, 26 February 1991, vol 186, col 459WA
HC Debs, 20 November 2012, vol 553, col 445
HL Debs, 19 December 1940, vol 118, cols 191–2
HL Debs, 21 November 1956, vol 200, col 423
HL Debs, 28 April 1980, vol 408, col 1121–2WA
HL Debs, 18 June 2014, vol 754, col 76WA
HR Debs, 22 November 1979, vol 116, 3506 (question No 4917)
'Multilateral Treaties Deposited with the Secretary-General, status as at 1 April 2009' (2009) vols I and III, UN Doc ST/LEG/SER.E/26
'Spanish Diplomatic and Parliamentary Practice in Public International Law, 1992' (1992) 2 SYIL 121

Brown, Jonathan (ed), 'Australian Practice in International Law 1988 and 1989' (1992) 12 AYIL 319
Brown, Jonathan (ed), 'Australian Practice in International Law 1990 and 1991' (1992) 13 AYIL 195
Caggiano, Giandonato (ed), 'Diplomatic and Parliamentary Practice' (1978) 4 IYIL 212 (Italy)
Charpentier, Jean, 'Pratique française relative au droit international law' (1966) 12 AFDI 893
Galbraith J (ed), 'Contemporary Practice of the United States Relating to International Law' (2019) 113 AJIL 600
Guymon, CarrieLyn D (ed), *Digest of United States Practice in International Law* [2019], available at <http://state.gov/wp-content/uploads/2020/09/2019-Digest-Complete.pdf>
Hackworth, Green Haywood, *Digest of International Law*, vol 1 (US Government Printing Office 1940)
Hackworth, Green Haywood, *Digest of International Law*, vol 4 (US Government Printing Office 1942)
Hartmann, Jacques, Sangeeta Shah, and Colin Warbrick (eds), 'UKMIL' (2012) 82 BYIL 676
Hudson, Manley O, *International Legislation*, vol 3 (Carnegie Endowment for International Peace 1931)
ILC, 'Peremptory Norms of General International Law (*jus cogens*): Comments and Observations Received from Governments' (9 March 2022) UN Doc A/CN.4/748
Lee, Edward G, 'Canadian Practice in International Law at the Department of External Affairs in 1988–89/La Pratique Canadienne en Matière de Droit International Public au Ministère des Affaires Extérieures en 1988–89' (1989) 27 CYIL 373Marston, Geoffrey (ed), 'UKMIL' (1983) 54 BYIL 361
Marston, Geoffrey (ed), 'UKMIL' (1985) 56 BYIL 363
Marston, Geoffrey (ed), 'UKMIL' (1999) 70 BYIL 517
Marston, Geoffrey (ed), 'UKMIL' (2001) 71 BYIL 518
Moore, John Bassett (ed), *History and Digest of the International Arbitrations to Which the United States Has Been a Party*, vol 3 (US Government Printing Office 1898)
Moore, John Bassett, *Digest of International Law*, vol 1 (US Government Printing Office 1906)Salmon, Jean JA, and Paul-F Smets (eds), 'Practique du pouvoir executif et le

controle des Chambres Legislatives en matiere de relations internationales' (1968) 4 RBDI 520

Siekmann, RCR, 'Netherlands State Practice for the Parliamentary Year 1989–1990' (1991) 22 NYIL 237

Whiteman, Marjorie Millace, *Digest of International Law*, vol 2 (US Department of State 1963)

3.2 Communications by States to International Organizations

3.2.1 Organization of American States

'Letter from Juan Guaidó to the Secretary General of the Organization of American States' (8 February 2019), available at <http://oas.org/en/sla/dil/docs/a-41_note_Juan_Guaido_03-7-2019.pdf>

'Note from the Permanent Mission of Antigua and Barbuda' (3 October 2022) OEA Ser.P, AG/doc.5785/22

'Note from the Permanent Mission of the Bolivarian Republic of Venezuela Enclosing a Copy of the Letter Denouncing the Charter of the Organization of American States (OAS) Pursuant to Article 143 and Initiating the Permanent Withdrawal of the Bolivarian Republic of Venezuela from the Organization. April 28, 2017' (29 April 2017) OEA/Ser.G, CP/INF.7707/17

3.2.2 United Nations

'Cablegram Dated 29 June 1950 from the Deputy Minister of Foreign Affairs of the Union of Soviet Socialist Republics to the Secretary-General Concerning the Security Council Resolution of 27 June 1950 (S/1511)' (29 June 1950) UN Doc S/1517

'Kenya, Mauritania and United Republic of Cameroon: Draft Resolution' (24 October 1074) UN Doc S/11543

'Letter Dated 1 March 1993 from the Prime Minister of Bosnia and Herzegovina to the Secretary-General' (5 March 1993) UN Doc A/47/899–S/25360

'Letter Dated 17 March 1993 from the Charges d'Affaires A.I. of the Permanent Mission of Afghanistan to the United Nations Addressed to the Secretary-General' (19 March 1993) UN Doc S/25435

'Letter Dated 29 November 1995 from the Permanent Representative of the United States of America to the United Nations Addressed to the Secretary-General' (30 November 1995) UN Doc A/50/790–S/1995/999

'Letter Dated 21 November 2019 from the Permanent Representative of Yemen to the United Nations Addressed to the President of the Security Council' (25 November 2019) UN Doc S/2019/904

'Letter Dated 26 May 2020 from the Permanent Representative of the Bolivarian Republic of Venezuela to the United Nations Addressed to the President of the Security Council' (27 May 2020) UN Doc S/2020/444

'Letter from Ambassador Kyaw Moe Tun to Secretary-General Antonio Guterres' (14 May 2021), available at <http://myanmarmissionnewyork.org/post/letter-ambassador-kyaw-moe-tun>

'Note verbale Dated 25 November 1980 from the Permanent Mission of the Union of Soviet Socialist Republics to the United Nations Addressed to the Secretary-General', annexed to 'Letter Dated 25 November 1980 from the Permanent Representative of the Union of Soviet Socialist Republics to the United Nations Addressed to the Secretary-General' (26 November 1980) UN Doc A/35/660

'Note verbale Dated 22 December 1988 from the Permanent Representative of the United States of America to the United Nations Addressed to the Secretary-General' (22 December 1988) UN Doc A/43/989

3.3 Other Records of State Practice

'Afghanistan Response: Foreign Secretary's Statement' (6 September 2021), available at <http://gov.uk/government/speeches/foreign-secretary-statement-on-afghanistan-response>

'Appointment of Chargé d'Affaires ad interim of the UK Mission to Afghanistan: Hugo Shorter' (18 January 2022), available at <http://gov.uk/government/news/appointment-of-charge-daffaires-ad-interim-of-the-uk-mission-to-afghanistan-hugo-shorter>

'Application of the Convention on the Prevention and Punishment of the Crime of Genocide (The Gambia *v.* Myanmar), Verbatim Record' (11 December 2019) CR 2019/19 (Myanmar)

'Brief for the United States as Amicus Curiae Supporting Affirmance' in *Mohamed Ali Samantar v Bashe Abdi Yousuf et al*, available at <http://scotusblog.com/wp-content/uploads/2010/01/08-1555_us-amicus-supporting-affirmance.pdf>

'Canada's Statement on the Recent Vote by the Venezuela National Assembly to Dissolve the Interim Government' (6 January 2023), available at <http://international.gc.ca/country_news-pays_nouvelles/2023-01-06-venezuela.aspx>

Canadian Legal Bureau, 'Approaches to Recognition of States and Governments' (1988) 26 CYIL 324

'Case on Behalf of the Foreign Secretary' submitted as part of its intervention in The "Maduro Board" of the Central Bank of Venezuela v The "Guaidó Board" of the Central Bank of Venezuela [2021] UKSC 57, available at <http://assets.publishing.service.gov.uk/government/uploads/system/uploads/attachment_data/file/1003665/20210818_Foreign_Secretary_s_Case_18_June_2021.pdf> (UK)

Certificate of 28 March 1988 by New Zealand's Minister of Foreign Affairs, as reported in *Attorney-General for Fiji v Robert Jones House Ltd* (New Zealand, High Court, 4 November 1988) (1989) 80 ILR 1, 5

Clark, Jr, Warren, 'Efforts toward Peace and Reconciliation in Angola' in DSB [1989] vol 89, No 2153, 31

'Declaration of Señor Don Genaro Estrada, Secretary of Foreign Relations of Mexico, Published in the Press on September 27, 1930, Relating to the Express Recognition of Governments' (1931) 25 AJIL Supp 203

'Declaration Regarding the Defeat of Germany and the Assumption of Supreme Authority with Respect to Germany by the Governments of the United States of America, the Union of Soviet Socialist Republics, the United Kingdom and the Provisional Government of the French Republic' (5 June 1945), available at <http://avalon.law.yale.edu/wwii/ger01.asp>

'G7 Leaders Statement on Afghanistan' (24 August 2021), available at <http://gov.uk/government/news/g7-leaders-statement-on-afghanistan-24-august-2021>

International Law Commission, 'State Responsibility: Comments and Observations Received from Governments' (28 June 2001) UN Doc A/CN.4/515 and Add.1–3

'Joint Statement of the Participants in the Moscow Format Consultations on Afghanistan' (20 October 2021), available at <http://archive.mid.ru/en/foreign_policy/news/-/asset_publisher/cKNonkJE02Bw/content/id/4913908>

'Libya/National Transitional Council—Statement by Alain Juppé, Ministre d'Etat, Minister of Foreign and European Affairs' (7 June 2011), available at <http://in.ambafrance.org/Libya-National-Transitional>

'Lima Group Declaration' (4 January 2019), available at <http://international.gc.ca/world-monde/international_relations-relations_internationales/latin_america-amerique_latine/2019-01-04-lima_group-groupe_lima.aspx>

'Lima Group Declaration' (4 February 2019), available at <http://canada.ca/en/global-affairs/news/2019/02/lima-group-declaration-february-04-2019.html>

'List Compiled by the UK's Principal Secretary of State for Affairs Pursuant to the Diplomatic Privileges (Extension) Act 1941', reproduced in *Edinburgh Gazette* (24 July 1942) 295

'Ministerial Meeting in Paris (France + Germany + United Kingdom + Italy + USA + EU): Statement on Libya' (13 March 2016), available at <http://diplomatie.gouv.fr/IMG/pdf/statement_on_libya_13th_march_cle82f4c6.pdf>

President's Statement, 'US Severs Diplomatic Contact with Noriega Regime' (1 September 1989) in DSB [1989] vol 89, No 2152, 69

'Remarks by President Biden on the Administration's Response to the Coup in Burma' (10 February 2021), available at <http://whitehouse.gov/briefing-room/speeches-remarks/2021/02/10/remarks-by-president-biden-on-the-administrations-response-to-the-coup-in-burma>

Research Services of the German Bundestag, 'Legal Questions Concerning Recognition of the Interim President in Venezuela' (15 February 2019), available at <http://bundestag.de/resource/blob/827466/f4de0cf7eb1e74f552fb711f7d07fb76/WD-2-017-19_EN-pdf-data.pdf>

'Résolution portant sur la nécessité de reconnaître le Gouvernment d'unité nationale de Birmanie', *Sénat* (5 October 2021)

'Response to Order of the Court' (filed 17 November 2022) (Exhibit A in Cengiz v Mohammed bin Salman (District Court, District of Columbia, Civil Action No. 20-3009)) (USA)

'Statement by Ambassador Kyaw Moe Tun at the UN General Assembly Plenary Meeting Agenda Item 135' (16 May 2021), available at <http://myanmarmissionnewyork.org/post/statement-by-ambassador-kyaw-moe-tun-at-the-un-general-assembly-plenary-meetingagenda-item-135>

'The United States and Partners Announce Establishment of Fund for the People of Afghanistan' (*Media Note*, 14 September 2022), available at <http://state.gov/the-united-states-and-partners-announce-establishment-of-fund-for-the-people-of-afghanistan>

4. Other Materials

Institut de Droit International, 'La reconnaissance des nouveaux Etats et des nouveaux gouvernements' (1936), reproduced in (1936) 9 *Annuaire IDI* 300

International Law Association, 'Resolution 3/2018', available at <http://ila-hq.org/en_GB/documents/conference-resolution-sydney-2018-english>

Keesing's Contemporary Archives: Record of National and International Current Affairs with Continually Updated Indexes [1979]

'Observations by Professor Roger O'Keefe, Pursuant to Rule 103 of the Rules of Procedure and Evidence, on the Merits of the Legal Questions Presented in "The Hashemite Kingdom of Jordan's Appeal against the 'Decision under Article 87(7) of the Rome Statute on the Noncompliance by Jordan with the Request by the Court for the Arrest and Surrender [of] Omar Al-Bashir'" of 12 March 2018 (ICC-02/05-01/09-326)', ICC-02/05-01/09 OA2 (18 June 2018), available at <http://icc-cpi.int/CourtRecords/CR2018_03100.PDF>

Index

For the benefit of digital users, indexed terms that span two pages (e.g., 52–53) may, on occasion, appear on only one of those pages.

The manufacturer's authorised representative in the EU for product safety is Oxford University Press España S.A. of el Parque Empresarial San Fernando de Henares, Avenida de Castilla, 2 – 28830 Madrid (www.oup.es/en or product.safety@oup.com). OUP España S.A. also acts as importer into Spain of products made by the manufacturer.

www.ingramcontent.com/pod-product-compliance
Lightning Source LLC
Chambersburg PA
CBHW070551020425
24465CB00003B/75
* 9 7 8 0 1 9 8 8 8 2 9 2 3 *